BECOMING WILLIAM JAMES

William James, c. 1873

Becoming William James

Howard M. Feinstein

Cornell University Press

Ithaca and London

Copyright © 1984 by Cornell University Press

All rights reserved. Except for brief quotations in a review, this book,
or parts thereof, must not be reproduced in any form without
permission in writing from the publisher. For information, address
Cornell University Press, 124 Roberts Place, Ithaca, New York 14850.

First published 1984 by Cornell University Press.
Published in the United Kingdom by
Cornell University Press Ltd., London.

Printed in the United States of America

*The paper in this book is acid-free, and meets the guidelines
for permanence and durability of the Committee on Production
Guidelines for Book Longevity of the Council on Library Resources.*

Library of Congress Cataloging in Publication Data

Feinstein, Howard M.
   Becoming William James.

   Includes bibliographical references and index.
   1. James, William, 1842–1910.   2. Psychologists—United States—
Biography.   3. Philosophers—United States—Biography.   I. Title.
BF109.J28F44   1984   150'.92'4 [B]   83–45944
ISBN 0–8014–1617–5 (alk. paper)

TO MY PARENTS

The issue here is of the utmost pregnancy for it decides a man's entire career. When he debates, Shall I commit this crime? choose that profession? accept that office, or marry this fortune?—his choice really lies between one of several equally possible future Characters. What he shall become is fixed by the conduct of this moment. Schopenhauer, who enforces his determinism by the argument that with a given fixed character only one reaction is possible under given circumstances, forgets that, in these critical ethical moments, what consciously seems to be in question is the complexion of the character itself. The problem with the man is less what act he shall now choose to do, than what being he shall now resolve to become.

—William James, 1890

Contents

Contents

Photographs

JAMES FAMILY ALBUM

All of the photographs of each individual are in proper sequence though not necessarily from the same year as the other family photos in the group. Some are repeated either because no other is available (Mary Walsh James and Garth Wilkinson James in the 1850s) or to indicate their continued influence on the family after they died (Henry James, Sr., Mary Walsh James, and Garth Wilkinson James in the 1880s and 1890s).

Drawings

All drawings are reproduced by permission of the Houghton Library, Harvard University, and Alexander R. James. Unless otherwise indicated, the epigraphs that accompany the drawings are from William James, *The Principles of Psychology* (New York: Henry Holt, 1890).

Drawings

Preface

THE JAMES FAMILY has attracted considerable attention from students of American culture over the past fifty years. An extraordinary household, it simultaneously sheltered three men of genius: Henry James, Sr. (1811–82), a renegade theologian; his eldest son, William (1842–1910), who became a distinguished psychologist and philosopher; and his second son, Henry (1843–1916), who emerged as a major novelist and literary craftsman. Where is the reader to place this volume in relation to a multitude of others, many of them distinguished and graceful works of scholarship? First, this is a biography of William James that emphasizes the first three decades of his life. But more than a biography, it is a family drama that reaches back into the eighteenth century and across three generations and two continents for the telling. Neither a chronicle nor an encyclopedic compendium, the narrative traces relationships and core issues that were passed down from one generation to another. Thus, while William James is the protagonist, many others are also on the stage, as well as time itself.

My title, *Becoming William James*, is intended to call the reader's attention to this perspective, which, appropriately, is consistent with William James's own psychology and philosophy. His was a mind that emphasized process and movement rather than inert categories, empirical evidence rather than accepted canons, and the tension, often acutely painful for the young, between determinism (influence and historical possibilities) and the felt actuality of freedom of the will in the shaping of a life.

Some comments on the structure of the book may be helpful. The story begins with a Prologue set in 1874, when William embarked on the career that was to channel his prodigious talents for the next thirty-five years. Questions raised there about the complexity of his character and inconsistencies in his bearing are explored in the remainder of the book. The tale wends its way back into the eighteenth century and forward into the twentieth, and finally comes full circle in 1874, where it began. Despite the retrospective and prospective leaps, the narrative has a simple chronological line. Each of its three sections is written from the perspective of one of the story's leading figures: William James of Albany (1771–1832), Henry James, Sr., and William James.

Naturally, the sections differ in character because of the unique voices of their protagonists, the nature of their work, and the density of the sources. The story of William James of Albany is brief both because it introduces the thematic elements that structure the rest and because the handful of letters, speeches, and business documents that survive leave so many gaps. The elder Henry James, in contrast, was a prolific writer, and his section is fuller. The richness of the sources allows a reading of Henry's theology as the ideology of a rejected prodigal, and his journalistic pieces permit the construction of a map of his vocational world that directed and influenced his son William's search. This map emerges from responses to the intentionally naive question: What did the words "art," "science," and "philosophy" mean to this man whose son would turn first to art, then to science, and finally to philosophy in his efforts to locate himself?

The final section shows William finding his way within the territory defined by his father's map, guided by his own set of meanings. Here cameo career biographies of his siblings, friends, and teachers provide a contrast to William's development. The voice of William James of Albany reappears throughout as he continues to influence his grandson long after his own death.

In my research I have foraged omnivorously in the James archives as well as in published sources. Letters, diaries, wills, theological debates, drawings, short stories, lectures on psychology, books of philosophy, even physical illnesses give witness to the intergenerational struggle. This is primarily a story about men, not because women are unimportant, but because the sources tell it that way. Mary Walsh James, William's mother, appears as an important player in the third section. Alice, his sister, and his two youngest brothers, Garth Wilkinson and Robertson, do not appear in detail until Chapter 16. Analytic psychology and simple notions of fairness aside, I have accepted a historian's discipline and let the records speak.

Readers who are only casually acquainted with the James family and its history will, I hope, be intrigued by the literary quality of their lives. It is a story of mercantile success, rebellious prodigality, and the flowering of genius. Those already familiar with James will be pleasantly surprised, as I have been, to learn how much there is to discover while walking even this well-traveled path, where the glint of reflected light may still reveal a lost gem to reward the patiently curious.

The idea for this investigation of William James and his family emerged over a decade ago during many spirited discussions with Cushing Strout on the relationship between person and history.[1] It would not have been brought to its conclusion without the patient guidance and encouragement of Michael Kammen, Lawrence Malley, and Barbara Salazar, whose fine editorial hands helped shape it.

I am indebted to many other friends and colleagues at Cornell University for reading and commenting on preliminary versions of the manuscript: Richard Polenberg, David Brion Davis, Jonathan Bishop, R. Laurence Moore, Howard Kushner, Glen Altschuler, Robert MacLeod, Stephen Jones, Richard Reinitz, and the many members of the Group for Applied Psychoanalysis at Cornell who helped me clarify my thoughts about psychobiography. William Tucker Dean and Dr. Philip Lempert advised me on legal and medical technicalities.

Many librarians have generously given of their time, but I owe particular gratitude to Carolyn Jakeman, Martha Shaw, and Melanie Wisner of the Houghton Library, Harvard University, for their many kindnesses. Other scholars—Codman Hislop, Harold Larrabee, and Leon Edel—have aided my pursuit of James materials. The Josiah Macy, Jr., Foundation provided generous support for two years of research. I also had the benefit of a year as a Special Fellow of the National Institutes of Health and a year as a Fellow of the National Endowment for the Humanities, which freed me from clinical and teaching responsibilities.

Jonathan Feinstein, Eric Feinstein, and Rebeccah Paget verified quotations. Jonathan Feinstein aided in the preparation of the illustrations. Gloria Hennig typed the final manuscript with patience and remarkable accuracy.

The following institutions and individuals have kindly given permission for the publication of archival materials: the Manuscripts and Archives Division of the New York Public Library, Astor, Lenox, and Tilden Foundations; Special Collections, Colby College; the Trustees and Fellows of Harvard University; Henry James Vaux; and Alexander R. James, the literary executor of the James family papers. The late John R. James provided a memorable evening in the James family home at 95 Irving Street in Cambridge which helped to stimulate my biographical imagination.

I owe a special debt of gratitude to Edward W. Fox, teacher and friend, who introduced me as a Cornell undergraduate to the intellectual excitement of historical studies. My wife, Rosalind Sobelman Feinstein, has provided editorial assistance and warm encouragement throughout.

HOWARD M. FEINSTEIN

Ithaca, New York

Abbreviations

AJ   Jean Strouse, *Alice James: A Biography* (Boston: Houghton Mifflin, 1980).

AJL   Ruth Bernard Yeazell, *The Death and Letters of Alice James* (Berkeley: University of California Press, 1981).

CCNE   Henry James, *The Church of Christ Not an Ecclesiasticism: A Letter of Remonstrance to a Member of the Soi-Disant New Church* (New York: Redfield, 1854).

CER   William James, *Collected Essays and Reviews* (New York: Longmans, Green, 1920).

CLC   Henry James, *Christianity the Logic of Creation* (London: Appleton, 1857).

CWE   Henry James, *Charles W. Eliot*, 2 vols. (Boston: Houghton Mifflin, 1930).

DAJ   Leon Edel, ed., *The Diary of Alice James* (New York: Dodd, Mead, 1964).

EHJ   Austin Warren, *The Elder Henry James* (New York: Macmillan, 1934).

HJ   Leon Edel, *Henry James*, 5 vols. (Philadelphia: J. B. Lippincott, 1953, 1962, 1969, 1972).

HJL   Leon Edel, ed., *Henry James Letters, 1843–1875*, 3 vols. (Cambridge: Belknap Press of Harvard University Press, 1974, 1975, 1980).

LM   Henry James, *Lectures and Miscellanies* (New York: Redfield, 1852).

LRLHJ   William James, ed., *The Literary Remains of the Late Henry James* (Boston: James R. Osgood, 1885).

LSS   William James, Lawrence Scientific School Notebook, James Papers, Houghton Library, Harvard University, Cambridge, Massachusetts.

LWJ   Henry James, ed., *The Letters of William James*, 2 vols. (Boston: Little, Brown, 1926).

MC   Henry James, *Moralism and Christianity* (New York: Redfield, 1850).

MH   Houghton Library, Harvard University, Cambridge, Massachusetts: James Papers.

NE   Henry James, *The Nature of Evil, Considered in a Letter to the Rev. Edward Beecher, D.D., Author of "The Conflict of Ages"* (New York: Appleton, 1855).

NN   New York Public Library, New York: Manuscripts and Archives Division; Astor, Lenox, and Tilden Foundations.

NSB   Henry James, *Notes of a Son and a Brother* (New York: Charles Scribner's Sons, 1914).

PHJ   Frederic Harold Young, *The Philosophy of Henry James, Sr.* (New York: Bookman Associates, 1951).

PP   William James, *The Principles of Psychology,* 2 vols. (New York: Henry Holt, 1890).

S&S   Henry James, *Substance and Shadow; or Morality and Religion in Their Relation to Life: An Essay upon the Physics of Creation* (Boston: Ticknor & Fields, 1863).

SBO   Henry James, *A Small Boy and Others* (New York: Charles Scribner's Sons, 1913).

SRFM Henry James, *Society the Redeemed Form of Man, and the Earnest of God's Omnipotence in Human Nature* (Boston: Houghton, Osgood, 1879).

SS   Henry James, *The Secret of Swedenborg, Being an Elucidation of His Doctrine of the Divine Natural Humanity* (Boston: Fields, Osgood, 1869).

TCWJ Ralph Barton Perry, *The Thought and Character of William James,* 2 vols. (Boston: Little, Brown, 1935).

Vaux   Collection of Henry James Vaux.

VRE   William James, *The Varieties of Religious Experience: A Study in Human Nature* (New York: Longmans, Green, 1902).

WJ   Gay Wilson Allen, *William James: A Biography* (New York: Viking Press, 1967).

Prologue

IN THE AUTUMN OF 1874 a new instructor joined the Harvard faculty to teach comparative anatomy and physiology to upper-level undergraduates. He wore his beard closely trimmed, and his blue eyes flashed with vitality as he caught the students up in his enthusiasm. He was remarkably erudite for a teacher just past thirty and at the beginning of his career. He seemed to have read everything—not just anatomy, physiology, and medicine, but fiction, Shakespeare, and philosophy (much of it in the original French and German, which he spoke fluently). And he seemed to have been everywhere—Germany, France, England, Italy, even Brazil. The student who was intent on mastering the details of the physiology of the reflex arc or the changing structure of the bones of the forelimb in the lower orders of animals might have become impatient with the professor for his failure to march the class lockstep through the rudiments of biological science. Such mundane details were left to the textbooks, St. John Mivart's *Anatomy* and Thomas Huxley's *Physiology*. But the undergraduate who looked to the study of science for general cultivation was not disappointed. The class discussion ranged widely with the mind and mood of their lively new teacher, Dr. William James.[1]

A student who was as shrewd a judge of character as Dr. James had been when *he* was a Harvard undergraduate might have mused over the paradoxes in the man. Dr. James's younger brother Henry had recently written an allegorical tale ("Benvolio") about a character who was so divided that "it was as if the souls of two different men had been placed together to make the voyage of life in the same boat, and had agreed for convenience' sake to take the helm in alternation."[2] That engaging yet confusing tension seemed to capture Professor James exactly. He had been to medical school but had never practiced. He called his course Physiology but he kept nudging the class toward the borderland of psychology, where, he assured them, new discoveries in psychophysics promised to solve age-old riddles of the human mind. When it came to comparative anatomy, it was Darwin and the cosmological implications of evolution that excited him. Though Professor James was scientifically trained, he spoke passionately against the materialist's blithe conclusion that evolution made God superfluous in human affairs. Theologically sophisticated but no theist, scientifically expert but no materialist, aesthetically talented but no artist (when he drew illustrations for his lectures, it was clear that he was an accomplished draftsman), William James seemed to have a veritable host crowded into that single boat for his youthful voyage.

There were other riddles for the observant student to ponder besides paradoxes of mind. A hint of sadness could be seen in James's eyes. Tension around his mouth, which habitually suggested willful determination, sometimes relaxed into a look of despair. And there were moments when his energetic bearing felt forced, an expression of something that he wished for rather than someone that he was. One got the uneasy feeling that when the class left the room, the jaw loosened, the shoulders sagged, and a sigh of weariness replaced the tone of moral uplift that permeated the room when others were there. Yes, Dr. James was a brilliant, complex man, but there were many things one wanted to know about him.

BOOK ONE

GRANDFATHER

All the while the world *we* feel and live in will be that which our ancestors and we, by slowly cumulative strokes of choice, have extricated out of this [black and jointless continuity] like sculptors, by simply rejecting certain portions of the given stuff. Other sculptors, other statues from the same stone! Other minds, other worlds from the same monotonous chaos!

—William James, 1890

I

Tenants Become Landlords

Instead of tenants they become landlords . . . and fully enjoy the fruit of their labor in freedom, peace and plenty.

—Eighteenth-century broadside

[1]

IN 1789, the year of George Washington's inauguration, an eighteen-year-old Ulsterman named William James joined the crowds of immigrants from Northern Ireland searching for a new life in the United States. William James of Albany (for he settled in Albany, New York, and that is the designation used by historians to distinguish him from other Williams in the family) was first of his family to find his vocation in the new republic. A farmer's second son, he had no expectation of inheriting the family land in county Cavan. His parents prodded him to become a Presbyterian minister. According to family lore, he felt no calling for the career, rejected it as unsuitable, and sailed to America to build his fortune as a merchant.

Documentation of his early life is meager. Yet it is important to investigate, as best we can, the conditions that prompted him to leave, and uncover the wellsprings of his singleminded pursuit of the merchant's calling. For in that reconstruction lies the roots of a struggle over work choice that plagued the next two generations and tainted his abundance with bitterness. William James amassed a handsome fortune (estimated at $3 million when he died in 1832). But vocational conflict—father against son, son against grandson—marred the promise of his accomplishment. Worldly triumph proved inextricably bound to personal tragedy.

The Scotch-Irish—William's people—were dissenters from the Church of England. Tracing their descent from a Protestant effort to colonize the north of Ireland, they lived uneasily as a religious minority surrounded by Catholics and governed by an even smaller Anglican aristocracy. It was a poor land. Absentee landlords, exorbitant rents, and unpredictable harvests forced the farmers to supplement their earnings by weaving flax. Poverty was aggravated by inflation. The cost of land soared fivefold during the eighteenth century, and by 1770, when William James was born, four-fifths of all the linen marketed in Ireland was produced by farmer weavers who worked in the cottages of the northern counties to supplement their meager incomes.[1] Linen was the prop that kept them from economic disaster. When foreign demand fell in the 1770s, the trade collapsed and thousands faced starvation. William's boyhood was spent surrounded by children with pinched faces and swollen bellies. Sitting for hours in the lengthening shadow of the loom, watching the weaver hard at work, a bright boy couldn't help wondering why so few prospered. The grumbling of the old men made it clear that the landowners, the collectors of rent, regularly profited from the Lord's providence. Why not dream about being one of *them?*

Born into a time of starvation, James grew to young manhood in an age of revolution. He had ample opportunity to witness the parading of troops and sense the excitement of rebellion. When the Americans resisted London's discipline by disrupting the tea trade, and the first Continental Congress was convened to challenge George III's punitive response, the Ulster dissenters took sides with the colonies against the king. One loyalist observer reported bitterly to London that Ulstermen were "Americans in their hearts," and the talk among them was such "that if they are not rebels, it is hard to find a name for them."[2] The Scotch-Irish had also suffered from London's trade policies. And for more than one hundred years, a steady flow of Scotch-Irish had settled in British North America. The extensive family connections between the colonists and the Protestant community of the north assured their revolutionary sympathies. It was their brothers, uncles, and cousins that were wronged by the monarchy and needed defense. When the opportunity came for rebellion in Northern Ireland, Protestant volunteers marched with Irish patriots to topple the Anglican oligarchy that ruled them.

Emigration was a traditional response to economic hardship. The collapse of the linen trade made the James' neighbors vulnerable to broadsides that waved tantalizing promises before them. Newry was the port for departure from Cavan, and a boy would have had ample opportunity to go with his father to help neighbors and friends depart for America. For those who had the 3 pounds 5 shillings for passage, advertisements promised that no expense would be spared to make their Atlantic crossing "comfortable and agreeable." Those who lacked the money, and there were many, could exchange indentures for passage. Leaflets in the marketplace announced, "A FEW SERVANTS STILL WANTED," a lure to tempt the destitute. But the cautious hesitated. Despite the soothing assurances of the agents in the immigrant trade, an eighteenth-century voyage was hazardous. Shipwreck, pirates, starvation, and disease made the mortality rate frighteningly high, particularly among children. But William James was determined to leave when he came of age. The war between king and colonists interrupted the flow of immigrants temporarily. When naval hostilities ceased and peace was declared, he would be able to join them.[3]

If he were to remain with his family he would face unattractive prospects. The linen trade revived in the 1780s, so there was money enough for his education. Robert, the older brother, was heir to his father's property, and the younger son had to find a different vocation for the service of man and God. His father wanted him to become a minister. There is no record of how strenuously William was pushed toward the pulpit, but he steadfastly refused.[4] When he emigrated, he turned his back on Cavan, the threat of poverty, and the prospect of an unwanted career. For a man who had seen the labor of land and loom turn to nought, the broadsides were irresistible: "INSTEAD OF TENANTS THEY BECOME LANDLORDS . . . AND FULLY ENJOY THE FRUIT OF THEIR OWN LABOUR IN FREEDOM, PEACE AND PLENTY."[5] Drawn by that vision, he booked passage.

[2]

James had neither capital nor family connections to aid his start in business. He began as a merchant's clerk in Albany, New York.[6] He must have been frugal and diligent, for after two years as a clerk he opened his doors as a merchant in the tobacco trade. Two years more spent amidst the pungent aroma of cut tobacco on Mark Lane, and the young tradesman was ready to expand into the produce business. His second store was cleverly located near the water in order to ease the unloading of York farmers' crops.* He decided to manufacture his own tobacco products to enlarge his profit from that source. In 1800 he opened yet another store. This time he took a partner, Francis McCabe. Five years later, expanding into the transatlantic trade with Ireland, he formed a partnership with John Flack of New York City. Flack's partner, James McBride, acted as the agent for the shipment of clover and flax to Dublin for the firm.[7] McBride's brother handled the business in Dublin.

*John and Robert Barber, the publishers of the *Albany Register,* were Scotch-Irish immigrants, too. James's expanding enterprises were announced in their paper.

William James valued family loyalty. He was generous with assistance to relatives who followed him to the United States. His older brother, Robert, stayed in Cavan, but four of Robert's sons and the widow of a fifth came and settled with James's aid. He helped one nephew establish himself in business at Buffalo in 1819. Two more were given a start in New York City the following year.[8] In addition to advancing money, he used his influence to help younger members of the family. When his younger brother, John, wanted a commission in the U.S. Dragoons, William wrote to his friend Governor Daniel Tompkins on John's behalf. And blood relations were not the only relatives to benefit from James's wealth and position. He hired his brother-in-law, Moses De Witt Burnet, to manage some of his real estate interests. Burnet's experience with James provides a vignette of a man who was at once demanding and generous with his extended family.

Acting as James's agent, Burnet negotiated first with the Holland Land Company and then with Henry Eckford, a New York shipbuilder, to buy land along the Erie Canal. In 1824, property bordering the canal, including the village of Syracuse and a saltworks, was purchased for $60,000. Burnet was then sent to Syracuse to represent the newly formed Syracuse Company. He found the living conditions intolerable. During the summer, the salt swamps that surrounded the village filled the air with a miasmic stench. Illness added to the misery of homesickness. Burnet finally dared his brother-in-law's wrath by declaring in a letter that he would no longer live in Syracuse "for any consideration whatsoever." James traveled to Syracuse to deal with Burnet directly. That encounter was so convincing that Burnet remained to risk his life for James's capital in the Syracuse swamps. In the next eleven years he did not go to Albany at all, was seldom out of the town of Salina, where the saltworks were located, and only once left the county.[9] William James was a persuasive man.

There was a fortune to be made from real estate development in Syracuse. The Syracuse Company stumped and drained the land and sold it for building lots to the new residents who were drawn by the boom stimulated by the new canal. When the deal with Eckford made the Syracuse Company owner of the saltworks, James had one more outlet for his commercial energies. And he wanted to be in charge. The meeting at which the board of directors of the saltworks elected him president was its last. James took absolute control. The production of salt from the state-owned salt springs involved changes in technology and marketing that tested the new salt merchant's skills. Originally it required a large supply of wood to boil away the water. When the forests nearby were depleted, James shifted to solar evaporation. The new process solved one problem but created another: the resulting salt was coarse and its texture was unfamiliar to the public. Undaunted, James marketed the new product with characteristic assertiveness. He shipped 200 unsolicited barrels to a friend in Detroit. John R. Williams was in debt to him for $10,000 and could hardly refuse James's offer. James's marketing strategy was based on an aspect of human psychology that was to become central to his grandson's thought: habit. Since "habit becomes a kind of nature," Williams was instructed to compare equivalent barrels of beef and pork cured with fine and coarse salt to demonstrate the superiority of the latter for his customers and train the public to buy the Syracuse product. The shipment arrived with James's blithe assurance, "We have no doubt of your closing the consignment."[10]

[3]

James's real estate holdings extended far beyond the borders of New York State, but acquisition of distant land was intimately connected with his promotion of the New York canal. The canal was central to the James fortune. As early as 1819 he had negotiated for the purchase of western lands whose value was predicated on the completion of the inland waterways. "If your grand canal from Erie to Hudson is completed," his agent assured him, "they must become immensely valuable."[11] But not all of James's speculations were as successful as the holdings of the Syracuse Company. The appreciation of the western lands purchased in 1819 was dependent on the timely completion of links to the Erie Canal via the Illinois and Michigan Canal. This development was delayed for thirty years (until 1848) and was of interest only to James's heirs. In addition to the risk of delay, the supervision of property was difficult at such great distances. James had to be constantly vigilant against unscrupulous agents who paid taxes in inflated currencies, even though they had received the more stable York money from him. More than once he had nearly forfeited his investment because of their manipulations. Building a fortune required diligence and foresight.*

The opening of the Erie Canal was a personal triumph for William James. He had been promoting the venture from the first meeting at the Tontine Coffee-House, in 1816, to rally support from influential Albanians. He had earned his place, as head of the citizens' committee, to address the thousands who gathered to witness the first barge pass through the lock at Albany. When the echo of the national salute and fifty-four rounds honor-

---

*William's son Henry (1811–82) understood little about business and cared even less. He dismissed his father's achievement as a mere stroke of luck.

ing each of the counties had faded into the valley, the twelve-pounders were silent.[12] A portly man in his fifties with dark curly hair and blue eyes, he was handsome and, despite his bulk, robust. His lower lip protruded ever so slightly, creating an impression of determination mixed with disdain. His eyes seemed too small for the mass of his face, which rounded to a double chin pressed into the ruffles of his collar. Addressing the crowd in a thick Irish accent, James proclaimed his Democratic faith. "Was an empire such as ours to be established," he boomed, "the only emigrants fitted to do it were those who abhorred the profligacy, bigotry and slavery of European governments." He believed in the divine mission of the United States. "Americans ought to rejoice with gratitude to heaven; nothing but the torpid stupidity of atheism can prevent the reflecting mind from perceiving the special interposition of providence, in protecting and advancing our national honor and greatness."[13] To be sure, this was standard patriotic piety, but there was an especially poignant, personal note in his allegiance to his new country and his rejection of the old.

"It is said that pride or attachment to the land of our birth is natural; but . . . the cause or source of such feeling differs extremely with the degree of intelligence or moral structure of the mind." And James obviously counted himself among the advanced in moral development. "The less man is removed from the savage state, the stronger is the attachment to the mountain or glen that first witnessed his existence. . . ." But for educated men like him, "military and heroic achievements, moral elevation of character, and the love of liberty and the social happiness of the people, are the component principles of attachment to the country of our birth."[14] So complete was his identification with his new country that he spoke to the crowd as though he had been born in his adopted land.

[4]

It was important for a merchant with extensive investments in land to cultivate connections in the statehouse. It was essential for a salt manufacturer to do so. A tax on Syracuse salt was a major source of state revenue (by 1846, half of the cost of the canal had been raised in this way). Furthermore, the Salt Reservation and the Erie Canal dropped forty patronage positions into the arms of the ruling party faithful.[15] For a man in James's position, well-placed friends could make a good investment an excellent one. He knew Governor De Witt Clinton well, and was thus a powerful ally to be cultivated by the other Syracuse salt producers. During the 1824 election Joshua Forman wrote to assure him of Governor Clinton's prospects and alert him to the need for political favor after the victory was

William James of Albany, c. 1810

won.* "We are now in the midst of the elections—the prospects of giving a majority for Mr. Clinton *in this county* are very flattering. . . .As soon as that is over measures will be taken to have a proper statement of the matters relating to the future Salt works sent on to be used in *case* the Legislature should be disposed to anything in the business to reward their friends."[16] Clinton had been forcefully retired from his position as a canal commissioner by the "Albany Regency," and the rough handling of him aroused such a strong public reaction that it helped him win reelection. James's friend was in power once more.

[5]

The new canal enriched Mr. James' estate. It also provided him with an easier means of getting back and forth between Albany and Syracuse to oversee his properties. A ride aboard one of the speedy, eighty-foot packets that glided effortlessly eastward hour after hour behind the monotonous drumming of hoofs on the towpath was a vast improvement over horse and carriage.

Occasionally the tedium of the trip through the flatlands of the state, the "long level," was broken by the approach of another barge moving westward. The barge decks were often strewn with bedding, iron kettles, and the stacked chests of new immigrants, many of them Irish, with paste-white skin and shadowed, sunken eyes, the faces of poverty that James knew so well from his boyhood. The hopes that lured immigrants westward enriched Mr. James. A bargeload of immigrants meant more customers for Syracuse salt, Illinois land, and Albany capital.

William James's calling had brought him wealth and power. His personal life was equally expansive but far more troubled. He married twenty-two-year-old Elizabeth Tillman in the summer of 1796, when he was twenty-six. The following spring she gave birth to twin boys. But the joy of having sons was followed by the gloom of bereavement. Married one summer, Elizabeth was buried the next. A busy man with twin infants on his hands couldn't remain a widower for long. William married Mary Ann Connolly. She was even younger than his first wife. Her family had come from Ireland to settle in the Mohawk Valley. It was a match that linked two mercantile families and their growing fortunes. Mary Ann's uncle

---

*Joshua Forman (1770–1848) graduated from Union College and practiced law before becoming a judge in the Court of Common Pleas of Onondaga County in 1813. He was elected to the Legislature in 1807 and was active in supporting the project that later became the Erie Canal. As a founder of the city of Syracuse and a land speculator, he shared many political and business concerns with William James of Albany.

Michael was a large investor in New York State land. Mary Ann took charge of the James household and the twin boys. She became pregnant, and her daughter, Ellen, was born as the ground began to soften from the winter frost. Before it had hardened again, Mary Ann, too, was dead. Barely two years a wife and six months a mother, Mary Ann James was buried at her father's farm on the banks of the Mohawk. William had to explain as best he could to his twice-bereaved sons that their new mother had gone from this world to a place of everlasting life. Perhaps he worried over the fate of her soul: his wife had been Catholic and married out of her church.[17]

Once again, James married. His third wife, Catharine Barber, proved hardier than her predecessors. Between 1805 (when she was twenty-six) and 1828 she bore ten children—seven sons and three daughters—eight of whom survived to adulthood. But death continued to stalk the family. James had pinned his hopes for an heir and partner on one of the twins, Robert, who seemed drawn to his father's calling. In 1818 William turned over the supervision of his commercial affairs to his son. As head of Robert James and Company, Robert appeared assured of a successful mercantile career. He married well (his wife was the daughter of Governor Clinton's private secretary) and moved into a comfortable house on Green Street, near the family business. Inexplicably, he was struck down in his prime, as his mother had been. There was yet another summer funeral for Mr. James, and the loss of a partner as well as a son.[18] William, the second twin, was a source of grief too, but for a different reason: he had no flair for business. A dark-spirited youth who had been converted during the revival of 1815, he subsequently felt a call to the ministry. But he became despondent as a student at Princeton. Dr. Adam Alexander, a teacher with a gift for helping young men with morbid doubts about their spiritual condition, gave him counsel, and he completed college, becoming the first graduate in the family.* But that was a short-lived source of satisfaction. No sooner had the Reverend William James reached the point where he could begin to practice his profession than he fell ill. Immediately after being ordained as a Presbyterian minister, he left the country for nearly two years of recuperation and study in Scotland.[19] When he finally did return to practice his profession, the Reverend William James carefully avoided settling in Albany, his father's domain.

Even with such a prolific, sturdy wife as Catharine, James's need for a son to help manage his affairs was repeatedly frustrated. Of the first three sons born to this third marriage, only one, Augustus, survived. And Au-

---

*Professor Adam Alexander (1772–1851) helped to found Princeton Theological Seminary and became its first professor in 1812. He served on the faculty until he died in 1851.

Catharine Barber James, c. 1855

gustus nearly died from the pox.* Augustus had a strong inclination to follow his father's vocation. But was one business-minded son enough? After what had happened to Robert, it hardly seemed so. Henry, Catharine's fourth boy, was too much like his reverend half brother to be counted on. Besides, he had been crippled in an accident and his health was uncertain. No doubt the Lord would provide. But a father had to make plans.

[6]

By the time he addressed the celebrants at the canal opening, William James had exceeded even the wildest imaginings of a boy raised in poverty among the Scotch-Irish of county Cavan. A merchant, banker, and landowner, he now owned such vast acreage (40,000 acres in Illinois alone) that the holdings of the landed gentry of his boyhood paled by comparison. His children and heirs were very much on his mind when he stood to address the crowd. He expressed the hope that the canal would succeed, "for the honor of the state and the good of my children." They would have a much easier start in life than he had had. There was no longer any risk that they might have to struggle for mere survival. His sons would be educated and have all the benefits that wealth and power could provide in their chosen careers.

But a painful dialectic had been set in motion within the family that would turn success into bitter disappointment. When he abandoned Ireland, William James brought with him a deep conviction of the merits of hard work. Diligence was essential for worldly accomplishment and spiritual growth. But his success created a radically different world for his American-born children. He had accumulated so much capital that his children could question the value of diligence.

We can perceive the dim outlines of a pattern that began with the Reverend William James and was to be repeated many times. Instead of starting work at eighteen, as his father had done, young William delayed entry into the practice of his profession. Ill health justified study abroad for him, as it would for his nephews William and Henry (the children of his half brother Henry). When he was assured of an inheritance, at the age of thirty-eight, he abandoned the pulpit altogether, having worked a total of thirteen years—hardly a display of diligence in comparison with his

*Augustus James's deep pockmarks are evident in the portrait of him at the Houghton Library, Harvard University.

father's forty-four years as a merchant. Henry James had a stormier temperament than his older half brother, and his battle with his father was correspondingly more intense. Henry scorned the essence of William of Albany's world and waged open warfare against work, capitalism, and the God of Calvin. The wounds from that battle smarted for decades and left scars that would mark his children's lives.

BOOK TWO

FATHER

To suggest personal will and effort to one 'all sicklied o'er' with the sense of weakness, of helpless failure, and of fear, is to suggest the most horrible of things to him. What he craves is to be consoled in his very impotence, to feel that the Powers of the Universe recognize and secure him, all passive and failing as he is.

—William James, 1885

There are moments of discouragement in us all, when we are sick of self and tired of vainly striving. Our own life breaks down, and we fall into the attitude of the prodigal son. We mistrust the chances of things. We want a universe where we can just give up, fall on our father's neck, and be absorbed into the absolute life as a drop of water melts into the river or the sea.

—William James, 1907

2

A Crime against Childhood

When the child's natural instincts are violently suppressed or driven inward by some overpowering outward authority, a moral feverishness is
sure to result. . . .

—Henry James, Sr., 1881

[1]

THE HENRY JAMES who was to become the father of two
famous sons was the second of ten surviving children born to
William James and his third wife, Catharine Barber. Much that we know
of Henry James's childhood comes from a posthumously published "autobiographical sketch" written in old age at the urging of his children. In
characteristically vigorous prose, Henry indicted the severe religious atmosphere of his Albany boyhood. It had been burdened by moralizing at
home and at church. Children were coerced into mindless asceticism to
curry favor with a stern, omnipotent God. What was worse in his view,
Calvinism imposed a burden of guilt on a sensitive child, and made him
distrust his very being. "I cannot imagine anything more damaging to the
infant mind," he wrote, "than to desecrate its natural delights, or impose
upon it an ascetic regimen." The danger was pain for the child and deformity of the adult: ". . . when the child's natural instincts are violently
suppressed or driven inwards by some overpowering outward authority, a
moral feverishness is sure to result, which would finally exhaust or con-
sume every possibility of his future manhood."[1] In short, the Calvinist
belief in original sin was a crime against childhood.

James graphically depicted himself as a reckless youth bubbling with
animal spirits. "I was an ardent angler and gunner from my earliest remembrance," he recalled, "and in my eagerness for sport used to expose
myself to accidents so grave as to keep my parents in perpetual dread of my

39

being brought home some day disabled or dead."[2] For such a boy, the garden of Nature was a perpetual temptation. It finally provided a chastening scourge.

At the age of thirteen, Henry James was injured in a fire and crippled for life. He was a student at the Albany Academy, and Joseph Henry (later to become famous for his magnetism research) was supervising the boys' experimentation in the park in front of the school. They could make a paper balloon fly by heating the air inside it. The children launched their lighter-than-air craft and watched as it was lifted skyward by the heat from a ball of flaming flax. Eventually the paper balloon burst into flames and plummeted to earth, to be kicked by the shouting boys until nothing was left but ashes and the lingering smell of turpentine. The playful experiment was repeated over and over until one of the balloons floated into the hayloft of a nearby stable. Henry James scrambled into the loft, heedless of the danger. His pants caught fire, and with awesome speed the smell of turpentine gave way to the odor of charred flesh. A friend who recorded the accident said nothing of Henry's tears or screams of pain.[3]

Henry was confined to his home on North Pearl Street for three years as a result of that leap into the flames. The doctor decided that amputation was necessary (probably to prevent the spread of gangrene). He had to incise and saw on the draining limb, leaving a stump that stubbornly refused to heal. As late as the fall of 1827, his sister Jannett wrote the discouraging news: "Henry's leg is not as well at present as it was in the Spring. Instead of progressing it goes back and there is a greater space to heal now than there was before."[4] The surgery had to be performed again, this time above the knee. Henry's older brother Augustus described the procedure: "The operation lasted (that is severing) about six minutes, but the most painful part was the securing the arterys, tendons, cords &c. He is now thank God safely through it, and in a sound sleep, with every appearance of doing well."[5] In an era without anesthesia, Henry's suffering must have been hideous. It was more than enough to attract the attention of his busy father. As an old man Henry savored the recollection that "his tenderness to me showed itself so assiduous and indeed extreme as to give me an exalted sense of his affection."[6]

James's autobiographical sketch is not simply a memoir.[7] It was intended as a religious parable contrasting the life-giving truth of his brand of Swedenborgianism (his adopted faith after his conversion in 1844) with the death-dealing falsehood of Calvinism. It was written about a fictitious friend, Stephen Dewhurst, who allegedly presented Henry with letters and an urgent request that he turn them into a book. The use of Dewhurst as an alter ego enabled James to obscure biographical detail in order to highlight spiritual meaning. He made light of Dewhurst's injury, disguising it as a gunshot wound in his arm, and then noteworthy only because of the effect it had on his father. Yet his imagery of branding and fire inextricably ties Dewhurst's accident to his own. In recalling the Calvinist picture of a wrathful God whose hatred of Dewhurst's fallen nature disturbed the young man's sleep, Henry pointed to his own ordeal by fire. "This insane terror pervaded my consciousness more or less. It . . . made me loath at night to lose myself in sleep, lest his dread hand should clip my thread of life without time for a parting sob or penitence, and grovel at morning dawn with an abject slavish gratitude that the sweet sounds of Nature and of man were still around me. . . . The conviction of his supernatural being and attributes was burnt into me as with a red-hot iron, and I am sure no childish sinews were ever more strained than mine were in wrestling with the subtle terror of his name."[8] He also tied his experience to that of Jacob, another son who wrestled with God's angel and "strained" his "sinews." Writing from the vantage point of old age, Henry would have us believe that he, too, came out of that archetypal wrestling match triumphant. But, as we shall see, like Jacob, he was crippled by the encounter.

[2]

Three years of confinement would have provided ample opportunity for a theologically talented young man to speculate on the meaning of his misfortune. Was it punishment? If so, what was his transgression? Childish rebelliousness? Playfulness? Or was the disaster pure evil, an imperfection of God's creation? The amputation made him acutely aware of something else—the puzzling relationship between body and spirit, between material substance and spiritual reality. The flesh and bone were gone. He could see that, but his mind told him something different. He still felt his amputated leg as part of him, yet only one limb dangled over the edge of the bed when he tried to stand. Perhaps his senses were misleading him about the reality of other things, too. Perhaps "reality" was an illusion made meaningful only through revelation.

Possibly the blame for the accident lay with the fire. But could the laws of combustion operate in the world heedless of an omnipotent God's will? In his late thirties James alluded to this aspect of the moral problem posed by the accident of his youth (though not identified in the text as personally meaningful). As in the autobiographical sketch, he spoke of an upper limb instead of a lower, but the event with which he was struggling to make peace is unmistakable. "When the fire burns my incautious finger, I do not blame the fire, and why? Because I feel that the fire acts in strict obedience

Henry James, Sr., in his youth

to its nature, which is that of subjection to me, and that I alone have been in fault therefore, for reversing this relation and foolishly subjecting myself to it."[9] A boy might curse the flame for his misfortune, but the man had thought past that problem and accepted full responsibility for the leap into the flames.

Two incidents in Henry's later life show that his deformity had moral significance for him and for his friends. He and A. Bronson Alcott, the transcendentalist seer and schoolmaster, were once engaged in philosophic debate. James did not find Alcott's reasoning well founded and told him so. The incensed Alcott replied, "Mr. James, you are *damaged goods* and will come up *damaged goods in eternity*."[10] No doubt Henry's lighthearted presentation assured his listeners that the loss of his leg was an old hurt made insensitive by time.

Yet a second incident reveals just how much his injury preoccupied him. James was once asked by a grieving Julia Ward Howe, after her three-year-old son died, what his ideas were on the subject of immortality. She was clearly seeking consolation in a time of bereavement. By her report, "Henry illustrated his belief in a singular way. 'I lost a leg,' he said, 'in early youth. I have had a consciousness of the limb itself all my life. Although buried and out of sight, it has always remained a part of me.'"[11] Here we can see, in addition to Henry's insensitivity to the needs of a bereaved mother who could hardly welcome the comparison, how the amputation became emblematic of his mature theological belief. To Henry the Calvinists were misguided to believe that God would punish an innocent boy. And only a fool would mistake his amputation for damage to his immortal soul. His spirit came from God and could not be cut off from God. A sentimental mother might worry that she would be separated from her son, but Henry knew better. A loving God's creatures were eternally bound to him in spirit. So was a mother bound to her son. That was the only bond that truly mattered. Physical death and deformity were illusory. In old age, this spiritual truth reassured him that he was whole and at one with his Creator.

Henry's autobiographical sketch provides two inadvertent clues that bear directly on his vocational struggles with his father. Even at the end of his life, his battle with William of Albany and his ensuing vocational diffusion rankled. The Stephen Dewhurst of the autobiographical sketch was not simply an exact double whose differences could be erased by alteration of a few details of date and place (as his son William, the editor, suggested when he published the manuscript). Henry James had created a well-developed alter ego who had, in his youth, all the ideal qualities to which Henry aspired after a lifetime of spiritual struggle. Stephen Dewhurst was a spiritually undivided self.

Besides precocious spiritual development, Dewhurst had one significant characteristic that differentiated him from Henry: he was a worker. He chose a socially recognized occupation and participated in the major national crisis of his generation, the Civil War. James cited many parallels between his own life and Dewhurst's, but he was noticeably silent about his own career. They left school, married, and inherited in tandem, but only Dewhurst became responsibly employed in a fashion that William James of Albany would have sanctioned. "He had inherited a small patrimony, but as we neither of us contemplated a life of idleness, so he on this inevitable breaking up of his studies got a situation of trust in the Treasury Department at Washington, which his ability and probity qualified him to fill with advantage to the country. . . ."[12] Henry's implication that both were workers was decidedly untrue—an indication, I suggest, that the issue was still a sore point even in old age.

The second clue is even stronger evidence of a lingering problem. Henry James never completed his autobiography. For a man who wrote fourteen books and published scores of letters and book reviews, the failure suggests something more than lack of perseverance, some hurdle that could not be gotten over. The end of the text points to the problem of vocation. Henry recalled that he found friends suitable to a democrat of high animal spirits at a local shoemaker's shop. Unlike his Calvinist family, "they were so utterly void of all religious sensibility or perturbation that my mental sinews relaxed at once into comparative ease and freedom, so that the force of nature within me then felt, I may say, its first authentication." In this parable of democratic spirituality, representatives of the common man provided Henry James with the first confirmation and acceptance of his true self. As James recalled, the craftsmen appreciated the theater and were admirers of eloquence. He used to recite for them, and was particularly well received by "an old workman in the shop, an uncle of the principals, who sacrificed occasionally to Bacchus, and whose eyes used to drop very freely when I read. . . . He even went so far in his enthusiasm as to predict for the reader a distinguished career at the bar . . ." We shall soon see how frantically Henry resisted his father's attempts to make him into a lawyer, so that we can appreciate the irony of his final phrase: "but apparently prophecy was not my friend's strong point."[13] And on that note the manuscript ends. Try as he did as an old man to portray through his spiritual double the ideals of immortal life, it was on the very mortal question of worldly labor that the autobiography foundered. The problem of vocation aborted the life story as it haunted the life.

3

Flight from Union

Either subordinate your vocation to your life, or quit it forever: it is not
for you; it is a condemnation of your own soul.

—A. Bronson Alcott

[1]

THE FERMENT that was brewing between Henry and his father
was no mere family squabble. It was a clash between two men
of powerful will, one rooted in the religious orthodoxy of eighteenth-
century Ulster, the other rebellious, innovative, and optimistically American. One stood firm against the bulwark of the Presbyterian church, confident that worldly success provided ample evidence of God's favor; the
other was equally intransigent, first out of a conviction that he alone
should shape his life, and later in affirmation of an inner spiritual light.
The father championed hard work and moneymaking as a sign of grace.
The son found devotion to the God within more worthy than the multi-
plication of capital. He heard the clinking of silver as noise rather than
heavenly music. Money was at best useful to support contemplative leisure, at worst a temptation to human egotism, selfishness, and the soul's
perdition. Ultimately, living out the family dialectic they had generated,
the son dismembered the father's creation, reaping the harvest of what his
Scotch-Irish immigrant sire had sown while scorning the courage and skill
of the sower.

Having recovered from surgery, Henry James entered Union College as
a junior in 1828. The November before he was to graduate with the class of
1830, he provoked an open confrontation with William of Albany and fled
from the college to Boston. Then he made a serious effort to support
himself through work of his own choosing. Initially the frantic break for

freedom succeeded, but eventually the rebellious son returned to try the path that his father had chosen for him.

Union College was a natural choice for Henry's education. It was not far from the family home in Albany. Eliphalet Nott, the president, was his father's friend and former minister.* And perhaps most important, Nott had a reputation for skill in managing difficult boys. Nott's special sympathy for strong-willed boys grew out of his own childhood experience. Chaffing under the discipline of an older brother, he had resolved as a boy, "If I lived to be a man, I would not be like other men in regard to their treatment of children."[1] True to his boyhood promise, he introduced reforms that attracted students from all over the country to Union, and incidentally gave it a scandalous reputation among the older New England schools.†

Nott was in the twenty-fourth year of his presidency (he reigned for sixty-two years) when Henry entered, and many of his innovations had proved their usefulness. No matter how sympathetic he was to the plight of boys of high animal spirits under Calvinist discipline, however, even Nott was against open rebellion. He had been very successful in changing the atmosphere at Union to one conducive to study, with discipline removed from the faculty's hands. It was an atmosphere that seemed unlikely to provoke an independent young man like Henry James.‡ Yet Nott's

---

*The First Presbyterian Church in Albany—dubbed "the court church" because of the prominence of its parishioners—was the place of worship for the city's Scotch-Irish. Nott was minister there before he assumed the helm at Union (Cornelius Van Santvoord, D.D., *Memoirs of Eliphalet Nott, D.D., L.L.D.* [New York, 1876], 57; Codman Hislop, *Eliphalet Nott* [Middletown, Conn., 1971], 33–40). William James was one of his most important parishioners.

†New England schoolmasters informally agreed that they would refuse to admit students expelled from other schools for disciplinary infractions. Nott acknowledged his disapproval to a friend: "Though entirely disapproving that monopoly which the existing combination among the colleges is intended to secure, I have always acted in the spirit of the common law on the subject." Yet the reputation of Union as a haven for unruly boys persisted. "I cannot imagine the reason why there should be occasion, year after year, to say anything about us true or false," Nott lamented. "If we had ever in any case, during the troubles in other colleges, counteracted their plans, or given shelter to what they call their rebels, there might be a *reason*, if not a justification for this repeated complaint. But it is a truth that, though always applied to, we have always refused young men *revolting* from government elsewhere" (Van Santvoord, *Memoirs of Eliphalet Nott*, 154–55).

‡When Nott took over, the five-man faculty was the sole judicial authority, and suspensions and expulsions were frequent. "The faculty met and sat as a court: arraigned offenders; examined witnesses, and passed judgment with all the solemnity and formality of a civil tribunal." He was convinced (as anyone familiar with the keen sense of justice of adolescents would have predicted) that the process "was found practically to array students against faculty, to prevent mutual confidence, and to provoke rather than deter from transgression." The infractions that merited such judicial concern seem innocent by twentieth-century standards. A dispute between a student and a teacher over a forbidden light in the student's room, for example, led to expulsion. When the boy's parents made a plea to the president on his behalf, Nott seized the occasion to reform the entire structure (ibid., 150).

reforms would hardly seem an advance to twentieth-century students, as Nott made himself the sole judge and disciplinarian. Autocracy was hardly an improvement over oligarchy. But in Nott's hands, relationships between students and teachers gradually shifted from adversarial to familial.

He had taken the then unprecedented step of insisting that faculty and their families live with students. This innovation (instituted in the first decade of the century) bears directly on Henry's career at Union, as the president had been the first member of the faculty to follow the new program, and James lived in Dr. Nott's house. The idea had been so radical at its inception that the president had reassured the academic world that neither he nor any member of his family had received "either injury or insult" because of the new housing arrangements. Furthermore, the reform had led to "neither a general rebellion, nor an expulsion, nor any resistance in any way to the government of the institution."[2]

A contemporary of President Nott's recalled that many students "who seemed morally unpromising if not irreclaimable, went forth from his instruction bouyant and brave in the consciousness of powers which they hardly suspected themselves to possess, and with virtuous resolves which it was hardly thought possible to inspire."[3] And Henry badly needed such guidance. Besides being reckless and willful, he had become addicted to alcohol. The elderly shoemaker whom he had euphemistically referred to in his autobiographical sketch as "sacrificing to Bacchus" had in fact been feeding the boy and his friends "raw gin and brandy" morning and afternoon when they stopped by on the way to and from school from the time Henry was ten years old.* To compound matters, following his accident, Henry had been encouraged to use "all manner of stimulants" by his "parents, physicians and nurses," with the net result that (as he later confessed to his son Robertson, who was then struggling against alcohol addiction), "I emerged from my sick-room, and went to college . . . hopelessly addicted to the vice."† Henry's harried parents (by then there were five children at home and a sixth was about to be born) must have had high hopes as they dispatched their son to Schenectady and Dr. Nott's ministry.

---

*Drinking among children was not at all uncommon during the first third of the nineteenth century. Alcohol consumption in general was higher then than at any other time in the history of the country. During the 1820s the average adult male drank nearly half a pint of whiskey daily. Nine million women and children drank 12 million gallons of whiskey annually. The total per capita consumption of alcohol (a total of five gallons of wine, beer, cider, and whiskey) was three times what it is today. See W. J. Rorabaugh, *The Alcoholic Republic* (New York: Oxford University Press, 1979).

†Jean Stouse (*AJ*, 11) incorrectly implies that James fell in with professional gamblers before he returned to graduate from Union. In a letter written many years later Henry says, "I left Albany abandoning my studies and my profession, and . . . fell in with professional gamblers" (Henry James, Sr., to Robertson James, n.d., Vaux). This sequence obviously refers to the brief period when he studied law after his graduation from Union in 1830.

[2]

Unfortunately, Nott failed with Henry James. James continued "wild," and eventually fled from Union and Nott's reputed influence. Why Nott was unable to turn this boy around as he had so many others must remain an open question. But the surviving records hint at a possible explanation. James was not merely another difficult boy, but the son of the one man, William James, whose good name and financial resources kept the college from financial collapse and Nott from public disgrace. Henry James was a pawn in a complex financial manipulation that would have made it exceedingly difficult for Nott to take the boy's side in a clash with his father, even if such action had been warranted. Furthermore, Henry might have found it distasteful to open his mind and heart to Nott, whom he saw as vigorously pursuing greedy, marginally legal capitalist expansion of the kind that offended the youth's conscience. By the time Henry entered Union, his father and the president were bound together by long-standing political and financial ties that precluded successful influence on this prodigal's moral development.

When Nott became president in 1804, the college could barely pay its bills. At the end of his stewardship, Union was comfortably endowed, much enlarged, and graduating more students than the oldest colleges in the country. The cornerstone of the financial structure that moved Union from rags to riches was a courageous (Nott's critics would have said "reckless") political coup. At a time when the principle of state support for education was a novelty, he lobbied the legislature and won an $80,000 subsidy for Union. The sum was to be raised by lottery.* It took ten years for Union to get the money. The war and the natural reluctance of state-appointed managers on an annual salary interfered with a more rapid conclusion. Union's trustees had refused to sanction Nott's initial request of the legislature. They did not hold back, however, when he proposed to apply a second time for state funding. Through shrewd parliamentary maneuvering he won a new grant, this time for $200,000, again to be raised by lottery. The first lottery had caused Nott financial embarrassment because of the long delay in collections, but this problem was minor compared to the complications caused by the second lottery. Before it was concluded, Nott was drawn, along with Union's trustees and treasurer and

---

*It was a common practice in Europe and America to raise funds for worthy purposes through lotteries. In England, a lottery in 1753 provided a financial base for the British Museum. In the British colonies, Dartmouth, Yale, Harvard, and Brown received liberal lottery grants. The Continental Congress raised funds for troops in the field in this manner. See A. Franklin Ross, "History of Lotteries in New York," *Magazine of History,* February–June 1907, 96–100.

high state officials, into a vicious web of speculation, bribery, fraud, and blackmail that ultimately ensnared William James and made Henry, when he entered Union, the son of the one man whose liquid assets kept the college afloat.

The salaried managers ran the second lottery for eight years and "nothing was realized to pay a dollar of the principal sums granted, nor even enough to meet the interest."[4] Undaunted, Nott convinced the legislature that its salaried managers were no longer useful to Union or the four other institutions that by then had also been named as beneficiaries of the lottery. Nott gambled that he could select managers who would bring the matter to a close more quickly and, borrowing $33,000 from William James, bought out the other beneficiaries, leaving Union with all of the risk and all of the profits. James had lent Union $56,000 earlier to take the place of the grant that had been approved but not made available because of the slow performance of the managers. These two transactions, in 1821 and 1822, made James Union's banker. By 1823 the sum had increased to $71,000, secured by a mortgage on the land and buildings of the college. Eventually Nott won his gamble. His appointed managers completed the lottery and Union collected $276,000 plus interest, more than enough to repay James and add liberally to the endowment of the college. Behind the scenes, however, the president and his managers functioned marginally within the law, and sometimes beyond it, risking bankruptcy to enrich themselves as well as the college.

A committee of the 1819 New York State legislature concluded that the lottery system was impossible to divest of evil.[5] Graft, fraud, and theft flourished at every level. The Union lottery was no exception. Nott appointed managers who agreed to give him a commission, thus legally splitting the profits allowed by the state. Nott then secretly gave the managers permission to invest the lottery proceeds until they were needed for prizes instead of putting them in the bank, the expected procedure. Beginning in 1822, the managers speculated with these funds in Washington, D.C., and Pennsylvania real estate as well as in the Wellington Canal.[6] The investments went badly, and on January 4, 1826, the managers announced to the president that they had "no reasonable prospect of being able to pay the sum stipulated or even to pay the prizes in the lottery now pending." To make matters worse, the managers committed fraud by selling more tickets than they were legally allowed.[7] To aid them in this endeavor, they imported a Mr. Vannini from Italy to advise them on a new way of bilking the system. By 1830 their "consultant" had turned blackmailer and had to be given a $20,000 bribe to get out of the country.[8]

When the managers were unable to pay the prize money because of their speculation in 1826, they blithely suggested that Nott "should raise for our immediate relief $100,000."[9] It is possible that they thought they could make this seemingly outrageous request because they knew of William James's willingness to act as Union's banker. Nott was by this time hiding his manipulations from his trustees, and remained undaunted. The risks involved, the shady turn to the negotiations, and the imagined profits made him bold to the point of grandiosity. He advised Union's treasurer (who was a brother of the governor and one of the lottery managers as well), "You and I have such unlimited powers and have used them so boldly and so frequently without ever consulting the resident trustees, who are a standing committee with powers on all emergencies, that I feel anxious in the first place to arm ourselves and prepare for our justification in case of the worst—and having done so to prevent disaster contemplated—and if going further than we have gone will prevent it—my advice is to go still further and to stick at nothing but impossibilities. . . ."[10] The day before, he had induced William James to restore liquidity to the managers.*

At this point in the financial manipulation, William James's capital was secure. Rather than being precariously placed, as some biographers have suggested, he held power over Nott, his managers, and the fate of Union. As one of the managers put it to Nott, "We are now, as it were situated on a *Magazine of Powder* with a torch in the hand of a man who is our *friend* today, but we know not how long, and he can *blow us up* when he pleases. . . ."[11] By the time Henry entered Union, in 1828, the lottery scandal had become public knowledge through the published findings of a legislative committee of grievances.[12] Union ultimately got its grant in full, with interest; Nott personally earned $322,779, part of which had to be obtained through litigation against the managers (he ultimately made this money a gift to the college under threats from the legislature); and John B. Yates and Archibald McIntyre, the managers, retired as wealthy men. In the ironic words of a contemporary political chronicler and critic who was fully aware of the shady character of the entire affair, "They made, as was to have been expected, and indeed, as perhaps was right they should have done, a splendid fortune out of the enterprise."[13]

*Previous biographers have been confused about this $100,000. Gay Wilson Allen, for example, wrote: "Once when the college was near bankruptcy he lent the president one hundred thousand dollars, taking as security a mortgage on all the grounds and buildings, which he later cancelled without having received any payment" (*WJ*, 4). Allen is wrong on all three counts. The college lands were security for previous loans, James never lent the president $100,000, and all loans owed him were repaid. The confusion arose because James endorsed notes so that the managers could borrow money from someone else. James had securities and written assurances from Nott, Union's treasurer, and the managers that, should they default, he would not have to make up the loss from his own resources (*Documents Relative to the Dispute between the Trustees of Union College and Yates and McIntyre* [Schenectady, 1834], para. 137).

Set against this background, Henry's rebellion was the concern of three powerful men who were intent on taming him for their own reasons: his father, the president, and Archibald McIntyre (the lottery manager), acting as a friendly intermediary. It must have occurred to William James many times in his long business career that it would be expedient for his financial empire if he had a son who was a lawyer. A son with legal training could oversee his extensive real estate transactions and keep the fees within the family. William tried to force Henry in this direction, but Henry would have none of it. Not only did he refuse the law, he also spent his rich father's money liberally without permission. McIntyre wrote anxiously in mid-November 1829: "Your friends generally have heard enough of your conduct to cause us much pain and solicitude for your safety and future usefulness."[14]

There is no way of knowing what McIntyre had in mind by the phrase "future usefulness," but there can be little doubt that William James's good offices were still essential to the lottery managers, and that a rebellious son jeopardized an already precarious situation. The rebellion needed to be put down. Though pretending sympathy with Henry's point of view, McIntyre was obviously troubled by his rejection of a career at the bar (McIntyre was a lawyer himself). He supported William James's demands: "You intimated to me that you disliked the law, I regretted it, but yielded the point to you. On speaking to your father on this head, however, I found him inflexibly fixed on your studying the law. . . ."[15]

The issue of Henry's vocation was intertwined with that of his prodigality. Henry had spent about $100 for "segars and oysters . . . and cloth from taylors" without his father's consent.[16] Knowing, as we do, that McIntyre and his partner had been reckless with sums a thousandfold greater, we can only wonder at the strength of his moral indignation over Henry's fiscal indiscretions. Though the words were intended for Henry, they applied with even greater force (if the amount swindled is to be weighed in the moral balance) to McIntyre himself, who had been speculating with public funds since 1822 and was inextricably mired in deceit, duplicity, and fraud. "I consider you on the verge of ruin, and am well satisfied that if you do not without delay stop short in the career of folly that you have for a time indulged in, (if you have not already stopped) and pursue with sincerity a different path, you are lost to the world. . . ." By then McIntyre knew full well the wisdom of the path he urged on the youthful offender. "Lose not a moment then, my dear Henry, to convince your father, by every future act of your life, that you repent of the past, and that you determine to act entirely conformably to his advice and wishes." He closed with a threat that underlined how important the respectability attached to the owning of property (if not to the method of gaining it) was to him. "If you do not, you will lose all respectability, all support, independence, everything valuable in life."[17]

Henry James decided that he had had enough of Union, its president, McIntyre, and his father. He ran off, leaving his bills unpaid and his seniors uncertain of his destination. It is an indication of how seriously their relationship had deteriorated that William James expected the worst of Henry. He wrote to McIntyre of the "arts of low vileness and unblushing falsehood" practiced by his son, who "was reared not only by anxiety and prayer but with liberality to profusion." William announced that Henry had "so debased himself as to leave his parents house in the character of a swindler." This was a gross exaggeration. Apparently Henry had prepared for his flight from Union by ordering a suit that was appropriate to a big-city adventure. The tailors in Albany turned him down, but those in Schenectady were more trusting. They presented their bill only to find that Henry had left town. His distraught parent prophesied gloomily, "His mind and concett [conceit?] being given to such low pursuits I fear there is no hope for him."[18]

"Swindler" was a harsh judgment. True, Henry expected his father to pay for the clothes without first having approved of the expenditure. That hardly constituted a swindle, but clearly Henry was rebelling against parental government. So irate was Mr. James at his son's behavior that he was ready to believe that Henry had given his creditors a false destination to avoid being brought to account. In fact, Henry made no secret of his plans to go to Boston, but his father did not believe it was his true destination. "Townsend Sons—and others from the College have reported through the City—that H is gone to Boston—and I understand he told the man who gave the cloth—that he was going there—but deception is of no consequence—in his case—they will find him and he will find his reward, poor being. . . ."

President Nott was under the impression that Henry was heading for New York City. Nott and McIntyre both saw Henry's flight as a financial issue—their dependence on William James—and failed completely to consider the young man's wish to dissociate himself from a vocation that was devoted to the acquisition and preservation of property. The president's remarks show how thoroughly he had taken the father's side against the son. "I perceive that young James did not stay in New York as was expected. And had he, unless he could have been induced to return to his father, no good would have resulted. He must become convinced himself, that money has some value, and that economy is a virtue, before he will be induced to look to his father for support or for counsel."[19]

Nott's letter to McIntyre contains the earliest prediction (or was it a wish?) that the struggle between father and son would lead to Henry's breakdown. "I hope he will get into business immediately; or else break down immediately—the sooner his business comes to a crisis; the better for him and for his friends." Nott considered independent work an alternative for Henry, but despite his reputation for understanding difficult young men, he was unsympathetic. He repeated the breakdown alternative a second time to McIntyre several weeks later. "I hope he will either get into business that will support him or break down quick." By then he did consider the possibility that some good might come of this episode for Henry's moral development. "He is a bright boy, but has defects of character; adversity may be of use to him." When word did come that Henry had found work in Boston and was not breaking down, Nott refused to believe it. "I have just heard from young James," he reported; "he professes to have to get into business, but fear he is not doing well—nothing can be done for him till he learns the worth of a father's house."[20] Nott the educator was as unsympathetic to Henry's desperate attempt to find his own way as McIntyre the lawyer and James the merchant. From their point of view, it was unthinkable that a youth with great expectations of paternal bounty would gamble his (and Union's) future to work as he chose.

[3]

For an intellectual youth in search of freedom and adventure, Boston was as good a choice as the republic offered in 1829. Its 60,000 residents made it the third largest city in the nation, and huge by comparison with Albany's 20,000 and Schenectady's 4,000 citizens. He could see Edwin Booth perform *King Lear* (if he arrived early enough in December, as the famous tragedian suffered a "mental derangement" that temporarily interrupted his performance after the first week) or Mrs. Austin in *The Tempest* at the Tremont Theatre. He could also hear concerts at the Tremont and timely lectures sponsored by the Boston Society for the Diffusion of Knowledge at the Athanaeum. But Boston held attractions even greater than high culture for a youth in flight from Presbyterian moralism. Boston was the center of Christian liberalism, represented by the Unitarian church.

When word finally arrived in Schenectady that Henry had found work and was enjoying his independence in Boston, it came in a letter to Isaac Jackson, a friend and tutor at the college, rather than to President Nott. The letter suggests that Jackson may have had advance knowledge of Henry's plan. It was the jaunty letter of a young man who had begun to sense his own abilities. Significantly, he saw his situation in religious rather than materialistic terms. "After all," he declared, "the great step has been taken, and I am alone in my pilgrimage." He had found work as a proofreader for *The Christian Examiner* and lived with the editor's family. He described every detail of his new world with the exuberance of a prisoner set free. "Here I am in the good town of *Bosting* very comfortably situated on the first floor (not the basement) of a four story house in Hancock Street, occupied by Mr. Jenks. The room contains a very valuable and curious library (4 large cases). My bed stands in a near recess, on either side of which opens a handsome closet. I am sitting on a snug sofa. . . . On my left is a cheerful Lehigh fire; under my feet a warm carpet and over my head a painting of Lorenzo de Medici, by Mrs. Jenks. This room is sacred to me." Unfortunately, his tenure in that sacred room was to be brief.

He outlined the advantages of the new experience for his education. It was not "drudgery," as McIntyre charged (apparently McIntyre had heard of the job and was scornful of it), but a new life that awakened his abilities.

> Mr. Jenks ranks high as a scholar, and is very liberal in encouragement. He will afford me during the first year of my stay about $200 exclusive of my board and lodging in his own family. I am occupied about 8 hours per day, in reading proofs, etc. This has been called by Mr. McIntyre "drudgery." But it is quite a misnomer. I have to search out every quotation (say in Paley's Nat. Theoly. which Mr. J. is now publishing) and ascertain whether it be correct; and if it be not, to amend it. When a short notice may be wanting for the Examiner etc. I am expected to prepare it. . . . I now go on with the study of languages much more thoroughly than I should have found it necessay had I remained at home. It is indispensable that I should. My ambition is awakened; I have here every advantage, and the least shall not be slighted.[21]

Though the letter was not written directly to the president, it is likely that Henry expected his message to reach Dr. Nott, and his father as well. The remarks about foreign languages would have fallen on sympathetic ears, as Nott had radically altered Union's curriculum to include the study of modern foreign languages in addition to the traditional Latin and Greek.[22] The letter was also artlessly designed to flirt with Unitarian apostasy in a manner calculated to reassure while at the same time tweaking the paternal nose. "Mr. Jenks is, you know, a Unitarian, but no way anxious to direct me in the choice of a preacher. I hear Dr. [William Ellery] Channing occasionally and I should never wish a higher treat than one of his practical sermons." So much for temptation. Reassurance followed hard upon it: Alonzo Potter, who was Union trained and reliably orthodox, "Has numbered me amongst his hearers." As if that were not enough, the young diplomat who was not ready to burn his Union bridges closed with a theological buttering up that would have warmed Dr. Nott's heart and softened his judgment of the prodigal. The lady referred to as Mr. Potter's wife was none other than the president's daughter Sarah. "Mrs. Potter is what Eve might have been before the Fall. Listening to and looking upon her sometimes, I am apt . . . to wish with the Psalmist, neither poverty nor riches, but just such a wife as Mrs. Potter." But the irrepressible truth teller could not help adding a fly to sully the mix: "by the way, what a horrid name for *that* woman)."[23]

One must admire the ability of this rebellious youth (and perhaps rebellious youth in all times) to choose a direction that was a happy compromise (happy for him) between his independent aspirations and the choice most likely to inflame parental sensibilities. If it was work his father wanted of him, he would work, but as a laborer rather than a learned professional. If it was sanctity he insisted upon, Henry would give it to his father in good measure, but not the Presbyterian sort. He would place himself as an apprentice to the learned voice of Boston Unitarianism, working to spread doctrine that ran counter to much that his father held sacred. To the triumvirate intent on proving the worth of a father's house, he could fling at them the comfort, stimulation, and generosity of Mr. Jenks, who offered him shelter and tender parental concern. How Henry found this situation we will never know. The Boston papers carried few requests for apprentices. Those advertisements that did call to aspiring youths offered to teach the mercantile trade without pay. Perhaps it was just the good fortune of a young man who dared to leave well-marked channels.

Henry may have learned of Jenks by reading the *Examiner* in his search for a less cramped version of Christianity. Jenks's editorials challenged Calvinist doctrine as "repugnant" to an independent mind and contrary to the simple teachings of Jesus. To the Calvinist vision of a God who applied his irresistible will without regard to his creatures' deserts, a God who was "cruel and remorseless," a tyrant who laughed with "fiend-like joy" to see men sinking into perdition, Jenks retorted resoundingly, "Oh it must be false! scripture tells us, reason tells us, our own hearts tell us, it must be false!"[24] We can imagine Henry's hearty amen.

Henry could also have found evidence in the pages of the *Examiner* that others like himself were searching for an authentic sense of vocation. In 1826 the *Examiner* had published a long review with extensive quotations from Sampson Reed's *Observations on the Growth of the Mind*. The implications of Reed's essay, which blended Swendenborg and German idealism in a popular form, were revolutionary. Lockean psychology, which assumed all knowledge to be built of sense impressions, depended on a passive view of a mind awaiting the imprint of the world. Reed countered that the human mind was unique from birth, and shaped the world through active perception. The implications of Reed's ideas were upsetting to conservatives. In deserting Locke, he undermined one rationale for parental and institutional control. If the mind was passive, then the agencies of home, school, and church could expect to mold children. Righteous indignation over deviance was justified. But if each individual had a God-given shape from birth, just as the shape of the tree is foreordained in the seed, oppressed children could appeal to their own natures to justify their challenges to their elders.

Reed labeled John Locke's view "an erroneous sentiment." "The mind must grow," he insisted, "not from external accretion, but from an internal principle." To be sure, human beings were subject to influence, but it should not be forgotten that from earliest infancy the mind possesses "a principle of freedom, which *should be* respected, and *cannot* be destroyed." Reed was well aware that forcing a man to act contrary to his nature (as William of Albany was doing to Henry) might stifle rather than encourage growth. The mind is like a delicate plant. "Its peculiar propensities may be discerned, and proper nutriment and culture supplied; but the infant plant, not less than the aged tree, must be permitted, with its own organs of absorption, to separate that which is peculiarly adapted to itself; otherwise it will be cast off as a foreign substance, or produce nothing but rottenness and deformity." Here was a clarion call to individualism and self-expression to excite the imagination of an eighteen-year-old on the verge of a daring break. "There is something which every one can do better than any one else; and it is the tendency, and must be the end, of human events, to assign to each his true calling."[25]

[4]

Henry succeeded in giving his father an unfamiliar taste of an all too human sense of helplessness. The perplexed James wrote to McIntyre: "It is difficult to conceive of the wound'd spirit of a man in my situation—my heart pities a poor unfortunate son—who has so perverted the mercies of a kind providence that with the most ambitious desires and means of making him one of the most respectable members of his family and of the community—all parental kindness only increases his progress in guilt, and contempt—any efforts of mine—" he lamented, "are as certain to produce evil to him—in his present course—as they would be to elevate him—if he pursued a correct course." William counted on conscience to bring Henry to his knees for his violation of the laws of private property and filial piety. In his bewilderment, he urged McIntyre to offer conciliation on terms that to Henry would have meant complete capitulation but must have seemed generous to this father who was trying to save his son from damnation. "I only wish to say one word—if you see him, tell him, that when he finds how base he has acted—and when deceiv'd and despised by himself and all others to come to me and I shall endeavor to screen him from infamy and as far as possible from reproach."[26]

We do not know why Henry capitulated and returned to Union. Perhaps the flight had been just one more attempt to draw the attention of his father. Clinical experience has taught us that estranged children may seek to stir their parents by sickness, careless daring, and rebellion. His behavior at Union had indeed roused his father's tenderhearted concern, as his accident had done four years earlier. But this time, of course, it had also provoked his anger. Even anger may have been welcome to a youth who craved love to make him whole. So Henry may have gotten what he wanted and seen the sense of return.

But it is also possible that he could just not stand up to the threat of disinheritance (a threat that was ultimately carried out) and the pressure that three such powerful men as William James, Eliphalet Nott, and Archibald McIntyre could mount against him. They may have shaken his youthful resolve. Proofreading may have been exciting for a while, but would it do for a lifelong career? How could $200 a year plus room and board compare to a share in his father's estate? A bright young man like Henry might even enjoy reading law. What was the harm in doing what his father wanted? Whatever the reason, Henry gave in. He returned to Union and graduated in June 1830, at the age of nineteen.

But judging from the tone of his letters, he violated his own strongest wishes. After graduation he made a brief show of reading law in Albany, fell in with professional gamblers, and began to drink even more heavily. By his own report to his son years later, he "rarely went to bed sober."[27] At no time in the subsequent years of his long life did he ever again write with the same assurance and sense of whole-souled enthusiasm about work as he did from that "sacred room" on Hancock Street. Thirty years later he would have a similar battle with his favorite son, William. And William, having completed a paternally forced scientific degree, would slip even more deeply into despair, as his father had done in *his* youth. William of Albany's descendants were heir not only to his vast fortune but to the struggle over vocation and the self-definition that it implied for the next two generations, if not beyond.

4

A Conflict of Wills

They must severally learn some one of the professions, trades or occupations usually pursued in this country as a livelihood and must assiduously practice the same.

—William James of Albany, 1832

[1]

IN THE SUMMER OF 1832, cholera broke out in Albany. Earlier that spring the dread disease seemed comfortably remote when it was brought to the attention of citizens by travelers' reports printed in the local newspaper. But then it struck passengers on an immigrant ship in Montreal. Soon cases appeared in New York City. Finally the papers carried daily accounts of the newly stricken and the dead from all over New York State. People read of the mounting toll with fear and then panic. More than 12,000 died in New York City in June alone. Mayor John Townsend quarantined Albany and forbade any vessel with cholera victims aboard to approach closer than one mile below South Ferry. The fear of contagion was so great that the Fourth of July celebration was canceled, and the occasion was marked simply by the firing of a national salute.[1] But still the disease spread. Eleven deaths were listed in Albany. Then fourteen more quickened the terror that dominated the city. Many residents fled. Business was suspended. The streets were strangely emptied, providing clear passage for the burial carts bearing the latest victims to the cemetery.*

* "Cholera was the classic epidemic disease of the nineteenth century, as plague had been in the fourteenth." The 1832 outbreak was the first of three—1832–34, 1848–49, 1866—that terrorized the entire country. In the 1830s the population thought the outbreak was a consequence of sin; by the 1860s, with the development of medical science and public health, it was looked upon as a water-borne infection, the result of poor sanitation and therefore under human control. The specific organism that causes the disease was not identified until 1883. See Charles Rosenberg, *The Cholera Years: The United States in 1832, 1849, and 1866* (Chicago: University of Chicago Press, 1962), 1–4.

William James was sixty years old. It must have been a difficult summer for him. Business was bad, but the slump was only temporary. The imminence of death was not. If the cholera did not take him, something else would. If not this year, then perhaps the next. At first the disease was limited to the poor; new immigrants huddled in the miserable sections of the city were the first to fall ill. The paper reported that in Paris the poor were irritated by the seeming invulnerability of the rich, and they greeted the funeral of the first cholera victim of rank to enter Père Lachaise Cemetery with shouts of rejoicing.[2] But the summer heat wore on and disease proved democratic. Unfortunately, medical science was of little help. Doctors were warned to avoid familiar remedies, as bleeding, purges, and alcohol were definitely harmful. Laudanum and rest were of some use. The papers repeatedly described the symptoms of the disease. It would have been hard to keep from worrying that the appearance of any one of them meant the end was near: "a diminution of appetite, furred tongue, indigestion, oppression about the stomach and heart, a dingy complexion. . . ."

Science was a weak reed, but the devout could turn where they always had turned for strength and reassurance, to God. The ministers urged fasts and prayers for divine mercy. If James had dared to expose himself to the crowd of other worshipers, he could have heard Bishop Benjamin T. Onderdonk's prayer, "O Almighty God, who by the many instances of mortality which encompass us on every side, and the warning, now especially urged upon us, of our exposure to the sudden stroke of death, dost call upon us seriously to consider the shortness of our time here upon earth, and remindest us that in the midst of life we are in death, so teach us to number our days, that we may apply our hearts unto wisdom."[3] For a man of property, "wisdom" was not just a spiritual matter. One had to get one's financial affairs in order. On Tuesday, July 24, 1832, William James drew up his will.

[2]

Henry turned twenty-one that summer. He had made a brief try at reading law in Albany, and had worked for five months helping to edit *The Daily Craftsman,* an Albany paper of Jacksonian persuasion. But his plans were still unsettled. His behavior continued to be too loose to suit his father. William James had to account in his will for two other sons who had reached their majority, the Reverend William and Augustus. He also had to provide for six minor children, two grandchildren, and his wife, Catharine. The instrument that he fashioned is a key to an understanding of the subsequent history of the family. The language of the will emphasized James's religious values. Throughout, he repeated a litany in praise of labor and in condemnation of prodigality and vice. He punished Henry and the Reverend William by cutting them off from a substantial participation in the estate. When his father died six months later, Henry interpreted his disinheritance as one more arbitrary authoritarian act against youth and innocence. First God, through his injury and amputation, and now his own father had issued a punishing decree. Considering the shame and outrage he must have felt (not to mention the fear that he might have lost his chance at a leisured life), one cannot wonder that when he became a father, the disinheritance was kept secret from his children, though it festered (as family secrets often do), insidiously shaping their lives.

In preparing his will, William James was torn between a desire to protect his capital from his heirs and the wish to protect his heirs from the evils of capital. He set up a trust to mediate between these conflicting interests. Had he succeeded, he would have created a fabled fortune of the kind that now supports large foundations. He directed his executors to turn all of his capital into investments in real estate, which were to be held in trust for twenty-one years—the legal limit. He was so intent on keeping his capital intact that he left his wife too little for her needs. She was given the house on North Pearl Street with its furnishings and an annuity of $3,000, out of which she was to provide for herself and her six minor children. Understandably, Catharine James was the first to challenge the will. Recently enacted legislation of the State of New York entitled her to one-third of her husband's real property as her dower portion.[4] The court granted her petition, recognizing that William had not left his wife what was due her. The court further recognized that the support of their minor children had to be provided by Mr. James's estate, and was not to be drawn from Catharine's share, as he had intended.

William James hoped that work would protect his heirs from the dangers of money. He reminded his trustees that his aim was "to discourage prodigality and vice, and to furnish an incentive to economy and usefulness." The trustees could provide funds for education or to establish his sons "in any reputable profession or trade." Preparing for work was one way his heirs could get money from the trust, and work was obligatory if they were to participate in the final distribution twenty-one years later. To be eligible then, "they must severally learn some one of the professions, trades or occupations usually pursued in this country as a livelihood and must assiduously practice the same." Furthermore, he set his trustees as moral judges over his heirs. Any who led "a grossly immoral, idle or dishonorable life" would be cut off at the trustees' discretion. In sum, throughout his will William James sounded remarkably like the bookkeeping Calvinist God with whom Henry would wrestle for the remainder of his life.[5]

[3]

William James of Albany died on December 19, 1832, not from cholera but from a stroke. But the litigation over his will was not over until 1846, fourteen years later. And the will's provisions controlled Henry from the time he came of age until he was a man of thirty-five, with a family of his own.*

Henry went to Princeton Theological Seminary in 1835. Though he had an intense interest in theology, and Scotch-Irish sons with a theological bent tended toward Princeton, the timing of his stay at Princeton can be linked directly to the question of financial support. Henry's attack on the will was initiated by his lawyers in 1834, but in 1835 it was still unclear whether he was to inherit a substantial amount of money. He still had to live up to the standards specified in his father's will (that is, prepare for a profession) if he was to share in the final division of the estate in the event that the suit failed. As the will specifically provided for the support of further education, why not give Princeton a try until the Court of Chancery decided his financial fate? On July 21, 1835, a judgment by the court did give him a partial victory, but he did not get any substantial amount of money until March 28, 1837.[6] After that he left Princeton and turned his back on a career in the ministry forever. The sudden influx of cash in 1837 financed his first trip to Europe. Another major distribution of capital

---

*Scholars have already described the special treatment accorded Henry (he received an annuity of $1,250 but no guarantee of participation in the final division of his father's capital). And the breaking of the will is well known. Austin Warren's position is typical: "Two years after Henry's graduation from Union, the redoubtable William James departed this life. In spite of his efforts to cut off with small annuities his two theologically minded sons, Henry and William, both of whom he regarded as unsound in the faith, the will was broken, and Henry, along with his brothers, found himself, upon coming of age, 'leisured for life,' and consequently able to work out, as he chose, his cultural and spiritual salvation" (*EHJ*, 21). Warren mistakenly implied that the death of the sire, the breaking of the will, and becoming "leisured for life" occurred with convenient simultaneity.

Depending on their focus, previous James scholars have left out various parts of the story linking the will with Henry's vocational problem. Ralph Barton Perry neglected the fact that Henry and the Reverend William were singled out for moral rebuke. Furthermore, he suggested that the will was of interest only to lawyers, a position that must have discouraged others from reading through the extensive legal opinions on the case. "The elder William James thus did his best to transmit a blend of piety and acquisitiveness to his surviving offspring; but partly because there were too many of them, partly because the strictness of his rule was compromised by his own indulgence, partly because his children inherited their father's temperament without inheriting his opinions, and partly for technical reasons known only to lawyers and courts of equity, his plans, in sum, miscarried" (*TCWJ*, 1:6).

C. Hartley Grattan merely reported that the will "proved unworkable," and incorrectly asserted that the heirs "became independently wealthy as they came of age" (*The Three Jameses: A Family of Minds* [New York, 1962], 17). Leon Edel was the first to pinpoint William's intent to punish Henry. He was also the first to note that the litigation over the will was not finished until 1846. But he took no meaningful account of that fact in telling the story of this period (*HJ*, 1:21). Gay Wilson Allen is more precise about who broke the will, but otherwise follows the traditional view (*WJ*, 7).

directed by the court six years later coincided once again with a decision to live abroad. By then Henry was married and had two sons.

While abroad the second time, Henry had a nervous collapse that was partially relieved by a Swedenborgian conversion. Here, too, the will litigation was of critical importance. In 1844 the litigation reached a milestone with considerable symbolic significance for this thirty-three year-old man who was still without work. On September 16, 1844, a bill was filed to force partition and sale of the James holdings in Syracuse. At this stage the court forced Augustus, the son who was willing to follow his father's vocation and who was clearly the favored son in the will (both by property settlement and by his trustee position), to advertise the saltworks and the Syracuse Mill property for sale. Henry's assault on the will had worked so well that Augustus had to buy what his father had meant him to have by inheritance.[7] At one stroke Henry dismembered his father's estate and displaced a favored son. He spent several years in Europe recovering from his breakdown. This period coincided with the initiation of the Syracuse partition suit* and the final distribution of the estate, which took place in 1846. The prodigal who had defied his creator did finally triumph, fourteen years after his father's death. Then, and only then, was he legally in a position to be master of his own future.

The instrument that William James fashioned to control his son was broken, yet it succeeded almost as well as the testator intended. For fourteen years Henry had to cope with the fact that he had been judged idle, and consequently cut off by his father. For fourteen years he had to fight, brother against brother, to win his rightful share and undo his father's punishment. By 1846 he had finally, belatedly, reached his majority. The conflict of wills was over. But he had been crippled by the battle. His first encounter with unreasoning authority left him without a leg. This second round left him without self-respect—a wound that made the first hurt even more unbearable. When Henry finally found his vocation as a publicist of a unique version of Swedenborgian theology, the problematic relationship between the Creator and his creature became his obsessive concern. In letter after letter, lecture after lecture, book after book, the mystery of a God who would inflict evil on his own son goaded him on.

[4]

Henry's first trip to Europe was brief but significant. He was introduced to Sandemanian theology (and for a time espoused the sect's beliefs), he

---

*There is some time discrepancy. James's crisis took place before the partition suit was recorded in court. James broke down in the spring and the court record registered the suit in the summer. I assume that Henry was informed of his lawyer's intentions long before the matter actually got to court.

gathered material for his first book, and he visited his father's surviving relatives in Cavan. Joseph Henry, his teacher, accompanied him for part of the summer and probably arranged for him to meet Michael Faraday, the eminent scientist, who was a devout follower of the Sandemanian creed. The Sandemanians preached a return to the simplicity of the early church. It is easy to understand the appeal of their ideas to a young man in rebellion against his father's materialism and orthodox religious principles. The sect had developed in opposition to the Presbyterian church in eighteenth-century Scotland. Its followers preached love instead of hatred, and the "kiss of brotherhood" was central to their ritual. They preached against moralism, claiming faith and not works as the true justification of a Christian. They rejected a licensed professional clergy, preferring to be governed by unpaid elders, pastors, and bishops chosen without regard for education and equal in authority. The private accumulation of property was restricted, and personal wealth was ever liable to be called upon to meet the needs of the poor, not locked in trusts to grow and feed on itself. By rejecting the God of moralism, materialism, and hierarchy, they attacked much that William James and Princeton Theological Seminary held dear, and invited the allegiance of an angry son.

Two sources enable us to reconstruct Henry's 1837 visit to Europe: correspondence with Joseph Henry concerning travel arrangements, and a family legend recorded by his son Henry, the novelist, in *Notes of a Son and a Brother*. The correspondence is remarkable for the listlessness of its tone. Though he made a brave show of enjoying himself, the words carry little conviction. The hollowness is even more dramatic when it is contrasted with the ebullient, iconoclastic style of his later correspondence. Henry's mentor had written a letter of introduction for him, mentioning the young man's crippling injury. "He has had the misfortune to lose one of his legs and on this account will be somewhat unpleasantly situated among strangers." But the old wound was not Henry's major burden that summer. He could manage with an English prosthesis, "a good cork leg" that he had ordered for himself. But no craftsman could hide the heaviness of heart in his remark "I feel a little homesick occasionally—but in the main do charmingly—spend my time pretty much in my room, and am as happy generally as the day is long."[8]

Instead of venturing onto the Continent, Henry decided to go to Ireland to visit his dead father's relatives. Whether this was a familial obligation made more insistent by proximity or whether the young American was hoping to touch ancestral roots that might anchor his aimless life is not clear. One of Joseph Henry's friends invited him to France instead, but he refused. "I should very much like to go on to Paris with Bache," he wrote, yet politely withdrew in favor of his familial tie: "but fancy I shall be obliged to go into Ireland, and spend a few weeks with an uncle's family there."[9] Though the visit to his father's boyhood home must have been an emotionally stirring experience, the young American left no written account of it.

What does survive is the legend that his son remembered in his autobiography as a favorite and oft-told tale. Henry James, Jr., recalled his "inveterate, childish appeal" to his father "in early New York days, for repetition in the winter afternoon firelight, of his most personal, most remembered and picture-recovering 'story'." It is impossible to separate the glow that Mr. James infused into his epic retelling from the work of his son's hand, which was ever tempted to shift either frame or detail to suit the imagination of the master craftsman. But one or both made the story into the visit of a much younger man. It was believed to have been "a visit paid by him about in his nineteenth year." In fact, he was twenty-six. Furthermore, the story was told (or remembered) as having taken place when William of Albany was still alive. The legend of that summer visit evoked the image not of a disinherited son but of a gilded youth sent as an emissary by his wealthy sire. Children are often confused about the chronology of their parents' lives, and the error may be of no consequence. It is consistent, however, with another puzzling fact. Henry, Jr., though a man near the end of his own life, wrote as if he knew only vaguely of his grandfather's will and nothing of the harsh judgment imposed by that document. This suggestion raises the distinct possibility that the gilded youth rather than the prodigal son was his father's public version of his younger self.

The son's account suggests that he did not know that his father was cut off by his grandfather's will and had to resort to litigation to recover his just portion. While reading a newspaper clipping of his grandfather's obituary, Henry, Jr., was reminded of the troubling questions that surrounded the fate of William of Albany's fabled wealth. It may only be the autobiographer's art, but a reader has the very strong feeling that he is watching the writer's puzzled face as he reads the number of heirs mentioned. The obituary cited nine. He "corrected" the number to twelve, thus including his father as a beneficiary. But even that increase in number did not solve the mystery. "Which fact, however, reduces but by a little the rich ambiguity of the question that was to flit before my father's children, as they grew up, with an air of impenetrability that I remember no attempt on his own part to mitigate. I doubt, for that matter, whether he could in the least have appeased our all but haunting wonder as to what had become even in the hands of twelve heirs, he himself naturally being one, of the admirable three millions."[10] Henry, Jr., changed the facts to make them consistent with his boyhood understanding, not just to fulfill the demands of the storyteller's art.

Though it appears that Henry James, Sr., hid the shameful details of the will from his children, they suspected that something seamy was connected with that moment in their father's life. Henry, Jr., reported his childhood suspicion. "There had been, by our inference, a general history—not on the whole exhilarating, and pressure for information could never, I think have been applied. . . ."[11]* Apparently the will was a taboo subject, a topic laden with mystery and danger. The children had to avoid their father's sore point and behave as if no mystery at all surrounded their grandfather's estate. The autobiography also shows how loyal the aging novelist was to his childhood part in the family charade. As an old man he still kept the affair shrouded in vagueness, though he could easily have inspected reports of the litigation over the will, which were a matter of public record. Instead, he chose to guard his father's secret.

Though Henry James as autobiographer "knew" nothing of the details of his father's disinheritance, as a young novelist he created a fictive character with a similar problem of inheritance. Rowland Mallet was described in Henry's first novel, *Roderick Hudson,* as a man who "had sprung from a rigid Puritan stock, and had been brought up to think much more intently of the duties of this life than of its privileges and pleasures." Mallet's father was a man with "an icy smile" who, whenever he looked at his son, "felt extreme compunction at having made a fortune." He was "determined it should be no fault of his if the boy were corrupted by luxury." Not only does Henry's character have a wealthy parent concerned about the deleterious effects of wealth on his son's soul, but Mallet's father created a will that led to litigation. Henry, Jr., emphasized that Rowland went to court not merely for money but because of "an angry desire to protest against a destiny which seemed determined to be exclusively salutary." Contrary to his father's view, Mallet felt that he could make good use of luxury. "It seemed to him that he should bear a little spoiling."[12]

It may be imagined that the young author was simply reaching for a stock character, for after all, stories of testamentary conflicts abound in literature. But the strong resemblance between Mallet and the author's

*The younger Henry's uncertainty raises intriguing methodological problems. My conclusion is based on a close reading of this text, and is at odds with the opinions of previous scholars, who have fallen into what I consider a chronological fallacy. It is tempting to assume that what one knows as one reconstructs the chronology of a life was necessarily known by the subject in the same sequence. A historian writing of the intrigues of politics would naturally wonder about his subject's knowledge of an event that the scholar knew had already taken place. But no such awareness has informed James's biography on this point. Parents consciously and unconsciously deceive their children. It is easy to understand why Henry, Sr., would have wanted to hide the true details of the story from his children. His shame is evident throughout the writings of a lifetime. By binding oneself to linear time, one obscures an element important to an understanding of the James family vocational evolution. It becomes clearer if the researcher adheres to psychological (or experienced) time instead.

father suggests a different conclusion. As a boy, Henry Jr., was exquisitely sensitive and perpetually observed his family from behind a facade of reticence. Though the details of the will were taboo, he may well have heard bits and pieces of the story and intuitively put them together without being certain of the accuracy of his construction. He may not have "known" of the disinheritance—Mallet is not cut off but gets one-third of the estate, the rest going to "various public institutions and local charities"—but he sensed the fundamental antagonism between his father and his grandfather and accurately assessed the passion attached to litigation over the will. Whether Henry was hiding what he knew when he wrote *Notes of a Son and a Brother* in his seventies (a doubtful conclusion if we respond to the convincing quality of vagueness and confusion in that recounting) or had "forgotten" what he knew in his thirties when he wrote the novel is impossible to decide. But one thing is clear: the bitterness generated by William James's will did not stop when it was probated in 1832. On the contrary, it could still stimulate the imagination of his grandson more than forty years later.*

[5]

When Henry returned home from his visit to Ireland in 1837, he was twenty-six and the question of vocation was still unsettled. He was sufficiently inspired by the Sandemanian creed to try his hand at writing, and published an edition of Robert Sandeman's *Letters on Theron and Aspasio*. He did not sign the two-page preface, but the Jamesian imprint is unmistakable. He extolled the *Letters* as "a far more faithful exhibition of Gospel

---

*This interpretation raises interesting epistemological issues for the biographer. My argument runs counter to common-sense psychology. On the one hand, I say that Henry James didn't know, and on the other, I say that he wrote as if he knew. Common sense suggests that by far the simplest explanation is that Henry knew all about it and was intentionally obscuring the details out of a sense of Victorian propriety. While that is an attractive alternative and one that appeals to the model of the mind conventionally used by biographers, it ignores some of the data and does not allow for the complexity that we know, following Freud, attends the process of memory. When issues are taboo, knowledge of them may be repressed. While Freud dealt with issues that were of more frankly sexual or aggressive character, repression may equally attend knowledge of other kinds. The adult continues to behave as if he knew what he consciously does not know. In this instance, the James children acted as if they knew of their father's shame, thought they did not have the details. Henry, as an artist, reached beyond his conscious awareness in telling the story of Rowland Mallet, but doing so did not necessarily alter his conscious knowledge of the family secret. And the story that he told in old age was still the conscious story that kept the family secret of his boyhood. The common-sense version ignores the frank confusion that still persisted in Henry's mind and that comes through as authentic in the autobiography. Without written evidence to the contrary, this conclusion remains suggestive and is consistent with the rest of this analysis.

truth than any other work which had ever come to his knowledge." He flaunted the "severity of censure which Sandeman saw fit to indulge towards the most venerated names of his day." Rootless and in search of direction, Henry James found that Sandeman temporarily met his need.

Sandeman espoused a view of God that would have attracted a young man smarting under the judgment of his disinheritance. He preached that God accepted *all* of his sons, not just the good ones. In his view, "the whole New Testament speaks aloud, that as to the matter of acceptance with God, there is no difference betwixt one man and another;—no difference betwixt the best accomplished gentleman, and the most infamous scoundrel; . . . no difference betwixt the most fervent devotee, and the greatest ringleader in profaneness and excess."[13] Here was a picture of a heavenly Father who could be counted on to rise above the petty moralism of Henry's earthly one. *He* would not cut off one son irrevocably because of his sins. *He* would not choose one son over another because he was compliant. Perhaps Sandeman's God would sever the ties of conscience that inexplicably continued to cut and bind him though his father had been dead for five years.

[6]

Henry James, Sr., returned to Europe a second time in 1843. By then he was married and the father of two sons. He had spent the intervening years oscillating between Albany and New York City, between the home of his mother and that of his mother-in-law. He read widely in theology but was still without vocation, as his late father had feared. The second decision to leave for Europe, like the first, was dependent on the advance of the will litigation.* By 1842 the basic structure of the original will had been broken (because it violated the statutes that limited perpetuity). Instead of the intended small annuity, Henry James was an heir at law. In July 1843 "a large amount of bonds and mortgages and contracts" was divided (the

---

*He told Professor Henry on July 9 that his trip was contingent on the sale of his house in New York City. "I am advertising my house for sale and shall be guided by circumstances connected with its sale as to whether I shall go into the country or go for a couple of years to Europe" (*TCWJ*, 1:17). Henry had purchased a home on Washington Place in New York City from his younger brother John for $18,000 the year before. In its original form, William James's will provided that each heir might purchase "real property in the city or town where he may reside or intend to reside for his own accommodation." John was thus entitled to funds from the trust, but Henry was not. John had probably purchased the Washington Place house under this provision. Henry's purchase of John's house was probably a means of transferring capital to which Henry was by then entitled from his brother, who had received more than his share under the new circumstances.

income alone amounted to $187,467).[14] Only then could Henry afford such an expensive trip.*

The James family spent two years abroad, all but three months (for a trip to Paris) in England, where Henry enjoyed jousting verbally with such leading intellectuals as Thomas Carlyle, Alfred Tennyson, and John Stuart Mill. These distinguished literary figures provided unwilling subjects for James's caustic wit but had little impact on his mind. It was a private crisis, an emotional upheaval from the depths of his soul, rather than public encounters that captured his imagination and focused his energies for the rest of his life. In 1879 Henry described the startling breakdown in characteristically vivid prose.

> In the spring of 1844, I was living with my family in the neighborhood of Windsor, England, much absorbed in the study of the Scriptures . . . my health was good, my spirits cheerful, and the pleasant scenery of the great Park and its neighborhood furnished us a constant temptation to long walks and drives. One day, however, towards the close of May, having eaten a comfortable dinner, I remained sitting at the table after the family had dispersed, idly gazing at the embers in the grate, thinking of nothing, and feeling only the exhilaration incident to a good digestion, when suddenly—in a lightning-flash as it were—"fear came upon me, and trembling, which made all my bones to shake." To all appearance it was a perfectly insane and abject terror, without ostensible cause, and only to be accounted for, to my preplexed imagination by some damned shape squatting invisible to me within the precincts of the room and raying out from his fetid personality influences fatal to life. The thing had not lasted ten seconds before I felt myself a wreck; that is, reduced from a state of firm, vigorous, joyful manhood to one of almost helpless infancy. The only self control I was capable of exerting was to keep my seat. I felt the greatest desire to run incontinently to the foot of the stairs and shout for help to my wife,—to run to the roadside even, and appeal to the public to protect me; but by an immense effort I controlled these frenzied impulses, and determined not to budge from my chair till I had recovered my lost self-possession. This purpose I held to for a good long hour, as I reckoned time, beat upon meanwhile by an ever growing tempest of doubt, anxiety, and despair, with absolutely no relief from any truth I had ever encountered save a most pale and distant glimmer of the divine existence, when I resolved to abandon the vain struggle, and communicate without more ado what seemed my sudden burden of inmost, implacable unrest to my wife.[15]

James's description invites belief, but the text owes more to John Bunyan's seventeenth-century *Pilgrim's Progress* and Holy Scriptures than it

---

*His share in the estate was enlarged again when the court ordered the sale of the Syracuse property, including the saltworks. In November 1845 Augustus purchased the property from the estate and the proceeds were divided among the heirs.

does to material fact. Though Henry's crisis and conversion experience were well known to his family and friends and oblique references to it had appeared in earlier writings, the above text was not published until late in his life (*Society the Redeemed Form of Man,* 1879), thirty-five years after the episode he described. By then the experience had been refracted by evangelical imagery, and, like all of his mature works, the tale was intended to illustrate a well-developed theological position. He begins as a "natural man," well fed, comfortable, successful, and conventionally religious. Like Bunyan's "Christian," he needs to be awakened to abandon "safety, friendship, and content" and follow the more difficult path of the spiritual pilgrim.[16] The sequence of James's story is Bunyan in microcosm: reading the Bible, being cast into despair, hiding the matter from his family, and then telling them the awful truth that launches him on his solitary quest for the Heavenly City. James's last sentence is virtually a copy of Bunyan's: ". . . as he read, he wept and trembled; and not being able longer to contain himself, he brake out with a lamentable cry, saying, 'What shall I do?' In this plight, therefore, he went home and refrained himself as long as he could, that his wife and children should not perceive his distress; but he could not be silent long, because that his trouble increased. Wherefore at length he brake his mind to his wife and children."[17]

James's episode of "fear and trembling" was intended as spiritual reality and not historical actuality.* The distortions that he made are noteworthy. He may have been in good health, as he alleged, but before going abroad Henry had referred to his poor health as one justification of his decision to travel.† Since he had confided his vocational dilemma to his friend Ralph Waldo Emerson the year before, the impulse to flee to Europe in 1843 came as no surprise to him. "Here I am thirty-one years in life, ignorant in all outward science, but having patient habits of meditation which never know disgust or weariness, and feeling a force of impulsive love toward all

---

*The reference to "fear and trembling" has many biblical resonances. In Job 4:14 it marks the onset of a mystical experience, a revelation of man's inability to understand God's ways. Swedenborg wrote authoritatively about such "holy fear," using the imagery of fire and lightning. In *The Apocalypse Revealed,* for example, he remarked that "a holy fear, which is sometimes conjoined with a sacred terror of the interiors of the mind, and sometimes with the hair rising, supervenes when life from the Lord enters in place of one's own life." To illustrate the point he referred to Daniel, who was placed in a state of holy fear when he came upon a man whose face was "as the lightning, His eyes as lamps of fire" (Emanuel Swedenborg, *The Apocalypse Revealed; Wherein Are Disclosed the Arcana There Foretold, Which Have Hitherto Remained Concealed* [Boston, 1907], 1:100–101).

†Henry wrote to Joseph Henry, "My health has got unsteady from deprivation of fresh air and confinement to my chair" (*TCWJ,* 1:17), and then announced his intention to travel to Europe. A few months later he was more specific about his symptoms to Emerson: "I think it probable I shall winter in some mild English climate—Devonshire, perhaps—and go on with my studies as at home. My chest is in an unsound condition someway, and if I can find a superior climate for it in England than I have at home, I think I shall then be much furthered also in my pursuits" (*TCWJ,* 1:50).

humanity which will not let me rest wholly mute—a force which grows against all resistance that I can master against it. What shall I do?"[18]

"What shall I do?" The plaintive cry of Christian over his soul's fate was also the cry of a thirty-one-year-old man burdened by aimlessness. He considered two alternatives, withdrawal to the country in order to live a bucolic life (like Emerson), far from the "talking kind," save for communicating "a fit word once a year," or learning science, which would bring him "first into men's respect, that thus I may the better speak to them." He characteristically rejected both alternatives (he would foist science on his son William in 1860) and dared "the invisible Emerson" to come up with "some heart-secret-law" to help him.[19]

Emerson understood the desire to help humankind in general, but he also knew that Henry was running from a particular culture with specific occupations, none of which appealed to him. Emerson shrewdly reminded him that while travel "may easily silence all contradictions, . . . it will not do that which you will ever hold before you to be done, but that will remain to be achieved afterward as now."[20] The travel solution was at best temporary.

It is possible that James recovered his health abroad, and the alleged good health of the crisis story may have been historically accurate, but the successful lectures to "good audiences" were certainly fabrications. In fact, his words typically reverberated in uncomfortably empty halls. After one of these poorly attended lectures in 1841 he had complained to Emerson: "I came home tonight from my lecture a little disposed to think from the smart reduction of my audience that I had about as well not prepared my lectures, especially that I get no tidings of having interested one of the sort (the religious) for whom they were wholly designed. And now I say to myself 'the first step in your outgoing to the world having thus failed you, no second step of course offers itself, but you must come back to your perch, and look around the horizon for some other flight.'"[21]* And that flight was to Europe.

In his turmoil, James, like Bunyan's Christian, turned for help to his version of Mr. Worldly Wise—physicians who could formulate his spiritual crisis only in materialistic terms. "I consulted eminent physicians, who told me that I had doubtless overworked my brain,—an evil for which no remedy existed in medicine, but only in time and patience, and growth into improved physical conditions. They all recommended by way of hygiene a resort to the water-cure treatment, a life in the open air,

---

*Perry dated this letter incorrectly as 1842, because James says he is "thirty-one years in life" in the text. I think this means he was in his thirty-first year, and so had not yet turned thirty-one. In any event, the letter is from the period vaguely referred to by James as "two or three years" before the crisis.

cheerful company, and so forth, and thus quietly and skillfully dismissed me to my own spiritual medication." What James wanted was not the water cure that ministered to the body, but a spiritual baptism, a diving into the depths, heedless of the warnings of the wordly wise. In the crisis tale, he claimed that he was directed to Swedenborg by a friend, Mrs. Chichester, who told him that Swedenborg described an experience such as he seemed to be having as a "vastation," and suggested that he read about it. He purchased some of Swedenborg's works, yet was afraid to read them because of the doctor's warnings against overworking his brain. But finally he took the leap: "I resolved in spite of the doctors, that instead of standing any longer shivering on the brink, I would boldly plunge into the stream, and ascertain, once and for all, to what undiscovered sea its waters might bear me." Swedenborg and not the water cure could cleanse him after his descent into the Slough of Despond.

It was essential for the structure of Mr. James's Christian myth to report that he had heard Swedenborg's word while in the depths of despair, so that the encounter would demonstrate saving power. Here, too, as in the description of his health and success, the story bears little relation to the details of his life. It is likely that James was familiar with Swedenborg long before he went to Europe, and it is all but certain that he had read him before the crisis.*

He definitely knew the work of J. J. Garth Wilkinson, Swedenborg's English publicist and translator, before the crisis. Wilkinson's article in the *Monthly Magazine* in 1841 elicited a letter from Mr. James that initiated a lifelong friendship.[22] While in England in 1843, James visited Wilkinson. At the time, Wilkinson's translation of Swedenborg's *Economy of the Animal Kingdom* was in press. He wrote to James about it in February, four months before the crisis. It is possible that James and Wilkinson never discussed Swedenborg's views of "vastation," and that the story of the "discovery" guided by Mrs. Chichester took place as James described it.

---

*James could have come into contact with Swedenborg's ideas as early as 1830, during his flight from Union. Sampson Reed's *Observations on the Growth of the Mind* could have been found at Mr. Jenks's home (if he hadn't read the reviews in *The Christian Examiner*). In the 1840s many intellectuals were attracted to the teachings of the Swedish seer, and it is extremely likely that Henry, who was devoting himself completely to biblical study by then, had heard of him and read his works. Furthermore, James's letters preceding the 1843 voyage abroad show that he had already arrived at a theological position that he later credited to Swedenborg. In his letter of July 9, 1843, to Joseph Henry, he outlined ideas that were, if not influenced by Swedenborg, certainly congruent with his teaching. "Again and again I am forced by Scriptural philosophy to the conviction that all the phenomena of physics are to be explained and grouped under laws *exclusively spiritual*—that they are in fact only the material expression of spiritual truth, or, as Paul says, the visible forms of invisible substance." It is possible that Henry reached this conclusion himself and was well prepared to embrace the Swedenborgian doctrine of correspondence.

But it is more likely that the "discovery" was one more piece of stage machinery in a Christian morality play, and that the personage of Mrs. Chichester was a Victorian bow to the saving power of woman.

Henry and his newfound friend had much to talk about besides Swedenborg. Wilkinson was in the throes of a vocational crisis himself, and Swedenborg promised help for the Englishman as he did for the American. Wilkinson had wanted to be a lawyer but his father had forced him to study medicine, using money as a wedge. According to Wilkinson's biographer, the reluctant physician hated surgery and "drugging," and his career began badly. "The routine education of an unwilling pupil left him ever hostile to the *Profession* into which it introduced him." The slow start of an unwanted practice left him ample time to translate Swedenborg's works.[23] James must have known of his friend's vocational dissatisfaction, because he urged him to move to America—a plan that was abandoned as too risky—and introduced him to homeopathy, a theory of medicine more harmonious with his spiritual inclinations. Once Wilkinson was launched on his career as a homeopath, his practice flourished.

One final element in James's 1879 description of his crisis bears critical scrutiny: the impact that it allegedly had on his work. He said that he had discovered that "the book of Genesis was not intended to throw a direct light upon our natural or race history, but was an altogether mystical or symbolic record of the laws of God's *spiritual* creation and providence." After his crisis, he claimed, he abandoned all interest in the discovery. "It struck me as very odd, soon after my breakdown, that I should feel no longing to resume the work which had been interrupted by it; and from that day to this (nearly thirty-five years) I have never once cast a retrospective glance, even of curiosity, at the immense piles of manuscript which had erewhile so absorbed me."[24] Once again James made use of an allusion to underscore the spiritual significance of the crisis. Bunyan's Christian never cast a backward glance once he decided to leave his unawakened life in the City of Destruction.* The allusion is biblical as well. The fate of Lot's wife, who was tempted to look back as she fled from the destruction of Sodom, was different from Christian's. She looked back "and she became a pillar of salt."[25] In actuality, that was Henry James's fate. His theological writing shows clearly that he was obsessed with the problem of creation, the topic that he allegedly abandoned. If, as he says, he turned his back on a mountain of manuscript, he cast his glance back

---

*"So . . . the man began to run. Now, he had not run far from his own door, but his wife and children perceiving it, began to cry after him to return; but the man put his fingers in his ears, and ran on, crying Life! Life! Eternal life! So he looked not behind him, but fled toward the middle of the plain" (John Bunyan, *The Pilgrim's Progress* [New York and London, 1848],5).

again and again in an attempt to make sense of the flames and the bitterness of his father's rejection.

[7]

The Jamesian rendition of the crisis of 1844 was clearly a parable, artfully based on the author's experience. Though consciously shaped to highlight spiritual reality instead of historical actuality, it contains clues unconsciously left by the author which tie the crisis to his disinheritance. The biblical allusion to Job and to Lot's wife, for example, both refer to loss of property.* Even more important, he made direct reference to the parable of the prodigal son. Henry recommended Swedenborg's nourishing doctrine for the spiritually hungry who, like the prodigal son, "are secretly pining for their Father's house where there is bread enough and to spare. . . ."26 The parable of the prodigal son spoke directly to Henry's plight. It treats of a younger son who "wasted his substance with riotous living," but was welcomed back by his father as a lost sheep. Not only did Henry cite the parable, but he spoke of his desire, during the throes of his torment, to change places with the sheep grazing in the park at Windsor—to exchange their natural simplicity for his despair, and, I presume, their fate at the hands of a shepherd who rejoiced in the return of one lost from the fold.

Henry wrote an earlier version of the crisis tale (*Substance and Shadow*, 1863). Even more compelling connections with the testamentary rejection are to be found in this version, published sixteen years before the one found in *Society the Redeemed Form of Man*. The early version lacks the archetypal quality of the later one, but the details give a much more vivid impression of Henry's scrupulosity during his breakdown.

> The more I strove to indue myself in actual righteousness, the wider gaped the jaws of hell within me; the fouler grew its fetid breath. A conviction of inward defilement so sheer took possession of me, that death seemed better than life. I soon found my conscience, once launched in this insane career, acquiring so infernal an edge, that I could no longer indulge myself in the most momentary deviation from an absurd and pedantic literal rectitude, could not, for example, bestow a sulky glance upon my wife, a cross word upon my child, or a petulant objurgation on my cook, without tumbling into

---

*Job had been deprived of all his flocks. Lot's wife was, according to Luke 17:31–32, moved to look back because she was overly concerned with property: "In that day, he which shall be on the housetop, and his goods in the house, let him not go down to take them away: . . . Remember Lot's wife."

an instant inward frenzy of alarm, lest I should thereby provoke God's personal malignity to me.[27]*

The early rendition contains a long version of the parable of the prodigal son rather than a brief reference. It is, to say the least, peculiar to James:

> Surely if I have a family of children the eldest of whom is alone legitimate, and therefore alone entitled to my name and estate, while all the younger children are bastards, and consequently destitute of all legal righteousness, I should be a worm and no man, if while according to the former his fullest legal consideration, I did not bestow my tenderest and ripest affection and indulgence upon the latter. If my acknowledged heir, conceiving himself prejudiced by this action on my part, should grow angry and reproach me thereupon, saying, "Lo! these many years do I serve thee, neither have I transgressed thy commandments, and yet thou has never given me the slightest expression of thy heart's delight, such as thou art now lavishing upon others who have wasted thy substance with riotous living;" . . . I should say, "My son, I leave it to yourself to estimate the claim which the service you boast of exerts upon my heart, now that your shameless inhumanity to your less fortunate brethren reveals even to your own eyes the spirit which has always animated that service; . . . You shall have accordingly your legal deserts to the utmost, all that I outwardly possess shall be yours, while I bestow myself, all that I inwardly am, upon your humbler brethren."[28]

By imagining himself a father with only one heir legally entitled to his estate, he placed himself in a position comparable to that of his own father, with one grown son, Augustus, entitled to inherit by his father's interpretation of the moral law. But Henry will behave like the father in Jesus' parable rather than like his own father. The moralizing speech that he delivers to the rightful heir shows that he was quite capable of dealing out humiliation. He would, he indicated, give the legitimate son his material wealth, as the law required, but he would cut him off from his spiritual legacy—his affection—taking instead the illegitimate offspring to his bosom. As a man in his fifties, father and creator himself, Henry rewrote the parable of the prodigal son so that he could simultaneously win out over his father's favorite, Augustus, prove himself a better father than *his* father had been, and undo the testamentary rejection that still rankled.

The crisis tale and the revised parable are not unique. Whenever Henry James, Sr., wrote about the importance of conscience for his religious

---

*When William James edited his father's manuscripts for *The Literary Remains of the Late Henry James,* he placed this passage just before the 1879 crisis tale, and I assume saw the connection between the two.

development, metaphors of inheritance and property repeatedly surfaced. A passage from *The Secret of Swedenborg* (1869) makes the link irrefutable: "Thus deeper than my intellect, deeper than my heart, deeper in fact than aught and all that I recognize as myself or am wont to call emphatically *me*, is this dread omnipotent power of conscience which now soothes me with the voice, and nurses me with the milk of its tenderness, as the mother soothes and nurses her child, and anon scourges me with the last of its indignation, as the father scourges his refractory heir."[29] Careful attention to Henry's language—the metaphors and associations of a lifetime of theological speculation—point unequivocally to the plight of the prodigal son.*

*It may be argued that the strength of this construction depends on associations and metaphors that are widely separated in the same text or from different texts widely separated in time. Fortunately Mr. James provides us with a single text that links the crisis with his father's will. In it he condenses a period of seven years, joining the period of study at Princeton Theological Seminary with the crisis that led to his Swedenborgian conversion—the period of vocational floundering, from 1837 to 1844. "I was born in the bosom of orthodoxy, and never knew a misgiving as to the perfect truth of its dogmas, until I had begun to prepare myself for its professional ministry. Then I could no longer evade the enormous difficulties which inhered in its philosophy. . . . I was sure that while orthodoxy had somehow succeeded to a celestial inheritance, it was yet a most unrighteous steward of the inheritance; but how to dispossess it God alone knew. It was at this crisis of my intellectual fortunes that I encountered Swedenborg, . . . and found in his doctrine of nature a complete extrication from my trouble" (S&S, 121–22). Lawyers rather than God helped Henry to dispossess the unrighteous stewards. Swedenborg gave him vital help in his efforts to cope with the emotional consequences of his rebellion.

5

Ideology for a Prodigal

It were a wise inquiry . . . to compare, point by point, especially at
remarkable crises in life, our daily history with the rise and progress of
ideas in the mind.

—Ralph Waldo Emerson, 1836

[1]

HENRY JAMES was thirty-four when he returned to America
in 1845. He moved his enlarging family restlessly back and
forth between Albany and New York. The birthplaces of his children mark
his movements. Garth Wilkinson James was born in New York in 1845,
Robertson James in Albany the following summer, and Alice James in
New York in August 1848. Finally the family settled into a home that
Henry purchased at 58 West Fourteenth Street in New York. They remained there for seven years.

Henry befriended many artists and writers, and his New York home
became a familiar gathering place for luminaries of the transcendentalist
and associationist movements. Waldo Emerson, Henry Thoreau, Arthur
Brisbane, Parke Godwin, Charles Dana, and George Ripley were his
guests. Like many of his intellectual friends, Henry was enthusiastic about
the ideas of François Fourier, the French utopian socialist, who proposed
social reform through "scientifically" ordered associations that he called
phalanxes. His program was seized upon as a practical blueprint for spiritual harmony, the goal that drew many people to Swedenborg's vision in
the 1840s and 1850s. *The Harbinger,* George Ripley's associationist weekly,
trumpeted a call to the establishment of the kingdom of heaven, and
Henry James added his voice to the multitude in a series of articles written
from 1847 to 1849.

Henry's writings make it perfectly clear that the parable of the prodigal son was more than an apt biblical allusion. It had become a self-image impressed on him by William James and sealed by his testamentary rejection. Henry would carry it as a mark of shame for the rest of his life. But in his social commentary and his theological speculation, he tried to lighten that burden by fashioning an ideology to justify a rejected prodigal.*

The primary issue between Henry and his father had been Henry's refusal to bow to paternal authority. Understandably, this rebellious son was drawn to a social theory that sanctioned individual freedom unfettered by social conventions or filial piety. Socialist and democratic ideas were blended in his mind into a utopian alloy seemingly strong enough to bear this ideological load. But there were fractures beneath the surface. Individual freedom had to be weighed in the balance against Henry's equally insistent demand for nurture. On the one hand, he stormed at any interference with his will; on the other, he demanded that God and society (and his father) support him *without fail*. Obviously the severe Calvinist God of his father's generation was unsuitable for this purpose. Nor was the aloof God of deism satisfactory. A Creator who set the world machine in motion and then sat idle and remote from his creatures held no appeal for James. He would acknowledge only a Heavenly Father like Swedenborg's, who loved *all* his creatures generously and unconditionally. Such a God promised forgiveness to this uncertain, intermittently contrite prodigal.

Henry presented many of his ideas from the lecture platform. In a lecture arranged by Emerson and delivered in Boston in November 1849, he exhorted his audience to embrace his socialist vision of human nature. He contrasted the conservative's (Calvinist) view with the socialist's. "The socialist affirms the inherent righteousness of humanity. . . . The conservative, on the other hand, . . . affirms the inherent depravity of man." The distinction was important. With different premises about human nature, the conservative and the socialist had very different attitudes toward individual freedom. The socialist "affirms that man is sufficient unto himself, and needs no outward ordinances for his guidance. . . . The conservative . . . affirms that he is insufficient unto himself, and requires dominion

---

*Clifford Geertz has aptly categorized the type of ideological analysis used in this chapter as the "strain theory." According to this approach, ideologies are understood "against the background of a chronic effort to correct sociopsychological disequilibrium." Since the theory is based on a medical model by implication, it treats an ideology as a "symptom." I do not believe that this metaphor necessarily depreciates creative work. The term *ideology* can call attention to the functional evolution of ideas without necessarily labeling the thought pathological. Geertz suggests that the study of ideology should be extended by an exploration of transformation of ideological symbols within a given culture. Chapter 6 pursues this idea. See Clifford Geertz, "Ideology as a Cultural System," *Ideology and Discontent* ed. David Apter (New York, 1964), 52, 60–65.

of tutors and governors all his appointed days upon the earth."[1] As a socialist, James affirmed that human beings have a God-given right to be free of all institutions, whether family, church, or state. And anyone who dared to impose a lifetime of compliance was evil and ought to be resisted with all one's strength.

James warned his audience that parents had no right to expect lifetime obedience from children. Parental care must be freely offered without expectation of perpetual obligation. Of his own parents he said, "I acknowledge gratefully the kindness I have received at their hands. But if they ask any other reward for this kindness than the satisfaction of seeing me a man, if they expect me to continue their humble satellite and partisan, instead of God's conscript and votary solely, I am bound to disappoint them."[2] How well a God that freed him from parental control and the dictates of a scrupulous conscience suited his ideological necessity! When such a God called, a father's internalized voice might be stilled.*

Henry proclaimed a democratic vision that harmonized with his utopian socialist ideas. Democracy "supposes men are capable of so adjusting their relations to each other as that they will need no police or external force to control them, but will spontaneously do the right thing in all places and at all times."[3] This sentiment was not anchored in any firsthand familiarity with democratic political structures or constitutional theory. James's attention rarely descended to practical affairs. He was concerned with spiritual ideals. Indeed, he complained to an 1851 audience that society (and practical affairs) interfered with his spiritual development. "The incessant action of society is to shut up all my time and thought to the interests of my mere visible existence, to the necessity of providing subsistence, education, and social respect for myself and my children. . . . My true divine selfhood is completely swamped in transient frivolous cares."[4]

---

*The idea that James's theology was intimately connected with his personal history is not new. His son William was the first to note that his "father [seemed] in his early years to have had an unusually lively and protracted [religious crisis], and his philosophy indeed is but the statement of his cure" (LRLHJ, 55). Frederick Harold Young, who has written a thorough analysis of the formal structure of James's theology, found that "his works read as though they were produced out of an autobiographical necessity, and for no other reason" (PHJ, 283). Henry James, Sr., rejected passionless, abstract thought as so much "worthless wind," and he explicitly denied theology a source beyond personal experience (Henry James, "On the Philosophical Tendencies of the Age—J. D. Morell," Harbinger 7 [1848]:3). "It is true the old theologians will tell you that they derive their views of the divine character and of human destiny from revelation, but it is none the less true that every one's perception of revelation is exactly moulded upon his experience of life, or the amount of science it has engendered for him" (Henry James, "Theological Differences in Association," Harbinger 6 [1848]:26. See also Dwight W. Hoover, Henry James, Sr., and the Religion of Community (Grand Rapids, Mich.: William B. Erdmans, 1969), 43–73; Giles Gunn, ed., Henry James, Sr.: A Selection of His Writings (Chicago: American Library Association, 1974), 3–32.

If only government and parents would cease their interference with individuals' divine selfhood, surely the kingdom of heaven would be at hand. All that the inward human spirit "asks of the outward [law and government] is to serve or obey it by immediately ceasing to restrain or govern its outflow." *Then* society would reshape itself to provide "the affluent satisfaction of every human want," and humanity's deepest spiritual longings as well.[5]

Henry expected society to give him what he had demanded from his father: generous support. And if the moral outcome was evil, it was not *his* doing, but the fault of social institutions. People were good, and were made evil only by imperfect society. In his most radical frame of mind (in his thirties), James followed that premise to an extreme, declaring that criminals were really heroes because they expressed the God within, heedless of society's strictures. In anticipation of Nietszche's idea of the superman, he lauded the criminal who, "instead of contenting himself . . . with the bare supply of his physical wants . . . [has] instincts of infinitude . . . [that] drive him to seek their *excessive* gratification, and . . . hurry him into vice and crime."

It is easy to understand the ideological appeal of this version of the doctrine of the holy sinner. The youthful excesses that brought his father's (and God's) wrath upon him were transformed from signs of depravity into proofs of spiritual talent. Rather than the mark of Cain, they were the stigmata of immanent grace. "Vice expresses his attempt to actualize his ideal and essential infinitude, without concurrence of nature. Crime expresses his attempt to actualize it, without the concurrence of society." He urged his audience to join him in pardoning sin, since "the very vices and crimes of man place him above nature, deny his essential finiteness, proclaim his true subjection to an ideal and infinite object only."[6]

In effect, a prodigal son could not lose. He was either a saint or, failing that, a blameless sinner because society made him so. "No man is evil save for want of free development, save for want of a closer walk with God than the existing Church and State agree to tolerate. . . . [The criminal] does all this in the way of a mute unconscious protest against overwhelming social tyranny, which would otherwise crush out the distinctive life of man under the machinery of government and caste. . . . Let us view them as unconscious martyrs of humanity."[7]

James's paean to sin may have suited his inner logic, but it was not favorably received. His friend and usually sympathetic reviewer James Freeman Clarke, for one, could not resist parodying what he considered an absurd position. "The only danger, in fact, is of not being as bad, as mean, as false, as base, as cruel, as selfish as we need to be, in order to be loved by God."[8]

Henry James retained a measure of utopian optimism to the end of his days. But a subtle shift took place through the 1850s. He gradually acknowledged the importance of social constraints. As the glow faded from associationism, the Calvinist flame within him was rekindled. This shift was due in part to the experience of parenthood.* He could not continue his battle with William James of Albany on exactly the same terms in middle age as had appealed to him when he fled from Union College, twenty years before. He had five children and knew that parental authority was necessary. "It is well for me," he reluctantly admitted, "when my will is purely sensual or devilish—when it insists upon overriding everything to compass a momentary gratification—when in short I am an infant in culture and manifest the disposition of an infant—then it is well for me to obey the will óf a superior. Devotion then is both profitable and honorable."9

If the shade of William James of Albany hovered in the back of the sparsely filled hall, listening to this admission, he might have taken comfort from the change in his son Henry. But the satisfaction would have been momentary, for Henry's rebellious self was also there in all its irritating vigor. He simply could not discuss private property without swiping at his dead father. He minimized his father's accomplishment in acquiring his wealth while maximizing his own spiritual superiority in using it. "A man of very large possessions, unless he has come into them by inheritance, is almost wholly absorbed by them. Instead of being rendered free and careless, his life is a perpetual servitude. His whole energy becomes demanded by the care of his property, while he himself gradually lapses from unqualified manhood into the mere man of money." Henry weighed William James on the scales of an ungrateful heir. "As a general thing therefore we may say, the larger the possessions the smaller the man."10

Though he relished the good use he made of his father's money, Henry was apparently uncomfortable with the newness of the James family for-

---

*James told his 1851 lecture audience about the difficulty he had getting his young children to share their toys. "Do you take home with you as you go from your occupations in the evening, or return from a journey, a picture book or child's toy of any sort, and expose it to the gaze of your children: you all know how furious a storm of entreaty will greet you on every hand for the sole possession of the bauble. You may assure the little circle that each shall possess it in turn, that each shall enjoy it to the full. But no, each must call it his own absolutely, each must have complete possession of it, and then of course he will do the generous thing toward the others." How does a father with a firm belief in his child's divine nature cope with this naked declaration of evil? Mr. James confessed frankly that he retreated to await the opportunity of a better day: "You are glad to purchase the final quiet for yourself by bestowing it out and out upon the noisiest lungs of the group, promising the others that their turns shall come next time" (*LM*, 53–54).

tune. No matter how large his inheritance, he was still a merchant's son with no tradition of leisure or letters to draw upon. Society, he implied, would not let him forget it: "So true is this, that if by chance a lucky investment in real estate makes his descendants rich and leaders of fashion, society is sure to visit them with perpetual recurrence to the ancestral wax-end, or at least a very frequent prick of the paternal needle."[11] Dismissal of forty years of real estate development and financial planning as "a lucky investment" was the privilege of a son who knew little of the business that paid for his leisure. Though Henry was more sensitive to parental problems in the 1850s, his battle with his father was far from over.

[3]

Independence and dependency needed to be accounted for in James's theology just as he had balanced them (to his satisfaction) in his social theory. Individuals are morally independent of God yet totally dependent on him, just as they are independent of society though they rely on its generous support. Henry's theory of creation became the central doctrine of the theological side of his ideology. He was at his best rhetorically as a critic, and the Reverend Edward Beecher (son of Lyman Beecher, the "pope" of conservative Congregationalism) was a convenient adversary.* James attacked him in *The Nature of Evil* (1855) for falling prey to the errors of "natural theology," the derivation of one's conception of God from a study of nature. According to James, conservative natural theology was misguided because it emphasized the physical act of creation as an event in space and time. He preferred to call physical creation "formation," and blithely assumed it as a necessary precondition of spiritual creation. For him, a creation theory had to account for man as a moral creature straining toward redemption with a benign, patient Creator. His emphasis was more psychological than cosmological. Henry was quick to point out that the conservative focus on physical creation in time and space had logical implications that were unacceptable. He was convinced that it made moral responsibility impossible.

If one is to be morally responsible, one must have freedom to choose between good and evil. If God created man in time and space—a physical

---

*Edward Beecher was a prominent minister of a conservative congregation but he became a theological renegade. In his efforts to defend Calvinism, he transformed it and roused a storm of criticism. In *The Conflict of Ages*, he argued that the Fall had taken place in a preexistence. It was this view, anchored in natural theology, that drew the elder Henry's barbs. See Marie Caskey, *Chariot of Fire: Religion and the Beecher Family* (New Haven: Yale University Press, 1978), 123–39.

act—and if by definition God has the attributes of omnipotence and perfection, then he and not man is reponsible for what follows. "If creation be an outward act of Deity, an act of His arbitrary power or will, it is instantly clear that He alone is responsible for all its contents, and the creature is pronounced *ipso facto* incapable of drawing a moral breath."[12] Such a relationship between Creator and creature was not fitting. It was not moral freedom but moral slavery, and in James's impassioned view *any* crime committed in an effort to break free was justified, even murder. "Deprive a man of self-mastery or the arbitrament of his own actions, that is, reduce him to slavery, and you destroy his morality. He may kill you, or do what he will towards you without reproach, because you have previously debauched his moral instincts, or robbed him of his moral growth, and consequently inaugurated purely brute relations between you."[13]* James's gift for hyperbole did not always serve his theological argument well, but it revealed the intensity of his indignation.

The same logic that made thieves into heroes now, in theological context, justified a murderous rage toward one's Creator. Henry warmed to the battle as he slashed at his foe's inhumane diety. Every strike at such a Creator was a blow against tyranny, and James relished the combat. Beecher's God created people evil and then punished them for the very acts that were forced on them by their God-given natures. By any standards of human decency, James declared, such a God was an outrage. "A very pretty temper of mind, for men to ascribe to the fountain of all perfection!" he chided. "God angry with a person for being empty of all goodness, of all knowledge, of all power! Angry with a person for not displaying His own exclusive attributes, a person whom He himself summons into existence, and who therefore is completely dependent upon Himself for all that he has been, is, or shall be! What incredible petulance! What incredible inhumanity to ascribe to God!" For James, the ideological assault on his father and his father's God were one. He concluded, "I would renounce my own father as cheerfully as I would eat my daily bread, did I conceive him capable of a pretty malignity like this."[14] Did any of his readers appreciate the tragic irony of that brave declaration? He had effectively turned his father's basis for judgment against the judge himself. If conventional Calvinism was correct (and Henry thought it was not), then he could not be responsible for his prodigal actions, and his father had no right to punish him.

---

*Two decades of abolitionist pamphleteering on the moral crime of slavery and the recent upset of the equilibrium of national politics by the Kansas-Nebraska Act of 1854 made the image of the murder of a master by a slave a compelling one for his audience.

[4]

James preferred an entirely different conception of God and creation to solve the dilemma of God's omnipotence and man's moral agency. If man was to have moral responsibility, then creation had to be an ongoing spiritual process and not an act in the physical world. Creation is not, he insisted, "the power of making THINGS," but is "exclusively a rational power . . . of making PERSONS."[15]* And this relationship between a loving Creator and his dependent creature allowed the creature to sin yet promised forgiveness and redemption. For Henry a loving and obedient son was inconceivable without a loving father. The Calvinist God that James abhorred would choose one brother over others because he had been obedient. But a humane God would care about all of his children because they were dependent on him, not because they had done his bidding. Men are not "servants, but sons," he argued, "and the son does not feel himself related to the father by desert or merit, but by want, by infirmity, by essential dependence, and a confidence which is bounded only by the father's truth."[16] It could not be the will of God "that one brother enjoy the servile and sycophantic devotion of all the rest."[17] That one compliant son should be favored with a greater portion and granted power as a trustee to judge his brothers' tendencies toward "profligacy and vice" was outrageous. It must be wrong.

As spiritual creation became more central to his thinking, Henry moved away from Fourier and the hope that social reorganization by itself would bring on the kingdom of heaven. An 1855 letter in the *New York Tribune* marked his complete abandonment of Fourier's social mechanics. Society, he now believed, was a spiritual relationship that depended on the process of spiritual creation. Fourier and other socialists (such as Saint-Simon and Comte) were wrong because they "all suppose [society] to be the product of purely natural laws." He was particularly critical of Fourier, who talked "of organizing society as glibly as you would talk of organizing a military company."[18] Henry was no longer an advocate of such social experiments.

Though James argued heroically for independence, he also longed for

---

*James was perpetually reminding his audience that creation was an invisible process that proceeded by the liberation of inner resources rather than the imposition of external form. Using a favorite transcendentalist metaphor, he cautioned, "It is not like the power of a carpenter or sculptor modifying pre-existing materials, and proceeding therefore from the circumference to the center of his work: it resembles rather the phenomenon of natural growth which proceeds upon the liberation under suitable conditions of an invisible spiritual germ, and its subsequent orderly expansion into root and stem, branch and leaf, flower and fruit" (*CCNE*, 46).

fusion with the Creator. How could he balance the two? On the one hand, he declared that the aim of spiritual creation is "not to make [a man] the likeness of his father. . . . It is simply to make him himself."[19] Yet on the other, he did not want to be cut off from his Creator. Surprisingly (given the intensity of his youthful radicalism), he came to believe that this much-vaunted and logically necessary independence was an illusion. Man eventually discovered that God was the source of his powers, and far from being independent and alone, he was inseparably fused with his Creator. God was within him, making his presence felt in his spontaneous attractions. "Here preeminently do I find God. Here alone do I perfectly lose and perfectly find myself. Here alone, in short, do I feel empowered to say, what every true creature of God is bound to say, 'I and my father are one.'"[20] Absolute freedom, the *sine qua non* for the radical of the 1840s, had been transformed into a necessary illusion.

[5]

While Henry James's theology can be read as a criticism of his father, it may also be understood as a statement of his own parental aspirations.* God the Creator was an ideal model for him to emulate in raising his own children. He had balanced independence and dependency, separation and fusion in his social theory and in his theology. The tension had to be addressed at home as well.

Man's independence "no more separates me from God," he asserted, "or renders me independent of Him, than the freedom I allow my child renders him properly independent of me." As a more experienced father, James saw the necessity of tempering that freedom. It was not absolute (as he had demanded as a younger man), but a "rational freedom" that aimed at "the development of a manly character in the child, and consequently involves on my part the administration of a strict discipline." Though a liberal parent may surround his child with an atmosphere of freedom that fosters his dignity, he also must recognize that "the child has certain natural or inherited tendencies which . . . tempt him to the inordinate indulgence of his natural appetites." To allow such indulgence to go unchecked would amount to moral indifference. And a responsible parent had to blunt the force of a child's evil inclinations by punishing him.

---

*When James reviewed Horace Bushnell's *Views of Christian Nurture* in 1847 for *The Harbinger*, he had four sons under five years of age. He shared Bushnell's view that the proper relation between parent and child is "a spiritual relation, elevating the merely natural relation in which the parties previously stood, into a truly human one, or one which accurately images the relation of the Creator to the creature."

Henry James, Sr., and Henry James, Jr., 1854

Indeed, he now believed that punishment could free a child "from the bondage of his nature," which tempts him to "plunge into every lawless lust."[21]

When William James of Albany chastised his son for his extravagent tastes and his alcoholism, hadn't restraint of "lawless lusts" been his intention? When he urged a learned profession on his son rather than boundless leisure, wasn't he intent on directing a high-spirited son toward responsible manhood? Wasn't disinheritance a father's reluctant final discipline, an act of concern and not indifference? It was not *necessarily* narrow materialism, as he originally thought. A father might inflict pain on his son *because* he loved him. In sober passages such as these, Henry James reluctantly joined hands in middle age with all parents enmeshed in the tense cycle of connectedness and separation between generations.

As Henry illustrated his theological tracts with incidents from his own family life, we can glimpse his paternal ideal in operation.* He would not be overly judgmental toward a child whose inclinations were wild, or overly complimentary toward a son whose nature was "celestial." To the naturally good child he would say, "Yes, these are very sweet traits, my child, and they make you sweet and beautiful to your father's heart; but we must both remember that all these things come from God to us through the medium of angels, and are not intended therefore to make us proud or vain." He would try to make the child aware that his talents were not to inflate his own sense of importance, but were a means to "realize your eternal conjunction with God." A child who was deceitful, wild, and bad-tempered would be disciplined by his father, yet encouraged "for that these dispositions are exclusively an influx from evil spirits, and do not belong to him, save in so far as he heartily cherishes and indulges them."[22] An ideal father would understand evil characteristics as trials to bring his erring son into spiritual conjunction with his Creator.

What parent would not be happy to fulfill his responsibility with such compassion? The ability to communicate love without indulgence and discipline without vindictiveness is a high ideal that is, unfortunately, difficult to attain. If these passages were at all representative of Henry's behavior with his children, he succeeded, at least at moments, in being the father he wished he had had, and the father he wished to be.

[6]

As we reconstruct the family atmosphere in which Henry's son William grew to manhood, it is convenient to identify Henry's shifting inclinations

---

*When Henry published *The Nature of Evil* he was forty-four. His son William was thirteen years old.

as different voices—different emotional tones matched to conflicting positions toward human nature, moral responsibility, and punishment.* In defining Henry's ideology, I have emphasized the voice of the disinherited prodigal. When writing or speaking in this mode, Henry was shrill, rebellious, and outraged by any interference with his inward impulsion. This was the dominant voice in his twenties and thirties, and it never completely subsided. I have also indicated Henry's ideal parental voice. In this mode he was compassionate yet aware of his responsibility to provide direction and discipline to the young. This is a voice filled with tenderness, yet free of indulgence. It is a voice that met the ideological necessity of the rebellious son, not by berating his Creator but by treating his children as he wished his father had dealt with him.

The third voice, which became more and more prominent in his forties and fifties, was disturbingly like the severe, judgmental God (and father) he had rebelled against in his youth. His exclamations in this mode have the content of a renascent Calvinism and the scourging, moralizing tone of his father's testament. As his son William approached thirteen, the same age at which Henry's crippling encounter with God had occurred, Henry James began to sound more like that despised, punitive father. He spoke vividly of man's sinful nature, "which descends to us from all our past ancestry . . . and attaches to all mankind without exception." And he transformed what in his prodigal voice had been a primary goal—independence—into a defect that was the essence of man's fallen state. "What is called the Fall of man consisted in no change of his intrinsic nature from good to evil. He never lapsed from a state of goodness-in-himself into one of evil-in-himself, for the simple reason that he never was and never could have been good-in-himself." James was eloquent in his disgust with man for believing in his own independent powers. "His fall was his elevation in his own conceit, and hence it was pure mercy upon the part of God to endow him with conscience or the faculty of self condemnation." Speaking in this voice, he was convinced that natural man gives himself "airs of self sufficiency," but is "a fool" when he "unlearns his dependence."[23]

"The truth of our creatureship," he asserted, "the great truth that in the Lord alone we live and move and have our being, perfectly reconciles us to the fact of our essential and intrinsic destitution, by quieting every ambitious aspiration, or divorcing us from all desire to be any thing in ourselves."[24] James's new emphasis scorned man's belief in his own powers but it also relieved him of the need to strive. If independent selfhood was illusory, then Henry could not be condemned for failing to make his worldly mark.

---

*It is appropriate to speak of different voices, because that is how they would have been heard by his children.

We can only imagine how Henry's renewed Calvinist voice sounded to his teenaged son. Though the boy was philosophically gifted, it is likely that his father's fine theological distinctions escaped him. What he probably heard and responded to was the passion of denunciation—"Evil is what one is . . . man cannot be good-in-himself . . . he should be grateful to God for condemning his airs of self sufficiency . . . it is sinful to be independent . . . a good man is without ambition and has no desire to be anything"—a prophetic harangue that echoed the voice of William James of Albany. To be sure, Henry continued to say other things as well. In the voice of the rebellious prodigal, he said that it was important to be independent and it was criminal for institutions to block human efforts. And the ideal father's voice spoke of love, and patience, and the cultivation of manly qualities. It was a bewildering babel of tongues that had little logical consistency beyond its roots in Henry James's experience.

From an intellectual-historical point of view, we can recognize the new cuttings grafted onto the old—romantic individualism, liberalism, and Swedenborgianism were added—but the roots and the trunk were tenaciously Calvinist. The new graftings gave hope and placated a punitive conscience. But natural depravity, predestination, and submission to God's will increasingly blighted the fruits. It is a tragic irony that after struggling mightily to fashion an ideology for a prodigal, Henry James revived the atmosphere that poisoned his own youth, and he, too, undermined the manliness he was trying to nurture and, despite vigorous efforts to the contrary, pitched himself along with his son William into a mire of confusion and conflict over the choice of a vocation.

6

Words and Work

The mind, in short, works on the data it receives very much as a sculptor works on his block of stone.

—William James, 1890

[1]

WILLIAM JAMES would flounder for twelve years (from 1860 to 1872) in search of his vocation. Beginning when he was eighteen, he made transient forays into painting and natural science. He hesitatingly completed a medical degree but never practiced, and his medical studies were frequently interrupted by trips abroad to recover from recurrent depressions that plagued yet guided his search. Belatedly, in 1873, he began to teach at Harvard, first anatomy and physiology, then psychology, and finally philosophy. William James was a gifted young man, and the length of time required before he found his direction could be considered natural for a youth with multiple talents and a family with ample financial resources to support his wanderings. By comparison with the lives of his friends, however, William's prolonged search for a vocation was atypical. And his frequent illnesses—often timed to prevent final commitment to undesirable work—suggest a different conclusion. The ordinarily difficult task of vocational choice for a man of his age and station in nineteenth-century America was unusually complex in his case. The ideology that Henry James constructed in order to defuse, if not resolve, *his* father's judgment proved a stumbling block in the path of this eldest and favorite son.

As we have seen, Henry James challenged human authority, then exaggerated God's; insisted on unfettered independence, then rejected independence as illusory; scorned the making of money, yet demanded unlimited support; and absolved criminals of penance, yet finally affirmed guilt as a necessary stage in the redemptive process. These views naturally shaped Henry's behavior toward his son.

In addition to his socialist and theological tracts, Henry James wrote extensively about the nature of work, particularly during his Fourierist phase. By the time his son considered a career as an artist, scientist, or philosopher, Henry had vigorously declared his estimate of each of these fields. Thus, by studying the way the meanings of these terms shifted in Henry's writings, we can reconstruct the work world as he presented it to his son.

In his Fourierist phase, Henry James spoke of the artist in laudatory terms. Yet when his son wanted to be a painter, he scorned the choice. Then he glorified science, and at first encouraged his son in that direction. But when William became a scientist, his father was full of foreboding about the impact of a scientific career on his moral development. Henry James was devoted to philosophy throughout his adult life and he nurtured his son's philosophic talents. Yet when William turned to philosophy in his mature years, his father vehemently condemned academic philosophers. The changes of meaning of the terms of vocation reveal the ties that bound and the chasm that separated this devoted father and son.

[2]

Had he been alive to read *The Harbinger* in 1848, William James of Albany would have been shocked to read Henry's declaration that "no man dislikes labor." He would have been pleased, no doubt, that his son finally agreed with him that work "is in every man a divine inspiration which he can no more resist, than he can resist the attraction of the earth."[1] Work as a law of nature was close enough to his own belief in work as a divine duty. But that apparent shift was illusory. The young socialist had split two functions that earlier Protestant writers considered unified—work as an expression of the self was cut off from work as a social necessity. According to the older Calvinist view, religious devotion was central to labor.[2] Due recognition was given even so to the need to match individual talents and interests to gainful employment, but personal satisfaction was secondary to the obligation to fulfill one's God-given place in society. By contrast with this tradition, Henry James made human spontaneity the center of his worker's universe. Labor was good if it expressed a persons's impulse to act in the world. Though a religious intensity permeated this romantic view of labor, duty, the need to earn one's bread, was peripheral. "We repeat it no man dislikes labor, free labor, labor which is the outgrowth of his own spirit, and expresses himself. But every man dislikes to labor for his *living*." In short, Henry was prepared to admit the importance of labor, but he was not at all interested in earning a living. We can easily see how this break from traditional Calvinism suited his circumstance as wealthy would-be man of letters who was freed from the necessity of earning his bread because his father had labored so well.

William of Albany might have been startled to learn a detail about the life of Jesus that had captured his son's attention. Even Jesus was not gainfully employed! "I find no instance in all his history, in which he ever did a stroke of work whereby to gain a living. On the contrary," he assured his readers, "so far as *any* light is shed upon the question, he seems to have preferred living by the free-will charity of his followers, some elderly women being incidentally designated as those who ministered to him of their substance."[3] If it was permissible, even admirable, for Christ to live by another's substance, why not Henry James? He, too, would labor, but his work, like Jesus', would be the spreading of the Word, rather than conventional work for bread or social position.

When we note the romantic shift away from the Calvinist view of work, we should not overlook two important continuities. Henry still considered work (as he defined it) a virtue, and idleness was still a vice for man and God: "God is God to us, and worthy of our rational adoration," he proclaimed to his *Harbinger* readers in 1847, "not because of His infinite love and wisdom merely, but because this love and wisdom are *actually productive*. . . ." He praised God as a worker. "God is a mighty Artist, not a dreamer, nor a speculator but an actual doer."[4]

In his late thirties, Henry aspired to productivity, and on occasion even entertained the idea of earning a living by his pen. Encouraged by the sale of *Lectures and Miscellanies* (which he published at his own expense), he informed a friend of his ambition to "live abroad . . . on the income of my writings. How much more honorable this than upon one derived from the merciless warfare of Cedar and Wall Streets?"[5] But that brave hope was never realized.

Though he scorned worldly work, Henry James never overcame a sense of failure for not having supported himself. His judgment of idleness became increasingly severe until it culminated in a flood of vituperation that could only signify deep self-loathing. Sixteen years after the *Harbinger* articles he declared, "No one of my readers is capable of feeling the least respect for an idle God any more than for an idle man. Everyone respects labor; everyone respects the man who does something more to vindicate his human quality, than just live upon his ancestral fat."[6] Henry James was in his fifties by then, and still living on his patrimony.

Though he rejected Cedar and Wall Streets as vociferously as he had done in his youth, Henry ironically cast his religious message in the imagery of commerce. He urged his readers (and himself) to pursue a spiritual capitalism, investing their gifts for profit. Idleness, he argued, was a bad investment. "Everyone despises idleness; everyone despises the man, who being endowed as every man is by his maker with one talent or two talents or ten talents as the case may be, yet buries this Divine endowment in a napkin instead of putting it out to profitable use."[7] William James of Albany had been dead for more than thirty years at that writing; and this son that he had warned and threatened and finally punished had come to accept his father's judgment, and pronounced it in his father's language of increase.*

Six years later, Henry scourged himself publicly for living extravagantly on inherited wealth. "From the day of my birth till now I have not only never known what it was to have an honest want, a want of my nature, ungratified, but I have been able to squander upon my mere fantastic want, the will of my personal caprice, an amount of sustenance equal to the maintenance of a virtuous household." But here, too, his father would not have been entirely happy with his son's remarks. Henry criticized his extravagance out of a sense of social justice rather than economic good sense. William of Albany had worried about damage to his capital and his son's soul. Henry scorned his son prodigality because others lacked economic necessities. It was perfectly just that he should have his needs taken care of, but it was "monstrous" that he "should be guaranteed, by what calls itself society, a life-long career of luxury and self indulgence, while so many other men and women every way my equals, in many ways my superiors, go all their days miserably fed, miserably clothed, and die at last in the same ignorance and imbecility, though not alas! in the same innocence, that cradled their infancy."[8] So Henry had arrived at the same conclusion as his father, but by a different route—prodigality was still a sin, and he was still a sinner. The cross was made of gold, but it remained a cross nevertheless.

Henry James's view of work held within it contradictions that he never resolved. He placed a high value on work that was self-expressive, and (by his own example) work of this order required wealth and leisure. Yet he condemned those who lived on ancestral fat while others lacked the bare necessities of life. If a son wanted to follow his admired father's map of the work world, which way was he to go? Was it permissible (or admirable) to use his grandfather's resources as his father had done, for a prolonged

---

*A similar use of capitalist metaphor is found in his last book. "A man *is* in the long run so much as he *does* . . . our only chance therefore for immortality lies in no stored-up capital of goodness and truth we possess, but in the acute life or character we daily witness in putting all our accumulations of goodness and truth out to active use" (*SRFM,* 332).

search for vocation? What was to be the test of its value? Utility? Self-expression? Should an eldest son make his forays brief to save resources for the younger children? But why follow such worldly signposts when the quest for authentic labor beckoned him down yet one more tantalizing path?

Henry James was not a systematic thinker. Yet he was aware of the tension between his individualistic faith and his increasingly insistent Calvinist assumptions. He solved the problem intellectually by assuming that in a properly organized society, a worker would want to do what he had to do—a condition that, unfortunately, did not match either his or his son's experience. But it was a logical solution, nevertheless. If spontaneity is an unquestioned good, and social duty is an equally compelling imperative, the man who spontaneously desired the social good would usher in James's millenium. The saint of his spiritual community would be "the man who cheerfully abounds in social uses, who diligently pursues his lawful calling, who . . . manfully confronts every duty, aspiring with his whole heart to be worthy of the great and beautiful society in which God has placed him."[9] By 1854 he had hesitantly begun to knit back together the elements of the older work ideal, adding earning a living to what in the 1840s had been his solitary concern—spontaneity of self-expression.

This spiritual alchemy promised a new age, when "man will work no longer to life but only from it, no longer with a servile but only with a filial spirit. . . ." But as he knew all too well, this was an unrealized ideal. When talents and aspirations did not harmonize with existing institutions, romantic individualism ran head on into the Calvinist ideal. William James was about to discover this for himself. What if he didn't want to do society's bidding? What if work performed in a filial spirit turned him to stone? What if he wanted to be like his father and avoid *any* lawful calling? As he approached each of his choices—art, science, philosophy—William had to find his way through a labyrinth of contradictory paternal injunctions.

[3]

For a brief period in his late thirties, Henry James considered art as the expression of divinity, and the artist as a hero grandly enthroned at the pinnacle of spiritual development.* The artist was the quintessential spon-

---

*Henry's earliest formulation placed the artist at the top of a spiritual developmental scale that consisted of three stages. In the first stage, the individual is "instinctual" or "infantile"; selfhood is controlled by nature, the soul by the body, and the spirit by the flesh. In the second, more advanced stage, one has achieved more voluntary control of one's life. This is

taneous human being. Yet when Henry's son William decided to be a painter, he would meet vigorous resistance from his father. This apparent contradiction becomes a little less mysterious when we examine Henry James's writings. His essays make it perfectly clear that when he proclaimed the divinity of the artist, he did not have painters or sculptors in mind. It is also obvious that he believed his *Harbinger* contributions were art, and that he himself was an artist in the pure (his) sense of the term.

His 1851 lecture "The Principle of Universality in Art" stated this position in both positive and negative forms. "Art" does not refer to any particular occupation, but to a quality of spiritual relationship to work. "The sphere of Art properly so called, is the sphere of man's spontaneous productivity." Negatively stated, it was to be distinguished "on the one hand from his *natural* productivity, or that which is prompted by his physical necessities, and on the other by his moral productivity, or that which is prompted by his obligations to other men." In short, "Art embraces all those products of human genius, which do not confess the parentage either of necessity or duty."[10]

But a painter was not necessarily excluded from the sphere of art. He might be an artist in James's sense if he did not have to paint to support himself. Henry illustrated his idea: "Round the corner lives a portrait painter. . . . Now this man follows his vocation for a subsistence, and it may very well be therefore, that it by no means indicates his true or predominant attraction." But a painter in other circumstances might well approximate his ideal. Such a man would always have been "beyond the reach of want," and would have been well educated "to ensure a comparatively free development of his faculty." If such a man were devoted to his art, then James allowed that "the very highest happiness he is capable of lies in the untrammelled exercise of his calling."[11] By 1860, when William was eighteen and decided to launch himself on a painter's career, he fulfilled the criteria of his father's ideal case. He had never known want. He had been educated in the best schools his father could find in Europe and America. He had considerable talent for drawing, a faculty that had

---

the "adult" or "moral" level in the developmental sequence, when selfhood controls nature, the soul controls the body, and the spirit has dominion over the flesh. Though the "adult" stage is an advance over the "infantile" stage, both periods are characterized by conflict between selfhood and nature, soul and body, spirit and flesh. James labeled the third stage "mature" or "spontaneous," since it was characterized by the resolution of tension between the previously warring elements: "All controversy between these things has become Divinely reconciled, the body, flesh, or nature being by its own momentum reduced to the cordial allegiance of the higher and Diviner element." This was the acme of the process of spiritual creation, the "perfected" stage when the individual was in finished form, a suitable vessel into which "the Divine Love and Wisdom can flow . . . without measure" (*CCNE*, 86, cited in *PHJ*, 184).

been developed under the guidance of good teachers. And he frankly described the moments of artistic creation as high points of happiness for his inmost self. Yet his father balked at a plan that seemed to match his ideal itinerary of 1848. Unfortunately, by the time William was old enough to fulfill that promise, his father's map of the vocational world had changed.

Henry's paean to art was orchestrated to his own vocational needs. To be sure, he copied from Swedenborg and Schopenhauer and Schelling; but he was using them to make sense of his own life.[12] He offered himself as an example of the artist to his *Harbinger* audience. "Take for example, my present employment. It does not spring from any necessity of the natural life, for I have bread for all my physical wants. Nor does it spring from any sense of obligation to my neighbor, for being addressed to the universal reason of man, it is not fitted to promote any specific or individual interests. It is exclusively the offspring of my own delight or attraction towards this kind of labor."[13] If his journalism was art, then he was an artist in the grand sense rather than an unemployed writer in a work-oriented society. As an artist and man of genius, he did not have to seek public approval. His natural superiority put him beyond competition. "For the Artist is not good by comparison merely, or the antagonism of meaner men. He is positively good, good by absolute or original worth, good like God, good in himself, and therefore universally good."[14] Thus enthroned, Henry James could see himself as a prince rather than an idler.

The period of Henry James's enthusiasm for art and the artist covered William James's early school years. From the time he was six until the time he was eleven or twelve, the praise of aesthetic man flowed from his father's pen. William had a talent for drawing, and his brother's recollection of him in their Fourteenth Street home emphasized the ease with which he spontaneously turned to that occupation. "As I catch W. J.'s image, from far back, at its most characteristic, he sits drawing and drawing, always drawing, . . . and not as with a plodding patience, which I think would less have affected me, but easily, freely, and, as who should say, infallibly."[15] We can only imagine how his father's praise of the artist sounded to a son with a talent for drawing. He was too young to be concerned with the question of his future vocation, although, in boyish fashion, he may have wanted to emulate Mr. Coe, his drawing teacher. It is doubtful that William was able to follow his father's philosophical view of art. What would have made an impression on him was the aura of excitement and parental approbation surrounding the word in his admired father's discussions. To be free, spontaneous, and creative was mysterious, grand, and admirable. To be an artist was something fine that he might do someday.

In the next thirty years Henry James rarely wrote of art or the artist, except in minor asides to compare the work of the artist unfavorably with the handiwork of God. In the scale of Henry James's adult life, this period of enthusiasm for the artist as a hero was a brief moment, a transient experiment in his own search for vocation. It was probably much more important for his artistically talented son.* Such is the disparity between time sense and the ability to comprehend the adult world that an ephemeral paternal experiment may become fixed in an impressionable son's mind. What parent has not had the experience of having his own ideas recited back to him by a child who has made them his own, with an intensity that belies their source and a content that no longer represents the parent's current beliefs? Uneasily one views a fossil encased in time, recognizable but no longer oneself. As Henry James struggled with his demons, the concept of aesthetic man was temporarily useful. Ironically, when William decided to be a painter, he would use his father's old arguments to try to move him out of his way.

[4]

In Henry James's map of the world of work, art was not discrete from science. His earliest usage blended the two so that science could be encompassed by art and a scientist could be seen as an artist. The bridging idea that linked art and science in his early *Harbinger* formulation was technology. Technological advance was art, since it was expressive of "the actual life of God in man." He was convinced that this particular expression of the "perfect marriage between Creator and creature" had important theological implications. He thought that "every railroad refutes Calvinism, and the electric telegraph stultifies Apostolic succession."[16] Technology authorized a new theology because it could bring about two important changes in the human condition: it could subjugate nature, and it promised, through that subjugation, to solve the problem of evil. James's gift for hyperbole was rarely more deftly employed than it was in his praise of scientific technology. It made the horizon glow with the millennial promise of a new day.

He reminded his fellow associationists that "science has at last brilliantly solved the problem of human destiny, and demonstrated in a thousand superb and palpable forms the truth of immemorial prophecies, that that

---

*William was of an age when young people are eager to learn about the work world of adults as they imaginatively prepare themselves for the life that awaits them beyond childhood (Erik Erikson, *Childhood and Society* [New York, 1950], 226–27).

destiny involves the complete subjugation of nature." And he underscored the implications of that achievement. "We find that science makes no advance but in the ceaseless direction of human welfare, in the ceaseless vindication of man's essential dignity; we find that the things which we have all along called evil and noxious, have at bottom a heart of the tenderest love to man, and exist only for the purpose of developing the otherwise inconceivable resources of his divine and omnipotent genius."[17] Thus rendered, a scientist was a worthy peer to share the pinnacle of James's spiritual hierarchy.

In his Fourierist writings Henry used the term "science" in yet another sense. This second meaning also had theological implications. By "science" he also meant a rational program for political and social reorganization. In the 1840s he believed that a social program modeled on Fourier's phalanxes would overcome man's natural depravity and undermine this basic Calvinist tenet. Thus, broadly conceived, "science" was a term that covered many popular reform movements at mid-century, from temperance to abolitionism. To Henry these were not isolated political movements, but proof that the old institutions that obstructed man's spiritual unification were being superseded. It was perfectly clear to Henry in his thirties that the only adequate expression of man's divine nature was "the organization of the whole race in perfect fellowship, . . . by God's legislation which is SCIENCE [Fourier's social science]."[18] Science held the promise of a society based on spiritual community rather than force, convention, or human legislation.

The advance of science authorized a new theology because it showed that the Calvinist vision of God was false. Man was not evil and God had not created an evil world. Instead of viewing nature as a tyrant, the scientist shows nature to be a servant of man, with secret forces "charmingly friendly" and intended by God for his "consummate benediction." Henry would happily work alongside fellow scientists (membership in the associationist movement made him a scientist in *his* scense) to clear the vestiges of an outworn Calvinism from the American landscape.

James was not inclined to draw clear boundaries, and he did not hesitate to blur the language of vocation if it suited his rhetorical intent to do so. We have seen that in his lexicon, a scientist could be an artist and a painter might not be. James was also prepared to anoint his scientist ally into the priesthood of the new age. In an 1851 lecture he suggested that his clerical brethren resign from their posts in favor of the priesthood of science. "Then at least *we* shall be well off: that is to say, we shall stand a chance at last of getting a capable or real priesthood of men of science, who ask no tithes . . . but are yet amply able to instruct us in all the conditions necessary to inaugurate the divine life on earth."[19] He embraced the scientist as a brother, a comrade in arms in the fight against moribund religion. In sum, this near minister who loathed the professional clergy espoused the priesthood of science.

As he moved beyond his Fourierist enthusiasm, Henry James significantly altered the meaning of "science." He wrote of it as one element in his theory of knowledge. James delineated three realms of human life: body, mind, and spirit. Each realm followed its own principle of organization. The organizing principle for body is sense. The principle for mind is science, and for spirit it is philosophy.* Henry outlined this theory in the 1860s, and it shows how much science had declined in his estimation. The scientist has given ground to the philosopher, who James now thought was the only man who could be trusted to speak authoritatively on matters of the spirit. Philosophy does not challenge the discoveries of science. But it is not limited by science, any more than science is limited by sensation. Following Copernicus, for example, science and reason may persuade man that it is wrong to believe that he is the center of the solar system, as his senses suggest. But it is only philosophy, following the light of revelation, that uncovers a superior truth. God is at the center of Creation and man is his dependent creature.

James placed science in an ambiguous position that reflected his appreciation of its potency, and his intention to limit that power. In his mature years he occasionally emphasized the importance of science for the spiritual development of humankind with as much conviction as he had done in the 1840s. But more often he reserved his enthusiasm for philosophy as the highest form of truth. Science was necessary to analyze the finite relative dimension. But scientists must be made aware that their "laws of nature" are merely the laws of the human mind and not God's. James still looked upon scientists as allies in the fight against superstition in religion, but scientists had to bend their knees to philosophers.

Henry James praised the priesthood of science during William's later school years. In 1860, after William declared that he wanted to become a painter, his father confessed to a friend that he had "always counted upon a scientific career for Willy." His son insisted that he be allowed to study painting and his father gave in, but not without a revealing reservation: "I hope the day may even yet come when my calculations may be realized in this regard."[20] When he was enthusiastic about science, Henry James had

---

*In addition to having a separate principle of organization, each of the three realms is illuminated by its own unique light. The light of sense is the sun, for science it is reason, and for philosophy it is revelation. The three realms form a three-tiered hierarchy, building in ascending order from body-sense-sun to mind-science-reason, and culminate in spirit-revelation-philosophy. Each level in the hierarchy builds on the knowledge of the one below, but is not bound by the limitations of the inferior realm.

encouraged his son's scientific studies in Europe and America. He persisted in his preference for science over art, and William ultimately abandoned painting and entered the Lawrence Scientific School at Harvard in 1861. But Henry's high opinion of science had begun to wane. The hierarchy of knowledge that he explicated the year his son entered Harvard to become a scientist unseated science from its elevated position. At the outset, the shift was one of emphasis, and left much that was admirable to science and the scientist. But the trend gathered momentum as William became more enmeshed in a scientific career, and culminated in Henry's frank declaration in 1879 (six years after his son began to teach science at Harvard) that "if a man's mind determine itself towards science or the senses, the result to one's spiritual understanding cannot help being disastrous in the extreme."[21] The priesthood of science had been a glorious career, as Henry James mapped the work world in the 1850s. By the time William actually became a scientist, the luster had tarnished. Indeed, rather than a glorious vocation, it had actually become dangerous for the soul.

[5]

Henry's usage of "philosophy" changed through his adult life along with the changes in the meaning of art and science. In the late 1840s, during his Fourierist years, it was a term of opprobrium. It meant abstract thinking that "perpetually balks the intellect instead of satisfying it."[22] In the 1860s, as he elaborated his formal doctrine of spiritual knowledge, philosophy became a field of the utmost importance, and the term became one of approbation. Philosophy was the dicipline that synthesized the lesser realms of science and sense into a reconciling form of Truth. He contrasted it more and more with the narrowness of science. "Philosophy deals only with the essence of things, that is with the spiritual realm, . . . where science never penetrates—to which indeed she is incapable of lifting an eye."[23] As he reworked and expanded his doctrine of spiritual creation in his later years, Henry James undoubtedly thought of himself as a philosopher in the highest (his own) sense of the term. He was certain that philosophy had not "an hour's honest vocation upon earth" other than doing what he had been doing for two decades.[24]

When we place Henry James's speculation on art, science, and philosophy in biographical context, it is evident that he was intent upon dramatizing his own search. He was most enthusiastic about art when he could conceive of himself as an artist. He praised science as one of the elect publicizing Fourier's program of social science. He happily embraced the scientist as an admired ally laying waste the pretensions of conventional religion. He devalued science as he abandoned Fourier and directed his speculative efforts to his theory of spiritual creation. Then he admired philosophy and thought of himself as a practitioner of that elevated vocation.

Each step along the way, as Henry was shifting and expanding his ideas, William James had to cope with his father's confusing map of the world of work. He must have found it disheartening to discover that he could never catch his mercurial sire. When he aspired to be an artist, a heroic figure depicted by his beloved father in glorious hues, Henry James was unhappy. When William reluctantly shifted toward science his father lost his enthusiasm for scientists. When William changed from science to philosophy, which his father praised as the highest degree of knowledge, his field was labeled "technical philosophy" and judged to be inferior to his father's own spiritual doctrine. In effect, no matter how much acclaim the world might give William James, the development of his father's ideas kept him kneeling before him as the elder Henry gazed heavenward.

BOOK THREE

SON

The identity which the *I* discovers, as it surveys this long procession can only be a relative identity, that of a slow shifting in which there is always some common ingredient retained. The commonest element of all, the most uniform, is the possession of the same memories. However different the man may be from the youth, both look back on the same childhood, and call it their own.

—William James, 1890

7

A Painter's Vocation

I have come to the conclusion that "Art" is my vocation.
—William James, 1860

[1]

THOUGH HENRY JAMES only briefly regarded the artist as an ideal type, he remained interested in writing throughout his life, and his robust style is the work of a literary craftsman. Though he never showed any inclination to pursue the plastic arts himself, he did arrange for his older sons to be exposed to painting and sculpture in the museums of Europe and America. Having overvalued the artist in the late 1840s and early 1850s, he had no intention of sanctioning a painting career for his son in 1860. There is some evidence that after reluctantly approving William's painting experiment, he aborted it covertly by threatening suicide—a threat that a dutiful son could not ignore. Despite his liberal protestations, Henry was determined to force William into science, no matter how strongly his son felt a painter's calling.

[2]

On August 15, 1860, William James triumphantly announced to his friend Thomas Sergeant Perry, "We are to return to Newport!! . . . I have come to the conclusion that 'Art' is my vocation." But his obvious enthusiasm was tempered by a young man's uncertainty about his talent. "At any rate I am going to give it a fair trial, and if I find I have not the *souffle* give it up." He was returning to study with William Morris Hunt, an American painter trained in Europe, and he looked to Hunt to guide him, like Virgil, into that dangerous underworld. "I don't hope to be anything *great,* but am pretty sure with good old Hunt as a guide, philosopher and friend, to commit nothing bad."[1] His ambiguous hopes for Hunt's protection from wrongdoing echoed his father's moral judgment. By "nothing bad" did he mean poor craftsmanship or moral transgression? To another friend he wrote that the experiment might take a year or two. If at the end of that time it turned out that he was not suited to a painting career, nothing would have been lost. The letter, written in French, expressed the same ambiguity in regard to lack of skill and moral evil. "There is nothing in the world so despicable [*déplorable*] as a bad artist [*méchant artiste*]."[2]

William's estimate of a year or two was wide of the mark. In fact, after less than six months in Hunt's studio he suddenly turned away from painting. Whatever the reason for stifling his artist self, in the fall of 1861 William entered the Lawrence Scientific School at Harvard to prepare for a career in science. Like his father's abortive experiment with *The Christian Examiner* in 1830, William's painting career could be pursued only in rebellion. Like Henry, he, too, turned from a paternally despised career to one that was sanctioned (at least temporarily). After this change of direction, unfortunately, William began to exhibit a mysterious and disturbing physical frailty that would worsen and end in crippling invalidism.*

[3]

Henry James, like many reformers of the 1840s and 1850s, had placed great emphasis on the importance of his children's education. His impatient search for a suitable education for his son reflected both the limitations of American educational institutions of the time and the brevity of Henry's patience. By the time he was eighteen, William had attended nine schools in four countries. He rarely stayed in any of them for a full school year. His father's repeated, impulsive disruptions were smoothed over by a haphazard parade of governesses and tutors, some speaking French and others English, but all commending themselves to Mr. James's anarchic design. It is little wonder that in later years William complained that he

---

*Since psychological symptomatology is used to illuminate William's vocational conflicts, precise dating is important. The earliest evidence in regard to the onset of William's symptoms is found in the recollections of Charles William Eliot, his teacher during his first year at the Lawrence Scientific School. This recollection is completely cited in *LWJ*, 1:32. Ralph Barton Perry cited the Eliot recollection incompletely and neglected to include the comments on William's physical frailty (*TCWJ*, 1:207). Perry did say that frail health made it impossible for William to join the Union army in 1861, though he cites no authority for this statement. Henry James, Jr., is the probable source of Perry's assertion, as Henry commented that the connection between William's ill health and his failure to take part in the war was "too clear to occasion discussion in his letters" (*LWJ*, 1:47).

had never had an orderly education to build upon—a smattering of Latin, arithmetic, and natural science plus the knowledge of French and German acquired abroad (six of his eighteen years were spent in Europe) were all that he felt he had gained from his random schooling.

But the James children had been exposed early to painting. According to William's younger brother Henry, their home on Fourteenth Street contained a modest art collection. Mr. James selected a Thomas Cole landscape to hang in the front parlor. Cole ("the American Turner") was well known for his landscapes of the elder Henry's native Hudson Valley, but apparently Henry preferred to be reminded of Italy, for he chose instead one of Cole's scenes of Florence. A painting by Jules-Joseph Lefebvre in the back parlor added to what the younger Henry recalled as the "great abundance of Italy" that graced the James home. The romantic landscapes were relieved by sculpture in a different mood. A classic marble bust of a bacchante (by American craftsmen working in Rome) attested to the European taste of the elder Jameses.[3]

The boys' experience with painting reached beyond their Fourteenth Street home. New York offered many possibilities for aesthetic training in the 1850s. It was by no means as rich with possibilities as the major cities of Europe, but by comparison with other American cities it was an artistic center. The National Gallery, the American Art-Union, the New York Gallery of Fine Arts, and numerous temporary exhibitions displayed a variety of works that would have been unimaginable in the elder Henry's boyhood.[4] European treasures of the medieval period were shown at Bryan's Gallery of Christian Art, and the boys devoted many evenings to the worm-eaten diptychs and triptychs there. Emanuel Leutze's famous painting of Washington crossing the Delaware provided a memorable evening that Henry, Jr., recalled for the double pleasure of the dramatic power of the scene, bathed in "a marvel of wintry light," and permission to stay up later than usual to attend the public viewing.[5]

William's formal training in drawing was sparse and erratic, although, like other elements of his experimental education, it was genially provided by his father. Benjamin Coe, a well-known teacher who exhibited at the National Academy, was his first drawing master. A man of immense stature and dramatic presence, with a shock of thick white hair and a great cloak with a vast velvet collar, he inspired intense admiration of the sort commonly reserved for a military hero. Coe's miniature rural scenes and larger oil paintings on wood were scattered throughout his Washington Square studio. Student and teacher appreciated each other. William admired Coe's panel paintings and praised them to the family, and Coe encouraged William to draw and develop his talent. But the instruction was of short duration—less than a year—because the boys inexplicably left the school where Coe taught and moved on to another for the winter of 1854.[6] William's next teacher was European and more distinguished. Léon Coignet's work had been exhibited at the Luxembourg Museum. The fact that he admitted William to his Paris atelier in the winter of 1857 (William was fifteen) suggests that the young American had a promising talent for the painter's craft.

Though William's formal instruction was minimal, visits to the great European museums during the family's three-year stay abroad from 1855 to 1858, stimulated his aesthetic development. The boys were drawn by the mystery of art. The younger Henry recalled a favorite walk across the Champs-Elysée to the river. They crossed over the nearest bridge leading to the Rue de la Seine, where old bookshops and printshops, their wares spread out in long cases on the parapets, beckoned them to an art world that seemed both sinister and immensely attractive. "Art, art, art, don't you see?" they seemed to say. "Learn little gaping pilgrims, what *that* is!"[7]

The boys preferred recent works to recognized old masters. In London's Pantheon they found Benjamin Robert Haydon's historical canvasses, painted in the grand manner, more attractive than the works of Rubens and Titian. According to Henry, Haydon was more approachable. Having lived closer to their own time (he had died a decade earlier), he pointed the way to an artistic career. As Henry recalled, the old masters "seemed to meet us so little half-way," while Haydon suggested "something that *we* could do, or at least want to."[8] To be sure, the James brothers experienced the moral uplift that nineteenth-century American travelers sought in the museums of Europe, but they were also groping for a future.

Haydon became of even greater interest to the boys when their father bought them the painter's recently published three-volume autobiography. There is no way of knowing whether the gift was a casual indulgence or was prompted by more complex motives. The latter possiblity suggests itself because Haydon's book served both as a model for entry into a painting career and as a cautionary tale of the moral dangers of such a career. Haydon had intended to write a guide for young artists. "I wish this Life for the student," Haydon proclaimed. "I wish to show him how to bear affliction and disappointment by exhibiting the fatal consequences in myself who did not bear them. I wish to give him spirits by showing how rashness is to be remedied, vice resisted and a great wish persevered in, when the last resource is a prayer to the Almighty."[9] Haydon's blend of uplift and degradation matched Mr. James's own feelings about art and artists.

He, too, believed that painting was a vocation dependent on the God within. He, too, scorned moneymaking and believed that art must be socially useful. Haydon's ambition as an artist was appropriately grand: to "enlighten the understanding of the English people and make Art in its higher range a delightful mode of moral elevation."[10] If Haydon matched the elder Henry's higher view of an artist's calling, he also matched his lowest. He was personally grandiose, vain, and prodigal in the extreme. He personified the natural man who was so preoccupied with his own selfhood that he stifled the God within even as he invoked his name. If a father wanted to provide a morality tale to warn his son away from an artistic career, Haydon's autobiography served admirably. It began with grandiose self-indulgence and ended in a hyperbole of self-murder. In a fit of rage and despair over neglect by the very public he was trying to save, Haydon had fatally shot himself in the head after slashing his throat twice with a razor.

According to his novelist son, it was not unusual for the elder Henry to tell his sons stories about people who ended badly. Henry, Jr., remembered this as the typical scenario for his father's stories about his boyhood friends. Though his father did not indulge in scandalous gossip, "it somehow rarely failed to come out that each contemporary on his younger scene, each hero of each thrilling adventure, had, in spite of brilliant promise and romantic charm, ended badly, as badly as possible."[11] As a grown man, Henry, Jr., recognized that his father's repetitive plot had shaped their boyish expectations. "This became our gaping generalization—it gaped even under the moral that the anecdote was always, and so familiarly, humanly and vividly, designed to convey." Disaster was in store for any youth who was exposed to pleasure instead of being immediately launched "in business of a vigorous sort." Paradoxically, as a storyteller their father had more in common with William of Albany than with his own rebellious youthful self. *He* might transcend the dangers of living on paternal bounty while he pursued his speculative pleasures, but the ill-fated peers that he paraded imaginatively before his impressionable sons had succumbed to an unhappy and much-to-be-avoided fate.

If one may judge from Haydon's autobiography, it was not uncommon for middle-class British families to oppose painting as a career for their children. Yet Haydon overcame his own family's opposition, and his book provided a model dialogue that artistic sons might use to defend themselves against other bourgeois parents: "'Who has put this stuff in your head?' 'Nobody: I always have had it.' 'You will live to repent.' 'Never, my dear father; I would rather die in the trial.'"[12] William was to write a challenging letter to his father in 1859 declaring his wish to be a painter, and his argument, though more elaborate, was essentially Haydon's.

The notorious Haydon also illustrated the use that illness might serve in the evolution of an artistic career. After Haydon declared his intention to paint, his family tried to force him to change his mind. He fell ill. "Luckily, I had an illness, which in a few weeks ended in chronic inflamation of the eyes. For six weeks I was blind and my family were in misery."[13] William James would also fall ill under familial pressure to abandon painting. And he, too, would develop an inflammation of the eyes that played an important role in his career. It would be overstating the matter to suggest that William consciously imitated Haydon, yet it is certainly an odd coincidence that both had inflammatory eye disease. And Haydon's life did provide a neophyte with ambiguous caveats against the spiritual dangers of art and at the same time offered a script for the successful launching of a painter's career. A generous father could not be certain how a talented son in love with painting would make use of his gift.

[4]

In addition to viewing the works displayed at the Pantheon, the boys visited Marlborough House, where they saw paintings by Daniel Maclise, William Mulready, Sir Edwin Landseer, Sir David Wilkie, and Charles Leslie, all contemporaries of Haydon but very different in style and subject matter. Their works ranged from genre to animal studies. The boys found them inspiring but curiously out of reach.[14] The Pre-Raphaelites were a very different matter. The Academy show at the National Gallery in 1856 included paintings by Sir John Everett Millais, a founding spirit of the Pre-Raphaelite school. Millais joined with W. Holman Hunt and some fellow students in an effort to break free of the constraints imposed on English painting by the neoclassic style. They experimented in suiting composition to the subject rather than following a classic formula. They studied nature, paying close attention to irregularity and variety, rather than imitating unrealistic abstractions. They abjured brown foliage, smoky clouds, and dark corners of canvass that, in their view, marked the decline of painting after Raphael. For them, Raphael represented the acme of High Renaissance painting. William and Henry found their initiation to the new school "momentous."

The Pre-Raphaelite aesthetic embodied tendencies that would emerge in William's later work as a psychologist and philosopher. The Pre-Raphaelites emphasized the psychological element in subjects that had hitherto received symbolic, allegorical treatment.* Observation of the people around them was as important as learning the painter's craft. Fur-

---

*When Hunt painted *Christ and the Two Marys* (1847), for example, he aimed to capture the women's surprise on meeting a man who had come out of the grave (W. Holman Hunt, *PreRaphaelitism and the Pre-Raphaelite Brotherhood* [London, 1905], 1:85).

thermore, the Pre-Raphaelites' use of color and emphasis on realistic detail gave their painting a characteristic hard edge, creating a visual world of shapes with impermeable boundaries, like so many pieces of stained glass.[15]* When, as a psychologist, William James studied the emotions and mental life, he would prefer minute, phenomenological descriptions of minds in action. When, as a philosopher of pluralism, he explored the relationship of personal worlds, he, too, emphasized the hardness of edge that divides human experience as decisively as lead separates the fragments of stained glass. Though William was initially drawn to the Pre-Raphaelites as an artist, the kinship of mind and method that he found in them was to be developed in his own fashion after he abandoned painting.

William found the Pre-Raphaelites important in yet another way. They led him to the ideas of John Ruskin. Ruskin's vigorous support had helped to win them a following. In *Modern Painters* he had advised young artists to go to nature trustingly, "rejecting nothing, selecting nothing, and scorning nothing." He welcomed the Brotherhood as his followers and he praised their efforts in *Pre-Raphaelitism* (1851). William James studied Ruskin's pamphlet closely and copied quotations from it into his notebook in 1859 (he was seventeen), when he insisted on studying painting. He copied Ruskin's advice about work rather than his aesthetic principles. He was obviously puzzled about the relationship between effort and talent. "It's no man's business whether he has genius or not: work he must, whatever he is, but quietly and steadily; and the natural and unforced results of such work will be the things that he was meant to do and will be his best. No agonies or heart-rendings will enable him to do any better. If he be a great man, they will be great things; if a small man, small things; but always, if thus peacefully done, good and right; always if restlessly and ambitiously done, false, hollow, and despicable."[16]† Here was reassuring guidance in the romantic mode that echoed his father's Fourierist declaration.‡ Both

---

*An outraged critic of Millais's *Ophelia* (1852) wrote, "There must be something strangely perverse in an imagination which souses Ophelia in a weedy ditch . . . while it studies every petal of the darnel and anemone floating on the eddy" (Jeffrey Maas, *Victorian Painters* [New York, 1969], 126).

†William's copy was slightly inaccurate. Where Ruskin said "things that God meant him to do," James wrote "things he was meant to do." He was self-conciously struggling with the problem of determinism but apparently found Fate a more recognizable opponent than Ruskin's (and his father's) God. In the same notebook he copied, "'Tis writ on Paradise's gate, Woe to the dupe who yields to fate" (MH).

‡(Henry James and John Ruskin were both sons of successful merchants. Both had experienced the strain of class mobility and had ideal solutions for that tension to recommend to their readers. The Englishman recommended that gentlemen should enter the laboring and mercantile occupations to prove that the personal qualities of the aristocracy were a function not of work but of character. The American urged that all men be freed from the need to work—a livelihood being guaranteed by society—so that they would be free to follow their inclinations for spiritual development. In effect, the democratic American proposed an up-

Ruskin and Henry James agreed that God intended all men to work. Both insisted that man was intended to be happy in his work.* And both cautioned against overwork.†

But Ruskin's belief that "a great thing can only be done by a great man, and he does it *without* effort," created as many problems as it solved. A doctrine of election applied to art, it left the would-be painter with a gnawing uncertainty. Though Ruskin was quick to point out that he did not mean to excuse neophytes from discipline and he eschewed "the favorite dogma of young men, that they need not work if they have genius," the question still remained: How much work is enough? When is intense effort to achieve one's artistic ambitions an unnatural forcing of genius? Ruskin begged that question, as Henry James did. He simply assumed that a man of genius would want to do what he had to do. "The fact is that a man of genius is always far more ready to work than other people, and is often so little conscious of the inherent divinity in himself, that he is very apt to ascribe all his capacity to work."[17] For a young man who was about to begin a painting career, Ruskin's insistence on steady, happy labor could have been reassuring. But the strain between Calvinism and romanticism remained. Salvation through organic growth was no more certain than salvation through God's grace. Whether intense labor flowed from talent or from the lack of it was not at all clear. And whether illness was an obstacle for genius to overcome or a sign of strain from too much work and too little talent was also obscure.

[5]

William was attracted by the paintings of Delacroix during the family's stay in Paris in 1856–57. He admired Delacroix's work so much that he tried to reproduce his pictures from memory. According to his brother, he singled out the *Barque de Dante* for special attention. Like the inscriptions in his notebook, his attachment to the *Barque de Dante* and the art of Delacroix offers an opportunity to glimpse William's inner concerns as he

---

ward leveling solution that turned every male citizen into an independently wealthy gentleman, while the class-bound Englishman urged a downward leveling that dignified labor. Ruskin's solution would have been of more practical use to William, as his grandfather's money would not support another leisured generation. For him, a gentleman worker was a more realistic ideal than a universal brotherhood of independently wealthy sons.

* "It is written, 'in the sweat of thy brow,'" said Ruskin, "but it was never written 'in the breaking of thine heart,' thou shall eat bread" (John Ruskin, *Pre-Raphaelitism* [New York, 1851], 7).

† "Now in order that people may be happy in their work, . . . they must not do too much of it" (ibid., 8–9).

approached a confrontation with his father over a painting career. His strong personal response and the lifelong persistence of Delacroix-like imagery in his writings suggest a deep affinity of theme.

The *Barque de Dante,* inspired by Canto VIII of *The Divine Comedy,* depicts Dante and Virgil being ferried across the marsh of Styx. Their boat is surrounded by tortured figures of the damned desperately clutching at them. The painting may have appealed technically, as a blend of neoclassical composition (the figures were organized in planes parallel to the surface, after the style of David) and romantic intensity of color, in the manner of Géricault. But from a psychological point of view, the most remarkable thing about the scene is its intense violence. The crime for which the souls were condemned to the marsh of Styx was rage—bitter, sullen rage that had poisoned their earthly existence. Their punishment was to spend eternity in the muck, biting each other and beating against each other "with head and breast and heels that spurn."[18] Delacroix's rendition was a vivid image of destructive oral rage surging from below.* Significantly, James's own sketches of 1859 show the same thematic preoccupation with the menace of biting rage, as we shall see. And his drawings dramatize the same frightening power of one enraged creature trying to destroy another with his teeth.† It is instructive to note that this unconscious resonance between William and Delacroix anticipates the onset of William's depressive symptoms by about three years and points to his early vulnerability.

When William wrote to Sarge Perry announcing his plan to study painting with William Morris Hunt in Newport in 1859, he spoke of Hunt as a figure in the Delacroix painting. He looked to the American painter to act for him, as Virgil did for Dante, as "a guide, Philosopher and friend." This description suggests yet another quality of *Dante* that may have appealed to William and may account for the ease with which he linked Virgil with Hunt. The painting depicts an inchoate mass of figures surrounding Dante and threatening to block his way across the marsh. Each victim in the tortured mass touches and blends with the next, with one exception—Virgil. He is cloaked in gray-black, wears a vivid red cap, and is distinctly separate from the rest. The painting can be viewed as emblem-

---

*The violence of the *Dante* was not unusual for Delacroix. Many of his paintings portray rapacious attacks by animals (as in *The Lion Hunt*) or of men (as in *The Death of Sardanapalus*). Delacroix himself was painfully aware of the black depths within him that sought expression in paint (Phoebe Pool, Delacroix [London, 1969], 8). The painter's characteristic melancholy as he brooded over the eternal struggle between the forces of light and the forces of darkness struck a responsive chord in William James.

†In the *Dante* a figure hangs onto the stern with bared teeth fiercely clamped to the boat. Psychoanalytic experience demonstrates a firm connection between such oral-sadistic tendencies and depression.

atic of the problem that faced William: to extricate himself from his father's entangling mass of contradictory ideas. A teacher and guide, Hunt might help a young man to separate definitively, to individuate rather than be sucked down into the muck of his father's struggle with *his* father. Perhaps William's painter's eye saw more in the Delacroix than he knew.

Delacroix-like imagery persisted in William's imagination for many years after he abandoned painting as a career. In a lecture delivered to Harvard divinity students when he was renowned as a psychologist and philosopher, he captured the eternal struggle between good and evil with an image worthy of Delacroix. "Not the absence of vice, but vice there, and virtue holding her by the throat, seems the ideal human state." And metaphorically he placed himself on a boat, adrift like Dante and Virgil in a sea of evil. "Our moral horizon moves with us as we move, and never do we draw nearer to the far-off line where the black waves and the azure meet."[19] To James, the mature philosopher seemed eternally adrift on the marsh of Styx, like the central figures of Delacroix's painting. He had abandoned the painter's craft almost a quarter of a century before, yet his mind turned easily to imagery supplied by an admired master who had once seemed worthy of emulation. He had made Delacroix's moral vision his own.

[6]

It is one of the painful ironies of an open society that the hard-won gains of one generation often alienate newly successful parents from their children. William James of Albany triumphed in the age of Washington, and raised a son whose views were congenial to the age of Jackson but antagonistic to his own. Henry James, Sr., grew to manhood with the comfort and opportunities that his father's wealth provided, rejected the source of that wealth, and introduced his son William into an international world that was aesthetically rich far beyond his own experience. He, too, found himself at odds with his son by virtue of the very opportunities he had created for him. He, too, found himself fighting with his son over a chosen career that grew out of the very impulses he had nurtured and followed the ideology he had proclaimed. As we follow the extension of William's experience with art that enriched its meaning for him, and as we see his father's continuing struggles with his own continuing vocational diffusion, we can witness this tragic dialectic at work.

The Jameses ended their three-year sojourn in Europe in the summer of 1858 and returned to live in Newport, Rhode Island. For Henry, Sr., Newport was a place where a man of means but of uncertain position might be inconspicuous among other leisured intellectuals. For William it was a town where he could find American friends who shared his artistic interests and a teacher who modeled the possibility of a career as an artist in America. The boys made friends with James MacKaye, Thomas Sergeant Perry, and John La Farge, all aesthetically talented young men who were to become famous in the literary and artistic world.

The James family's Newport years split into two separate periods, the first from the summer of 1858 to the fall of 1859, and the second (a year after the family returned to Europe to separate William from Hunt) from September 1860 to the following autumn. When Henry James, Jr., wrote about this time, he tried to mask his father's "aimless vacillation" by ignoring the first stay in Newport.[20] Though he was willing to make some effort to cover up for the elder Henry, his description of the Newport period was remarkably revealing of the battle that was brewing between his brother and his father. As Henry, Jr., remembered it, the decision to return to America was prompted by his father's failure to gain an audience in Europe. He had recently published *Christianity the Logic of Creation* without drawing any great notice. When the family returned to America, "it may have been with illusions not a few for him . . . about the degree of sensibility of the public, there awaiting him."[21] So Henry thought his father had his own reasons for leaving, and that his brother's desire to study with Hunt was merely a "pretext given him by his so prized and admired eldest son."

Newport also appealed in 1858 because cousins of the family had settled there recently—Mr. and Mrs. Edmund Tweedy—and because it was a popular gathering place for New England intellectuals. Henry, Jr., looked back on it as an ideal choice, for Newport was a haven where one could find shelter from the oppressive American work ideal. They had learned to appreciate leisure in Europe, and had become disconnected from an America where leisure was a crime to be confessed rather than good fortune to be enjoyed. As Henry recalled, to "confess to disconnection was to confess by the same stroke to leisure—which involved also an admission, however rueful at once and deprecatory, of what might still at that time pass in our unregenerate country for something in the nature of 'means.'"[22] Whether a family's money was new or old, America was not an easy place to be without work—except perhaps in Newport, where the fortunate could take cover with others whose bank accounts were ample and whose occupations were comfortably vague.

But in America once again, the prodigal son was forced to face the problem of career that he had left behind. Henry, Sr., could joke about it from Newport in a letter to his brother Howard, but beneath his humor, the field of battle between William James of Albany and his son still smoldered. "I have established my financial reputation afresh: by buying a house at half its worth," he chortled (in fact, the family lived in a rented house). "I shiver to think how soon I may be elected a director, and next President of the Newport Bank; and how sure an elevation of that sort is, to lead to my being called to one of the great cities to preside over financial circles there. I shan't go. People who would like their interest presided over by me, may come to Newport. I think it altogether probable they will. But it is absolutely certain that I shall not go away." There can be little doubt who was the intended butt of his joke. To be sure, the country was recovering from the panic of 1857, and the need for financial counsel was on many minds. But it was banker William James's shuttling back and forth between New York, Albany, and Syracuse that was being mocked. Henry playfully enlarged on the imagined picture of himself as a successful financier. "The ocean breeze shall fan my fevered brow and lift my flowing hair (or rather my flown hair) [James was bald] while I live; and when I die it shall pipe a pleasant requiem over my grave paying due respect at the same time to the roses which my grateful fellow-citizens will no doubt keep planted there."[23]

Though the imagined figure was clad in an antic costume, there is no mistaking the ghost of William James of Albany, who was ready to leap out of the shadows and pose as a negative model for his jesting heirs with a vividness that does credit to his son's literary gifts, and makes the three decades that had passed since his death collapse into yesterday. Unhappily, the issue that set off their fight thirty years before was still very much alive. "So you see," the elder brother confided to the younger, "I know what I am about at last." It was a brave but unhappy joke. He was no longer a young prodigal, and the time had come for *him* to be father to a rebellious son, yet the earthworks of his own bitter engagement with his father were still in place.

There was an ideological component to James's line of defense. His views on work, art, science, and philosophy were attempts to articulate his growing understanding of his battle with William of Albany. But another element must be added before we can appreciate the web that was spun around Henry's son: character style. Vagueness and the blurring of boundaries between ideas, institutions, and persons typically prevented Henry's father and later opponents from pinning him down. He avoided specificity as though any firm commitment threatened to compromise his freedom. His theological opponents could ignore him (they did),* his

---

*James had objected to the establishment of the Swedenborgian church in the 1850s, insisting that when Swedenborg spoke of "the Church," he was referring to a spiritual relationship, not a tangible institution. James's assault on the sectarian's urge toward the concrete and the specific has the same structure as his argument with his son. "The true

readers could winnow the seed of hopefulness and wisdom from the chaff of vague idealism, and his friends could chide him for erratically flitting from place to place instead of taking root. But his children were much more vulnerable.

When Henry James, Sr., had fought with his father, the issue was out in the open, the lines of battle clearly drawn. William James of Albany asserted his paternal prerogative to force a vocation on his son. Work was the issue, obedience the demand, and disinheritance the price of rebellion. When William's son fought with *his* son, the conflict was shrouded in vague benevolence.* Spiritual perfection was the apparent issue, self-fulfillment the apparent injunction, and rebellion was ostensibly unnecessary. But covertly Henry James was asserting his paternal authority as his father had done before him. And in this intergenerational battle, as in the one before, work was the issue, obedience the demand, and guilt over hurting the father the price of rebellion.

Henry James, Sr., was well aware that inconsistency could lead to parental tyranny. Indeed, he offered a vivid example to his readers a full decade before his son's decision to paint. To illustrate the defects of the Calvinist God's gift of free will, he wrote, "If you give your child permission to go to Cambridge or Roxbury as he pleases, and then denounce him to the constables for going to the latter place, you make yourself unworthy of the child, proving yourself not a parent but a tyrant."[24] But intellectual understanding was not enough to deflect him. Ten years later that is exactly what he did. William took him at his word that the choice of vocation was his own, and opted for painting. Henry acceded superficially

---

Christian," he declared, "allows others to separate from him as much as they please, as much as their unfortunate narrowness makes it inevitable to them, but feels it necessary to separate from no one. His mission is one of love, and therefore of fusion and unity, instead of separation or disunity" (*CCNE*, 12). The "true Christian" was like God in James's theory of creation. Separation required *his* permission—permission that was refused in fact, although allowed in illusory fashion.

In 1863 his friend and perceptive reviewer James Freeman Clarke criticized the same impulse toward fusion that he detected in James's most recent book, *Substance and Shadow*. "We do not see," admonished Clarke, "why the individual soul of man is not as much a real creation of God, as his substantial life. When God makes Peter, James, and John, what does he do. He makes three individual souls, wholly distinct from himself, from nature and from each other—each soul with its special power of self-development for ever and ever" (*Christian Examiner* 75 (1863):222). One might easily substitute other names and find that Clarke was pointing to a difficulty of Henry's style of paternal government.

*Henry, Jr., recognized his brother's plight because he shared it. He remembered his own puzzlement at his father's inclination to discourage any specific steps his children might take because they were cutting themselves off from "any suggestion of an alternative." No matter what they seemed to want, it did not suit father. "What we were to do instead was just *be* something, something unconnected with specific doing, something free and uncommitted, something finer in short than being *that*, whatever it was, might consist of" (*NSB*, 50–52).

but, as we shall see, threatened illness and suicide. In so doing he set the constable of William's conscience after him for disturbing his father's peace. Try as he did to approach his fatherly ideal, Henry was trapped behind the advanced line of his own failed rebellion. Instead of wearing away with time, it had petrified into a formidable obstacle blocking his son's path.

8

The Murdered Self

. . . he may sometimes doubt whether the self he murdered in that decisive hour might not have been the better of the two. . . .
—William James, 1897

[1]

WILLIAM MORRIS HUNT taught William and Henry painting in Newport. During the family's first fifteen-month
stay, the contact was casual, as William and Henry still attended school
during the winter of 1858–59 (the Berkeley Institute, a "classical and commercial school" run by the Reverend William C. Leverett, curate of Newport's Trinity Church). But the encounter was enough to stimulate
William's desire to paint. A Vermonter who had been educated at Harvard
and then in Europe, the artist was an intriguing blend of New England
work consciousness and leisured European sophistication. Hunt was a
musician as well as an accomplished painter and sculptor, a mature artist
firm in his aesthetic convictions and scornful of rigid academic procedures
for the training of the young. His presence in Newport was a fortunate
accident in William's accidental education.

There were intriguing congruities between this tall, bearded teacher and
his new pupil. Each was the oldest of five children. Each had a next
younger brother who surpassed him in artistic success (Hunt's younger
brother Richard was an architect who designed many mansions for
wealthy clients in New York City and Newport). Both enjoyed playful
exhibitionism. One of Hunt's capers was to empty his wineglass and perch
it on his shiny bald pate while his amused guests watched and listened to
his head-nodding conversation.[1] Both had mercurial temperaments and
slid precipitiously from the heights of excitement to the depths of unhap-

piness. Both seriously contemplated suicide in moments of despair. Hunt did eventually kill himself. Each, in choosing a vocation, found his way through illness toward the fulfillment of a failed parental ambition.

William Hunt's mother had had a talent for painting which had been stifled by her father. When her son turned out to be an unenthusiastic student at Harvard and fell ill, she whisked him off to Europe in search of a more healthful climate and richer prospects. Hunt was placed in studios in Rome, Düsseldorf, and Paris. His painting and health flourished abroad, and he abandoned all thought of returning to Harvard to study medicine, as he had originally planned. The educational needs of both Williams was the germ around which the lives of James and Hunt families crystallized—the needs of the younger children being interpreted as naturally in harmony with those of the eldest. If Europe was good for William Hunt's health and career, the whole family must go to Europe. If Newport was where William James wanted to study painting, the whole family must return there as well.

When Hunt decided to return to the United States in 1855, he left two influential teachers behind. He had been a favorite pupil of Thomas Couture in Paris but had grown weary of his academic method. He was attracted instead to the genre painter Jean-François Millet, and moved to Barbizon in search of a respite from the Parisian art world and the accoutrements of aristocratic life—splendid horses, fine hounds, and the pastimes of a Parisian gentleman. Wealthy enough to become Millet's patron, the fatherless American found in him a teacher and friend who revived a seriousness of purpose that Hunt had submerged in elegant Parisian living. Perhaps it was Millet's peasant figures, which seemed to grow out of the ground they tilled, or the somber straight-lipped faces uncomplainingly working the land that attracted him. Though the French were unenthusiastic about Millet's subjects, they brought the American back to the spirit of his New England boyhood.[2] Millet's blend of egalitarianism, biblical sobriety, and romantic love of nature touched him deeply. When Hunt returned to New England, he took with him a large collection of Millet's paintings. Hunt's Boston friends responded as he did and made Millet their own.[3]

William made three other important friends in Newport: James Steele MacKaye, Thomas Sergeant Perry, and John La Farge. All three had strong artistic inclinations. Among them they represented the possibilities of sons of newly rich and more well-established families. MacKaye and La Farge painted. Perry became a literary critic.

During that first Newport summer, William James fished, rowed, and swam with Steele MacKaye. Like William, Steele was a third-generation American from a family that had made its wealth in the Hudson Valley.

When the two youths met, MacKaye had just emerged from a prolonged illness and convalescence following a battle with his father. Colonel James Morrison MacKaye organized Wells, Fargo & Company (he was the "Company") and Western Union. His fortune was a generation newer than the Jameses'. Steele MacKaye's boyhood had been much less sheltered than William's. After his mother died, when he was seven, he was shuttled back and forth between the family home in Buffalo and assorted relatives or boarding schools (which he hated).

An adventurous Tom Sawyer–like boy, he had run away repeatedly—once to hide in the church steeple, and on another occasion to work as a telegrapher in Albany, having first covered his tracks by floating his jacket and hat downstream in an empty canoe. His father, Colonel MacKaye, had been trained as a soldier and he marked his son for a military career. He sent him to military school for two years to prepare him for West Point. But the boy's training ended abruptly after he threw an inkwell at a teacher and fled. When the runaway finally turned up at his father's house, he was placed on a strict regimen of home tutoring. But he soon fell ill with "brain fever"—a turn of events that ended plans for a military career.

Sickness may have helped Steele to avoid one paternally directed career, but it did not discourage his father from trying to shape his life again. The colonel was also enthusiastic about painting and was an active patron of the Academy of Design in New York City. If Steele MacKaye would not be a soldier, he would be a painter. Unfortunately for Colonel MacKaye's plans, though Steele loved painting, he grew to love the theater even more. And for the remainder of his life he would fight against the colonel, often living on the verge of starvation to pursue what his father labeled "that fickle jade, the Theatre."[4] His bout with "brain fever" was merely the first of many puzzling attacks of "nervous exhaustion" that marked the struggle.*

Thomas Sergeant Perry was younger than William and closer in temperament to Henry, Jr., but he shared William's intellectual and aesthetic enthusiasms. Like Steele MacKaye, Perry had only one living parent. His father Christopher Grant Perry, had died four years before. The son of the naval hero Oliver Hazard Perry (victor in the Battle of Lake Erie in 1813), Christopher Perry had not shared his father's affinity for a conspicuous place in public affairs. Beginning as a lawyer, he found the work unsatisfactory and changed to medicine. When medicine became too demanding physically, he switched back to law, and practiced as an attorney

---

*In his New York debut as Monaldi, a mad artist, MacKaye fainted after acting out the hallucinatory murder of his imagined foe. He abandoned a European tour of his widely acclaimed *Hamlet* in 1874 because of another fainting episode.

till he died at the age of forty-two. His son Thomas Sergeant Perry was a voracious reader. Turning himself loose in the world of books, he clearing whole shelves like a woodsman felling trees. He had the most famous forebears of the band of friends (in addition to Commodore Perry, he was descended from Benjamin Franklin on his mother's side). When he graduated from Harvard, Perry humorously weighed his alternatives in a mocking letter to his sister that showed the shadow that fame had cast. He was not sure, he wrote, whether "the laurel wreath or the cotton nightcap of obscurity" was to be his lot.

For a Harvard graduate considering career options in the nineteenth century, the learned professions were obvious alternatives. Medicine, law, and divinity had to be considered, however mockingly, before one followed an academic career. Perry listed them all when he told his sister he was in doubt "whether to grasp the keen, trenchant scalpel of the chirurgeon, the light rapier of the jurisconsult, . . . or else retire to the fortress-like calm of metaphysics, not unmingled with theologic lore." But he was much more decisive than William. After graduation, Perry went to Europe for two years of study and travel to prepare himself for an academic career. "America needs above all things educated men particularly in its best colleges," he wrote, and assured his sister that his was "no hastily formed vagary."[5] Perry began to teach at Harvard five years before William. Though he had never shown any inclination to become a painter, his family would not have objected if he had. An older brother was a painter, and his sister married the painter John La Farge.

La Farge was a welcome addition to this group of aesthetically talented young men when he burst into their midst. Obviously much impressed, William rushed from Hunt's studio and trumpeted, "There's a new fellow come to Hunt's class. He knows everything. He has seen everything— paints everything. He's a marvel!"[6] La Farge was seven years older than William and made a fabulous impression on him and his friends. To the mix of their English and Irish, he added a leaven of French—linked on one side to the ancien régime and on the other to the armies of Napoleon. He posed very much as the cultivated European, but La Farge, like MacKaye and James, was a New Yorker supported by a mercantile fortune (New York and Louisiana real estate).* He had been educated in American schools through college and had not visited Paris until he was twenty-one.

---

*The La Farges had been slaveholders in Santo Domingo. John's maternal grandfather, Binsse de Saint-Victor, owned one of the largest plantations there. He fled to the United States for safety after a slave revolt destroyed his mansion. La Farge's father took part in a French attempt to capture the rebel leader Toussaint L'Ouverture, was wounded running a British blockade, and then captured. He, too escaped to the United States (Royal Cortissoz, *John La Farge: A Memoir and a Study* (New York, 1911), 26, 45, 50, 57.

But his parents made his home an island of French culture set apart from the raw Washington Square scene.

La Farge demonstrated a talent for painting quite early. When he was six, his grandfather taught him to paint. He had lessons from an English watercolor painter when he was ten, but in retrospect labeled these efforts "nothing but the fancy of a youngster for something else than his usual occupation." He found college "an extinguisher of art" and turned toward a legal career after graduation. After reading enough law to convince himself that it was not his calling, he left for Europe with no clear goal other than self-cultivation. His father feared for his son's moral development, but he did not share Henry James's dour view of painting. Quite the contrary, when he suspected that John was living "faster" than he liked (the son denied that there ever had been any justification for his father's concern), he urged him to study painting in order to learn discipline. John reluctantly entered Couture's studio, but after a few weeks he set off on a tour, preferring to copy in the museums of France, England, Denmark, and Belgium rather than study with the master. He told Couture he was not interested in becoming a painter, and furthermore, he was not seriously seeking a vocation. In 1858 he was recalled to the United States to attend his father's final illness. Still uncertain about his future, he resumed the study of law. Yet he was still lured by art and spent many stolen hours in his own New York studio, drawing and visiting with artist friends. When he and William James met in Newport, La Farge was still unsettled about the direction of his life.

Having avoided Couture earlier, John craved further training from him now. Richard Hunt sent him to Newport to do the next best thing—to study with Hunt's brother William, who had been Couture's apprentice. But La Farge was a young man who refused teaching. He found Hunt too much influenced by Millet and too far from the style of Couture to suit his taste. He stayed to paint in Hunt's studio, but not to learn from him.* With the firing on Fort Sumter, La Farge abandoned the hope of returning to study in Europe. Nearsightedness kept him out of the fighting, so he moved back to New York and his seemingly aimless drift.[7]

Set beside the attitudes of the MacKayes, the Perrys, and the La Farges, Henry James's hostility to painting as a career was atypical. Other parents of his station encouraged or even tried to impose a painter's vocation on their sons. All of the young friends save MacKaye considered the learned

---

*William later remarked on La Farge's supreme self-confidence in a letter to his brother Henry. In his more mature view, it made his friend a less desirable companion than he had been during the Newport experiment. "John La Farge came in a few nights since. My affections gushed forth to meet him, but were soon coagulated by his invincible pretentiousness, that no one can teach him anything that he does not know already" (*TCWJ*, 1:294).

professions of medicine, law, and divinity before choosing other work. A specific early sense of vocation was unusual. Perry was the only one who knew clearly what he wanted to do when he finished college. Drift rather than decision shaped their lives. And neurasthenic illness played an important part. William Morris Hunt, Steele MacKaye, John La Farge, and William James all fell puzzlingly ill. Clearly the freedom that wealth and mobility provided was also a great strain on these privileged young Americans.

[2]

The James family abruptly left Newport in October 1859. Hunt's influence was far too strong and Henry wanted to sever that tie. He didn't admit it at first. Instead, when he wrote about the matter to friends, he gave two other reasons for dragging the family off to Europe once again: suitable housing was not available in Cambridge (where he hoped to place William to study science), and the social atmosphere of America made young people rebellious. In July 1859 he had written, "We are anxiously thinking of embarking for that educational paradise [Europe]. We can't get a house in Cambridge, and are disposed to think it would not be the place for us in all respects if we could." Henry did not explain why Cambridge would not suffice, but he did make it clear that William's scientific education was uppermost in his mind, "our desire after Cambridge having been prompted by the wish to get my oldest boy in the Scientific School."[8]

Henry proceeded to lay the groundwork for William's scientific career, even as his son's intention to paint gathered force. Perhaps it was this contradiction that made him slide off into a bewildering run of theological platitudes in the remainder of his letter. He comforted himself with a statement of faith in divine guidance, which to his mind made the decision to uproot his family cosmically insignificant. "The truth is, . . . I have but one *fixed mind* about anything; which is, that whether we stay or go abroad, and whatever befalls my dear boys in this world, they and you and I are all alike, and after all, absolute creatures of God, vivified every moment by Him, cared for every moment by Him, guided every moment by an infallible wisdom and an irreproachable tenderness, and that we have none of us therefore the slightest right to indulge any anxiety or listen in any conceivable circumstances to the lightest whisper of perturbation."[9]

The ease with which Mr. James moved from "we" to "I" to "Him" in the flow of discussion about William is indicative of his characteristic blurring of boundaries. He might justifiably fuse his own and his wife's judgment into "we," but when it came to equating God's infallible wisdom and irreproachable tenderness with his own attempt to shape his son's life, he was bound to get into difficulty. And he did.

Something happened between July and September that made him shift the ground of justification for another trip to Geneva. Judging from his note to Samuel Ward, his banker and friend, he feared open rebellion. "I have grown so discouraged about the education of my children here, and dread so those inevitable habits of extravagance and insubordination, which appear to be characteristic of American youth, that I have come to the conclusion to retrace my steps to Europe, and keep them there a few years longer."[10]

If the reasons Mr. James gave his children were anything like those he gave in his letters, his sons must have found it bitter indeed to be wrenched from their newfound friends and American roots by a parent who claimed to be making sacrifices for their good. "My wife is completely of the same mind," he assured Ward, "and though we feel on many accounts that we are making personal sacrifices in this step, the advantages to the children are so clear that we cannot conscientiously hesitate." Having rationalized the step, Henry confessed only one source of guilt about the matter—he was admitting that he considered Europe superior to America, and that attitude didn't fit easily with his view of himself as a democrat. Characteristically, he resolved the inconsistency with a good-humored turn of phrase that suggested that there was, after all, no inconsistency. "I am a good patriot, but my patriotism is even livelier on the other side of the water."[11]

It was not until a full year later, after William insisted on returning to Newport for his painting experiment, that Henry told a friend what was probably clear to the older boys all along. "Willy especially felt, we thought, a little too much attraction to painting—as I suppose from the contiguity to Mr. Hunt; let us break that up, we said, at all events."[12] He did not want to be separated from his sons, so he wouldn't send them off to Europe alone. But physical separation was only part of what troubled him. The closeness to Hunt threatened to give his son a mentor who would turn his life in a direction other than the one Henry had planned. If William did not become a scientist and succeed where he himself had failed, Henry James would be left to wrestle more directly with William of Albany and his own barely quieted demons.

Between October 1859 and September 1860, the James family lived abroad once again. All but three months were spent in Geneva, where William was enrolled in the Geneva Academy and excelled in scientific courses. Unfortunately, Henry, Jr., was misplaced in a school that specialized in mathematics and science. He was miserable. Though the trip abroad was allegedly for his educational good as well as William's, his father seemed to have had little appreciation of the different quality of his mind. On the surface, William went through his Geneva experience in high spirits. He was popular with his peers and was invited to join a student drinking club. His brothers and sister described his letters as playful. Alice, his twelve-year-old sister, reported that he had composed mock sonnets to her and read them dramatically for the amusement of the family. In retrospect, Alice's jocular aside has an ominous ring: "We have all come to the conclusion that he is fit to go to the lunatic asylum."[13]

Though William complied with his father's efforts to cut him off from Hunt and the lure of painting, he was torn by angry feelings that threatened to overwhelm his lighthearted facade. The conflict that was germinating beneath the surface bursts through his drawings. The sketches that survive from his stay in Newport and Geneva are at first glance casual experiments or playful cartoons with little personally dramatic import. The first group of six sketches dates from 1859–60. Five were tossed off to amuse a young cousin, Frank Tweedy. They appear to be illustrations for some fairy tale. Two more groups were drawn in his school notebooks. The first from the Geneva notebook are little more than doodles, the idle wanderings of his pencil to escape the boredom of a lesson in physics. The second group was done more carefully and represents the artist's observations in an anatomy class that he attended at the Geneva Academy.

The most striking commonality among all of the sketches, aside from William's skill, is his preoccupation with violence—an extension and elaboration of the theme of Delacroix's *Barque de Dante*.* Figure 1 represents two fleeing hunters about to be pounced upon by an elephant charging from behind. They have apparently set out, one with spear in hand, to hunt, but have suddenly found themselves fleeing as the hunted. There is a marked contrast between the massive beast, with its gaping mouth and threatening tusks, and the puny humans. The more distant figure is balding and has the suggestion of a beard, and his right foot appears to be detached from the leg. The clothed, younger figure, with a full head of hair, is about to scream; his gaping mouth echoes the awesome mouth of the attacking beast. In the spirit of play, James wrote at the bottom, "Done by Willy James for Frank 1859." The artist and the child imaginatively acted the roles of creator and patron.

Figure 2 sustains the theme of violence. Here two figures, a bear and a man, face each other in mortal combat. Again there is the suggestion that the hunter has been surprised and is about to be overwhelmed by the hunted. The surprised hunter is forced to defend himself with a dagger.

---

*It is remarkable how James's *Principles of Psychology* (1890) provides epigraphic commentary for his youthful drawings.

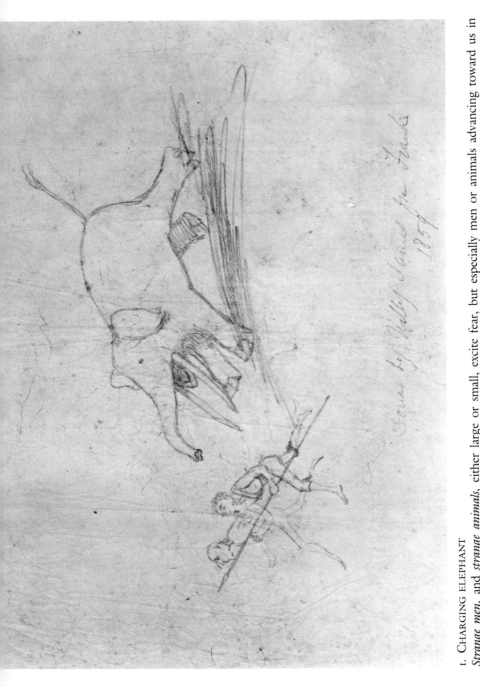

1. CHARGING ELEPHANT

Strange men, and *strange animals*, either large or small, excite fear, but especially men or animals advancing toward us in a threatening way. —W. James, 1890

2. BEAR

We both fear, and wish to kill, anything that may kill us. . . .   —W. James, 1890

The bear has more human proportions than the elephant in Figure 1, but the beast is still more massive and powerful than the man. As in the first sketch, the most vicious attack is obviously coming from his gaping mouth. The victim's mouth is also open in an expression of pain and horror that echoes the screaming mouth of Figure 1. There is an odd dancing quality to the figures, which would appear, were it not for the knife wound and bared teeth, to be in an embrace. That William could draw more accurately is evident in later figures, so the distortion suggests a backing off from the violence of the scene.* Apparently Frank was bothered by the darkness of the scene, too, because he added his own sun to William's, so that two suns shine down on the grisly scene.

*There is no way of telling the order in which the drawings were produced. My numbering is intuitive, and the drawings are organized to enhance the argument.

3. OGRE
In many respects man is the most ruthlessly ferocious of beasts.   —W. James, 1890

Figure 3 depicts an act of cannibalism by a mythical ogre, whose body has the same squat, massive quality as the bear in Figure 2. The giant carries a dead bear, perhaps the animal from the previous drawing. The ogre's head is ringed with hair that rises in points, suggesting horns or flames that contribute to his diabolical appearance. The eyes are crossed, the nose is snubbed, the jowls are heavy, but the most menacing feature is the mouth, which is sawtoothed and cavernous, as in the earlier drawings. An arm and head have been torn from the victim, whose remains are about to be eaten. As in Figure 2, it is the head that is the target of attack. It is obvious that primitive aggression is the theme of these drawings, and their intensity suggests the proportions of the wish the artist is defending against. William's aggression is least defensively disguised in Figure 3. It is no longer animals that bite and destroy, but an oversized mythical man. What is beastly in Figures 1 and 2 becomes human—mythically displaced—but recognizably human, like the artist himself.

Figure 4 appears to be from an entirely different tale. There are no animals, but two men, one of whom is terrified of the other. The threatening older figure is a cloaked, bearded man with a high hat and staff, suggesting a wizard-scientist. This impression is enhanced by a large flask near the doorway, the sort of flask commonly found in a chemistry laboratory. The younger man is literally cornered. He cowers, trying to make himself as small as possible. But there is no way out.

The last scene in the series (Figure 5) is the most carefully drawn, and demonstrates that William could render the human figure in complicated combative stances. The theme of violence continues. This drawing is less gruesome than the others because the aggression has social definition—a battle with swords and daggers rather than tooth and claw. A solitary young man is under attack by four assailants, one of whom has already been slain. A white-bearded older man with a turban hovers in the background, waiting to see the outcome.*

Considered as a group, the drawings are the products of a talented draftsman who was struggling against murderous wishes of mounting

---

*There were five children in the James family, all vying for father's sanction and approval. One visitor described the family at table as follows:

> The adipose and affectionate "Wilkie," as his father called him, would say something and be instantly corrected and disputed by the little cock-sparrow Bob, the youngest, but good-naturedly defend his statement, and then, Henry [Jr.] would emerge from his silence in defence of Wilkie. Then Bob would be more impertinently insistent, and Mr. James would advance as moderator, and William, the eldest, would join in. The voice of the moderator presently would be drowned by the combatants and he soon came down vigorously in the arena, and when, in an excited argument, the dinner knives might not be absent from eagerly gesticulating hands, dear Mrs. James, more conventional, but bright as well as motherly, would look at me, laughingly reassuring, saying, "Don't be disturbed, Edward; they won't stab each other. This is usual when the boys come home." [*TCWJ*, 1:171–72]

4. WIZARD

Our shyness before an important personage may be complicated by . . . "servile terror," based on representation of definite dangers if we fail to please. —W. James, 1890

5. DUELING MEN

Constrained to be a member of a tribe, he still has a right to decide, as far as in him lies, of which other members the tribe shall consist. Killing off a few obnoxious ones may often better the chances of those that remain. —W. James, 1890

intensity. The disproportion between man and animal indicates the felt inequality between rage and the means of controlling it. William apparently feared impending disaster from some hidden source, perhaps his own destructive impulses. The theme of the hunter who becomes the hunted anticipates the retribution that would ensue if the aggression that is directed outward in the drawings were turned against the artist himself. The emphasis on the head as both agent and target of attack implies an emphasis on intellectual, verbal modes of aggression. The older male figure, a constant element in his imagination, is experienced as ineffectual (Figure 1), or confronting and overtly destructive (Figures 3 and 4), or remote and covertly destructive (Figure 5). The half embrace of hunter and bear (Figure 2) is indicative of his ambivalence—affection and rage prod him toward a warm embrace and murder simultaneously—but the balance is tipped toward destruction. The figure of the magician-scientist may represent his sense of being trapped in science by that awesome older man.

In sum, the handiwork of unguarded child's play pulls back the facade of compliant good humor. Not that the picture of a dutiful son is untrue; rather it is incomplete. And the additional element that William's drawings add to the picture make his depression after he abandoned painting less mysterious. The drawings anticipate by many months William's rebellion and insistence on his painter's vocation, and they plumb the depths of his rage over the bind he was in. There are some hints of arguments with his father in his correspondence. But they are only hints, a barely audible whisper. The artist has amplified them into a shriek of terror and a snarl of rage.

The two sets of sketches from the Geneva notebook of 1860 are also scenes of violence. The first group fills the bottom of a page of notes on physics and the whole of the opposite page (Figure 6). At first glance the drawings on opposite pages appear unrelated, but in fact they represent a continuation of an earlier preoccupation, the beastly attack on the unsuspecting. A partially sketched head stares pensively into the distance, and a barely visible bewhiskered second head below looks in the same direction. Behind and between the heads a heavily outlined panther or mountain lion is about to spring on its unsuspecting prey. The scene opposite depicts the next stage of the attack, but a giraffe is substituted for the human prey. Here is a Delacroix-like rendition of a savage attack on unsuspecting innocence. The stalking cat has leaped on the back of a fleeing giraffe. The giraffe, elegant and graceful, is caught in mid-air as the cat sinks its teeth deep into its flank. The artist apparently attempted a preliminary drawing of the cat below before mounting it on the back of the giraffe. All of the animal figures convey a sense of primitive power and energy about to be unleashed.

taken overcome is equivalent to a sum of momenta destroyed one after another. How are we to measure a sum of momenta destroyed? $M(vt + v't' + v't$ $+ \&c \&c)$. Now this quantity in parenthesis is nothing else than the expression of the distance

$d = \frac{1}{2} wt \cdot t$ $w = $ elementary increment of velocity.

Now we can not by direct observation learn nothing not learn the magnitude of w, the "acceleration" We can by arresting the accelerating force at the end of the first second + noting the space described during the second second space of time t, learn the magnitude of $wt \cdot t$

$\frac{w}{v} = \frac{t}{1\,second}$

6. GIRAFFE

Thus a hungry lion starts to seek prey by the awakening in him of imagination coupled with desire; he begins to stalk . . . he springs upon it, . . . he proceeds to

tear and devour it the moment he gets a sensation of its contact with his claws and
fangs.   —W. James, 1890

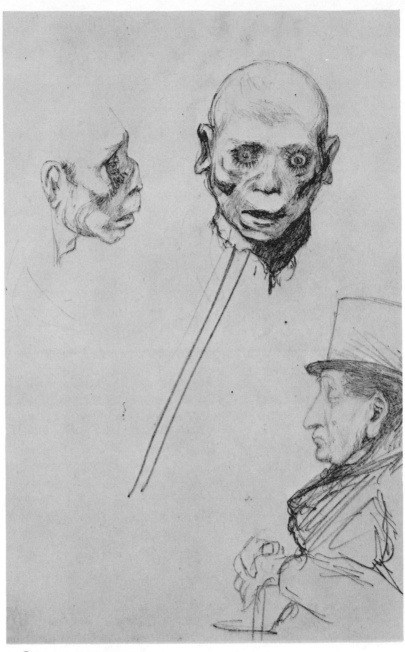

7. CADAVER AND BURGHER

Such different characters may conceivably at the outset of life be alike *possible* to man. But to make any one of them actual, the rest must more or less be suppressed.   —W. James, 1890

134

The second set consists of three heads—two studies of a cadaver and one of a top-hatted and formally jacketed burgher (Figure 7). The skin of the corpse is drawn taut over the skull. One cheek seems to have been gashed by a knife. Both eyes and mouth create a grim, frightening impression of evil. The side view of the cadaver's head looks beastlike, the nose flattened, the eyes barely visible. The clothed figure of the burgher is in sharp contrast. His eyes are closed, his mouth is pursed, his hands rest on his cane—all elements that contribute to the impression of smug, self-satisfied repose. Though his features are not deformed like those of the cadaver, this virtuous citizen appears more dead than the corpse.

One can almost follow the line of William's thought as he mused over the meaning of his dissecting-room experience in Geneva. Death held a fascination for him like the fascination of animal-like violence. How did it come about that a gaping corpse looked more alive than the smug burgher napping in the corner? This cadaver, perhaps a pauper or criminal who died a violent death—did he express more of the animal within him that his more fortunate neighbor? Should a young man follow his instincts, even if they are violent, or should he fit himself into the straitjacket of civilized somnolence?

Though continuous in theme with the 1859 drawings, the Geneva drawings of 1860 no longer emphasize the immense disproportion between animal and man, between the attacker and the victim, that contributed to the earlier impression of an overwhelming of the artist's controls. The shift away from the grotesque to the tragic implies that William had more of a sense of mastery and aesthetic distance by 1860. Perhaps these drawings were made when William had decided to insist on painting. He would risk his father's disapproval and dare to live on the vital edge rather than subside into a conventional life. But he reckoned without his father. And, as he feared, the attack came from an unexpected quarter.

[3]

The family left Geneva and moved for the summer to Bonn, Germany, where the boys were placed with German families to learn the language. William finally told his father what had been brewing in his mind. Oddly enough, Henry James was surprised by what he heard. He reported the "change" to a friend: "We had hardly reached here before Willy took an opportunity to say to me—what it seems he had been long wanting to say, but found it difficult to come to the scratch—that he felt the vocation of a painter so strongly that he did not think it worth my while to expend any more time or money on his scientific education! I confess I was greatly startled by the annunciation, and not a little grieved."[14] He reluctantly agreed, and plans were made to return to Newport in the fall. But nominal approval was one thing, paternal blessing quite another.

In arguing with his father in his correspondence, William tried to draw him onto the high ground of rational discourse to persuade him of the wisdom of his choice. But he was too well acquainted with the workings of his father's mind to expect much from the effort. He wrote to Henry, Jr., in Paris: "I wish you would, as you promised, set down as clearly as you can on paper what your idea of the nature of art is, because I do not probably understand it fully, and should like to have it presented in a form that I might think over at my leisure."[15] What depth of indictment hides behind the apparently deferential phase "as clearly as you can"! This was a son who had virtually teethed on philosophic discussion with his utopian father, and he knew all too well by then that clarity was not one of the elder Henry's virtues. When the reply came, it was predictably vague, and set Henry up for a vigorous, well-reasoned pummeling by his philosophic son.

William challenged him for not answering the question. "Your present letter simply points out the spiritual danger. . . . It does not, therefore, cover just the ground I had expected." Of course he had heard all of his father's arguments before, so he rebutted the missing refrain. "I do not see why a man's spiritual culture should not go on independently of his aesthetic activity, why the power which an artist feels in himself should tempt him to forget what he is, any more than the power felt by a Cuvier or Fourier would tempt them to do the same." William was right. There is no *logical* reason why aesthetic activity is any more dangerous to the process of spiritual creation than the biology of Cuvier or the social science of Fourier. But no matter how well he knew the structure of his father's argument against art, he could not have understood the prodigal origins of his father's stand. Judging from the family correspondence, that entire episode was still kept secret from the children.

Having shown that Henry's argument had no logical power, William proceeded to turn his father's basic assumption—that spiritual impressions reflect God within man—against him. "I am sure that far from feeling myself degraded by my intercourse with art, I continually receive from it spiritual impressions the intensest and purest I know. So it seems to me is my mind formed, and *I can see* no reason for avoiding the giving myself up to art *on this score*." So the prodigal who more than a decade before had bravely sounded the clarion call of his own unfettered self-expression now had to listen as his son blasted away on the same horn.

But if Henry James could not win logically, he could count on his son's conscience to get him his way. William turned from his high-spirited, incisive argument to reveal his vulnerability to the elder Henry in a manner that ominously presaged the outcome of his painting experiment and his decline into illness. "Of course if you even agree to let this pass, there remain other considerations which might induce me to hesitate,—those of utility, of duty to society, etc. All these, however, I think ought to be weighed down by strong *inclination* towards art, and by the fact that my life would be embittered if I were kept from it."[16] Achilles was pointing at his heel: a sense of responsibility and love of his father. As he begged that he not be forced away from painting, he showed his father where to strike.

[4]

The decision to leave the art center of the Western world in order to study painting in an American village does seem strange. It is tempting to jump to the conclusion that the return to Newport from Europe to study painting was unquestionably a self-defeating choice. Henry, Jr., found it so odd that he remembered being embarrassed to tell such an absurdity to his friends. "I alone of the family perhaps made bold not to say quite directly or literally that we went home to learn to paint. People stared or laughed when we said it, and I disliked their thinking us so simple."[17] Though European study had been a coveted goal of American artists for well over a century, by 1860 there had been a substantial improvement in the American art world. Painting had evolved beyond a trade of wandering, poorly educated artisans into a more organized profession. The polite drawing classes of early-nineteenth-century schools that catered to provincial aristocratic aspirations had been superseded by more serious professional institutes, particularly in New York and Boston. True, American artists still considered themselves fortunate to study in Europe, but on the eve of the Civil War, when William made his decision, Hunt was not the only serious American painter, and William was not the only student who chose to cast his lot with artists in his native land.[18] Though in Europe art was more a part of daily life than an isolated luxury, the Newport plan offered compensations. The children could give up the tiresome routine of their hotel existence. William knew Hunt and liked him. And there were friends to welcome him back.

If William had decided to study in Europe and the rest of the family had returned to America without him, the outcome of the painting experiment might have been different. But such a separation was unthinkable in the Jamesian scheme. The elder Henry's personal fate was too closely bound to that of his eldest son to permit him to allow William to travel and study alone, as the parents of James MacKaye, Thomas Sergeant Perry, and John La Farge had already done.

Intuitively William sensed this psychological side of the problem. Before leaving Germany, he described a scene in the household where his brothers were living that underscored his keen awareness of the risks of psychological fusion. The tutor's wife and sister-in-law were, he thought, perfect characters for Dickens. "They have been so shut out from the world and have been melting together so long by the kitchen fire that the minds of both have become confounded into one, and they seem to constitute a sort of two-bodied individual. I never saw anything more curious than the way in which they sit mumbling together at the end of the table, each using simultaneously the same exclamation if anything said at our end strikes their ear. The boys say they always speak together, using the same words or else one beginning a phrase, the other ending it. It is a singular life."[19] It hardly seems an accident that his eye should see and his pen should capture the disastrous psychological consequences of the failure to recognize and affirm the boundaries between persons as he was trying to set a course different from his father's.

[5]

William entered Hunt's studio in October 1860 and painted there every day but Sunday. He, John La Farge, and Theodora Sedgwick had the master's exclusive attention, except when he would descend from the upstairs studio to comment encouragingly to Henry James, Jr., who had as always followed in his brother's tracks and was copying from plaster models below.* As Henry remembered that time, art still had the quality of a forbidden pleasure. The hours in the studio were "hours of Art, art definitely named, looking me full in the face and accepting my stare in return—no longer a tacit implication or a shy subterfuge, but a flagrant unattenuated aim."[20] William led the way to the temptress and Henry followed.

Since the family was together, there are no letters to chronicle the background of William's abrupt decision in the spring to abandon Hunt and head for Harvard to study science. In his autobiography, Henry, Jr., merely said that conditions for William's artistic career were not "pro-

---

*Theodora Sedgwick (1851–1916), the youngest daughter of Theodore and Sara Ashburner Sedgwick, moved to Cambridge after her father died in 1859. She and her brother and two sisters were neighbors and friends of the Jameses during the 1860s. Her older sister, Sara, became Alice James's closest friend.

William James at Newport, c. 1861

pitious." He did remark how strange it was that his brother suddenly quit. "Nothing meanwhile could have been less logical, yet at the same time more natural, than that William's interest in the practice of painting should have suddenly and abruptly ceased." Though Henry did not specify what was "natural" about the decision, we may infer from the fact that this remark preceded his discussion of his father's penchant for undermining particular career choices that he associated the two. From his vantage point as an aged biographer and successful novelist, he thought it an "interesting case," but left the matter cloaked in mystery. "He at a given moment, which came quite early, as completely ceased to ply his pencil as he had in his younger time earnestly and curiously exercised it; and this constitutes exactly the interest of his case."[21]

Scholarly opinion has been divided and speculative about the cause of the sudden change, as no evidence pointed to a clear solution to the mystery. Lack of talent, the Civil War (the firing on Fort Sumter in April), ill health, and discouragement by Hunt have all been offered as possible reasons.* But a previously unpublished letter from Henry James,

---

*Ralph Barton Perry concluded that William stopped "because of a growing conviction that he could not excel in a field in which mediocrity would be intolerable." He based this conclusion solely on a remark made before the episode. It is a major leap from William's intolerance of a bad artist to the conclusion that he abandoned painting because he thought *he* was mediocre. Perry may be right, but there is no other evidence to support his conclusion. He was most certainly wrong in the remark "Having once rejected painting he rarely looked back, and never with profound regrets" (*TCWJ*, 1:200). It may seem reasonable to believe that a man who distinguished himself as a philosopher and psychologist had no misgivings, but the language of symptomatology tells another tale.

Leon Edel suggests that it was the Civil War that made painting an untenable occupation. But as no evidence exists either to support or to refute this contention, he states it in tentative terms. "It is impossible to judge what role the Civil War played in this decision; certainly it was difficult for him to remain painting in the studio under the pressures and tensions of the time" (*HJ*, 1:170). But why would study at the Lawrence Scientific School qualify as a more suitable occupation than painting for a young man who was old enough to fight in the war? Both occupations were remote from battle, and young men were leaving Harvard to sign up just as they were leaving Newport.

Gay Wilson Allen (*WJ*) wrote that William had told his painter son Billy that Hunt had diverted him from painting by complaining that America did not value its painters. William may have offered this explanation, but the alleged complaint is puzzlingly inconsistent with Hunt's character and reputation as a teacher. His pupils typically found him full of encouragement despite the difficulties to be overcome. "When I was a little boy I wanted to learn the violin, but a certain man discouraged me. 'Don't learn the violin! It's *so hard!*' I could kick that man now! It is easier to eat dip-toast than to play the violin; but it doesn't meet the same want." Hunt urged his students to place feeling before duty. "Do as you feel—Hang duty— in drawing and painting! Duty never painted a picture, nor wrote a poem, nor built a fire. Do it *as it seems to you to be!*" And Hunt shared what later came to be a characteristic attitude of Jamesian psychology. "Don't talk of what you are 'going to do!' Do It! . . . It's the doing of the thing that's important! Doing is bad enough; but not doing is worse" (William Morris Hunt, *Talks about Art* [London, 1890], 4, 6, 8, 30). It is hard to believe that this man who was full of muscular exhortations to work hard to master the painter's craft discouraged one of his first students. This story may contain a partial truth told by a father to a son who had

Sr., to his brother the Reverend William James adds significant new information that helps to explain that abrupt termination.* Two new elements are added to our picture of the James family scene during that fateful winter: Henry James, Sr., had unexplained fainting spells, and he warned the family that he would soon be dead, though he informed his brother that he was not concerned about his survival. "I have tumbled over in the street, and feel myself wheeling about in unconsciousness every little while, as if the next moment would probably be my last: but I know very well that it is a passing symptom of overwork merely, and that if I hold off for a day or two I shall survive." He urged various remedies on his ailing brother (whom he pronounced a sufferer from "nervous exhaustion"), including stimulants ("a little Bourbon" or coffee) and electric treatments of galvanism.

He sermonized, reminding his correspondent that all was in God's hands, that "these mundane affairs will be quite as well transacted without as with us," and he underscored the moral with the following vignette: "I often tell Mary when I come thundering down into her dovecote scattering her and the children's innocent projects of pleasure, perhaps, merely because I happen to be indisposed to enjoy myself, that I have no doubt they will all get along much better without me than with me: and I have made the same admission to the juveniles. But they all scoff at the idea: they all seem to think that if I should go, the day of doom would arrive for them. I know vastly better." The picture of Henry upsetting the household with death threats is peculiar to the second Newport 'winter, when William was painting. Henry closed his letter with a characteristic insistence that failure is the only divinely inspired truth. "Life is not by any

---

persevered where he had not. Could he confess that he had given up painting—work that now gave his son so much pleasure—because his father opposed him? Perhaps a discouraging teacher was a compromise more acceptable than a discouraging parent.

Besides suggesting that Hunt discouraged him, Allen wrote that William suffered from ill health and therefore gave up painting. I think that illness is part of the picture, but Allen has confused the facts so that time is distorted, leading him to a false conclusion. He claimed that William's eye trouble "would have taken much of the pleasure out of painting, and painting or sketching out of doors where the ocean reflected the dazzling sunlight would have been harmful to sensitive eyes." There is no evidence that James developed difficulty with his eyes before May 1865—four years after the decision to stop painting. Allen is aware that William was in good health up until his return to Newport, and he quite rightly ties the symptoms that arose then to "psychic disturbances of serious proportions" (*WJ*, 70).

The earliest mention of William's illness is in the recollections of Charles W. Eliot, his first teacher at Harvard. Eliot's reminiscence places the onset *after* the decision to abandon painting and at the commencement of his preparation for a career in science. It is curious that Perry left out this crucial sentence when he cited that memoir (*TCWJ*, 1:207).

*The importance of the letter has not been recognized because it was not dated. Internal evidence places it at December 21, 1860 (Howard Feinstein, "An Application of the Concept of Identification for the Historian," *Journal of the History of Science*, April 1970, 147).

Mary Walsh James, c. 1870

Henry James, Sr., c. 1860

means a victory, but simply a battle: and the battle ends so disastrously for no one as for him to whom it *seems* other than a defeat."[22] He was in the process of teaching his eldest son that lesson.

William had told his father that duty might make him change—might force him to abandon painting even if to do so would embitter his life. His father had taken him at his word, and transformed the apparent victory of the return to Hunt into defeat. A painter's vocation was no longer a matter of self-expression but one of duty to an ailing father who might die at any moment by God's (or his own?) hand.* The stakes were high in this internecine battle. If William had his way, the father's hope for justification through the son would be lost. William feared that if the elder Henry won, he would be embittered for life. In Mr. James's boundary-blurred world, paradox softened confrontation, but from this head-on collision only one of them could emerge whole.

"Self-murder" seems too strong a label for William's decision to end what was after all simply a vocational trial. But the imagery is William's own. Twenty years after Newport, he lectured about free choice to an audience of young men at Harvard. He selected a vocational crisis to illustrate his point. "Whether a young man enters business or the ministry may depend on a decision which has to be made before a certain day. He takes the place offered in the counting-house, and is *committed*. Little by little, the habits, the knowledge, of the other career, which once lay so near, cease to be reckoned even among his possibilities. At first, he may sometimes doubt whether the self he murdered in that decisive hour might not have been the better of the two but with the years such questions themselves expire, and the old alternative *ego*, once so vivid, fades into something less substantial than a dream."[23] He substituted business for science, but the personal experience that gave the illustration force is unmistakable. In resigning himself to science, William had murdered a part of himself as decisively as his sketched ogre decapitated his victim two years earlier. Unfortunately, the outcome was not so happy for him as for the hypothetical young man he described. Like so many other elements of

---

*Suicide was not proscribed by Henry's theology. As early as 1849 he described suicide as a reasonable option for socially frustrated genius. "Both nature and society may prevent me following my genius, may keep it completely latent and undiscovered, by holding me in incessant bondage to themselves, but while God remains supreme they cannot make me actually resist it. Insanity or suicide would speedily decide that controversy in my favor" (*Lm*, 50). When his daughter Alice threatened suicide in 1878, he said he was not opposed to the act if she felt it necessary (*DAJ*, 149). When Henry offered condolences to his cousin Katharine Barber James after the suicide of her husband, Dr. William Prince, he derided conventional attitudes toward suicide (Henry James, Sr., to Katharine Barber James, Colby College Library).

the healthy-minded philosophy he would develop, the tale was the statement of an uplifting wish rather than a faithful description of his own experience. His painter self, the alternative ego that he stifled, did not fade away. Instead it insistently reappeared through symptoms that plagued him for the remainder of his life.

9

Evolution at Harvard

We have reached the point where the results of science touch the very problem of existence, and all men listen for the solving of that mystery.
—Louis Agassiz, 1862

[1]

ACCORDING TO the elder Henry James's vocational map, science as technology was the harbinger of a new day, and a welcome ally in his efforts to break free of Calvinism. But he had no firsthand experience with the actual world of science that he forced upon his son. William's entry into the Lawrence Scientific School in the fall of 1861 brought him into contact with the institutional structures, the influential teachers, and the intellectual atmosphere that made up the reality of his father's abstract, theologically inspired plan. The school was young and primitive, the atmosphere was electric with the conflict over Darwin's *Origin of Species* (1859), and three of Harvard's scientists—Louis Agassiz, Jeffries Wyman, and Asa Gray—were men of distinction whose career line defined the possibilities for an aspiring scientist in America.

William soon found himself under pressure to choose between basic science and medicine, and in 1863, when the decision had to be made, his drawing showed once again a preoccupation with violence. Insanity surfaced as a recurrent theme in his correspondence as he felt himself impelled by duty and circumstance into what he quickly labeled the "humbug" of medicine. Though he continued to make occasional drawings in his science notebooks, the Atlantis of his artist self remained effectively hidden.*

---

*John Jay Chapman, a friend and admirer, wrote as he mused over the death of William James in 1910: "It has sometimes crossed my mind that James wanted to be a poet and an artist, and that there lay in him, beneath the ocean of metaphysics a lost Atlantis of the fine

Yet these surviving drawings, like those of 1859–60, faithfully monitored the inner tempest unleashed by his murdered self.

Cambridge was very much a rural community in 1861. Harvard Square was still unpaved. A horsecar ride down Cambridge Street linked the town with the larger world of Boston. For all of Henry James's scorn of the world of business, his son could study science in America because of a new industrial fortune. Abbott Lawrence provided financial backing because he recognized that America (and his mills) needed men with advanced technical training. A gift of $50,000 provided an initial endowment. Lawrence insisted that the school focus exclusively on science and practical technology (engineering, mining, and mechanical drawing).[1] The school had been open for fourteen years by the time William entered, but despite the founder's aspirations, it still offered casual training to a poorly prepared student body.

There was no entrace examination, nor was a student expected to have any prior training. If a boy was eighteen years old and interested in studying with a particular member of the faculty who accpeted him, he was admitted. There was no course common to all of the students because they worked exclusively with one professor. A shift of field meant a shift of professor. James, for example, started with Charles Eliot in chemistry, and then shifted to Jeffries Wyman when he wanted to study comparative anatomy. The terminus was as variable as the program in this loosely organized structure. Most students stayed from eighteen to thirty months but never bothered to complete the work for a B.S. degree which was conferred after an examination by the professor following at least one year of residence. The quality of training was entirely dependent on the maturity of the student and the caliber of his chosen mentor.[2] While some graduates lauded their educational experience, the days of such loose organization were numbered. When Charles Eliot became president of Harvard in 1869, he instituted a four-year graded curriculum for all students, no matter what their field, and no one was admitted without having passed an entrance examination. By entering in 1861, William escaped the impact of this reform.[3]

Another institution that shaped William's scientific opportunities was the Lowell Institute. Here he was dependent on the forward vision of another manufacturer of cotton fabrics, John Lowell, Jr. The Lowell Institute sponsored a lecture series that brought eminent scientists to the

---

arts; that he really hated philosophy and all its works, and pursued them only as Hercules might spin or as a prince in a fairy tale might sort seeds for an evil dragon, or as anyone might patiently do some careful work for which he had no aptitude" (John J. Chapman, "William James," in *The Selected Writings of John J. Chapman,* ed. Jacques Barzun [New York, 1957], 203).

Boston platform. Louis Agassiz, the distinguished Swiss naturalist and one of William's most influential teachers, was lured to Boston by the Lowell lectureship. He was secured in place at Harvard in 1846 by Abbott Lawrence's willingness to adapt his mandate to accommodate Agassiz so he would join the faculty. Since he did not study with Agassiz when he entered, William's first chance to hear him was in the Lowell lecture series of 1861. In later years, James became a frequent Lowell lecturer himself.

[2]

Louis Agassiz's arrival was a major event in American science. A naturalist of international reputation, a polished lecturer and inspiring teacher, he was the personification of a scientist for the American public, and a model for such aspiring young men as William James. As Agassiz had been trained in Europe, his career offers an interesting contrast to the line of development of his American peers. He was from modest middle-class circumstances and had to fight a continuous battle against lack of funds and parental conservatism concerning his chosen work. Rather than rebelling, as Henry James had done, he succeeded in winning reluctant parental support for a most uncertain future. His talent for observation had appeared early, and his ambition was firmly set by the time he was fifteen. He knew he wanted to study science. By the time he was twenty he declared his ambition to become the "first naturalist of his time." But he also stated his intention to be a "good son" and accepted the high value his parents placed on learning, social position, and hard work.[4] With the help of his teachers, he dissuaded his parents from forcing him into a commerical apprenticeship. When they insisted that he prepare for a practical vocation after two years of college, he entered medical school, this being a common compromise in the nineteenth century between the wish for more training in natural science and the need to earn a livelihood. A brilliant student, Agassiz was given access to his professors' private libraries and collections in recognition of his talent. By the time he was twenty-three, he had published a book, *Brazilian Fishes,* which was accepted for his Ph.D. He completed his M.D. at the same time. His mother gratefully applauded him for entering "a career as safe as it is honorable."[5]

The tension between applied and basic science was a typical conflict for young scientists. When Agassiz wanted to go to Paris to study with Cuvier, practical medicine provided the pretext for the trip. The Paris of Louis-Philippe was besieged by the same cholera epidemic that had prompted William James of Albany to write his will. There is no evidence that he actually paid any attention to the epidemic while in Paris, but cholera did affect his career in an unforeseen way. Cuvier, his teacher, died of the disease in 1832. Agassiz's success in scientific circles had been spectacular. Baron Alexander von Humboldt, the Prussian naturalist and explorer, had also taken him under his wing. Agassiz's practical-minded mother was unimpressed by his prospects; she characterized him as living "on brilliant hopes in relation . . . with great people."[6] He returned to Switzerland as a professor and curator of a museum of natural history. Contrary to his parents' fears, by the age of twenty-five he had achieved an international reputation and a secure position, and was free to pursue his ambition. During the next thirteen years he married, turned his home into a scientific factory with a staff of twelve supported by him and living under his roof, started his own scientific publishing company, produced his masterwork, *Poissons fossiles,* and achieved his ambition of being the first naturalist of his age.

It was a hollow victory. His wife would not put up with the penury and lack of privacy indefinitely, and finally she left him. His publishing house collapsed from indebtedness. Worst of all, at the age of thirty-eight he felt he had exhausted his intellectual resources. The Lowell lectureship led to a renewal. In America he found a new continent to explore, a new academic post with wealthy men anxious to support his research, and, after his wife died, a new marriage to a well-connected Bostonian fifteen years younger than he. By the time William James entered Harvard, Agassiz had been shaping its science program for nearly fifteen years.

Jeffries Wyman, the professor of comparative anatomy, also came to science through medicine. Both his father and his older brother were physicians. Like Agassiz, Wyman had been an avid collector of natural history specimens in his boyhood. After preparatory study at Exeter Academy, he entered Harvard. The standard curriculum held little interest for him and he was an indifferent student, graduating fiftieth in a class of fifty-three. But poor undergraduate performance was no bar to a medical career then. In 1837, after two years of medical study and a year as an assistant at the Massachusetts General Hospital, he qualified for the M.D.; but lack of money was a constant source of worry for him. He had to supplement his paltry earnings from his practice and his post as a demonstrator in anatomy at Harvard by working as a fireman for the Boston Fire Department.

The Lowell Institute was critical for Wyman's career, as it had been for Agassiz's. It was not until he was made curator of the Lowell Institute and earned the munificent stipend of a Lowell lecturer that he had enough money to go abroad for advanced study. Unfortunately, his father's death forced him to return prematurely to America and medical practice. The practice did not go well. After teaching for three years at Hampden-Sydney Medical College in Richmond, Virginia, he returned to Harvard as professor of anatomy in 1847. He supplemented his salary by teaching at the Museum of Comparative Zoology and at a private medical school in Cambridge. Wyman had welcomed Agassiz to the Harvard scientific scene. But when William James entered the Lawrence Scientific School in 1861, a gulf of bitterness had developed between them over Darwin's theory.[7]

Wyman had Asa Gray as an ally in this controversy. Gray had also proved that it was possible to become a research scientist in America after one had prepared for a medical career, and throughout the 1860s, he advised aspiring scientists to get a medical degree.[8] Gray, like James, was a Scotch-Irish New Yorker. When he was fifteen he attended the canal celebration addressed by James's grandfather. The eldest son of a merchant farmer, he had been given the best education that the Mohawk Valley offered. He entered the district school at age three. His public school education was supplemented by a year of study with the village pastor's son before he entered the Clinton Grammar School, a preparatory school connected with Hamilton College, when he was thirteen years old. He followed a favorite teacher to Fairfield Academy for an additional year of study that emphasized science and English letters. Because his family was short of funds, plans for a college education were abandoned, and he entered the medical school attached to Fairfield Academy directly at the age of sixteen.

Youthful entrants to the school were not unusual. According to school rules, a student was expected to have "studied medicine and surgery, for the term of three years after the age of sixteen, with some physician duly authorized to practice his profession" before qualifying for a medical degree. In addition to the apprenticeship, students were required to attend two sixteen-week courses of lectures and be at least twenty-one years old to graduate.[9] All but one of the faculty at Fairfield were itinerant teachers. They traveled a circuit of frontier medical schools, starting at Dartmouth and Berkshire and moving on through Fairfield to Geneva, Buffalo, and Cleveland. Students bought tickets for each course, the fee going directly to the professor, who traditionally allowed any student who had completed two courses and wanted to benefit from another hearing to attend free.

Fortunately, Gray found a teacher, the professor of chemistry, who encouraged his passion for botany, and he took time away from his apprenticeship to gather specimens for his own herbarium. Gray graduated, opened a practice, and did miserably. Though financial support from practice was one of the lures of a medical education for young scientists, the prospects were uncertain. After his first year, the young doctor complained to a friend, "It is very healthy and Doctors have fair prospects of starvation."[10] Ironically, his first substantial salary came from teaching a summer course in botany. He found a position as a naturalist in a boys' high school and became so involved in his botanic interests, and so disenchanted by medicine, that he headed south to Pennsylvania by stagecoach to collect fossil plants while cholera raged around him.[11]

It is clear that financial support had been a problem in the beginning for Agassiz, Wyman, and Gray, and had justified medical training. Yet Wyman and Gray failed at practice, and Agassiz never tried. And all three ultimately supported themselves by teaching. Institutional support for research had been sparse for their generation. Such learned societies as the American Philosophical Society and the American Academy of Arts and Sciences, legacies of eighteenth-century devoted amateurs, gave some support. And in the Jacksonian era, state legislatures had begun to fund government surveys of natural resources. These activities supported others.[12]

While these three professors modeled the possibilities for a life in science at mid-century, some important changes were in store for William's generation. The move toward specialization had begun. It was no longer feasible to be a "naturalist" and encompass the entire range of knowledge as Agassiz had attempted to do. And educational institutions began to recognize the need to support basic research in science. Asa Gray's career serves as a benchmark for both of these shifts. When he arrived at Harvard in 1842, it was understood that he would teach botany and leave zoology to someone else. Furthermore, the college supported his research. Such men as Agassiz and Gray had to beg and borrow from other collectors to do their work. Not so in William's generation. In 1860 Agassiz opened a zoological museum with specimens, gathered from all over the world, that students could actually handle and study. Students of James's generation did not have to curry favor to study biology, as their teachers had done. And there was even the possibility of a $1,000 stipend for a select few students at Agassiz's museum. Men of the previous generation had started work at one-quarter as much. The Lawrence Scientific School was rightly characterized by Henry James, Jr., as "a gray and scant little scene,"[13] but William's opportunities were more abundant than those that had been open to his mentors two decades earlier.

[3]

It did not take William long to make contact with Agassiz. By the second week in September, he announced to his parents that he was going to Boston to hear him lecture. To hear Agassiz lecture was to watch a master performance. He lectured without notes in a charming French accent, illustrating his talk with spontaneous drawings. Large crowds, unsettled by the implications of Darwin's work, came to hear his authoritative, reassuring brand of natural theology. He proclaimed biological and geological science to be reflections of a divine intelligence at work in the universe. He assured his audience that "a coherence binds all the geological ages in one chain . . . a stability of purpose that completes in the beings born today an intention expressed in the first creatures that swam in the Silurian ocean . . . a steadfastness of thought . . . between the facts of nature and . . . the results of an intellectual power."[14] For Agassiz, studying nature was a holy act, and the scientist's discoveries were a source of revelation.

It is not likely that this natural theology impressed James. His father's harangues had already inoculated him against its influnce. The Bostonians who had crowded into the Tremont Temple listened carefully when the professor announced "We have reached the point where the results of science touch the very problem of existence, and all men listen for the solving of that mystery." The debate over Darwin's theory had ruffled their religious sensibilities, and the devout were relieved to hear this professor, whose forebears had been ministers of the Gospel for six generations and who was a recognized scientist of international repute, assure them that man was not bound by his animal nature, though his body might be classified among the vertebrates. "Man is the crowning work of God on earth. He may sink as low as the lowest of his type, or he may rise to a spiritual height that will make that which distinguishes him from the rest far more the controlling element of his being than that which unites him with them."[15]

The lecture series must have captured William's imagination. By November he was outlining his idea of spending "five or six years with Agassiz," and by Christmas he was making plans with his parents to move the entire family to Cambridge to implement this project. It is significant that his first note of enthusiasm for Agassiz came when he felt that he could appreciate him as an artist. One of Agassiz's students described the professor's teaching method to him, and William discovered, much to his delight, that the career of a naturalist depended on the ability to see and experience the world afresh, like an artist. "I had a long talk with one of his students the other night and saw for the first time how a naturalist could feel about his trade in the same way that an artist does about his. . . . He must be a great teacher."[16]

While Agassiz's gift as a lecturer won him a huge popular following, he was not in good standing with his scientific colleagues at Harvard. Evolution divided them. Evidence that undermined Agassiz's conception of biology had been accumulating during the 1850s. Trained in the tradition of old-fashioned German *Naturphilosophie,* he believed that the order of nature was the result of the continuous intervention by a Supreme Being for the realization of an ideal plan. He steadfastly rejected any theories or evidence that suggested that change was merely the result of physical laws. He labeled such materialistic ideas the "curse of science."[17] He was convinced that every animal conformed to a divinely ordained type from the beginning. When geological evidence showed that many such catastrophes as the Ice Age had occurred in the past, Agassiz explained the reappearance of similar species as the result of multiple creations that repeated the divine plan. He also insisted that the distribution of plants and animals was static. Ideal species, multiple creations, catastrophism, and static geographical distribution formed his canon, and he branded Darwinism a materialistic heresy, no matter how well supported.

Though Asa Gray, too, was a religious man, he remained more open than Agassiz to scientific evidence. His own research in Hawaii confirmed Darwin's conclusion that independently created species were a myth. He openly challenged Agassiz before the scientific community. He criticized Agassiz's penchant for "always writing and talking *ad populum.*"[18] Increasingly he and Wyman saw Agassiz as an obstacle to the development of science at Harvard.

The battle gradually shifted from the high ground of science to personal invective. Agassiz criticized Gray publicly for adopting "a pleasing but false theory," and Gray threatened "to stop Agassiz's mouth with his own words." The bitterness reached such a pitch that Agassiz challenged his distinguished colleague to a duel.[19] Darwin's *Origin of Species* had been published just two years before William entered, but the fault that split the faculty had appeared more than a decade before. James would take sides with Wyman, who was the first to teach him about evolution.

10

Basic Science vs.
the Humbug of Medicine

Medicine would pay, and I should still be dealing with subjects which interest me—but how much drudgery and of what an unpleasant kind is there!

—William James, 1863

[1]

WILLIAM HAD the sense that he had taken a wrong turn from the very beginning of his career at Harvard. He inscribed a proverb in his notebook that tellingly summarized his plight: "On ne va jamais si loin que lorsqu'on ne sait pas où on va."[1] (One never travels so far as when one does not know where one is going.) He did not like chemistry. He was bewildered, and complained that "I have to employ most all my time reading up." Though the small class of twelve students (Harvard recitations often had as many as eighty in a class) promised "a very cosy time," his letters were humorous on the surface but unhappy. He joked with a cousin that "writing in the middle of the week is an unheard-of license, for I must work, work, work." He mockingly bewailed his fate that "relentless Chemistry claims its hapless victim."[2] By the spring he had become adept at laboratory work and reported the alchemical transformation of cloth into sugar. "I am now studying organic chemistry. It will probably shock mother to hear that I yesterday destroyed a handkerchief— but it was an old one, and which, though rather brown, is very good."[3] The good humor could not hide the general lack of enthusiasm. Though he would continue his study with Eliot into a second year, the reading lists that he kept show that intellectually he was living elsewhere.

As Charles Eliot remembered him, "James was a very interesting and agreeable pupil, but was not wholly devoted to the study of Chemistry." Judging from William's correspondence, that was an understatement. Eliot went on to report on James's ill health: "During the two years in which he was registered as a student in Chemistry, his work was much interfered with by ill-health, or rather by something which I imagined to be a delicacy of nervous constitution."[4] William confided to his cousin Kitty Prince that "the first flush of [his] chemical enthusiasm" had, after a year and a half of hard work, been "somewhat dulled."[5] Since his brother Garth Wilkinson had outlined some of his plans for the future to their father, William mockingly did the same. "As Wilky submitted to you a resumé of his future history for the next few years, so will I, hoping it will meet your approval. Thus: one year study chemistry, then spend one term at home, then one year with Wyman, then a medical education, then five or six years with Agassiz, then probably death, death, death with inflation and plethora of knowledge."[6]

Two themes recur again and again in his correspondence from the Scientific School, a growing preoccupation with insanity and a mounting sense of the urgency of earning money. He maintained his usual jocular surface but his humor barely covered his fear that he, like his father, might break down. The concern about money was initially his parents' worry, but he soon made it his own. This anxiety added to the discomfort caused by the scientific direction he had taken. Why his parents, particularly his mother, became so worried about the money William was spending is unclear. Perhaps it was the Civil War inflation that made them feel uneasy. Perhaps their losses in the panic of 1857 and the high style in which they had been living for twenty years had finally depleted Henry's share of the estate. In any event, both parents made it clear that William had to make plans to earn his own living. Both the fear of insanity and the pressure to earn money quickly crystallized into a decision to study medicine, as Agassiz, Wyman, and Gray had done before him. But he was as unhappy as they had been in giving up basic science. Given his preoccupation, it is not surprising that psychiatry was the branch of medicine that most attracted him.

[2]

In William's early Cambridge letters, his tone was typically jocular and energetic, but his eye was ever ready to notice rational order overcome by divisive, malignant evil. The theme of his drawings now surfaced in black humor about himself and his correspondents. A letter written during his first week in Cambridge pictures him as a divided self, swinging between elation when a letter arrived from home and gloom when the mailbox was empty. The issue is common enough for a college freshman, but the imagery is not. "Never did the same being look so like two different ones as I. . . . Gloomily, with despair written on my leaden brow I stalk the street along towards the P.O. [post office], women, children and students involuntarily shrinking against the wall as I pass,—thus as if the curse of Cain were stamped upon my front. But when I come out with a letter an immense concourse of people generally attends me to my lodging attracted by my excited wild gestures and look."[7]

Included in the letter are two drawings that illustrate the poles of elation and depression. One figure looks more fierce than despairing, with piercing eyes, bushy brows, and set jaw as he strides angrily off the page (Figure 8). The second is dancing. His balance is precarious, his face wears an insane grin, and his hat is literally blown off his head by his exuberance. The lips grin but the eyes are puffy and the face is lined, as if it belonged to a prematurely aged man. If the mark of Cain (violence) is on the face of one, the cost of hiding that violence with a mask of jocularity is on the face of the other.*

Later in the month he received a picture of his cousin Minny Temple, who had cut her hair very short. In his reply, he pictured himself as a madman worthy of study by his medically trained professors. "As I read on unconscious of the emotion I was betraying, a vast crowd collected. Profs. Agassiz and Wyman ran with their notebooks and proceeded to take observations of the greatest scientific import." The sight of the picture of his cousin bereft of her tresses got him so excited that the fire engines were called. "Up came the fire engines; but I proudly waved them aside and plunged bareheaded into the chill and gloomy bowels of the night, to recover by violent exercise the use of my reasoning faculties. . . ." Even at this early date, long before he became a physician and psychologist, William humorously prescribed the treatment for "insanity" that was to become characteristic of his later therapeutic philosophy: vigorous activity. Action and the strenuous life were antidotes to the poison of the irrational for the student, as they would be for the psychologist he would become.

---

*The theme of madness is especially difficult to follow because of the manner in which previous scholars have edited the correspondence. Ralph Barton Perry, Henry James the novelist, and William's son Henry James have published various sections of this letter. William's brother is the only one who included this particular section, and he blended it with another letter of a different date.

letters. Never before did I know what mystic depths of rapture lay concealed within that familiar word. Never did the same being look so like two different ones, as I going in and coming out of the P.O. if I bring a letter with me. Gloomily, with despair written on my leaden brow I stalk the street along towards the P.O. women, children and students involuntarily shrinking against the wall as I pass, – thus. But when I come out with a letter an immense concourse of people attends me generally to my lodging attracted by my gestures and look. excited wild and look.

8. Elation and anger

In self-satisfaction the extensor muscles are innervated, the eye is strong and glorious, the gait rolling and elastic, the nostril dilated, and a peculiar smile plays upon the lips. This whole complex of symptoms is seen in an exquisite way in lunatic asylums. . . . —W. James, 1890

His playful characterization of Minny's "madness" shows that he was familiar with the science of physiognomy, the study of mind and personality as revealed in the structure of the face. "I have often had flashes of horrid doubt about that girl. Occasionally I have caught a glance from her furtive eye, a glance so wild, so weird, so strange, that it has frozen the innermost marrow in my bones; . . . I have noticed fleeting shades of expression on her face, so short, but ah! so piercingly pregnant of the mysteries of mania—*unhuman,* ghoul-like, fiendish-cunning! . . . Madness is plainly lurking in that lurid eye, stamps indelibly the arch of the nostril and the curve of the lip, and in ambush along the soft curve of the cheek it lies ready to burst forth in consuming fire." William invoked many of the images found in his 1859–60 drawings when he wrote this letter. "Wild," "weird," "unhuman," "ghoul-like" impulses were "lurking in ambush" to overturn reason. The appearance of depression and despair must have made William wonder whether he was doomed to break down as his father had done twenty years before. To the extent that he cooperated with the strategies that his father had developed to cope with his own guilt, he unwittingly marched himself down that frightening path. William closed with a reference to Dr. Prince, a relative by marriage, and a psychiatrist at the Northampton State Hospital for the Insane.* He was sure that "Dr. Prince has her by this time."[8]

Two years later, Dr. Prince was on his mind again as he approached the decision to enter medical school. Once again he joked about his insanity, suggesting to his cousin Katharine that he hadn't visited when he had had the impulse because he didn't know "whether you would chain me up in your asylum." This sally might have been received as a poor joke had William not gone on to explain that he was thinking of becoming a psychiatrist. "Of all departments of Medicine, that to which Dr. Prince devotes himself is, I should think, the most interesting. And I should like to see him and his patients at Northampton very much before coming to a decision." He told his cousin frankly that medicine attracted him because of the pressure he felt to earn a living. "After all, the great problem of life seems to be how to keep body and soul together, and I *have* to consider lucre." There was a note of envy over the favored position of women. "I suppose your sex, which has, or should have, its bread brought to it, instead of having to go in search of it, has no idea of the awful responsibility of such a choice."[9]

---

*Katharine Barber James (1834–90) was the fourth child of the Reverend William James. In 1860 she was hospitalized at the Northampton (Massachusetts) Hospital for the Insane, where Dr. William Henry Prince was her physician. They married in October 1861. "Kitty" Prince continued to be intermittently ill for the rest of her life. Dr. Prince committed suicide in 1883.

William's mounting tension over money is chronicled in his letters, as is the puzzling shift in his parents' attitude toward it. Mary James raised the issue of money early, insisted on fiscal responsibility, and provoked her son's humorously veiled ire. His plea on September 7, 1861, "Please tell Father to send me some money immediately," brought her down on him. She told him to keep a record of the funds he received and how he spent them. This was hardly a remarkable request of a young man away from his family for the first time, no matter how much money they had. What was notable was the picture of the family structure that stood out in William's reply. Though Henry, Sr., dispensed the money, Mary James felt responsible for keeping track of it. William thought this arrangement odd and inconvenient.

He showed his mother's demand to Wilky, who was visiting him from school in Concord. Wilky didn't hesitate to come up with an explanatory theory. William slyly jabbed at his mother with his brother's words, though he dissociated himself from them, branding them "naive." "Wilky . . . amused me 'metch' by his naive interpretation of Mother's most rational request that I should 'keep a memorandum of all moneys I receive from Father.' He thought it was that she might know exactly what sums her prodigal philosopher really gives out, and that mistrust of his generosity caused it." Apparently reluctant to say such a thing directly to his mother, he confessed that it did "a little sound that way" to him, too.[10] What is so telling about Wilky's theory is that "prodigality" was a label that Henry's children easily attached to him, despite the vagueness of his youthful history. Furthermore, Mary James was cast in the role of policing her husband's vice and eradicating any early signs of the defect in her son. To be prodigal was a negative identity—something *not* to be—and was so recognized by the rest of the family. A family joke pointed to a family tragedy. And William James found himself, for reasons unknown to him, about to be tarred with his father's brush.

[3]

As William James looked forward to his first Thanksgiving vacation from college, he acknowledged his willingness to accept that judgment. Again he mocked the rejection he felt, but beneath the humor lay two generations of family history that were about to engulf him. "Thanksgiving in less than two weeks and then, oh, then!—probably a cold reception, half repellent, no fatted calf, no fresh-baked loaf of spicy bread,—but I dare not think of that side of the picture."[11] How easily the parable of the prodigal son came to mind! And for what trifles compared with his father's "wild" youth!

At first William tried to cajole his mother out of her fear. "My dear Mother don't let yourself fret about me unnecessarily. Have confidence that I will not go through any very reckless squandering for *a long time* together at any rate." He was annoyed with what seemed to him to be undue concern about his college expenditures, but he veiled his feelings with good humor. "I appreciate your solicitude my dear mother lest your children should think you a bore for 'harping on the disagreeable subject forever,' but I hope you don't think I have any such feeling towards you. I know I have often called you so in banter but you must know it was the merest joking." Had the ghost of William James of Albany been peering over her shoulder as she read that letter, he might have commiserated with Mary James and urged her to stand firm. He had tried and failed with *his* son; perhaps she would have better luck with his grandson. Had he been of an ironic turn of mind, he might have shaken his head at one of the items on a page listing William's expenditures. Twenty-five cents had been squandered on oysters with the lame explanation "I could not resist the temptation on getting back from Boston without my dinner and nothing for tea but bread, preserves & cake."[12] Apparently thirty years had not changed the aura of self-indulgence that hovered over the shellfish that Professor Agassiz found scientifically so interesting.

Mary James was not fooled by her son's humor—or at least she didn't think it was funny. William made a drawing of the family in a November letter. Perhaps she noticed that she was drawn with a particularly malignant expression on her face, in contrast to the more benign, tottering figure of her husband (Figure 9). She insisted that Henry write to their son and back her up. Father's letter brought a shamefaced reply. "I received your letter with exquisite delight the other evening, altho it was put so strongly as to make one feel rather ashamed than otherwise at having to receive it." His contrite note went on to explain that he "made more fuss about it than was necessary" because Wilky had told him that father "is going to break your head for spending so much!"[13]

He managed his expenditures more carefully thereafter, and the battle subsided. He even tried to keep accounts: "sixty-one cents for prestidigitation and treat, twenty-five cents for photog. of negro babe, thirty-three cents for carfare and to hear Wendell Phillips." But the effort faltered, and after failing to keep any records for three months he solemnly promised to "turn here over a new leaf." He struggled into a second year without being able to balance the figures. "One dollar and ninety-eight cents left in hand, one dollar and eighteen cents actually in hand—deficit eighty cents." The following month's discovery, "Theoretically in hand fifty-four cents, actu-

to us. The radiance of Harry's
visit has not faded yet & I come
upon gleams of it 3 or 4 times a day
in my farings to and fro, but it
has never a bit diminished the
lustre of far off shining Newport
all silver and blue & this heavenly
group below

(all being more or less fatuous, especially the two outside ones). The more
so as the above mentioned Harry could
in no wise satisfy my cravings to
know of the family and friends as he

9. FAMILY PORTRAIT
Though in a general way he cannot live without them, yet, as regards certain
individuals, it often falls out that he cannot live with them either.
—W. James, 1890

161

ally in hand eight-two cents," led to the happy conclusion "Gained some-how twenty-eight cents" and brought forth an unrestrained "Hallelu-jah!"[14]

After successfully bargaining with his landlady for a fifty-cent reduction in his rent, William cajoled his mother: "I now lay my hand on my heart, and confidently look towards my mother for that glance of approbation which she *must* bestow. Have I not redeemed any weakness of the past?"[15] He clearly saw her as the cause of all the fuss. So when he began to study botany, he gave this joking aside a hostile edge: "I have been looking a little into Botany too—and have no doubt will end by pursuing that science upon my mother's grave, such is my ardor."[16]

But despite the pressure exerted by Mary James, it was Henry that dispensed the funds, and William was more solicitous when he wrote to his father. "I am sorry to appear before you once more in my old character of a beggar. . . . I am in very great want of stockings. . . . Please send me the money immediately."[17]

When William wrote to Katharine Prince and emphasized his economic strain, he jokingly outlined his career alternatives: "I have four alternatives: Natural History, Medicine, Printing, Beggary. Much may be said in favor of each. I have named them in the ascending order of their pecuniary invitingness." The list showed how strictly he defined his options in his father's terms. Natural history and medicine were scientific pursuits—the direction his father intended for him. Printing had been his father's first vocational experiment (we don't know how much, if anything, William knew about the prodigal flight of 1830), and at the time he wrote the letter, he was helping his father to choose type and put *Substance and Shadow* through the press. The last alternative, humorously considered the most lucrative, was a ghost of the past and a prophecy of his future. A beggar, like an heir, lives by another's substance. William had already experienced two years of advantages (and humiliation) of being supported as a college student. And he knew his father would continue to pay his bills as long as he was studying. In effect, he chose beggary as the most practical way open to him to emulate his father's life as a gentleman of leisure.

Though he would make a show of choosing medicine, his heart was never in it. He told his cousin, "Medicine would pay, and I should still be dealing with subjects which interest me—but how much drudgery and of what an unpleasant kind is there!"[18] He blamed his mother for pushing him toward "the flesh pots." "I fancy there is a fond maternal cowardice which would make you and every other mother contemplate with compla-cency the worldly fatness of a son, even if obtained by some sacrifice of his 'higher nature.' But I fear there might be some anguish in looking back from the pinnacle of prosperity (*necessarily* reached, if not by eating dirt, at least by renouncing some divine ambrosia) over the life you might have led in the pure pursuit of truth. It seems as if one *could* not afford to give that up for any bribe, however great."[19] Basic science now represented his heart's desire, as painting had done before. And medicine stood for duty, as science had done three years earlier, when his father's threats had tipped the scales against art. In 1864, money, maternal pressure, and perplexing family edginess about prodigality forced him against himself once again.

[4]

During the fall of 1863, when he felt so much pressure to make a decision, William worked in Wyman's comparative anatomy laboratory. He wrote of the experience to Alice, describing the lab as a scene of Gothic horror. "I work in a vast museum, at a table all alone, surrounded by skeletons of mastodons, crocodiles, and the like, with the walls hung about with monsters and horrors enough to freeze the blood. But I have no fear, as most of them are tightly bottled up."[20] No doubt he was trying to frighten his sixteen-year-old sister, in the long-standing tradition of nascent medical students. But note the return of the grotesque that characterized his drawings of 1859–60. Two sketches from 1863 underscore the reemergent theme. They depict a snapping turtle, one a front view (Figure 10), the other a view from the side (Figure 11). The perspective of both drawings gives the impression that the animal is at eye level or hovering above the viewer as an overwhelming destructive force. The animal energy of Figure 10 draws to a focus in the wild eyes and menacing mouth, echoing the bear, the ogre, the elephant, and the mountain lion of the earlier series. The frontal view, with the mouth agape, echoes once again a scream or bellow, a blending of the cries of the hunter and the hunted of the previous drawings. Seen from the side, the beast peers maliciously from on high, poised to fall mercilessly upon its prey.

William's view of nature differed markedly from his father's and Agassiz's conception. Evil had a place in Henry's world, but primarily as an illusion unmasked by science. When the legions of science had done their holy work, pain and destruction were transformed into divine concessions to man's fallen state. By contrast, William's beast peered maliciously from above, like Henry's Old Testament God, but its malice had no tie to a moral order. It was merely vicious. To the figures on high that watched him and menaced his movement, William dared to offer only veiled jibes. But once again his sketches tell a different story.

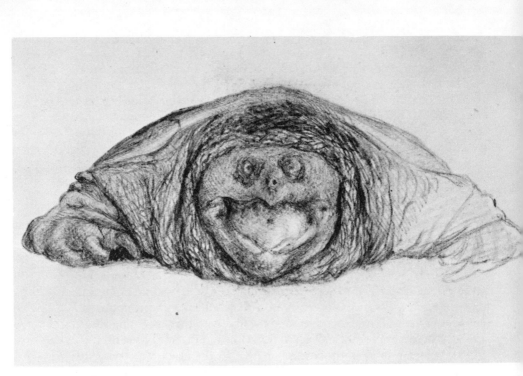

10. SNAPPING TURTLE, FRONT VIEW
Our ferocity is blind, and can only be explained from *below*.   —W. James, 1890

[5]

With Wyman's encouragement, William reluctantly entered Harvard Medical School in January 1864. The medical school was as loosely organized as the Lawrence Scientific School. There were no stringent admission requirements, no admission examination. William had no degree, as he had not graduated from the Lawrence Scientific School. The medical school's connection with the university was tenuous, and the faculty of eight professors ran what was essentially a proprietary school. The core of the curriculum was a four-month winter term that ran from November through March. Students attended lectures for five or six hours a day. By the time William entered, an additional three-month summer term, from April through June, had been added to provide clinical experience under faculty guidance in place of the older apprenticeship system. Visits to the Massachusetts General Hospital and clinical lectures with case presentations were already part of the curriculum.*

*A two-year graded course had been introduced in 1857. Anatomy, pathological anatomy, surgery, chemistry, practical anatomy, and physiology were studied the first year. The second

II. SNAPPING TURTLE, SIDE VIEW
Cadaveric, reptilian, and underground horrors play so specific and constant a part
in many nightmares. . . . —W. James, 1890

Two months after entering, William tartly declared to a friend, "I embraced the medical profession a couple of months ago. My first impressions are that there is much humbug therein, and that, with the exception of surgery, in which something positive is sometimes accomplished, a doctor does more by the moral effect of his presence on the patient and family, than by anything else. He also extracts money from them."[21] He was obviously unhappy to have abandoned the "ambrosia" of pure science for the "flesh pots" of medicine.

Charles Eliot lectured at the medical school as well as the Lawrence Scientific School, and he, too, was critical of the profession. "An American physician or surgeon may be, and often is, a coarse and uncultivated person, devoid of intellectual interests outside of his calling, and quite unable to either speak or write his mother tongue with accuracy." He vigorously assailed the practice of allowing poorly trained doctors loose on the public. "The mistakes of an ignorant or stupid young physician or

year was devoted to botany, zoology, the theory and practice of medicine, midwifery, the diseases of women and children, medical jurisprudence, materia medica, practical anatomy, and clinical observation (*The Harvard Medical School, 1782–1906* [Boston, 1906], 37–39, 74–77).

surgeon mean poisoning, maiming, and killing," and he was determined to do something about it. When he became president of Harvard in 1869, he initiated a demanding entrance examination and introduced a three-year graded curriculum. William barely escaped these reforms.[22]

Anatomy was one of the first courses William took when he shifted from Cambridge to the medical school on North Grove Street. He had already studied some anatomy in Geneva, so he was no neophyte in dissection. The class was presided over by Oliver Wendell Holmes, Sr. Happily the day had long passed when "body snatching" kept the class supplied with cadavers; Massachusetts had passed the first law to provide a legal supply of bodies for dissection in 1831. Once again, William's sketches indicate that he was more interested in the problems of mortality raised by the gaunt cadaver than in anatomical detail. They are casual drawings, half-completed studies, perhaps done to amuse himself as he listened to Dr. Holmes point out the structures prepared by the demonstrator who had already done the dissection. The sketches include (Figure 12, counterclockwise from upper left) a partially drawn head, a horizontal corpse, a fully drawn head with mouth and eyes agape, a vertical figure that is partially covered by the horizontal figure and appears to be emerging from between its buttocks feet first, and a foot with overgrown nails that look like talons. A centrally placed cartoon profile completes the sequence.

We can imaginatively follow the artist's ruminations as Dr. Holmes presented his elegant lecture, heedless of the postlunchtime somnolence of the students (the class met at 1:00 P.M.). As the demonstrator pointed to the mesentery, Dr. Holmes likened it to the "shirt ruffles of a former generation."[23] Perhaps William shifted his gaze from the boyish face of the lecturer to the skeleton standing in the corner, the willed remains of Professor John C. Warren, Holmes's predecessor. (Warren had willed his body for dissection to encourage local citizens to do the same.)[24] He attempted a sketch of the corpse prostrate before him, a lean, muscular man whose body was forceful, even in death. The artist merely indicated the outstretched arms and stopped the line of the lower extremities so that the man seemed to have no feet. What was it like to lose a foot or a leg? Father had lost his leg as a boy. Thousands of young men had lost their limbs in the war, and many others lay buried on the Gettysburg battlefield. His attention shifted to the foot that dangled from the edge of the table.

Wilky had been severely wounded in the leg while leading a charge of Colonel Shaw's Negro regiment on Fort Wagner. He was brought home near death and lay for months recuperating (Figure 13). How blurred the line is between death and dying! William's artist's eye noticed the talon-like nails. Was it true, as some people said, that they continued to grow after death? Perhaps dissatisfied with the face of his horizontal figure

12. ANATOMY DRAWINGS
A human corpse seems normally to produce an instinctive dread, which is no doubt somewhat due to its mysteriousness, and which familiarity rapidly dispels. —W. James, 1890

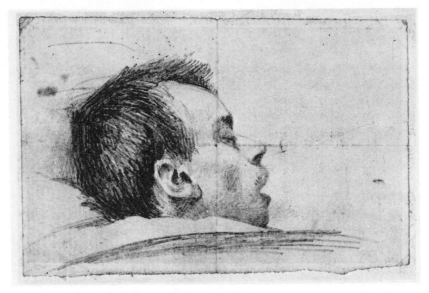

13. GARTH WILKINSON JAMES WOUNDED
Danger to the child blindly and instantaneously stimulates the mother to action of alarm or defence. Menace or harm to the adult beloved or friend excites us in a corresponding way. . . .   —W. James, 1890

because it looked alive and screaming, he attempted another detail to capture the impression of death. The head is shaved, the cheeks sunken. Its full weight bears down upon the table like a stone. The picture of death may have been too stark and he wanted to move back across the blurred divide. So he drew a standing figure with intact limbs but no head. It may have been an accident that he positioned the vertical figure so that it appeared to dangle between the buttocks of the horizontal one. Perhaps he mused on what Dr. David Humphreys Storer, the professor of obstetrics, had to say about the sight of a breech birth. But could the vertical and the vital transcend the horizontal and the inert? Could a man give birth to himself? In time, perhaps, when the anatomy lesson was over.

II

Vacation in Brazil

Twenty-five years ago, clerks and young employees hardly ever expected a holiday, except as a matter of particular favor. . . . That was a time when we lived under the dispensation of the favorite American proverb—no half truth even, but an invention of Sabbathless and unvacationed Satan—"Better wear out than rust out." But of those who repeated it with most faith, how many have since had enforced leisure to repent their short-sightedness. . . . Who that has traveled in Europe is not familiar with the type of the broken-down American businessman, sent abroad to recruit his collapsed nervous system? With his haggard, hungry mien, unfitted by life-long habit for taking any pleasure in passive contemplation, . . . these Americans have been brought up to measure a man solely by what he effects, hardly at all by what he is.

—William James, 1873

[1]

THE DARWINIAN controversy that undermined Agassiz's scientific reputation indirectly provided William with a welcome respite from the boredom of Harvard Medical School. As a result of the attacks of his scientific critics and the pressures of his expanding collecting and publishing ventures, Agassiz's health began to fail. His friends feared that the professor's prodigious appetite for work would drive him to an early grave. Fortunately, a remark made in his 1864–65 lecture series gave Nathaniel Thayer, a wealthy friend, a pretext to send him off for a much-needed vacation. Agassiz suggested that a naturalist who explored in Brazil would probably uncover evidence of the separate creation of species—evidence that would prove Darwin wrong. Wanting to give his friend an opportunity to rest, nurse his wounds, and perhaps uncover evidence that would vindicate his beliefs, Thayer offered to pay for such an expedition.[1] Agassiz accepted but characteristically expanded the venture into a full-fledged scientific project that required a staff of four professional naturalists from the museum and six students, one of whom would be William James. William was to have his opportunity to work with Agassiz after all, and well in advance of the time predicted in his 1861 timetable. And exploring with Agassiz would give him a chance to reassess a naturalist's career. Besides, the expedition smacked of high adventure and promised to be a stimulating interlude free of the "humbug of medicine."

Though the expedition had scientific objectives, it was also a voyage of personal discovery. Two generations boarded the *Colorado* in New York Harbor in the hope of resolving private uncertainties. Agassiz was fifty-seven and was seeking renewal. Adorned with the accoutrements of fame and power, he had spent himself on the lecture platform and in the in-fighting of scientific politics. Research had been the source of his youthful creativity. Exploration in Brazil, a country whose prehistoric fishes had been the subject of his first book, was "a scheme deferred for want of opportunity, but never quite forgotten."[2] To his delight, he found work in the field rejuvenating (though he overdid it in his usual fashion), and returned to Boston vowing to stop wasting his energies. But the metamorphosis was incomplete, and he soon returned to the lecture platform and the public that admired him.

At twenty-three, William James hoped to recapture as a field naturalist the inner excitement that he had once known as a painter. Unfortunately, he discovered that field biology was boring physical labor. It was not exhilarating, it was tiresome. He concluded that his genius was better adapted to theoretical rather than practical pursuits, and promised himself that on his return he would devote himself to the study of philosophy. But, like his mentor, William was soon swept along by the momentum of the life he had left behind. He dutifully returned to medical school and the pursuit of his father's vision.

[2]

The *Colorado* set sail on April 1, 1865. (Passage for the entire professional company was free, a gift to Agassiz from the steamship line.) Ironically, one of the passengers was Bishop Alonzo Potter, the son-in-law of Eliphalet Nott of Union, who had been host to Henry James, Sr., when he fled to Boston in 1829. Now the consequences of that failed rebellion worked themselves out in yet another generation, with Bishop Potter once again a witness. The bishop was ill and hoped the voyage would restore his health.

His hopes were not fulfilled, either. He died soon after the ship docked in San Francisco.

With disparaging good humor, William reported to his parents that Potter remembered his father from his youth. "The Bish. tells me he knows Father and Father spent some days in his house when he came to Boston years ago." Had he questioned Bishop Potter about that episode "years ago," William might have unveiled his father's shameful secret. But he did not. Instead, he stood aside and watched, fascinated by the interaction between Potter and Agassiz, the priest and the scientist.

> He and Prof. Agassiz furnish as good an illustration of the saying: "You caw me and I'll caw you" as I ever saw—though I think Agassiz will be left a little in the debt of the worthy Bish. unless he makes it up tomorrow. . . . Last Sunday he preached a sermon particularly to us "savans," as the outsiders call us, and told us we must try to imitate the simple child-like devotion to truth of our great leader. We must give up our pet theories of transmutation, spontaneous generation, etc. and seek in nature what God has put there rather than try to put there some system which our imagination has devised, etc., etc., (*Vide* Agassiz *passim*). The good old Prof. was melted to tears, and wepped profusely. . . . I am sure the words . . . were as heartfelt as anything in such a wooden man can be.[3]

James's letters are replete with evidence of the future psychologist's grasp of character as well as the painter's love of the visually exotic. But they show no enthusiasm for collecting. He seemed more intent on penetrating Agassiz's personality than on absorbing the professor's biological theories. At the beginning of the voyage he caught the professor in a revealing predatory moment:

> This morning he made a characteristic speech to Mr. Billings. . . . Mr. B. had offered to lend him some books. Agassiz: "May I enter your stateroom and take them when I shall want them, sir?" Billings, extending his arm said genially, "Sir, all that I have is yours!" To which Agassiz, far from being overcome, replied, shaking a monitory finger at the foolishly generous wight, "Look out, sir, dat I take not your skin!" That expresses very well the man. Offering your services to Agassiz is as absurd as it would be for a South Carolinian to invite General Sherman's soldiers to partake of some refreshment when they called at his house.[4]

A month later William tried again to capture his mentor's essence. "Professor is a very interesting man. I don't yet understand him very well. His *charlatanerie* is almost as great as his solid worth; and it seems of an unconscious childish kind that you can't condemn him for, as you would most people."[5]

By September, however, like so many others, William succumbed to Agassiz's charm, though he remained less interested in Agassiz's science (with which he disagreed) than in his personal style.

> I have profited a great deal by hearing Agassiz talk [he informed his parents], not so much by what he says, for never did a man utter a greater amount of humbug, but by learning the way of feeling of such a vast practical engine as he is. No one sees farther into a generalization than his own knowledge of details extends, and you have a greater feeling of weight and solidity about the movement of Agassiz's mind, owing to the continual presence of this great background of special facts, than about the mind of any other man I know. . . . I only saw his defects at first, but now his wonderful qualities throw them quite in the background.[6]

The arrival in Rio de Janiero excited William's artistic sensibilities. He was ecstatic over the grandeur of the mountains and the lush green of the foliage. The port fulfilled his image of a picturesque "African" town in its architecture and effect. There were many native "Africans" on the streets, and he sketched them with word and pencil. "The men have white linen drawers and short shirts of the same kind over them; the women wear huge turbans, and have a peculiar rolling gait that I have never seen any approach to elsewhere. Their attitudes as they sleep and lie about the streets are picturesque to the last degree" (Figure 14).[7] Travel into the back country was even more aesthetically stimulating. "Only savage inarticulate cries" could express the gorgeous intensity of the experience. "The brilliancy of the sky and the clouds, the effect of the atmosphere, which gives their proportional distance to the diverse planes of the landscape, make you admire the old gal Nature. I almost thought my enjoyment of nature had entirely departed, but here she strikes such massive and stunning blows as to overwhelm the coarsest apprehension." It is no wonder that he headed his letter, "Original Seat of Garden of Eden."[8]

From the outset William showed little enthusiasm for the work of the expedition, and as he collected fish from the bay he soon grew skeptical about the entire project. "Although several bushels of different things have already been collected, *nothing* has been done which could not have been done just as well from Boston."[9] He seriously considered returning home. Like many a young research assistant, he found his work menial and not in keeping with his scientific aspirations. "My whole work will be mechanical, finding objects and packing them, and working so hard at that and in traveling that no time at all will be found for studying their structure." He disgustedly realized that the entire "affair reduces itself to so many months spent in physical exercise."[10]

The best that he could say for it was that it was good for his moral

14. BRAZILIAN PIPE SMOKER

. . . here all is so monotonous, in life and in nature, that you are rocked into a kind of sleep. . . .   —W. James to Mary Walsh James, December 9, 1865

development. "If there is anything I hate, it is collecting. I don't think it is suited to my genius at all; but," he assured his family, "for that very reason this little exercise in it I am having here is the better for me. I am getting very practical, orderly, and businesslike."[11] And this moralizing tone on the sweetness of adversity persisted. At the end of the expedition he would assure his "darling old Mama" that he regarded it as one of the best-spent portions of his life, but "enough is as good as a feast."[12]

[3]

In May he became seriously ill and had to be hospitalized. What had started out as a lighthearted adventure turned into a life-threatening disaster. At first it was feared that he had smallpox, but the illness was finally diagnosed as varioloid, a mild form of the disease. The attack blinded him briefly and he became depressed.* The blindness eventually subsided, but his eyes remained painful and "weak"—symptoms that would recur for the remainder of his life. He feared that he might once again be accused of prodigality, as his hospitalization had cost "nearly $200.00." But money was not his main concern. In a penetrating self-assessment while he lay recuperating, he confessed that he had had serious doubts before the *Colorado* sailed from New York in April. "I had misgivings . . . before starting; but I was so filled with enthusiasm, and the romance of the thing seemed so great, that I stifled them. Here on the ground the romance vanishes and the misgivings float up. I have determined to listen to them this time."[13] He formulated his sense of inauthenticity in terms consistent with the lesson he had learned from Ruskin in 1860. Genius should not be forced. The romantic appeal to self-expression in work that had justified his painting experiment now served to support his decision to abandon field biology.

"On the steamer I began to read Humboldt's Travels. Hardly had I opened the book when I seemed to become illuminated. 'Good Heavens, when such men are provided to do the work of traveling, exploring, and observing for humanity, men who gravitate into their work as the air does into our lungs, what need, what *business* have we outsiders to pant after them and toilsomely try to serve as their substitutes? There are men to do all the work which the world requires without the talent of any one being strained.'"

Though Ruskin sanctioned the move, William was not entirely comfortable with it. He wished otherwise but sheepishly admitted he was not like

*The blindness was probably caused by a keratitis from variola.

those men whose "grit and energy . . . are called forth by the resistance of the world." He resigned himself to a more passive stance. "These lines seem to satisfy me, although to many they would appear the height of indolence and contemptibleness: "Ne forçons point notre talent,—Nous ne ferions rien avec grâce,—Jamais un lourdaud, quoqu'il fasse,—Ne deviendra un galant.'"*

He was all too well aware that lack of interest in practical affairs and unwillingness to push himself were qualities he shared with his father. They were both meant to be thinkers: "Men's activities are occupied in two ways: in grappling with external circumstances, and in striving to set things at one in their own topsy-turvy mind. You must know dear Father, what I mean." If nothing else, his Brazilian trip had taught him that aside from painting, philosophy was the work that suited his temperament most. "I am convinced now, for good, that I am cut out for a speculative rather than an active life," he wrote, but this shrewd appraisal would not be acted upon for many years. He was uncertain about his talent for philosophy. He described himself as "one of the very lightest of feather-weights," but that was not what made him hesitate.[14] He still had to fulfill his father's wish for a scientific son.

[4]

Throughout the trip, William oscillated between asserting the importance of self-expression and extolling the virtues of hard work. When recuperating, he longed to return home and argued against striving. After he decided to remain with the expedition and had done a share of practical work, pushing himself seemed advantageous. His descriptions of the Brazilians reflected his changing point of view. At the outset he thought their slower pace picturesque. But as he himself became drawn into Agassiz's frenetic wake, he compared them unfavorably with American workers.

> I am beginning to get impatient with the Brazilian sleepiness and ignorance. These Indians are particularly exasperating by their laziness and stolidity. It would be amusing if it were not so infuriating to see how impossible it is to make one hurry, no matter how imminent the emergency. . . . I had no idea before of the real greatness of American energy. They wood up the steamer here for instance at the rate (accurately counted) of eight to twelve logs a minute. It takes them two and one-half hours to put in as much wood as would go in at home in less than fifteen minutes."[15]

*Don't force your talent. One can't push oneself with good effect. A clod, no matter how hard he tries, cannot turn himself into a gentleman.

William James in Brazil, after the attack of "small pox" in 1865

If the Indians represented a negative standard of indolence when he was flushed with enthusiasm for work, Agassiz offered a negative model of excessive labor. William told his father, "I never saw a man work so hard. Physically, intellectually and socially he has done the work of ten different men since he has been in Brazil; the only danger is of his overdoing it." He might be prepared to push himself a bit, but he was wary of becoming an "engine" like Agassiz, who had turned "thin and nervous" from "working himself out."[16]

The professor was not content merely to sit for verbal portraits; he studied William with a critical eye, too. William swore his correspondents to secrecy, but Agassiz did not hesitate to tell the young men what he thought directly. "I am getting a pretty valuable training from the Professor, who," he told his mother, "pitches into me right and left and wakes me up to a great many of my imperfections." Despite his disagreement with his mentor's biology, he was prepared to listen to his estimate of his character. "This morning he said I was 'totally uneducated.' He has done me much good already, and will evidently do me more before I have got through with him."[17] Not only was Agassiz critical of William's erratic education; he also accurately assessed the handicap that lack of discipline and laziness placed on his ambitions. "'James . . . some people consider you a bright young man; but when you are fifty years old," he prophesied, "if they even speak of you then, what they will say will be this; that James—oh yes, I know him; he used to be a very bright young man!'"[18] William James of Albany had failed to inculcate the gospel of work in his errant son, and now Agassiz, *in loco parentis,* was belatedly preaching it to good effect to his grandson.

[5]

Despite his illness, William's stay in Brazil had been a peaceful time. Physical labor in the out-of-doors against brilliant tropical landscapes had provided a welcome diversion from medical school. His Brazilian drawings reflect the shift in his emotional world. Whereas his drawings from Geneva, Newport, and Boston show a preoccupation with biting rage, his Brazilian sketches are more tranquil. The human figures were drawn in moments of contemplation and repose (Figures 14 and 15), evoking a sense of quiet energy that is in sharp contrast to the nervous, macabre intensity of his earlier work. Despite his complaints about the languour of the Brazilians, his artist's eye took pleasure in the graceful, sensual outlines of an Indian musing over his hands and the sedentary satisfaction of a man smoking his gently cradled pipe. Even the animal drawings are different.

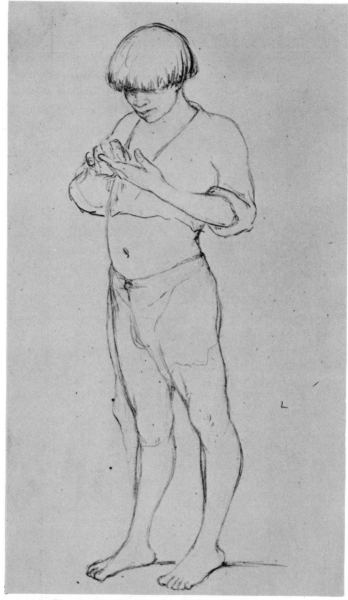

15. STANDING BRAZILIAN INDIAN
The men have white linen drawers and short shirts of the same kind over them; the women wear huge turbans, and have a peculiar rolling gait that I have never seen any approach to elsewhere. —W. James to Henry James, Sr., and Mary Walsh James, April 21, 1865

16. ANGRY MONKEY
We read anger in the face, though the blow
may not be struck. —W. James, 1890

Only one monkey projects a hint of angry intensity from its eyes and straightened mouth that is reminiscent of the drawings of 1859–64 (Figure 16). But the aggressive energy is muted and edges toward sadness. Two other monkey heads, one a frontal view, the other a profile, look human and remarkably philosophical (Figure 17). In contrast to the rapacious snapping turtle and lion in the mood of Dalacroix, the soulful and wise Brazilian monkeys made Darwin's theory of human origins believable.

In Boston, James had longed for leisure, but now that he had nine months of tropical ease behind him, he was eager for a change. Even a harsh Boston winter appeared admirable from his tropic paradise.

> I hardly think you will be able to understand me [he told his mother], but the idea of the people swarming about as they do at home, killing themselves with thinking about things that have no connection with their merely external circumstances, studying themselves into fevers, going mad about religion, philosophy, love and sich, breathing perpetual heated gas and excitement, turning night into day, seems almost incredible and imaginary. . . . I thrill with joy when I think that one short month and we are homeward bound. Welcome ye dark blue waves! Welcome my native slosh and ice and cast-iron stoves, magazines, theatre, friends and everything![19]

On the outward-bound journey abroad the *Colorado,* Professor Agassiz had given daily lectures to his staff. The last in the series was devoted to the subject of metamorphosis. As Agassiz read the evidence, an individual could undergo major structural transformation (metamorphosis) as it

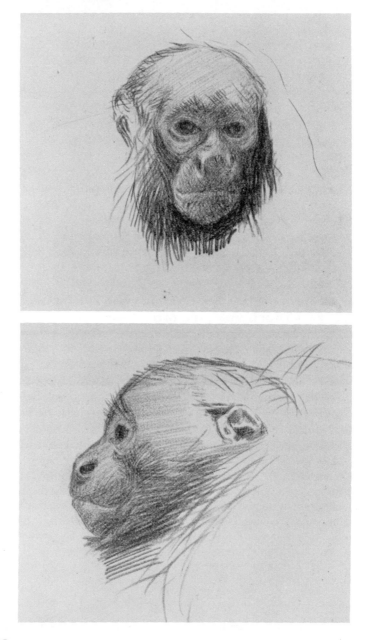

17. CONTEMPLATIVE MONKEY
I am convinced that the vulgar idea of a monkey being—a merely ludicrous creature is all wrong—There is a dash of the pathetic in them. . . . —W. James, 1865

grew, but adult offspring were indistinguishable from the parent; thus the fixity of the species boundary was confirmed.[20] Agassiz was speaking of physical structure, but the conception serves as well as a metaphor of psychological growth. The central personal issue that William faced was analogous to the scientific problem the expedition tried to solve. Was an offspring inevitably limited by a preexisting parental design? Did he have to follow the pattern set by his father? Was the Jamesian species fixed and immutable, or was there room for evolution and novelty? The Thayer Expedition searched diligently, but by 1866 both the scientific and the personal outcomes of the venture were still distressingly inconclusive.

12

The Use and Abuse of Illness

I know multitudes of people who are zealously seeking to ascertain the laws of health and conform themselves thereto: but I do not find that they succeed in securing health or cheerfulness. Thousands of lusty sinners on every hand enjoy enough and to spare of both, while these pale captives to anxiety, who make a conscience of every mouthful they eat, and daily soak themselves into superfluous cleanness, and go about the world gasping for pure air, grow only more spectral every day. . . . Let us forsake these purely individual methods of overcoming evil, and take at once to the social method, which alone is profitable. . . . We must all recover together, or recover not at all.

—Henry James, Sr., 1859

Geniuses are sensitive plants. . . . They have to be treated tenderly. They don't need to live in superfluity; but they need freedom from harassing care; they need books and instruments; they are always overworking, so they need generous vacations; and above all things they need occasionally to travel far and wide in the interests of their souls' development.

—William James, 1906

[1]

WILLIAM RETURNED to the longed-for Boston winter. Following a month of parties with his Cambridge friends, he applied himself once again to the lackluster task of completing his medical degree. When he started his medical studies in 1863, he had a low opinion of the profession, and he did not change his mind during the next three years as he pursued the M.D. degree. He informed a friend in the summer of 1866 that he was resigned to earning his living by plying the "physicking trade like any other tenth-rate man."[1] At the end of the year he described the process of getting a hospital appointment as if he had cynically sold his soul. "The present time is a very exciting one for ambitious young men at the Medical School who are anxious to get into the hospital. Their toadying the physicians, asking them intelligent questions after lectures, offering to run errands for them, etc., this week reaches its climax; . . . I have little fears, with my talent for flattery and fawning, of a failure."[2]

At the commencement exercises the following spring he was all too conscious of the low scientific quality of the theses read by the graduates. He interpreted the look on Agassiz's face as one of "mingled wonder, pain and disgust," confirming his own impression. In 1869, when he finally completed work for his degree, he summed up the experience with a mixture of relief and mild disdain. "So there is one epoch of my life closed. . . ." What the epoch yielded, beyond occasional flickerings of interest in the subject matter of medicine, was an opportunity "to see a little the inside workings of an important profession and to learn from it, as an average example, how all the work of human society is performed."[3] Medicine remained in his estimation the humbug trade of tenth-rate minds and unsuited to his genius.

When William resumed his training with a summer clerkship at the Massachusetts General Hospital in 1866, he was riding the crest of a wave of good health. But within a year he had completely exhausted the reserves built up during his Brazilian excursion. He fell ill. This time his back troubled him as well as his eyes. He fled to Europe to recover. For the next seven years ill health became central to his life as vague illnesses followed by prolonged periods of convalescence became an established pattern. A simple accounting tells the tale. Of the seven years between his return from Brazil and the start of his career as a teacher at Harvard, two were devoted to medical school and five to the search for health. What in the early 1860s had appeared to be a minor impediment to his career now threatened to become a career in itself. William shuttled nervously between Europe and America, between learning the healing art and becoming his own chronic patient. The pursuit of an inauthentic career threatened to end in lifelong invalidism.

[2]

It would be possible to describe William's invalidism, the uses that illness served, and the abuses that it brought about as a unique experience inextricably tied to his personal uncertainties. But he was not alone in his neurasthenic struggles. A twentieth-century reader of the James letters is startled to discover how many of their friends, not to mention family members, devoted themselves to, in Alice James's phrase, the "life-long occupation of improving."[4] During the Civil War and in the decades immediately following it, the environs of Boston were plagued by an epidemic of invalidism. Besides William, his brothers Henry and Robertson, his sister Alice, and their mother's sister Kate, who lived with them, dozens of others are described who fell ill and sought treatment abroad. The neurasthenic illnesses of Steele MacKaye and William Morris Hunt have already been mentioned. To add to this list, Mary James noted in the spring of 1867 that "John La Farge looks badly and says he had quite a breakdown after getting back to Newport."[5] That same spring she informed Alice that Elly Van Buren (an aunt married to the son of Martin Van Buren) was in Boston for treatment of her eyes, "which have been troubling her of late." In the same letter she inquired about Aunt Kate's back brace.[6]

William Dean Howells' wrist had become so lame "that his wife has to write for him."[7] Dr. Wilkinson's visit from England was occasioned by a "nervous American man, a patient of his, who had the possession to use the Doctor's own words, that no one could coach him across the intermediate sea but him."[8] Two years later, William informed his brother that "Gurney and Alex. Agassiz are the last two brain collapsers."[9] William's remark makes it clear that these two family friends were only the most recent additions to the swelling ranks of the nervously ill.

What caused so many privileged New Englanders to develop the disease that the New York neurologist Dr. George Beard labeled "neuraesthenia"? The James correspondence reveals conflicts that were unique to that talented family, but it also sheds light on larger societal issues. Both the familial and the social dimensions of the epidemic of neurasthenia share a common nexus: the problem of work.

Dr. Beard's preliminary papers were published in the late 1860s, when William's nervous symptoms reached their peak. He noted that patients suffering from nervous exhaustion were typically in their late teens to mid-forties. One out of ten, like William, was a physician. Beard described a variant of the disease that affected the eyes, causing weakness and difficulty in reading—symptoms that plagued William—and reported that it had a "contagious" quality. In fact, an epidemic had spread "through many of the colleges and seminaries of the country—in some instances compelling young men to abandon their plans of a liberal education." Beard disapproved of the fashionable treatment for functional disorders, which consisted of "recommending a trip to Europe." He recognized that work, far from being detrimental, was therapeutic for many of his patients. "Very rarely indeed do I advise a patient to change profession or occupation, whatever it may be, provided he is happy and successful in it." He was convinced that work was particularly important for young men who suf-

Henry James, Sr.
1811—

Mary Walsh James
1810—

William James
1842—

Henry James, Jr.
1843—

Garth Wilkinson James
1845—

Robertson James
1846—

Alice James
1848—

Henry James, Sr.
1811–

Mary Walsh James
1810–

William James
1842–

Henry James, Jr.
1843–

Capt. Garth Wilkinson James
1845–

Capt. Robertson James
1846–

Alice James
1848–

Henry James, Sr.
1811–

Mary Walsh James
1810–

William James
1842–

Henry James, Jr.
1843–

Garth Wilkinson James
1845–

Robertson James
1846–

Alice James
1848–

Henry James, Sr.
d. December 19, 1882

Mary Walsh James
d. January 29, 1882

William James
1842–

Henry James, Jr.
1843–

Garth Wilkinson James
d. November 15, 1883

Robertson James
1846–

Alice James
1848–

Henry James, Sr.
1811–1882

Mary Walsh James
1810–1882

William James
1842–

Henry James, Jr.
1843–

Garth Wilkinson James
1845–1883

Robertson James
1846–

Alice James
d. March 6, 1892

fered from the disease. "In a large number of cases I urge, especially upon young men, the necessity of obtaining some occupation; and I would rather have them work too hard than not work at all."[10]

While Dr. Beard was of the opinion that insufficient work, or at least insufficiently gratifying work, contributed to the development and persistence of neurasthenia, others argued that too much work was the core of the problem. On a visit to the United States, Sir Herbert Spencer, philosopher of evolution and James's later philosophic antagonist, took a traveler's privilege to comment on the malaise he saw about him: ". . . in every circle I have met men who had themselves suffered from nervous collapses, due to stress of business, or named friends who had crippled themselves by overwork." Spencer thought the danger was the outcome of evolutionary development. Americans had moved too far beyond the savage. The savage was incapable of monotonous daily toil, but "it is otherwise with the more developed man. The stern discipline of social life has gradually increased the aptitude for persistent industry until among us and still more among you, work has become with many a passion." And it was a passion with disastrous consequences for health. "Exclusive devotion to work has the result that amusements cease to please; and when relaxation becomes imperative, life becomes dreary from lack of its sole interest—the interest in business." Spencer preached a new gospel for the overroutinized, overworked American. "In brief, I may say that we have had somewhat too much of 'the gospel of work.' It is time to preach the gospel of relaxation."[11]

The American doctor and the British philosopher at least agreed that the phenomenon of neurasthenia was connected with work, whether too much or too little. The James family correspondence reflects both poles of the discussion and revolves about the same axis.

The elder Henry had spoken decisively for leisure and the enjoyment of his inherited fortune. He set the tone for the entire household, blending the romantic ideal of work as an expression of selfhood with a religious ideal of holy rest. "I am determined . . ." he had told his friend Garth Wilkinson in 1852, "to take holiday for the rest of my life [he was forty-one], and make all my work sabbatical, and expressive only of irrepressive inward health and impulsions."[12] Though he applied himself steadfastly to his literary labors, he maintained a lifelong suspicion of the dangers of overwork. Mary James, following her husband's lead, as she did in most intellectual matters, shared the suspicion. Of La Farge's breakdown she said, "He ascribed it to the cold rainy weather, but perhaps he had worked too hard in New York."[13] When William was abroad and undertook to write some reviews for publication as a gesture of self-support, she lamented, "I fear he is working himself to death to meet his expenses."[14]

When Professor Agassiz fell ill, she offered the same explanation. "He was attacked a day or two ago with a paralysis of the larynx. . . . His condition is thought very critical. He has been overworking very much of late."[15]* Of Wendell Holmes she remarked, "His whole life, soul and body, is utterly absorbed in his *last* work upon his Kent. He carries about his manuscript in his green bag and never loses sight of it for a moment. . . . His pallid face and this fearful grip upon his work, makes him a melancholy sight."[16]

A corollary to Mary's belief in the dangers of overwork was her conviction that physical exertion should be avoided by her frail children. Thus to Henry, Jr., who was enjoying an exhilarating walking trip in the Alps, she cautioned, "Of course I know you would not attempt any dizzy heights or any but well beaten tracks without a guide—But you might easily over estimate your strength and sink down with sudden exhaustion."[17] Again to Henry, who was enjoying horseback riding in Rome and finding it salutary: "Do not run any risks darling Harry, by staying too long in Rome, and do not overdo the horse-back exercise."[18]

This fear of work and exertion rested on an assumption that many people seemed to share. They were convinced that human energy was scarce and had to be expended parsimoniously, as it was easily exhausted. Capital and the laws that governed it seemed to be an unconscious metaphor that structured human action. Energy had to be saved rather than spent. If the principal was invaded and reduced, it might no longer adequately support life. Scarcity rather than abundance, weakness rather than strength, ill health rather than health were their natural expectations. Effort was an extravagance that threatened to deplete already strained resources.

William made the energy-supply problem explicit in a letter to his friend Tom Ward, who was momentarily reconciled to his business career and was working well. "How I envy you your fund of energy. I have a little spoonful ready for each day and when that's out, as it usually is by 10 o'clock A.M., I'm good for nothing."[19] His brother Henry used the capitalist metaphor as well when he was in Europe enjoying a vigorous grand tour in search of health. He had discovered that walking made him feel better, and feared that the hot Italian summer would prevent this kind of exercise. "I have laid in such a capital stock of strength and satisfaction in Switzerland," he told his sister, "that I shall be sorry to be compelled to see it diminished and if I find it is melting away beneath the southern sun I

*Agassiz had had a stroke. I am grateful to Dr. Edwin A. Weinstein for calling this fact to my attention. Though Agassiz had an organic illness, Mary James thought of his problems within the framework that she used for functional (i.e., neurotic) illness.

shall not scruple . . . to cross over from Verona into southern Germany."[20] Both brothers obviously shared the view that many people in their social group lived by.

As work depleted energy, it followed that it was bad for health. William did not hold to this view consistently, as he often came upon evidence to the contrary. In Germany the sight of hard-working peasant women led him lightheartedly to urge hard work on Alice. "The sight of the women here has strengthened me more than ever in my belief that they ought to be made to do the hard labor of the community—they are far happier and better for it. I only wish I had that pampered Alice here to see these little runts of peasant women stumping about with their immense burdens on their back . . . they are as active and strong as little lionesses, and work from morning til night. Seriously there is a great deal of good in it—and the ideal German woman of poetry (see Goethe, for instance) is a working woman."[21] It was not until the 1880s, when he became a spokesman for the strenuous outdoor life, that William James acted upon that advice himself.

To subscribe to the conception of limited energy was to embrace the belief that rest was a logical cure. But William was skeptical of the value of the extreme rest cures popularized by the Philadelphia neurologist Dr. Weir Mitchell. When a friend was undergoing treatment that amounted to bed rest with complete sensory deprivation, he remarked, "She seems to be suffering from a general nervous debility for the treatment they are now pursuing is one of absolute quiet and non-stimulation. She may not even talk much. Poor girl! I should think it wd. prey on her spirits more than it wd. rest her nerves."[22] He favored rest, especially from undesirable labor, but leisure without literature, repose without responsive conversation were out of the question.

Mary James shared her husband's belief that work was dangerous to health and cultivated that attitude in her children. Yet she operated under different laws herself. An 1873 letter to William, for example, reads like a list of wounded from the front. She reported the current status of "our invalids": Alice, "poor child," had one of her fainting attacks "from a little overexertion"; father had an attack of eczema of the face (apparently herpes zoster, or "shingles") and is "nervous and sleepless"; Aunt Kate "is progressing slowly" under Dr. Munro's care, and "certainly bears well much more fatigue." But she, like a surviving heroine surveying the slain minions strewn about her, proclaimed: "The poor old mater wears well I am happy to say; strong in the back, strong in the nerves, and strong in the legs so far, and equal to her day."[23]

Her strength and endurance were the more remarkable in juxtaposition to the weakness of the rest. It was apparently worthy of comment in 1873 that Alice returned from visiting a friend in Beverly for three days and "came home with her nervous system unimpaired." It was also notable that father was "remarkably well." Others were expected to be short of energy, but Mary remained stalwart and ever ready to shoulder her caretaking tasks. It is not surprising that this attitude extended to household servants as well. She complained of the unreliability of that "race by whom unfortunately we live," but even when she did have someone she could count on, she expected the worst. "I'm glad to say that Mary in the kitchen still proves reliable, but I am afraid almost to lean upon her, lest she too prove a broken reed."[24] William reported that sickness did not keep *her* from her household tasks. "Mother is recovering from one of her indispositions, which she bears like an angel, doing any amount of work at the same time, putting up cornices and raking out the garret-room like a little buffalo."[25] Obviously, each Victorian household in which invalidism flourished required a strong caretaker who would nurture the weak and defer to the mythology of scarce resources while remaining a fount of energy that miraculously never gave out. Among the Jameses, Mary James was that "protecting spirit." She was the "household genius" on whom father leaned "with the absolute whole of his weight."[26] It is not surprising that the children followed his lead.*

[3]

Though overwork did not appeal to these New Englanders, pleasure was also suspect. Puritanical zeal had noticeably waned in mid-nineteenth-century New England, but the suspicion that pleasure was evil lingered on. Sabbatarian scrupulosity over game playing or singing would have been unthinkable in Mrs. James's liberal household, yet the family showed a subtle lack of hospitality for pleasure that robbed experience of joy. In Mary James's correspondence, particularly in her letters to her daughter, puritanism often masqueraded as humor. In the summer of 1872 Alice was abroad, enjoying a grand tour. She found France especially to her liking, and her mother jibed: "My daughter a child of France! What has become of the high moral nature, on which I have always based such hopes for her

*Mary Walsh James had ample childhood training for this position in the family. At her father's death, when Mary was ten years old, her mother was overcome by grief and withdrew from society. This circumstance probably threw a burden of premature parenting on Mary, the oldest daughter in the family. It is interesting to note that when William James married, he chose a woman with a similar childhood background. Alice Gibbens' father died when she was a girl and her mother collapsed in grief. Alice became the head of the household and assumed responsibility for the survival of the family. After Mary James died, Henry, Jr., and Alice's close friend Katharine Loring shared this caretaking role for Alice James.

for this world and the next? That you should so soon have succumbed to this assault upon your senses, so easily have been carried captive by the mere delights of eating and drinking and seeing and dressing [unclear], I should not have believed . . ." Mother was bantering, but her humor cut deep. She went on to explain Alice's enjoyment in terms of the very theory that was popularly believed to account for her neurasthenia: "and indeed I see it all now, to be merely the effect of a little cerebral derangement produced by the supernatural effort you made in crossing the Channel."[27] Whether Alice was enjoying herself or suffering, it appeared that mother's world view locked her daughter into a prison bounded by "cerebral derangement" and weakness. Ordinary activity was thus a "supernatural effort." And sensual pleasure, even the innocent traveler's sort, still had a sulfurous smell about it.*

Work that is supposed to be sabbatical and leisure that is supposed to be uplifting both require money. Capital, not as a metaphor for human energy but as a limited supply of cash, was an important ingredient of the neurasthenic phenomenon. No matter how extensive the resources of a family, if it shared in a distrust of pleasure and leisure, money could not easily be spent on travel for amusement. It was far simpler to justify travel for reasons of health. Between 1866 and 1873 sickness became a means by which the James children struggled for their share of the family resources. Sickness had been the price the elder Henry had paid for seizing his rightful share, and now ill health became a weapon for his children to use to take theirs.

If both Henry and William wanted to go abroad but there was money enough for only one, then surely the sicker of the two should go. If both were equally ill, then the one who had most recently had his turn at the cure should remain behind. This calculus required careful balancing on the part of the invalid. If he were too sick, the effort of travel was out of the question. If he were not sick enough, he might not need the cure as much as another member of the household. If he responded too quickly abroad to the benefits of the cure, or seemed to be enjoying himself too much, his travel might be cut short because it was using limited family resources for pleasure while others required "treatment." Both Henry and Mary James kept a sharp eye on the letters written by their traveling invalid children to monitor expenditures and healthful returns.

A most revealing exchange took place between Henry, Jr., and his parents in 1869. William had returned from his quest for health in the European spas and it was Henry's turn. He traveled in England, France,

---

*Mary James's humor about self-indulgence was equally cutting when it was turned on herself. See Mary Walsh James to Alice James, August 25, 1872, MH.

Switzerland, and Italy, and, violating the precept of limited energy, found delight in walking, climbing, and horseback riding. He seemed to be enjoying himself too much and was criticized by his Cambridge-bound parents. He wrote a defense to father, whose side of the exchange can easily be inferred from the son's remarks.

> To have you think that I am extravagant with these truly sacred funds sickens me to the heart, and I hasten in so far as I may to reassure you. When I left Malvern, I found myself so exacerbated by immobility and confinement that I felt it to be absolutely due to myself to test the impression which had been maturing in my mind, that a certain amount of regular lively travel would do me more good than any further repose. As I came abroad to try and get better, it seemed inexcusable to neglect a course which I believed for various reasons to have so much in its favor.

Having made a show of concern about limited funds and the evils of idle pleasure, Henry deftly concluded that what he needed for *really* good health was *more* pleasurable travel. "I have now an impression amounting almost to a conviction that if I were to travel steadily for a year I would be a good part of a well man."[28]

Seven weeks later he replied to a remonstrance against extravagance from his mother's pen. Here, too, he balanced carefully between acceptance of parental warnings against pleasure and insistence on his need, as one weak in body, to cater to the pleasures of the spirit. He wisely commended his plan for its utility in increasing his capacity to work. "When you speak of your own increased expenses, etc., I feel very guilty and selfish in entertaining any projects which look in the least like extravagance. My beloved mother, if you but knew the purity of my motives! Reflection assures me, as it will assure you, that the only economy for me is to get thoroughly well and into such a state as that I can work. For this consummation, I will accept everything—even the appearance of mere pleasure-seeking."[29]

That Henry had learned well the puritanical judgment on selfishness and mere pleasure-seeking was clear. He had also learned that illness and the need for treatment made divine what might otherwise have been labeled diabolical, even in his parents' liberal household. Energy and capital flowed freely for healing, while the sluices were clanged decisively shut for pleasure and idleness, precisely as William James of Albany had decreed thirty-five years earlier.

> When I think that a winter in Italy is not as you call it a winter of "recreation" but an occasion not only of physical regeneration, but of serious culture too (culture of the kind which alone I have now at twenty six any time left for) I

find the courage to maintain my proposition even in the face of your allusions to the need of economy at home. It takes a very honest conviction thus to plead the cause of apparently gross idleness against such grave and touching facts. I have trifled so long with my trouble that I feel as if I could afford now to be a little brutal. My lovely mother, if ever I am restored to you sound and serviceable you will find that you have not cast the pearls of your charity before a senseless beast, but before a creature with a soul to be grateful and a will to act.[30]

A month later his mother assured Henry that he could do what he wished. He was so successful at the politics of invalidism that he got her to apologize for having questioned his motives. The coffers were wide open, and Mary James urged Henry to let his "prudent old mother" take care of everything. "If you were only here for an hour, and we could talk over this subject of expense, I could I know exorcise all these demons of anxiety and consciensciousness that possess you and leave [you] free as air, to enjoy to the full all that surround you, and drink in health of body and of mind in following out your own safe and innocent attractions." The only promise that she wished to extract was that henceforth he would "throw away prudence and think only of your own comfort and pleasure, for our sakes as well as your own."[31] Henry remained in Europe and traveled as he saw fit, gathering impressions for his literary career. He was intermittently plagued by back and bowel complaints, so that repeated convalescence was necessary.

Not all of the James children were equally adept or so intensely driven to succeed at the manipulative politics of invalidism. A note from Alice James canceling a visit to her friend Sara Sedgwick shows one way in which a "prudent old mother" could manage limited funds. If she decided to give money to support the illness of one child, she merely deprived another. Alice openly recognized illness to be a tactic of family politics, and she felt herself misused.

> Poverty reminds me of my visit to New York, or rather my non-visit. You must not mention this on your return in Quincy St. A vague rumour reached number 20 a few days ago. A package of dynamite suddenly introduced into the midst would have produced a less shattering effect on the family circle— parent and child torn literally limb from limb, but its true nevertheless if I go to New York I shall have to buy some duds [unclear], which in these rural districts I can do very well without. Mother is constantly throwing out dark mysterious hints upon the necessity of economy and now I am economizing? (is it spelt with an s or a z?) I am in a very robust condition of health so that I cannot wriggle out there, but I am strongly tempted to abandon virtue when I think of thee as a companion in vice and of the little parental encouragement which I receive. But I shall be rewarded, I have quite determined elsewhere.

As an apology for not answering Sara's letter sooner she pleaded, "Original sin is my only refuge; I was born bad and I never have recovered."[32] She had learned her mother's trick of participating in the abstemious atmosphere of Calvinism while rejecting it through humor. But virtue and vice, sin and redemption remained the same familiar points of the compass, whether called out in a moralizing tone or softened with a chuckle.

[4]

Within this familial and social context, illness could be seen in either a negative or a positive light. It was an unfortunate consequence of overwork, yet it justified the pleasure of travel and leisure to a carping conscience. It caused pain and suffering, yet to the romantically influenced it marked the sufferer as one possessed of unique sensibility, like a poet or a saint. Not just a physical evil, illness was to be cultivated as a romantic sign of grace. Alice James's diary provides an ironic illustration of this attitude. She had taken to her bed and required perpetual nursing care for "sick headaches." While her nurse was dressing her one morning, Alice was "suddenly flooded by one of those luminous waves that sweep out of consciousness all but the living sense and overpower one with joy in the rich, throbbing complexity of life. . . ." She was so taken with her own sensitivity in comparison with the "primitive rudimentary expression" of the nurse that she announced, "Oh! Nurse, don't you wish you were inside of *me!*" But the nurse disclaimed the wish: "Inside of you, Miss, when you have just had a sick head-ache for five days!" The caretakers in the serving class apparently looked upon the enterprise of invalidism with different eyes. Alice wryly noted, "Nurse and I had a good laugh but I must allow that decidedly she 'had' me."[33]

Men were believed to find sickness in women particularly attractive. A delicate woman was thought to be a desirable woman. With affectionate good humor Henry James, Sr., advised Samuel Ward's wife, then in Italy for her health, not to be too zealous in pursuing delicacy lest she do serious injury to herself.

I do wish you would let those Italian doctors alone with their croton oil, and forswear all experiments indeed till you get back to a Christian land, if Scotland may be so called. The Doctors will be sure to make you more ill if you give them their own way, and you are now ill enough to satisfy any reasonable woman. Nothing interests so much as a delicate woman, who at the same time behaves as you do in saintly manner: but you must not go too far, or the heart becomes pained as well as interested. Let the doctors understand therefore that you are bent upon keeping to your present stock of illness, and be off with their experiments to some more needy patients.[34]

The following fall he wrote again to Mrs. Ward, who was still ill and abroad for cure. This time he abandoned the romantic perspective and spoke instead of illness as Christian suffering. Within this long-standing tradition, illness is a trial to soften the heart and bring the soul closer to God. "Well dear . . . though Providence does not send us ill health, He yet permits it to overtake us in this present state of things; and therefore we will not complain. Hard as your sufferings may bear upon you, be patient, because they are not allowed idly, but are the best possible means toward a certain Divine end to be accomplished in your soul. . . . He permits us to suffer because we cannot otherwise be led in freedom to him."[35] Whether the tender rebuke of a divine Father in the Christian mode or the stigmata of delicacy and inspiration of the romantic, invalidism was to some minds an enviable condition.

[5]

In a work-centered, pleasure-shunning culture, invalidism made idleness socially acceptable. It also provided social definition, particularly to the young, who felt keenly the need to *do* something but found other social options unattractive. Henry, Jr., recalled that in his youth, "just staying at home when everyone was on the move couldn't in any degree show the right mark: to be properly and perfectly vague one had to be vague *about* something. . . ."[36] Invalidism was to show "just the right mark" for him for a decade and beyond. Like William's eye symptoms, Henry's back problem followed a clearly documented physical injury. He hurt his back fighting a fire at Newport in the autumn of 1861. As in William's case, subsequent medical examination revealed no physical damage. Henry's recollection of that experience is most revealing, alluding as it does to the embarrassing yet useful aspects of being ill in that early Civil War period. He admitted obliquely to his intent: "to have trumped up a lameness at such a juncture could be made to pass in no light for graceful." He was vague about the nature of his injury but was convinced from the outset that the disability would last a long time.

Physicians were unpredictable supporters of the invalid role. Dr. Henry J. Bigelow, the medical "oracle" Henry consulted, said that there was "nothing to speak of the matter."* Without the doctor's help, Henry's invalidism could not flourish. He quite rightly reasoned that the work of a

---

*Dr. Henry J. Bigelow (1818–90) was professor of surgery at the Harvard Medical School. He published the first report of the use of ether anaesthesia in a surgical operation in 1846.

law student could also offer "in the public eye, a season of some retirement." In his autobiography he extolled the virtues of law school. "The
beauty was—I can fairly see it now, through the haze of time, even as
beauty! that studious retirement and preparatory hours did after all supply
the supine attitude, did invest the ruefulness, did deck out the cynicisms of
lying down book in hand with a certain fine plausibility." In addition to
providing cover for his literary pursuits, invalidism created the illusion
that he participated in the national struggle. "This was at least a negative
of combat, . . . something definitely and firmly parallel to action in the
tented field."[37] For the young who, like Henry, were uncertain of their
direction or unhappy with their lot, invalidism provided a niche—a feeling
of doing one's share while refusing other conventional endeavors.

Illness protected leisure in America, but the strategy worked even better
for the American invalid in Europe. Europe offered many attractions for
the American in search of cure—the cultural benefits of the grand tour, the
accessibility of famous spas, the bracing effect of a novel scene—but
among its greatest appeals was the fact that leisure was not under suspicion
in Europe. Alice James was keenly appreciative of this difference. She
noted in her diary that "among this robust and sanguine people [she was
in England], I feel not the least shame or degradation at being ill, as I used
at home among the anaemic and the fagged. It comes of course in one way
from the conditions being so easy, from the sense of leisure, work reduced
to a minimum and the god *Holiday* worshipped so perpetually and ef-
fectually by all classes. Then what need to justify one's existence when one
is simply one more amid a million of the superfluous?"[38]

Henry was also enthusiastic about the superiority of Europe over America for the leisured pursuit of health. He urged his New York–bound
friend John La Farge not to look upon his ill health as misfortune. "I am
deeply delighted to hear that there is a prospect of your getting abroad this
summer. Don't let it slip out of your hands. That your health has continued bad, I greatly regret; but I can't consider it an unmitigated curse, if
it brings you to these parts. You must have pretty well satisfied yourself
that home-life is not a remedy for your troubles, and the presumption is
strong that a certain amount of Europe may be. . . ." La Farge was planning a trip to Europe without his family, and James offered Mrs. La Farge
what seemed like comfort to a young bachelor. "Give her my love and tell
her, persuasively, that if Europe does not wholly solve the problems of
existence, it at least helps the flight of time—or beguiles its duration."[39]

Alice James could appreciate the superiority of Europe, but that observation was confined to the privacy of her journal. Henry James luxuriated
in the ease of Europe, parading that pleasure in front of his friends, but he
had to be much more circumspect with his father. As he grew older and
honed his philosophy with greater precision, Henry James, Sr., was more

critical of a social system that made idleness possible for a few through a rigid class system for the many. In *The Secret of Swedenborg* he confessed moral indignation at his own youthful extravagance. It was wrong that he had been able to "squander upon my mere fantastic want . . . an amount of sustenance equal to the maintenance of a virtuous household."[40] He was inclined to berate any social system that did not provide democratically for the economic and spiritual needs of all. At a time when Alice, Henry, and William enjoyed European idleness at their father's expense, their father reviled both idleness and the system that made it possible.

Henry, Jr., wrote a placating reply to his father's most recent moralizing letter. "Be very sure that as I live more I care none the less for these wise human reflections of yours. I turn with great satisfaction to any profession of interest in the fate of collective humanity—turn with immense relief from this wearisome European world of idlers and starers and self-absorbed pleasure seekers."[41] Henry knew that he had to cast himself as an ailing democrat rather than an indulgent aristocrat to curry his father's favor and support.

Besides protecting leisure and making pleasurable travel socially acceptable, invalidism served admirably to convey feelings that would have been difficult to express directly without ruffling the surface calm called for by the social ideal of the Victorian family. In our post-Freudian age, we live more easily with ambivalence between intimates than would have been conceivable in the social group in which William grew to manhood. That one might hate the parent one also loved, resent the caretaker whose nurturing made invalidism possible, loathe the domestic scene whose apparent peace shielded one from wordly struggles was unthinkable—or at least unmentionable. But an invalid could refuse to improve, bemoan his long list of complaints, and inflict pain on his anxious relatives as if to say, "I hate you for what you have done *to* me by doing *for* me." The perplexed caretaker felt the impact of the blow yet was unable to strike back at one so weak and helpless.

Once again Mary James's letters provide vivid illustration. When William returned from a voyage of recovery, she was frankly irritated by the assaulting quality of his complaints. She told Henry, Jr., "Well, he seems *as yet* too much the old story to give us all the pleasure that we expected. . . . The trouble with him is that he *must express* every fluctuation of feeling, and especially every unfavorable symptom; without reference to the effect upon those about him."[42] Though she was an acute observer, Mary James could not admit what must have been obvious to others—that William's unhappiness at being home had something to do with the jibes she received in the form of physical complaints.

Father also received his share of barbs in the form of illness. Whenever

William and Henry were unhappy with him, they mocked his ideas, but Alice could not do so directly. She could play the part of adoring child to perfection, but when angry feelings threatened to erupt, sickness became her mode of expression. In 1867–68, when William and Henry were both actively nursing their backs, Alice was overwhelmed by "violent turns of hysteria" that left her as prostrate as her admired older brothers. No hint of the cause of her fainting spells appears in the family correspondence; they were blamed, as usual, on overexertion. But a diary entry written after Alice had read William's essay "The Hidden Self," over twenty years later, exposed what she had been trying to hide. She had felt barely repressed rage pushing her toward murder or suicide. She was flooded with waves of feeling very much like those revealed in William's drawings during the Newport experiment, and the object of her violence was also the same: father. She recalled that she had had to police her patricidal impulses and was terrified that her moral powers would be overwhelmed. "I saw so distinctly that it was a fight simply between my body and my will, a battle in which the former was to be triumphant to the end. Owing to some physical weakness, excess of nervous susceptibility, the moral power *pauses,* as it were for a moment, and refuses to maintain muscular sanity, worn out with the strain of its constabulary functions."[43] She was weak not from overwork but from the strain of holding back her deepest emotions. The diary entry gives a graphic description of her inner conflict but offers no clue as to the source of the anger she felt toward her father.

Her older brothers were stalled in invalidism while they made a show of seeking careers. Her younger brothers were off working a plantation in Florida, backed by a substantial portion of family capital.[44] She was trapped in what she felt to be a rural backwater, keeping her parents company as they passed into old age. There is no mention of education for her in the family correspondence, save what she might learn from medical treatment, or of efforts to introduce her to young men, except physicians who were called to treat her. She joked with her girlfriend Sara well into the 1870s about looking for a husband, but family interest and resources were committed to the boys. If one had been casting about for omens, one would have been disturbed to note, as Mary James did in 1869, that the occasion of Alice's majority was ushered in by a solar eclipse.[45]

The limited options of a woman of Alice's social class were rapidly closing for her during the 1860s. It is easy to see how she might have been infuriated by her beatific father, who promised glorious spiritual fulfillment but whose efforts to help her were hardly commensurate with those expended on behalf of her brothers. How could she dare express animosity toward a "benignant pater" who made brotherhood the test of redemption and ideal fatherhood a model for himself and God? She gave her father the discomfort of witnessing her invalidism. When her rage intensified, she had to use all of her powers of restraint to keep from killing him—or doing what Freud has taught amounts to the same thing symbolically, killing herself. Neurasthenia was a vector between moral rectitude and rage. Alice experienced this intrusion of violence into consciousness as a physical defect, a "breakdown in her machinery" or "muscular insanity," rather than a valid emotional response to her plight. "As I used to sit immovable reading in the library with waves of violent inclination suddenly invading my muscles taking some one of their myriad forms such as throwing myself out of the window, or knocking off the head of the benignant pater as he sat with his silver locks, writing at his table, it used to seem to me that the only difference between me and the insane was that I had not only all the horrors and suffering of insanity but the duties of doctor, nurse, and strait-jacket imposed upon me, too."[46]

Though an astute clinician, Dr. Beard shared the family ideal held by his patients. He showed little comprehension of the ambivalent relationship between parents and children. For him, violence toward loved ones was "insane" by definition. "The sane man murders those whom he hates, from whose death he expects to gain something; the insane man murders those whom he most loves—from whose death he can gain nothing. . . ."[47] The banishment of evil to the realm of unreason was a comforting distortion. Freud had to remind the Victorian world that murder was a family affair in real life as well as in Gothic novels.

[6]

If invalidism had obvious social and interpersonal utility, it was at best a compromise. The invalid might enjoy the leisure that illness provided, but he also shared in the social judgment of that enjoyment and felt guilty. If illness served as a niche for social participation, it was one that the sufferer judged to be inferior, and he felt shame. The quest for health was a lever for prying loose family funds, but the beneficiary knew that others were being deprived and was torn by a sense of responsibility to them. Sickness could express the unmentionable, but the sufferer judged his own feelings as evil. In sum, the cultivation of illness may have abetted transgressions against society, family, and self, but it also levied penalties for those acts. Invalidism was a compromise between crime and punishment.

Henry James's letters from Europe provide ample illustrations of the way that illness helped the sufferer do penance for the advantages he enjoyed. Sometimes the punishment was merely restriction of pleasurable activity. It was a modest penance, if the pleasures one sought were modest.

Early in his trip, Henry described to his brother William how improved health freed him for more activity, but remaining illness still set some limitations. "You musn't think of course that I am literally on the gallop from morning til night: far from it. . . . But when a man is able to break-fast out, to spend a couple of hours at the British Museum and then to dine and go to the play, and feel none the worse for it, he may cease to be oppressed by a sense of his physical wretchedness."[48]

When the pleasures desired were intense (and expensive), illness became correspondingly more painful and inhibitory. For an American traveler making the grand tour in search of health and recreation, Italy was a temptation and a danger. Charles Eliot Norton had put the matter this way to Henry: "Born and bred in New England as we were, where the air we breathe is full of the northern chill, and no other philosophy but that of utilitarianism is possible—it is not easy to learn to be content with the usefulness of doing nothing. Italy is a good place, however, for deadening the overactive conscience, and for killing rank ambition."[49]

A young man of artistic sensibility had every expectation of finding Italian travel a sensuous feast. Henry had successfully argued for the inclusion of Italy in his itinerary, pleading its salutary effects for health and its enriching influences for general culture. But having overcome parental opposition, he found himself strangely hampered in his enjoyment of the prize. "It's as if I had been born in Boston," he complained to William: "I can't for my life frankly surrender myself to the Genius of Italy, or the Spirit of the South—or whatever one may call the confounded thing; but I nevertheless *feel* it in all my pulses." He did eventually unbend and wrote excitedly, "If I might talk of these things I would talk of more and tell you in glowing accents how beautiful a thing this month in Italy has been and my bosom aches with memories." Unfortunately, as he opened himself to Italy, his health began to fail. "I'm very sorry to say that I am anything but well," he complained to his father. "Not that I have any new and startling affliction, but . . . ever since I have been in Italy I have been rapidly losing ground. . . . It makes a sad trouble of what ought to be a great plea-sure."[50] True, Henry James was not a Bostonian by birth, but to his chagrin, he was prey to the very attitudes that he mocked. Invalidism, though useful, was a restricted visa for such a traveler.

Doctors were important to the structure of invalidism. Sometimes un-wittingly but often with consummate skill they matched illness with treat-ment, as a judge might match a crime with a suitable sentence. It would take us too far afield to describe in detail the entire range of treatments mentioned in the James family correspondence. Lifting, hot irons, ice packs, blistering, galvanism, the water cure—each was justified by some medical theory, each was translated into the exchange of pain for pleasure, and all were tried in their turn by the members of the family in their search for health.

If illness justified the avoidance of work in a work-centered culture, logic dictated that the sanction for ill-gotten leisure should be hard labor. Whether the doctors understood this relationship or not, their invalid patients saw it that way. Too simply stated, treatment turned leisure into labor, either through the prescription of rest to a degree that tested one's endurance or by the recommendation of physical exertion to a degree that seemed like work. When Mary James reported on Alice's attempts at a rest cure, for example, she described it as labor. "Alice is busy trying to idle, and it is always very hard depressing work, this to her, but I think it will tell in the end."[51] Henry, Jr., was more self-consciously ironic when he described sightseeing in Rome as labor. "I have buckled down to my work with a fair amount of resolution. . . . The Vatican, the Museum of the Capitol, the Colisium and the Baths of Caraculla, the Pantheon, the forum, and the churches of the Lateran and St. Maria Maggiore—such are my special acquisitions."[52]

But Henry's uncle William was not joking when he described the water cure at Clifton Springs as work. The doctors had reassured him that his headaches were not a sign of impending apoplexy (his father's fatal illness), but the effect of "torpidity" of the glands, stomach, and nervous system, which they claimed could be relieved by prolonged water treatment. No matter what pathophysiology was seized upon by the physician, it could be translated into the language of industry by the invalid. "Let me give you each days work," the Reverend William wrote. And work it was, at least enough to compensate a puritan conscience for the leisure enjoyed. The day began at 5:30 A.M. Besides baths of total and partial immersion in water ranging from tepid to very hot, there were two periods of required exercise—bowling in the morning, "which brings streams of perspiration from every pore of my body," and a walk of "4 to 5 miles" in the afternoon. Apparently the good effects of the treatment were due in part to separation from home and family. "From the day I left home I began to be better and for a week past I have been well," he noted. This observation led to the conjecture "that it will be long before I can settle down at home again."[53]

Henry James, Jr., had an intuitive grasp of this relationship. Witness his playful query to a friend, "Have you ever a superstitious sense of having to give some *quid pro quo* for your particular pleasure?"[54] A good-humored judge, he condemned his correspondent to describe her travels to him in person when they met again. However magical he felt such an exchange to be, he, along with other invalids, bartered in that economy. The full cooperation of the medical profession was usually readily obtained. Supported by the theory of counterirritation (which hypothesized that therapeutically induced pain could relieve the underlying cause of existing pain), patients were shocked and blistered and boiled. When Alice James subjected herself to galvanism (the application of electric current to the skin), she wrote graphically of the painful experience to a friend. She was being treated, she said, "by Dr. Neftel, of whom I had heard great things & who certainly either in spite or because of his quackish quality has done me a great deal of good in many ways. . . . His electricity however has the starching properties of the longest Puritan descent. . . ."[55]* Like so many other remedies that she tried, it had only temporary effect.

Indeed, all of the cures were doomed to failure, though they succeeded admirably in supporting the structure of invalidism. No matter what the theoretical basis for their therapeutics, experienced healers have always known that invalidism is a complex creation. In mid-nineteenth-century New England it coalesced from a romantic and puritanical matrix into a durable social role. Salvation through work, condemnation of idleness, suspicion of pleasure, and a belief that suffering leads to grace flowed from the puritan source. Insistence on self-expression, a high valuation of leisure, and the admiration of delicacy and acute sensibility issued from the romantic. In such vigorous crosscurrents, illness had considerable utility. It provided social definition, sanctioned pleasure, prescribed leisure for health, protected from premature responsibility, forced others to care, and expressed inadmissible feelings while protecting vital personal ties. For the patient it was a compromise between the attainment of forbidden goals and punishment for that accomplishment. With the cooperation of their physicians, pain was balanced against pleasure, crime against punishment, and an uneasy equilibrium was maintained.

For some invalids the haven was temporary. Others made a port in the storm their permanent home. Still others found to their dismay that they had waited too long and the channel of exit had become clogged by time. Work was a problem for these Americans, and illness was one solution. It is no wonder that Dr. Beard considered successful treatment to be an act of cruelty for some invalids. "Some patients take a pleasure in their distresses; it would be cruel to cure them; their pains are their possessions. Any man wishing to make them well would be no better than a thief or a robber."[56] A doctor had to share the illusion of treatment along with his patient as the invalid worked out his own spiritual recovery. For some patients, that meant getting to work.

---

*Dr. William B. Neftel, a Russian émigré who specialized in the treatment of nervous diseases, practiced in New York City. He treated many prominent Bostonians with galvanic currents applied to their muscles and nerves to relieve neurasthenia.

13

An Invalid Physician

Not long ago I was dining with some old gentlemen, and one of them asked, "What is the best assurance a man can have of a long and active life?" He was a doctor; and presently replied to his own question: "To be entirely broken-down in health before one is thirty-five!"—There is much truth in it; and though it applies more to nervous than to other diseases, we all can take our comfort in it. I was entirely broken down before I was thirty.

—William James, 1891

[1]

I N APRIL 1867, William James interrupted his medical education and fled to Europe. His departure was unusually precipitous even for this well-traveled health-seeking family. And it was kept secret, as if public disclosure would have required embarrassing explanations even within the family. Alice received the news at the last moment in New York, along with a mild lecture from her mother on the need to accept life's disappointments. Mary James merely said that William was to go abroad, and "there is no wisdom in indulging in selfish regrets in the matter but accept cheerfully the fact, that life is made up of changes and separations from those we love. . . ."[1] The plan was also kept from Mary's sister Catharine Walsh (Aunt Kate) until it was a fait accompli. When Kate did find out, she was dubious about the reason given. "I don't think she believes that you hurt your back in dissecting," Mary reported, "but injured it when we moved into this house, nor do I think she has quite forgiven you for not having told her before you left."[2] Kate's suspicion that William's back difficulties could be traced to the autumn of 1866, when the whole family took up permanent residence in Cambridge, was consistent with other speculation. Some of his classmates thought that he fled because of the strain of living with his family rather than the strain of dissecting.

Mary James reported this rumor in a tone of hurt disbelief. Family dissension was obviously less palatable than illness as a reason for putting an ocean between them. "Your friend Pratt made his appearance last evening the first time we have seen him since you left. . . . The only reason he had heard given, was 'family reasons' which had evidently placed the whole thing in so equivocal an attitude to his mind that he had not dared even to speculate upon the subject—some dreadful family rupture had driven you to place the ocean between you and your offending family—this seemed the most natural solution of the mystery. . . ."[3] Obviously William couldn't obscure his unhappiness with medicine from everyone.

He confessed to Oliver Wendell Holmes, Jr., that he wanted to hide from friends and family alike. Holmes, a regular visitor in the James household and a friendly philosophic adversary, had not been told in advance, either. "I am, as you have probably been made aware, 'a mere wreck,' bodily. I left home without telling anyone about it, because, hoping I might get well, I wanted to keep it a secret from Alice and the boys till it was over. I thought of telling you 'in confidence,' but refrained, partly because walls have ears, partly from a morbid pride, mostly because of the habit of secrecy that had grown on me in six months."[4]* That Herbert J. Pratt's inference was closer to the mark than Mary James's explanation was confirmed in a letter to his friend Tom Ward: "I had to throw up my hospital appointment, and fly from a home wh. had become loathsome."[5] A year later he added another important detail: he had been "on the continual verge of suicide" that winter.[6] The reasons for his preoccupation with suicide can only be inferred. When the family moved to Cambridge, William lived with them and was exposed once again to his father's moralizing pressure to continue in a scientific direction. The hostility that a year in Brazil had done so much to quiet was rekindled, and James fled from Quincy Street before his repressed rage could overwhelm him.

William's correspondence from this period is remarkable for its frequent requests for secrecy. He closed a letter to Holmes with the comment "I'd rather my father should not see it."[7] He began a letter to his father with a similar plea: "I think it will be just as well for you not to say anything to any of the others about what I shall tell you."[8] He swore Tom Ward to silence: "This letter is of course intensely private & confidential."[9] Two

---

*As Mary James had informed Alice almost immediately, and the only other son at home was Harry (with whom William had carried on frequent correspondence from the date of his departure), the excuse to Holmes raises as many questions as it answers.

18. Cowled friar

But if tears or anger are simply suppressed . . . the current which would have invaded the normal channels turns into others, for it must find some outlet of escape. . . . Thus vengeful brooding may replace a burst of indignation.

—W. James, 1890

drawings from this period, one from his German notebook and another from his medical school notebook, focus on the penetrating eyes of his subjects, creating a disturbing impression of angry surveillance consistent with his secretive frame of mind (Figures 18 and 19). It was as if he had decided to keep his correspondents separated—he the hub and they like spokes of a wheel kept rigidly apart by a rim of secrecy, so that he could keep moving. If they ever got together, the whole false structure of ill health and preparation for an inauthentic career would collapse.

19. STARING EYES
Secretiveness, . . . although often due to intelligent calculation and the dread of betraying our interests in some more or less definitely foreseen way, is quite often a blind propensity. . . . Often there is added to this a disposition to mendacity when asked to give an account of ourselves. —W. James, 1890

[2]

From the outset William's trip to Europe had ambiguous goals. It was, as Mary James and William indicated to their correspondents, a voyage in search of health. It was also, as Pratt inferred and William confirmed, a flight from what was "loathsome" at Quincy Street. Finally it supported the illusion that he was furthering his scientific training.[10]

After a brief stopover in Paris, he headed for Germany, where he was to spend most of the next eighteen months. Germany was a happy compromise, catering to the multiple purposes of the venture. It was European but, as William frequently commented, close enough in atmosphere to America so that it was not too invigorating. He assured his parents that "there is not the slightest touch of the romantic, picturesque, or even *foreign* about living here."[11] It was a center of scientific research and he could study science, if health permitted, or revel in art and aesthetics if it did not. Living was inexpensive. All in all, Germany judiciously balanced desire and duty, art and science, health and disease, leisure and labor.

The outcome of this European venture was as inconclusive as the Brazilian holiday had been. William talked a lot about studying science but did little. He enrolled in a physiology lecture series in Berlin, but stopped after three months without finishing the course. He promised himself and his family that he would make up for that failure by studying science at Heidelberg with Wilhelm Wundt and Hermann von Helmholtz. But, in spite of much rest in preparation, he quit Heidelberg after only six days. He was far from idle, though, reading voluminously in literature and philosophy (much of it in German) with a seriousness of purpose, a breadth of understanding, and an ensuing mastery that a modern professor would applaud in a graduate student. He spent a total of six months undergoing five separate cures at Teplitz and Divonne. His comings and goings served with remarkable reliability to remove him from too much indulgence of his love of art or too much progress toward the scientific career he reluctantly pursued. When he finally returned to Cambridge after eighteen months, he had in fact taken large strides toward an academic career that was as yet only dimly perceived.

[3]

William's first note from Paris bubbled with excitement over the theater. "I thrilled, I burned, I overflowed with joy from beginning to end."[12] Enchanted, he succumbed to temptation and extended his stay a few days longer. But once he arrived in Dresden, his studious routine was beyond reproach. "I have, since I wrote my last letter, led a perfectly monotonous life. Read all the morning, go out for a walk and lounge in a concert garden in the afternoon, and read after tea." At the museum he was particularly attracted by the Venetian paintings. He read voraciously. "I have been having a literary debauch," he confessed, but reassured his parents that he was "getting down again to medicine."[13]

Despite his protestations that life in Dresden was monotonous, his letters record a deliciously leisured life seen through the eye of a landscape artist: "I get up and have breakfast . . . at eight. I read, till half-past one, when dinner, which is generally quite a decent meal; after dinner a nap, more *Germanorum* [studying of the German language] and more read til the sun gets low enough to go out, when I go—generally to the Grosser Garten, a lovely park outside the town where the sun slants over the greenest meadows and sends his shafts between the great trees in a most wholesome manner." He saw romantic scenes worthy of Thomas Cole's palette: "There are some spots where the trees are close together, and in their classic gloom you find mossy statues, so that you feel as if you belonged to the last century. Often I go and sit on a terrace which overlooks the Elbe and, with my eyes bent upon the lordly cliffs far down the river on the other side, with strains of the sweetest music in my ear, and with pint after pint of beer successively finding their way into the fastnesses of my interior, I enjoy most delightful reveries."[14]

Through July he continued in excellent spirits, enjoying the theater, the museum, and the luxury of intellectual exploration. When he mentioned health, he did so jokingly. "Another fortnight over and I ant dead yet." He was clearly delighted with his existence and so at ease that he let slip a comment that must have ruffled sensibilities at Quincy Street. "I would not share your fate at home for anything."[15] But joy for such a son had its limits. He soon fell ill and went to take the baths at Teplitz for the first time.

[4]

The cure at Teplitz was less rigorous than the American counterpart at Clifton Springs described by William's uncle. Instead of waking at six-thirty to drink the waters and walk with the others as a band played in the background, William chose to stay in his bed, "provided with three large and very soft fluffy pillows which meet over the eyes when I lean my head on them," and sip his water leisurely until nine. A walk through the park to a dairy for breakfast followed. "A little maiden like Henrietta Temple [his cousin] brings me my breakfast, *viz.,* a big bowl of curds and whey, a roll and a glass of yellow frothing milk. . . . I sit under the trees, absorb the milk, and the air, and music and let my eyes feed on all the wonderful details of green light which the woods yield. . . ." A week after beginning the regimen, he was pleased to announce, "I have been greatly reinvigorated by my stay here, and consider myself a well man."[16]

But that remark was deceiving. He told his father later about the back, bowel, and depressive symptoms that had made him decide to go to Teplitz, adding more sober details that justified the extraordinary expense. Since what he wrote to his father was so at variance with earlier letters to other members of the family, he urged him to secrecy. "I don't see what will be the use of impairing the family confidence in my letters by saying anything about it to them." In retrospect, he believed the conditions that made up his princely leisure had in fact been bad for him. "My confinement to my room and inability to indulge to any social intercourse drove me necessarily into reading a great deal, which in my half-starved and weak condition was very bad for me, making me irritable and tremulous in a way I have never before experienced." When he did make social visits, they aggravated his "dorsal symptoms" very much.[17] He became more depressed and thought of suicide once again: "Although I cannot exactly say that I got low-spirited, yet thoughts of the pistol, the dagger and the bowl began to usurp an unduly large part of my attention, and I began to think that some change, even if a hazardous one, was necessary." Why visits to the baths were hazardous he did not explain, but in looking back, he decided the treatment had been a failure, though the drives in the countryside were a great success. "While there, owing to the weakening effects of the baths, both back and stomach got worse if anything; but the beautiful country and a number of drives which I thought myself justified in taking made me happy as a king."[18]

There is no indication of the elder Henry's reaction to this news other than the fact that William continued abroad and was supplied with funds. The tortured logic that turned the pleasure of study and visiting into painful assaults on health must have been confusing. If William found the baths debilitating, why did he continue to take them? (That question was to become even more troublesome as his son returned again and again for ever-lengthening stays at ever greater expense.) The ingenious juxtaposition of the pain of treatment with the pleasure of his drives into the country probably reassured father that family funds were not being wasted on idle pleasure alone. Henry might have been upset by William's declarations, the first since his arrival in Europe, that poor health made the promised study of science during the coming winter doubtful. "My back will prevent my studying physiology this winter at Leipsig, which I rather hoped to do."[19] He would stay in Berlin instead. By the time he told Oliver Wendell Holmes, Jr., of his plans for Berlin, there was no longer any doubt that poor health would prevent him from studying practical physiology, as he could not stand long enough to do laboratory work. Ultimately, he would not study science in Europe at all.

William showed only one side of his life in Germany to his friend. Holmes's positivistic cast of mind intimidated him. To such a correspondent he emphasized effort rather than ease, pain rather than pleasure, ambition rather than uncertainty, and above all science rather than art. With remarkable candor he outlined the differences in their characters which made him reluctant to tell the whole story. "You have a far more logical and orderly mode of thinking than I . . ." he noted, "and whenever we have been together I have somehow been conscious of a reaction against the ascendancy of this over my ruder processes. . . . I put myself involuntarily into a position of self-defense, as if you threatened to over-run my territory and injure my own proprietorship."[20]*

Furthermore, Holmes was decisive and firmly committed to a career in the law. Holmes, too, had struggled to find work that joined his talents and ideals with the needs of the world. His decision to become a lawyer was based on the conviction that "law, as well as any other series of facts in this world may be approached in the interests of science and may be studied, yes and practiced with the preservation of one's ideals." Unlike James, once he had chosen a profession, he accepted the need to master all of it. "Since I wrote in December I have worked at nothing but the law. . . . It has been necessary,—if a man chooses a profession he cannot forever content himself in picking out the plums with fastidious dilettan-tism and give the rest of the loaf to the poor. . . ."[21] If he had intended to let loose a moralizing arrow, it could not have flown more directly to the mark. Holmes beckoned to a line of charge that he had already taken. William could only feel his own cowardice in hanging back.

Illness excused William from science, and he was sure it would free him from marriage and the responsibility of supporting a family as well. "I now see that I can probably never do laboratory work, and so am obliged to fall back on something else. The prospective burdens of a wife and family being taken off my shoulders simultaneously with the placing of this 'mild yoke' upon the small of my back, relieves me from imminent *material* anxiety."[22] Instead of a young man frantically running from inauthentic labor and premature responsibility, he was a Christian soldier bravely bearing his cross. Perhaps Holmes could understand and even admire that.

[5]

William showed yet another side to his friend Tom Ward, who had been on the Thayer expedition with him and was openly unhappy about work-ing for his father's banking firm. William knew that Tom was subject to mercurial mood swings too, and he preached a gospel of positive thinking for them both: "I always want when I write to you to ring a trumpet blast

---

*Holmes had served with distinction in the Civil War. The choice of a martial metaphor in which his friend appeared as an invading rifleman whose charge threatened to overrun the field underscored an invalid's feeling of inadequacy three years after Appomattox.

that will wake the echoes in your will and put you in fighting tune."[23] And he marshaled his ample literary talents for the task. "Remember when old December's darkness is everywhere about you, that the world is really in every minutest point as full of life as in the most joyous morning you ever lived through; that the sun is whanging down, and the waves dancing, and the gulls skimming down at the mouth of the Amazon . . . as freshly as in the first morning of creation; and the hour is just as fit as any hour that ever was for a new gospel of cheer to be preached."[24]

He could be more relaxed in discussing his dilemma with Tom, since both were unhappy. William admitted that he had abandoned the romantic apogee of self-expressed genius (in the manner of Ruskin) as his ideal. He was prepared instead to settle for more modest goals: work that interested him and gave him a feeling of engagement in the world. "Well, neither of us wishes to be a mere loafer; each wishes a work which shall by its mere *exercise* interest him and at the same time allow him to feel that through it he takes hold of the reality of things. . . ." He listed his possibilities in descending order of attraction. Art was first, philosophy next, and medicine last on the list. "Individuals can add to the welfare of the race in a variety of ways. You may delight its senses or taste by some production of luxury or art, comfort it by discovering some moral truth, relieve its pain by concocting a new patent medicine. . . ."[25] And Tom Ward was the first to hear him declare outright that a career in science did not suit him: ". . . it's the old story, the square peg in the round hole. . . . The fact is that I am about as little fitted by nature to be a worker in science of any sort as anyone can be. . . ." Yet he felt that he had to be a scientist. He was firmly bound to his father's plan. Paradoxically he complained that even though he was not suited for science, "I should feel as if all value had departed from my life if convinced of *absolute* scientific impotence. . . ." Once again suicide seemed a way out. And when he spoke of suicide to Ward, his words had a more serious ring than his report to his father a year earlier: ". . . sometimes when I despair of ever doing anything, I say: 'Why not step out into the green darkness?' "[26]

For Henry Bowditch, his medical school classmate, he played the frustrated scientist. Bowditch planned a career in physiology. He intended to go to Europe to study and asked William's advice. According to James's estimate, "the opportunities for study here are superb. . . . Whatever they may be in Paris, they *cannot* be better. The physiological laboratory, with its endless array of machinery, frogs, dogs, etc., etc., almost 'bursts my gizzard,' when I go by it, with vexation." For Bowditch's ear, William could muster some enthusiasm for the physiological laboratory—but only as he walked by it without entering. Instead of considering medicine "busted," as he did when he wrote to Ward, he spoke of finishing medical school. "Of course I can never hope to practice; but I shall graduate on my return, and perhaps pick up a precarious and needy living by doing work for medical periodicals. . . . I can't be a teacher of physiology, pathology, or anatomy; for I can't do laboratory work, much less microscopical or anatomical."[27]

He jokingly proposed that the two join forces and go into medical partnership, Henry to take care of the patients and William to read the literature and keep him informed. "This division of labor will give the firm an immense advantage over all of our wooden-headed contemporaries." But the need to divide the profits of the partnership reminded him of his recurrent concern about money. And he let slip another of those naked statements that reveal the mixture of conscious maneuvering with unconscious turmoil in the politics of invalidism. Bowditch was the only one to read his estimate of the financial support available for him as long as he was ill. "I have no very definite plans for the future; but I have enough to keep body and soul together for some years to come, and I see no need of providing for more." It is no wonder that he followed this disclosure with yet one more request for secrecy. "This talk of course is only for your 'private ear.'"[28]

[6]

William wrote to his father at the end of December of his plans to go to Teplitz again in March, when the term ended. He also spoke of plans to study with Wundt and Helmholtz at Heidelberg. Either he had forgotten his original estimate of the poor effects of Teplitz or he had changed his mind again. "If it does me then as much good as before, I think I shall probably be about whole." He claimed the baths would make him "well enough to do some work in their laboratory. I shall hate myself til I get doing some special work; this reading leads to nothing at all."[29] He did not wait until March, but instead dropped out of the physiology course and headed for Teplitz before the term ended. While there he continued to study philosophy despite his protestations that it led "to nothing at all."

Naturally his abrupt change of plans (and additional expenditure) had to be accounted for apologetically to his father. "My dear Dad,—Don't allow yourself to be shocked with surprise on reading the above date [Teplitz] til you hear the reasons which have brought me here at this singular season." He clearly anticipated Henry's dismay, yet his logic was so tortured that he must also have counted on his father's indulgent suspension of his critical faculties. "They are grounded in the increasing wear and tear of my life in Berlin, and in my growing impatience to get well enough to be able to do some work in the summer. I find myself getting more interested in physiology." So he had left the wear and tear of studying physiology in Berlin to go to Teplitz (which last time had injured his health) so that he could store up enough good health to return to study physiology once more. If the elder Henry had scratched his head in disbelief, it would have been no wonder.

And besides, hadn't William claimed his health was improving? William anticipated rebuttal on that score. "I hope you won't think from seeing me back here that my loudly trumpeted improvement in the autumn was fallacious. On the contrary, I feel more than ever, now that I am back in presence of my old measures of strength (distances, etc.), how substantial that improvement was—only it has not yet bridged the way up to complete soundness." So he was well, yet not well enough; interested in physiology in Heidelberg, but not in Berlin; and if he could only become even more healthy, through further rest and reading (which he said earlier was pointless), he could finally return home and get started on the scientific career that both he and especially father wanted. Then "I *may* be able to make its study (and perhaps its teaching) my profession. . . ." To put the finishing touches on his accounting, he made it an act of valor that he had finally come to Teplitz and an act of "effeminate shrinking" that he had tried to remain so long in Berlin.[30] Henry James had already added $350 to his son's account, and he renewed his letter of credit in the fall.[31]

William successfully rationalized his prolonged stay in Europe and gained the largess of the family purse. But he felt guilty that his gain was his brothers' loss. As the oldest, he was expected to lead the way toward financial independence. But by 1868 all of his younger brothers were passing him by. Henry had already begun to earn some money from the publication of his stories. Garth Wilkinson and Robertson, three and four years his junior, had already been to war as officers and were managing a plantation in Florida. Though still supported by the family, they were clearly more adult than he. William ruefully confessed to Robertson, the youngest: "I feel rather ashamed at my age to stand in the presence of you and Wilky without having earned a cent. But I have not been quite idle notwithstanding, and will, if health only returns, make my living yet."[32] He wrote to Henry of his hope that he might yet get enough improvement "from this cure this time to get into a laboratory," a step that would "turn me from a nondescript loafer, into a respectable working man, with an honorable task before him."[33] But strangely, each time he moved toward science, ill health moved that goal, like the grapes of Tantalus, farther away.

For the next three months James shuttled between Dresden and Teplitz, forty miles away. And he persisted in representing the experience in various ways to various correspondents. When he wrote to Henry, Jr., and Alice, he emphasized the advantages of the baths—advantages that obliged him, in all good conscience, to continue. As far as his brother and sister were informed, Teplitz was a haven, and a place of treatment that had proved successful in the past.[34] But he told a different truth to Bowditch. Teplitz was a bore; the treatments were useless. Yet he manfully returned to them again and again, stoically accepting pain and weakness in the hope of being able to study science.

When he wrote to his brother Henry from Dresden in April, he waxed enthusiastic over the treasures of the museum. "I have been a number of times in the gallery, you may imagine with what pleasure—like a bath from Heaven. . . ." His painter's eye appreciated an artist whose skill was "adequate to his universe; it is a touching thing in Titian and Paul Veronese, who paint scenes which are a perfect *charivari* of splendor and luxury, and manifold sensations as far removed from what we call simplicity as anything well can be, that they preserve a tone of sober innocence, of instinctive single-heartedness, as natural as the breathing of a child."[35]

In May he wrote to Bowditch from Teplitz again, emphasizing his sickness and scientific failure. "I have been totally demoralized for more than two months past . . . and have let medical science almost totally slide." He had returned to the baths, he insisted, to gather strength for his final assault on the stubborn citadel of science, and was cautious about the outcome. "How long I stay in Heidelberg will depend on what I find I can gain there, and on the state of my back."[36] In Dresden once again he abstemiously avoided the gallery, and at the end of June announced to Alice his impending departure. "In three days I start for Heidelberg. I am sanguine after this long lapse to rise in the scale of being . . . as soon as I come in contact with the stern realities of life."[37]

But the assault was stopped at the gate of the city. In six days he was back in Berlin, and another painful rationalizing letter to father had to be composed. "You will doubtless, after my last letter, be astonished to read the above address. The fact is I have been to Heidelberg and fled again under the influence of blue despair which seized me for a week. Now that I am cheerful again I do not think I did unwisely." He did not even make a pretense of contemplating further scientific study. "I have learned now by experience that . . . I require to be somewhere in reach of conversation, music, French and English newspapers, or at least the sight of rushing affairs that a large city gives to keep of sound mind."[38]

There were limits to his parents' complicity in the politics of invalidism. He was ordered home. After a trip to Switzerland and a stay at the baths at Divonne, he informed Bowditch in Paris that he was leaving Europe,

William James, c. 1866

mockingly fabricating a houseful of dependents who required his presence. "I have been urged by my weeping wife and family to return home without delay, and having sagaciously with finger on nose bethunk me, I believe my wisest course will be to do so." If Bowditch recalled the confidential plan to do nothing "for some years to come," he may have wondered why the sudden change: the rim of secrecy that William had constructed to smooth his way hadn't broken down. Rather, he had strained the limits of parental credulity until they snapped. He still clutched his illness tenaciously, like a talisman, to protect his return to the rigors of medicine and Quincy Street. "I have a better chance of getting well in the quiet of home, than in tossing about Europe."[39]

[7]

Upon his return William settled down to finish work for his degree. He continued to read fiction and philosophy, but by comparison with his activities during the previous year and a half he was working hard at science. He told Tom Ward he was even enjoying medicine and his return to Quincy Street. "I have now been home near four weeks and enjoy enormously being in a house where I can talk about the things I read . . . —a pleasure I have not enjoyed for many long months. . . . I am reading medicine in a lively manner. . . . It grows so interesting that I find myself regretting that there is no chance for me to stick to it."[40] By the end of May he had completed a thesis on cold, and although "ashamed of the fewness of the medical facts I know," had submitted his tickets for the examinations.[41] The early crest of interest in medical study was followed inevitably by a trough. To his brother he complained, "I'm oppressed . . . by the *ennui* of the damned mass of stuff."[42] Nevertheless, he submitted himself to the nine ten-minute oral examinations and passed enough of them (failure in up to four was allowed) to earn the degree and close the book on medicine for the rest of his life.

The significance he attached to his accomplishment is indicated by a journal entry that states simply, "June 21, '69 M.D." The entry is virtually buried by long lists of nonmedical books he had been reading.[43] He almost forgot to mention his degree in a letter to Bowditch. It seemed more important to describe the "deliciously windy and cool" climate at Pomfret, Connecticut, where he was swinging in a hammock under the pine trees, giving "the policy of rest" a fair trial once more. "I am forgetting all this while to tell you that I passed my examination with no difficulty and am entitled to write myself M.D., if I choose."[44] He did not so choose. He had succeeded in fulfilling his father's expectation. But it was a hollow gesture, a Pyrrhic victory to be followed by four more years of invalidism. Duty had triumphed over desire, but he was less whole than when he had started.

The indulgence of his artistic self in Europe served as a marker to that submerged Atlantis but had not uncovered it. It threatened to rise above the surface again at Pomfret in 1869, but the episode was brief and the last before it submerged forever. Elizabeth Boott, a young painter who became the model for Pansy Osmond in Henry's *Portrait of a Lady,* was at Pomfret that summer, and William spoke glowingly of her to Bowditch. "She has a great talent for drawing and was very busy painting here, which, as she is in just about the same helpless state in which I was when I abandoned the art, made her particularly interesting to me."[45]

Mary James made much more of the incident in letters to her son Henry, who was in Europe. She spoke of Lizzie's virtues but felt quite sure that it was art that lured William. "She has so much talent and so much capacity for work, and . . . the artistic atmosphere that this work brings about us suits Will exactly." It had a dramatic impact on William's health. "I hardly dare to say or predict anything about Will's improvement. . . . But he appears to have taken a great start the last two weeks." The artistic atmosphere was important, but she also speculated on William's romantic interest. "Possibly Will's susceptible heart may be coming to the rescue of his back."[46]

Two weeks later she was delighted to report that the improvement continued. "I am strongly in hopes Will has got through the worst, and that his present improvement will be permanent." Once again she speculated on the cause: "His interest in the artistic work that was going on around him, brought him out of doors, directed him from reading, and furnished him with a moderate bodily activity from which he could always rest. This benificent influence gave him a decided start from which he has gone on to improve so as to take walks of a half mile *every* day without too much fatigue."[47]

Elizabeth Boott was a welcome artistic companion. When she left, William stayed on, but the good effects left with her. In September Mary James sadly reported that "Will has gone somewhat back in Pomfret." He returned to Cambridge, where Dr. Wilkinson, their English friend, was visiting. After examining the invalid, Wilkinson prescribed "high dilutions of Rhus & Nux Vomica."[48] A homeopath, he believed that health could be restored by minute quantities of drugs that in much larger doses would produce effects similar to those of the disease. If Dr. Wilkinson had listened attentively as Mary talked about the Pomfret experience, he might have concluded that what his patient needed was more of the same—not nux vomica, but painting.

[[8]]

It is not surprising that a young man of William James's psychological acumen glimpsed the tragedy in which he had taken part. A loose sheet of paper in an envelope marked "Pomfret" recorded a moment of pained awareness. The style is laconic, the form logical. It was as if he had gotten down to bedrock and there was no farther to go. He wrote: "Man, a bundle of desires, more or less numerous. He lives, inasmuch as they are gratified, dies as they are refused." He cited two desires that he had "abridged": "natural history, painting." But desires can be in conflict. He could see that his "expansive" and "defensive" tendencies were both "modes of self assertion," one based on "sympathy," the other on "self-sufficingness." Pure self-expansiveness was not possible. To ignore the importance of a scientific son to his father (he knew it was vital but he didn't fully appreciate why) would be to inflict pain on a man he loved. Sympathy had to offset self-sufficiency if he was to preserve his own self-respect. Solemnly he noted that "in a given case of evil the mind seesaws between the effort to improve it away, and resignation." But he was not content to accept resignation indefinitely. "The solution," he concluded, "can only lie in taking neither absolutely, but in making the resignation only provisional." Resignation to a medical career had been a depressing sham, tolerable only because he believed it temporary. But he was determined not to deceive himself. "Resignation should not say, 'It is good,' 'a mild yoke,' and so forth, but 'I'm willing to stand it for the present.'"

Yet the conflict seemed irreconcilable. How could he follow his desires, which delighted in art and of late were drawn toward speculation on the borders of science and philosophy, and still give his father a scientist son? His wants and father's wants, both being essential, valid, and without any other ultimate appeal for legitimation, were unequivocally opposed to each other. The conclusion he reached was ominous for his future. "Three quantities to determine: (1) how much pain I'll stand; (2) how much other's pain I'll inflict (by existing); (3) how much other's pain I'll 'accept,' without ceasing to take pleasure in their existence."[49]

He had succeeded in reducing a decade of his life to hard, sharp elements, like nails to seal a coffin or fasten a cross. He could suffer or make father suffer. He could inflict pain on himself (suicide was a temptation). He could do as he wished and disappoint his father, perhaps causing his death. He could continue to comply and risk having his love turn to hatred. When William became a doctor in 1869, the only uncertainty was the limit of his capacity to suffer. He would have four more years after that artistic summer at Pomfret to test his endurance.

14

A Singular Life

> . . . man is essentially *the* imitative animal.
>
> —William James, 1890

[1]

THE STRONG BOND between father and son hamstrung William's efforts to individuate, to establish a psychologically separate self. Separation was also difficult between William and his younger brother Henry, and vocational choice was as significant here as it was to the difficulty of individuation between father and son. The language of symptoms bore witness to that fraternal strife. During the thirteen years from 1859 to 1872, two paths that had overlapped and earlier were destined to parallel each other were divided. William declared for science and America, Henry embraced literature and Europe.

[2]

In September 1867, in a letter to Tom Ward, William burbled, "I don't know whether you have heard or not that I found myself last November, *almost* without perceptible exciting cause, in possession of that delightful disease in my back, which has so long made Harry so interesting."[1] The announcement to Ward was intended to explain the reason for his flight to Europe the previous spring. It was also a declaration by this ever-self-aware young man that his illness was connected with Harry's illness in a puzzling manner. "It is evidently a family peculiarity." The problem with

223

his back was the latest in a long series of events that confirmed an especially close fraternal bond.*

When Henry described his brother's illness in his autobiography, he confirmed that tie by moving effortlessly and imperceptibly from "he" to "us." The reader was thereby invited to share in the belief that there was really no boundary between them. He remembered "a sharp lapse of health on my brother's part which the tension of a year at the dissecting table seemed to have done much to determine; as well as the fond fact that Europe was again from that crisis forth to take its place for us as a standing remedy, a regular mitigation of all suffered, or at least of all wrong, stress."[2] William and Henry both saw illness as a confirmation of their brotherly attachment.

That fraternal bond was of long standing, having been fostered by closeness in age, shared aesthetic interests, and the constant deracination of their childhood. In play, in school, and in family life, William was followed by his admiring younger brother. Henry wanted to be with him and to be like him. But much to his chagrin, William was "always round the corner and out of sight."[3] This closeness was intensified by their shared fate as the earliest subjects of their father's educational experiments. Henry, Jr., characterized them himself as mythological twins. They were, he recalled, "a defeated Romulus, a prematurely sacrificed Remus," served up to father's radical educational program.[4] Where William went, Henry followed, albeit in the shadows. William's artistic talents declared themselves first; and here, as in so many other areas, Henry imitatively tried his hand. "The gratification nearest home was the imitative, the emulative—that is on my part," Henry recalled. "W. J. drew because he could, while I did so in the main only because he did. . . ."[5] When William studied with Hunt, so did Henry. When William moved to Cambridge, Henry soon followed him to attempt a Harvard degree as well.

In the 1850s they had mined the treasures of the museums together and learned to depend on each other for an attentive ear and an appreciative eye. Shared aesthetic sensibility deepened their sense of we-ness. In this respect, too, the younger brother's autobiographical recollections consistently link them as a pair. They liked Haydon because he pointed to something that "we could do, or at least want to do. . . . We found in these works remarkable interest and beauty. . . . The very word Pre-Raphaelite . . . thrills us in its perfection. . . . We were not yet aware of

---

*Though William identified his "interesting" disease of the back as a link between himself and Harry, he was not entirely accurate in naming Harry as the first to suffer from this "family peculiarity." In 1856 Mary James wrote to her mother-in-law about the back trouble that had begun to plague the elder Henry. "The effort he has made in walking for so many years has occasioned a weakness in his back which at times gives him great trouble" (Mary Walsh James to Catharine Barber James, August 25, 1865, MH).

style, though on the way to become so. . . ."[6] In old age, when the division between them had been effected, recognized by the world, and praised, it was easier to say that William was meant for science and Henry for art. But in the searching time of youth they were aesthetic twins, and it seemed possible that they might remain yoked in that twinship and become artists in tandem.[7]

William was the first to fall ill, his nervous symptoms having begun when he entered the Lawrence Scientific School in September 1861. Henry injured his back at the end of October, less than two months later. When the doctors failed to find any organic basis for the illness, Henry followed William to Cambridge and tried a year at the Harvard Law School. Though unsuited to his talents, the law justified leisured study. Henry described his activities as an invalid variously to his correspondents as "eating of the lotus to repletion, . . . loafing and talking aesthetics all day," and the "pursuit of a dreary hygienic course of no work," depending on his mood. He didn't expose himself, as William had done, to a direct confrontation with his father over art. Perhaps he had learned from his brother's failure. Gradually the balance between them shifted, and as Henry gained strength and competence as an artist, he became the leader of the pair.

William's back problem emphasized his kinship with Henry and afforded an opportunity when he was abroad to revive the aesthetic interests they had once shared. On the surface, it appeared that he had put an ocean between them when he fled in 1867, but the letters that followed emphasized that one brother was always in the other's consciousness. Henry was a wished-for or an imagined witness to William's aesthetic revival. Delight in the Parisian theater prompted this exclamation: "Dear Brother, how much I would have given to have you by my side so that we might rejoice together." While enjoying the peaceful, cultivated landscape around Dresden, he confided, "I have wished so often, . . . that Harry might be here for an hour at a time just to refresh himself with a sight of something new. . . ." Harry should "read Goethe's Faust—it is a good piece. . . ." Harry would want to read Balzac's *Modeste Mignon;* Harry would understand his feelings if he read that "imperturbable old heathen Homer." Fresh from viewing Titian and Veronese, he pined, "I'd give a good deal to import you and hear how some of the things strike you."[8] The older brother obviously missed the younger as he rattled the door that he had closed on art seven years earlier.

William was well aware that Henry wanted to be in Europe too. This thought must have been in his mind when he emphasized the many similarities between Germany and the United States. He had managed to acquire Henry's "interesting" infirmity and was abroad because of it, enjoying the aesthetic stimulation that his brother craved. Henry was miffed.

Henry James, Jr., and William James, c. 1905

Rather than acknowledge William's literary or artistic observations, he irritatedly fastened on one of William's hortatory asides. "Don't try to make out that America and Germany are identical and that it is as good to be here as there. . . . Only let me go to Berlin and I will say as much." To underscore the point and prick the fraternal conscience, he added: "Life here in Cambridge—or in this house, at least—is about as lively as the inner sepulchre."[9]

It was not his style to fight openly with his brother, but the same symptom that enabled William to get to Europe before him gave Henry the opportunity to snipe back. He knew that William believed the illness they shared would follow a similar course in both. Since Henry had had back trouble first, it was assumed that changes in his health predicted changes in William's, improvement or decline in one to be followed by improvement or decline in the other. Henry spitefully minimized the improvement that had already been described to William by other family correspondents. "I am no worse but my health has ceased to increase so steadily, as it did during the summer. It is plain that I shall have a very long row to hoe before I am fit for anything—for either work or play." Ever mindful of what he was doing—and both of them were often penetratingly aware—he denied his intent. "I mention this not to discourage you—for you have no right to be discouraged, when I am not myself. . . ."[10] If William absconded with Henry's symptoms, he had to be prepared to suffer as his brother suffered.

The rivalrous fusion represented by that shared symptomatology at times degenerated into name-calling. Each accused the other of feigning illness, of "imagining" himself to be suffering from a physical injury. And when accused, each insisted on his sincerity and the dismal state he endured. First William admitted his suspicions when Henry was abroad in 1869. He was full of medical lore gleaned from cramming for his final exams and offered his professional opinion: "My diagnosis of it now wd. be simply dorsal insanity."[11] When Henry was abroad again in 1873, it was his turn. The accusation can be inferred from William's pained retort: "I don't know whether you still consider my ailments to be imagination and humbug or not, but I know myself that they are as real as any one's ailments ever were, and that with the exception of my eyes which can now be used 4 hours a day the improvement I have made in 12 months is very slight."[12]

[3]

Whether Henry saw William's back problem as imitation or a shared fate is not clear. But he could not avoid noticing that this once admired older brother was trying to copy him as a writer. And to make matters worse, Henry was entreated to provide editorial assistance for the imitative endeavor. If Henry had drawn because William could, why shouldn't William write because Henry could? William announced the project in a letter: "The other day, as I was sitting alone with my deeply breached letter of credit, beweeping my outcast state, and wondering what I could possibly do for a living, it flashed across me that I might write a 'notice' of H. Grimm's novel which I had been reading." He felt inadequate in comparison with his younger brother and complained that he had no facility as an author. After "sweating fearfully for three days, erasing, tearing my hair, copying, recopying, etc., etc.," he passed his work on to Henry and the rest of the family for judgment. "I want you to read it, and if, after correcting the style and thoughts, . . . and rewriting it if possible, . . . send it to the *Nation* or the *Round Table*."[13] The review was published, as were five others written during William's 1867–68 stay in Europe. Henry dutifully edited and proofread copy for him. In his uncertainty, William scrambled to keep pace with Henry and obscure the separation the younger brother was patiently trying to effect.

When it was Henry's turn to seek health in Europe, he was still very much aware of his ambivalent ties to William. Soon after going abroad he wrote, "Has Willie felt my absence in any poignant—or rather any practical degree; if so—if he misses me round the room he musn't scruple to send for me to return." The offer could hardly have been serious, as he had barely arrived and was thoroughly enjoying himself in London. But it marked the ambivalence of separation. As his health improved, he generously extolled the fact, knowing that William would consider it a good omen. But there is a distinct sigh of relief joined with a fraternal shove of "good riddance" in his query a week later: "I am of course especially anxious to hear from Willy—as I hope he has by this time understood. Who in the world does his share and runs his errands and me over here? It's terrible to think."[14]

He served willingly as an observer for the pair, as William had done. He knew where William's heart was and eagerly met the need. "What you will care most to hear about is the painters," and he described them in lavish detail. Giotto's Chapel in Padua made him "long for the penetrating judgment and genial sympathy of my accomplished William."[15]

Henry knew what he wanted far better than William. He was determined to exploit illness-protected leisure to the hilt to develop himself as an artist. "When you tell me of the noble working life that certain of our friends are leading, in that clear American air, I hanker woefully to wind up these straggling threads of loafing and lounging and drifting and to toss my ball with the rest. But," he resolved, "having waited so long I can wait a little longer." Whereas William's trip abroad served to stall his scientific career, it failed to rescue his artist self. Henry pursued his artistic craft steadily. He alone would attain the goal that had once seemed their shared destiny. There was a sharp edge to Henry's plea: "Envy me—if you can without hating!"[16] And there was a poignant note in the words that he would put in the mouth of Roderick Hudson in his first novel. Hudson's older brother having died, Roderick remarked, "I will tell you the perfect truth, I have to fill a double place. I have to be my brother as well as myself."[17] In 1875, when that passage was written, the "twins" had been divided and Henry was the sole emergent artist of the pair.

But in 1869, conscience set limits on artistic indulgence. In Italy for the first time, Henry became constipated to such a degree that intestinal obstruction was feared. He delicately alluded to the matter as "an old trouble." William seized on the complaint with the therapeutic zeal of a young physician and wrote graphically about the affliction, sparing no details.[18] He suggested the typical remedies of the time, croton oil, soapsuds enemas, electric treatments to the abdominal muscles, to the spine, or inside the rectum, and urged his brother to get further advice from his American medical-student friends who were studying abroad.

William's solicitude was prompted in part by the fact that he himself had the same complaint.* He entered into Henry's bowel difficulties with the enthusiasm of a neophyte physician and the compassion of a fellow sufferer. And when he wrote, there were moments when he slipped imperceptibly from "you" to "I" in a manner that, as we have already noted, suggests psychological fusion. "If it continued 3 months longer in spite of what Doctors can do for you in Italy I would post for Malverne again and see what England can do for me." The brothers traded remedies back and forth, but Henry never showed so intense an involvement with the subject as William, who at times reached rhapsodic heights. "You can with difficulty conceive of the joy with which I received . . . the news of the temporary end of your moving intestinal drama. If I could believe it to be the

---

*Readers who have followed the logic of Erik Erikson's epigenetic scheme correlating organic modes and normal psychological crises will not be surprised to learn that this pair of talented young men, who were so close yet needed to become uniquely themselves, suffered from constipation. As a child gains sphincter control—the organically patterned task of the toddler—his developing will further separates him from a previously imagined unity with his parent. The issue of autonomy, of dividing from significant others, meets its earliest heightened challenge coincident with and through control of the bowels. As Erikson has pointed out, psychological issues recur in later stages of the life cycle. Earlier crises are constantly reexperienced and earlier solutions perpetually reworked. In young adulthood, which Erikson has labeled a time of identity formation, following one's will becomes a paramount issue once more. In a family context that has made separation difficult, it may have to be fought out symbolically, once again through control of one's own stool (Erik H. Erikson, *Identity, Youth, and Crisis* [New York 1968], 107–14).

beginning of *the* end the happiness wd. be almost *too* great." He evidently caught himself overdoing and stepped back with the remark "I dare say you'll thank me at last for dropping the subject."[19] The issue symbolized by costiveness was one of discipline versus desire. William noted this connection in characteristically hortatory advice to his brother: "*Never resist a motion to stool* no matter at what hour you may feel it. That is a *hauptsache* in the discipline of the gut."[20] We can easily hear the psychologist of "Habit" in that brotherly advice. William had so thoroughly habituated himself to stifling his own desires with self-deforming discipline that he was no longer sure of the difference between holding back and letting go. Henry knew the difference. He wanted to be a writer and accepted the discipline of that craft. And the early stories that he wrote during this difficult period show how acutely aware he was of the pull of this psychological twinship and the need to disengage from it.

[4]

Three of Henry's short stories are particularly revealing because their brevity makes the author's preoccupations nakedly clear: "De Grey: A Romance" (1868), "The Romance of Certain Old Clothes" (1868), and "A Light Man" (1869). They were written when the pull of the attachment between the brothers was intense yet on the verge of being severed. Analysis of these tales shows the younger brother's understanding of their "singular life."

Henry built the De Grey romance with familiar Jamesian elements: a family that "enjoyed great material prosperity," a father who acted in such a manner "as to incur the suspicion of insanity," and a family curse that casts a "shadow of mystery" over the household. He represented William through the character of Paul, George De Grey's son and heir, and cast himself as Margaret, a young woman living as a companion to Mrs. De Grey. Henry was brutally frank in his evaluation of George De Grey, the father of this family. His insane temperament and idleness make him "not to be wished . . . as an example." Paul is urged not to imitate his father but to select a career instead, since "in America, in any walk of life, idleness was indecent." Paul goes abroad and spends his time, like William, "roaming about Europe, in a vague, restless search for his future."[21] On his return, he and Margaret fall in love and activate the De Grey curse. For generations, the first passionate lover of a De Grey son has inexplicably fallen ill and died.

This story expresses an obvious fear of sexual passion, but even more important is the portrait of the sibling bond between Paul and Margaret.* Though they occupy two separate bodies, the boundary between them is vague. When Margaret cries out in terror, Paul hears her though he is miles away. When one is hurt, the other feels the pain. When Margaret is told of the curse, she courageously refuses to be separated from her brother/lover. But this challenge leads to disaster. Instead of preventing the curse, she redirects it, and Paul falls ill. "As she bloomed and prospered, he drooped and languished." At the end, Paul dies despite Margaret's brave attempt to save him. But she does not escape. She becomes insane. James underlined their shared body/twin connection: "The sense had left her mind as completely as his body, and it was likely to come back to one as little as to the other."[22]

Henry was obviously weighing the cost of his intense attachment to William. In "De Grey" he imaginatively posed the troublesome question: Could he survive and still remain one with his brother? If he attempted to rescue his ailing twin, would both fall prey to the curse of illness and insanity? The writing of this story was a decisive step along his own literary path, yet in the tale he expressed his worry that he might condemn himself to paired invalidism with William's submerged artist self. If work output was any measure, Henry "bloomed and prospered" while William "drooped and languished" at the spas. Yet he winced when his twin cried out even though an ocean separated them.

In "The Romance of Certain Old Clothes," Henry presented another view of their "singular life."[23] With William abroad, thanks to Henry's back pain, writing tepid critical letters about Henry's stories and imitatively composing reviews that he expected Henry to edit (not without complaint: "My *schriftstellerisches Selbstgefühl* [writer's sense of self] was naturally rather mangled by the mutilations you had inflicted on my keen article about Feydeau . . ."),[24] Henry was furious. The pages of this romance bristle with barely concealed rage at an older sibling who wastes his opportunities in Europe or who usurps the life of the younger. William first appears in this tale as Bernard, a devalued older brother who is not very "clever," "the wit of the family" having been "apportioned chiefly to his [younger] sisters." While in Europe to study, Bernard accomplishes very little ("without great honor") but does have "a vast deal of pleasure."[25] (Henry's portraits are so thinly disguised that it is remarkable that the only comment William made on the story was to criticize its "trifling" quality.)[26] The main action centers on a pair of sisters, Viola and Perdita. Though "dissimilar in appearance and character," they have "but one bed"

---

*Though not consanguineous, Margaret and Paul stand functionally in a sibling relationship by virtue of having the same maternal protector.

and one objective—to marry the same man. Arthur Lloyd, a friend Bernard has brought back from England (the family lives in Massachusetts, like the Jameses), is a novel attraction that threatens to split the "twins." Arthur chooses Perdita, the younger, and makes Viola bitterly jealous. She is chided by the triumphant Perdita: "Come, sister, . . . he couldn't marry both of us."[27]

But as Henry crafted the story, that is exactly what happens. The singular life continues to the marriage bed, serially rather than coincidentally but no matter, it is with the same husband. James used the wearing of another's clothes as an emblem for usurpation of the other's life. And he acknowledged that the older sibling was more artistic and therefore more suited to the clothes (and the life) that awaited her sister. Viola has the very best taste in the world, and when the cloth for the wedding gown arrives, it matches her coloring better than the bride's. The bride-to-be admits as much with a blend of cunning and innocence. "Blue's your colour, sister, more than mine. . . . It's a pity it's not for you. You'd know what to do with it." Indeed she does know what to do with it. Immediately after the wedding, Perdita is horrified to discover Viola wearing her wedding clothes. Following Perdita's death (after childbirth), Viola takes her sister's place as Arthur's wife. But this undifferentiated twinship (like the love of Margaret and Paul in "De Grey") is destined for a violent end. Perdita's dying wish is to preserve some separateness for herself by preventing her rapacious older sister from wearing her clothes. She makes her husband promise that he will preserve them as a legacy for her daughter.* When Viola forces her husband to give her the key and opens the chest, Perdita's avenging spirit murders her. Henry was unusually graphic (and Gothic) in describing the corpse of the vanquished older sibling. "Her lips were parted in entreaty, in dismay, in agony; and on her bloodless brow and cheeks there glowed the marks of ten hideous wounds from two vengeful ghostly hands."[28] Significantly, soon after this story was written, Henry ordered a suit made of the same cloth used by William's tailor before William went abroad.[29]

"The Romance of Certain Old Clothes" can be read as an allegory of Henry's struggle to individuate from William. William may have had more artistic ability (that is, better taste in clothes) and may have been intended for the artistic career they both desired (that is, the cloth for the wedding gown was more Viola's color), but Henry was furious at William's attempt to usurp his place (that is, to become a successful writer/wear the wedding clothes that symbolized his triumph). As far as Henry was concerned, it was high time they stopped sharing the same bed. Or was it?

On the question of sexual identity, the romances are ambiguous in the

---

*Once again a legacy is a curse.

extreme. What are we to make of the fact that Henry represents himself as a young woman in both? Or that he makes Viola resemble Shakespeare's heroine (in *Twelfth Night,* Viola is a woman dressed as a man)? Or that the lover in "Old Clothes" is merely a pretext for displaying the attachment between two siblings of the same sex? Henry James's early stories can be read as the creation of a young artist who had become painfully aware of himself as a female consciousness masquerading in the body of a man. It is not surprising that the brothers' "singular life" blurred sexual distinctions between them. And it should come as no shock that in Henry's fictive world there is a strong homosexual strand linking him to his brother William.*

In "A Light Man" Henry wrote a story that is transparently homosexual and at times even pornographic. Where else in Henry James's works do we read of one man saying of another, "How I should like to give him for once, a real sensation!"? And where else in the Jamesian corpus do we watch as the orgiastic sensation is masterfully delivered, man to man?

> The remainder of this extraordinary scene I have no power to describe: . . . how I, prompted by the irresistible spirit of my desire to leap astride of his weakness, and ride it hard into the goal of my dreams, cunningly contrived to keep his spirit at the fever point, so that strength, and reason, and resistance should burn themselves out. I shall probably never again have such a sensation as I enjoyed to-night—actually feel a heated human heart throbbing, and turning, and struggling in my grasp; know its pants, its spasms, its convulsions, and its final senseless quiescence.[30]

This story was published in 1869, while Henry was abroad deftly manipulating his parents to keep the money flowing to support his traveling cure. From the outset gender is in question. The title is a reversal of a Browning poem, "A Light Woman," and alludes to a figure who is something other than what she may seem to be to her lover (like Shakespeare's Viola).† The triangle in James's version is all male. An inheritance plays an

---

*Richard Hall ("An Obscure Hurt: The Sexuality of Henry James," *New Republic* 180[1979], no. 17:25–28; no. 18:25–29) has called Leon Edel to task for leaving a "peculiar timidity" at the center of his monumental biography of Henry James (*HJ*). He quite rightly points to a tendency to "wash out the sexual content" of his analysis (particularly in the early volumes) in favor of the theme of rivalry and thus to obscure the fraternal incestuous strivings (whether acted upon or not) that were central to Henry's psychology. Following Edel, Hall believes that William's marriage in 1878 caused a shift in Henry's novels from male to female heroines. This change seems less striking when it is placed in the context of his early stories, which typically represent a female consciousness. From the very outset of his career in his twenties, Henry James's psychological core was ambivalently feminine and fused with his older, more masculine "twin."

†"And I—what I seem to my friend, you see— / What I soon shall seem to his love, you guess. / What I seem to myself, do you ask me? / No hero, I confess" (Robert Browning, "A Light Woman," in *Browning's Men and Women, 1855,* ed. G. E. Hadow [Oxford, 1911], 98).

important role, as it did in the previous two stories. In fact, the orgiastic scene that I have quoted was consciously intended to describe not homosexual intercourse but the effort of a ruthless young man (Maximus) to force his aged benefactor (Frederick Sloane) to put him in his will. (Henry's letters squeezing money from his father's inheritance were written in May 1869 and "A Light Man" was published in July.)

Maximus and his friend Theodore blend qualities that we have already noted in William and Henry. Maximus is at loose ends, plagued by the eternal questions of youth. "What am I? What do I wish? Whither do I tend?" He is also frankly opportunistic, "scanning the horizon for a friendly sail, or waiting for a high tide" to set him "afloat." Theodore rescues him with an invitation to stay at the home of his "eccentric" employer. Like William, Theodore has returned from scientific studies in Germany with the determination to pursue his vocation. But "the inner voice failed him."[31] He decides instead to follow a path set for him by another. He is at work helping Sloane to write his memoirs.

James places Sloane in a fatherly relation to the two young men by his age (he is seventy-two) and as a former friend of Maximus' mother and Theodore's father. In short, the two are brothers imaginatively set in place by James to battle for favor and money from their father, just as William and Henry were actually contesting when the tale was written. Maximus accepts the invitation, declaring unashamedly that at the least he will "obtain food and lodging" while he "invokes the fates."[32]

Theodore's sex is ambiguous. He greets Maximus with "formidable blushes" as his friend "strides into his arms—or at all events into his hands." The richly homoerotic tone of the meeting is projected onto the landscape as the two walk arm in arm from the town past a lake "lapping and gurgling in the darkness" as it offers "its broad white bosom to the embrace of the dark fraternal hills."[33]

Sloane has qualities reminiscent of Henry James, Sr. Besides being old, he is rich, in ill health, and "fancies himself as a philosopher." Henry has a harsh judgment to pass on this side of Sloane's life. In his view, "his mind is haunted by a hundred dingy . . . theological phantasms." What is worse, "he has never loved anyone but himself."[34]*

Sloane is ambiguously feminine. His library is "a sort of a female study." He is also "depraved," "unclean," and "immoral"—not in the fashion of "a *viveur*," but because "he's of a feminine turn." He has retired

---

*The elder Henry James's entire speculative life stood in judgment here. By 1869 he had published all but one of his major theological works, declaring that redemption depended on the transcendence of selfishness. From his son's perspective (sharper here because it is veiled in fiction), though Henry, Sr., urged the abandonment of self in theory, he never loved anyone *but* himself, and distorted his sons' lives by chasing after his theological phantasms.

to his country house and for the past ten years has entertained "an unbroken series of favourites, *protégés,* and heirs presumptive." Each, however, has made "some fatally false movement," and now the field is clear for Theodore and Maximus. Once again Henry constructed a plot with siblings as blushing lovers who fight to get into the same bed. This time the homosexual intention is blatant. Sloane plays his sadomasochistic part to perfection. When the new arrival fills in for Theodore, who has fallen ill, and reads and gossips with Sloane, the old man gives him "a venerable grin" and declares, "Max,—you must let me call you Max—you're the most delightful man I ever knew." This time it is Max that blushes. Sloane pleads with his new beloved: "I wish very much that I could get you to love me as well as you do poor Theodore." He wheedles and moans, "You'll not get tired of me and want to go away?" Sloane then turns on Theodore, his former favorite, and treats him with "brutality." Maximus senses that Sloane enjoys being treated the same way, so he makes sure that he is "beaten" and "bullied" and "contradicted." The old widower is "vastly thankful."[35]

When Maximus concludes that his money troubles would be over if he married, he says, "My only complaint of Mr. Sloane is, that instead of an old widower, he's not an old widow (or I a young maid), so that I might marry him." The story reaches a climax when Max threatens to desert Sloane unless the widower wills him all of his money. But the will gets destroyed and Sloane dies before he can execute another. Neither brother wins. Rather than destroying each other (as in "Old Clothes"), in this denouement the brothers declare their love. Theodore admits, "I loved you even as my rival." In spite of all the sadomasochistic byplay and blushing affection that has taken place, Maximus replies, "I don't understand the feeling between men."[36] His tone is unconvincing; he most certainly was not speaking authentically either for himself or for the author. Henry James imaginatively understood homosexual love all too well.

In later life Henry would retire to his country house at Rye, like Sloane, and entertain a series of young male favorites like Theodore and Maximus, the creations of his fraternal youth.

15

An Ontological Window

I may one day get a glimpse of things through the ontological window. At present it is walled up.

—William James, 1867

"It was a dull life for a growing boy, and a duller life for a young man grown, but I never knew it. I was perfectly happy." He spoke of his father at some length. . . . Mr. Pickering had been, to my sense, a cold egotist, unable to conceive of any larger vocation for his son than to become a mechanical reflection of himself. "I know I've been strangely brought up," said my friend, "and that the result is something grotesque; but my education, piece by piece, in detail, became one of my father's personal habits. . . ."

—Henry James, Jr., 1874

[1]

WILLIAM WORRIED more about dividing from his father than from his brother. Having been bred on the elder Henry's theologic discourse, he chose philosophy rather than fiction as his arena. In 1868 he had taken his opponent's measure from the comfortable distance of Germany. This time the older man did not hover on the periphery (as in Figure 5), he lustily joined in the fight. "I am sure," he declared, "I have something better to tell you than you will be able to learn from all Germany—at least all scientific Germany. So urge me hard to your own profit."[1] Both combatants gave a good account of themselves. The apparent topic was abstruse, Swedenborg's ontology (Henry, Sr., had just published his thoughts in *The North American Review*).[2] William criticized his father's logic and Henry said his son didn't know what he was talking about. Both were right. And when the dust settled, David had not slain Goliath, but father and son remained standing in a philosophic bear hug. Though they argued about the elder Henry's theory of creation,

236

the correspondence can be read as a covert struggle over fusion and individuation. Was man really separate from God? If freedom of the will was merely an illusion, as Henry seemed to imply, then the attempt of a son to break free from his beloved father/Creator was hopeless.[3]

William opened with a challenge from Berlin: "I must confess that the darkness which to me has always hung over what you have written on these subjects is hardly at all cleared up." He knew his father's habits of mind, and was sure that he would be accused of responding with the "head" rather than the "heart" and of confusing the material world with the spiritual, so he was prepared to parry these thrusts. "My questions, I know belong to the Understanding, and I suppose deal entirely with the natural constitution of things; but I find it impossible to step out from them into relation with spiritual facts. . . ." He chided Henry for using technical philosophic language so loosely that his ideas seemed "devoid of significance." If he had meant to write an argument instead of a prayer, Henry had to be held logically accountable and not allowed to retreat to the high ground of private revelation. William lunged, aiming at the heart of his father's theory of creation. "I cannot logically understand *your* theory."[4]

He was troubled by Henry's use of the word "phenomenal" to describe the "illusion" of complete separation between Creator and creature. "You posit first a phenomenal Nature in which the *alienation* is produced (but phenomenal to what? to the already unconsciously existing creature?), and from this effected alienation a *real* movement of return follows. But how can the real movement have its rise in the phenomenal?"[5]

The problem was verbal. Instead of describing a substantial or "real" world underlying the phenomenal world of "ideas" that is all that man can know (the more conventional usage), the elder Henry bent the words into neoplatonic shape with quite different meaning. The "real world" for him was not a material as opposed to a mental world, but rather a spiritual as opposed to a natural world. Following Swedenborg, he believed that man knows the spiritual world only through the natural world. And to acquire the spiritual knowledge communicated by sense and science, man is dependent on revelation. Here was the core of William's confusion. It was the spiritual world that had substance or reality for his father, and it was the material or natural world that was the world of appearances.* For

---

*This position is perfectly clear in the following passage in his father's *Christianity the Logic of Creation*, written in 1857 but not yet closely studied by William. (It first appeared on his reading list, along with *The Nature of Evil* and *The Church of Christ Not an Ecclesiasticism*, under the date 1870 [MH].) "The NATURAL WORLD, *which is the world of appearances or phenomena,* PRESUPPOSES THE SPIRITUAL WORLD, *which is that of substance or reality,* AND IS UTTERLY UNINTELLIGIBLE WITHOUT SOME LIGHT OR 'REVELATION' THENCE DERIVED" (*CLC*, 26, cited in *PHJ*, 113).

Henry, Sr., "real" movement is a creative spiritual process of redemption or return to God. That "reality" is prior to phenomenal experience (nature) and supersedes it. Given those assumptions, the elder Henry's assertion that "real" movement can develop from the "phenomenal" is not inconsistent, though it offers ample opportunity for confusion.

William's misinterpretation enabled him to strike a more serious blow. He knew that the protection of human freedom was one of father's central preoccupations. As Henry, Sr., had formulated the matter in 1863, the "total problem of Philosophy is, to reconcile freedom with dependence; or to show how finite may be incessantly vivified by inifinite, without necessary inflation to the lower inter st or necessary collapse to the higher."[6] In order for man to have freedom, he saw, there must be a discontinuity between the Creator and his creature. Otherwise human action would constantly be defined by its divine source. If father was wrong in describing a "real" movement from a phenomenal base (according to William's usage), then, William argued, "creation is the very arbitrary one you inveigh against; and the whole process is a mere circle of the creator described within his own being and returning to the starting-point."[7] In short, if there is no clear separation between Creator and creature (or father and son), then Henry's entire theory of creation collapses.*

This was no minor quibble. Both father and son realized that if Mr. James's theology collapsed, twenty-five years of ideological construction tumbled down with it. William misinterpreted his father's meaning and held firm to his materialist position: "Of course it is impossible to attempt to imagine the *way* of creation, but wherever from an absolute first a second appears, *there* it must be;—and it must be magical, for if in the second there be anything coequal or coeval with the first, it becomes pantheism."[8] He was obviously talking here about creation as an act, *ex nihilo,* in time and space (creation of natural theology = "formation"), which his father explicitly disowned in earlier writings that William had not yet studied.†

---

*Ultimately, for the elder Henry James (following Swedenborg), the existence of a creature separate from the Creator is true by definition. It requires no proof. "To create means to give being or communicate life to what assuredly is not oneself. . . . The creature must be absolutely and unchangeably himself, must possess identity, or real and conscious distinction from his creator: otherwise creation in any honest sense of the word must confess itself an unqualified sham, and tumble off into the bottomless abyss of Pantheism" (*S&S,* 440–501, cited in *PHJ,* 128).

†When William edited *The Literary Remains of the Late Henry James* fourteen years later, he understood his father's distinction between "formation" and "creation" and was able to give him a fairer hearing. "Creation is thus made up of two stages, the first of which is mere scaffolding to the second, which is the final work. . . . On the whole, 'formation' is the word he often applies to the first stage, and 'redemption' to the second" (*LRLHJ,* 18).

Father was quick to see the misunderstanding. He defended himself vigorously from the charge of pantheism, then counterattacked: ". . . it is very evident to me that your trouble in understanding it [his paper 'The Ontology of Swedenborg'] arises *mainly* from the purely scientific cast of your thought just at present, and the temporary blight exerted thence upon your metaphysic wit." William spoke as if he believed in a reality or material nature underlying sense impressions. This belief his father labeled an "instinct" of the natural mind which scientists follow thoughtlessly.

Henry pressed his advantage to skewer science in general, running through a former friendly ally: ". . . the man of science admits that every thing he observes by any sense is strictly phenomenal or relative to every thing else; but he is not disconcerted by this fact, because he holds instinctively to an *absolute substance* in which all these fleeting things inhere, this substance being Nature. . . . The difference between the philosopher and the man of science, between the man who *reflects* and the man who simply *observes,* is, that the former outgrows his intellectual instincts or disavows the bondage of sense, and attains to the exercise of free thought." The conclusion was inescapable (to him): "while we disbelieve in creation, we are . . . the dupes of our scientific activity. . . ." If William had any doubts about the target of these general remarks on the defects of scientific intelligence, they vanished with the final hit: "Now here it seems to me is exactly where you are as yet intellectually: in this scientific or puerile stage of progress."9

[2]

Henry might call him puerile, but in return William could call his father's philosophy irrelevant. Oliver Wendell Holmes, Jr., was his metaphysical confidant: "If the end of all is to be that we must take our sensations as simply given or as preserved by natural selection for us, and interpret this rich and delicate overgrowth of ideas, moral, artistic, religious and social, as a mere mask, a tissue spun in happy hours by creative individuals and adopted by other men in the interests of their sensations,—how long is it going to be well for us not to 'let on' all we know to the public?" Knowing how vital religion had been to his father's recovery, he asked Wendell to keep his letter private: "I'd rather my father should not see it."10

Father may have tolerated William's skepticism more easily than the imagery directed at his amputated limb. "Now ought not we (supposing we become indurated sensationalists) to begin to smite the old, hip and thigh. . . . If God is dead or at least irrelevant, ditto everything pertaining to the 'Beyond.'" What must have hurt Mr. James even more than this verbal attempt to complete the dismemberment of his youth was his favorite son's confident assertion: "It seems exceedingly improbable that any new *religious* genius should arise in these days to open a fresh highway for the masses who have outgrown the old beliefs." Much more was at stake here than metaphysics. The level of argument dipped from the elevated plane of metaphysics to the mundane yet critical ground of family finance. William needed more money for the baths, and a response to his request was woven into Henry's metaphysical reply. To illustrate his point that it is through the process of spiritual creation that man is raised up to the level of God, Henry wrote, "But how shall the creature command the necessary resources for this end? He is in himself absolutely without funds, being as yet utterly unconscious or non-existent, so that unless his creator is rich and gracious enough to make him a loan by making over *his* existence to him as it were, or allowing him to appropriate it as freely as if it were his own, he will never be able to bring himself up to the required level."[11]

The metaphor of paternal funds borrowed or appropriated succinctly summarized the earlier struggle between Henry and William of Albany and the current tension between Henry and William, his son. Borrowed or misappropriated capital was essential for the younger of the pair in both generations, but to what ends? And at what price? The elder Henry was not so rich but was more "gracious" than *his* father had been. Or so he must have thought, as he renewed the invalid's letter of credit. Like the Creator, he would allow his son illusory independence to discover his limits.

A month later William rebutted with his own financial metaphor. He appreciated his father's theology as "a history," finding it "beautiful and acceptable." But as a logical argument it failed to persuade him. He didn't see how "you ever come out with more than you put in, namely the sole Creator." And if the Creator gets his own way (a scientific son), the loan is not a sign of paternal generosity, as his father suggested, but an obligation incurred because of God's (and father's) superior power. "He, in the last resort, bears the whole expense of the operation."[12]

William was too affectionate a son to let the matter rest while the two of them were in opposition. Throughout he wavered between challenge (and misinterpretation), on one side, and protestations of affection and repeated admission of his limitations, on the other. "These are points . . . which . . . will doubtless make you smile at my stupidity. . . . You probably now see the state of my mind, and . . . it will now be easier than before for you to set me right." Though he might want to smite "the old, hip and thigh," he was sensitive to his father's plight as a publicly disregarded prophet. "You live in such mental isolation that I cannot help often feeling bitterly at the thought that you must see in even your own children strangers to what you consider the best part of yourself." Affection made him wish their beliefs were the same, that he and his father could be as one, standing on the same ground, rather than torn apart by the logic of creation. "But," he ruefully admitted, "it is a matter in which one's wishes are of little influence. . . ."13

[3]

Despite the deep affection and respect of the combatants, the duel would end tragically. Each seemed driven to pull away and hold on tight at the same time. Henry urgently required his son to succeed in a worldly profession—science—as he had not. Yet he also wanted him to appreciate his religious experience and validate his unique brand of Swedenborgian theology. William needed desperately to detach himself from his father, yet he worried about Henry's isolation. His pursuit of art would deprive his father of a scientific son. His pursuit of science cultivated a skepticism that threatened the religious belief that Henry held essential to life and sanity.

Where logic might have separated them by clarifying their metaphysical differences, the son's conclusions tended in the very opposite direction. For if William succeeded in proving creation a magical event wholly encompassed by the Creator, what had he gained but a logical proof that it was impossible for him to act independently? At least the elder Henry argued for an illusory independence. William ended up proving that he could have no separateness at all.

William knew that his father's 1844 crises had opened the "ontological window" for him. "I cannot attain," he admitted, "to any such inexpugnable testimony of consciousness to my spiritual reality as that you speak of, and that must be a decisive moment in determining one's attitude towards such problems."14 Here, at least, was one impediment to fusion. He had not had an experience like his father's crisis. But even that barrier would dissolve. In the fall of 1872, William broke down as his father had done.* When his moment arrived, the ontological window that had been walled up lay shattered around him.

There are many similarities between the elder Henry's crisis of 1844 and

---

*The date of this "crisis" can be fixed through internal evidence. William James referred to it in a letter (William James to Robertson James, April 26, 1874, typescript, Vaux) as a philosophical crisis associated with anxiety and despair which had taken place shortly before and during Robertson's last visit to Cambridge. Robertson and his bride had visited the family during their honeymoon. As they were married November 18, 1872, the breakdown occurred in the fall of 1872.

his son's a quarter of a century later. Each breakdown took place when the sufferer was seeking health and resolution of a prolonged vocational conflict. Though both were in their thirties when the crises occurred, neither breakdown was made fully public until its subject was in his sixties.* Henry proclaimed to all the world that his crisis was the basis of his spiritual understanding. William, by contrast, did not acknowledge his crisis as his own, but rather presented it as that of a French correspondent who supplied case material for his lecture "The Sick Soul," in the Gifford series.† Propriety may have dictated anonymity, but it was emblematic that in the retelling, William made it somebody else's experience and directed the reader via a footnote to the elder Henry. The breakdown was more his father's than his own.

The crisis tales begin differently. Henry pretended good humor while William admitted his earlier gloomy state.

HENRY:
I remember I felt especially hopeful in the prosecution of my task . . . my health was good, my spirits cheerful. . . .

WILLIAM:
Whilst in this state of philosophic pessimism and general depression of spirits about my prospects . . .

For both, the "other" whose presence personified what was most to be feared was a seated figure. Henry saw the sinister presence in religious terms. His son described a natural rather than a supernatural presence—an inmate of an asylum rather than a squatting devil.

HENRY:
. . . it was . . . to be accounted for by some damned shape squatting invisible to me . . . raying out from his fetid personality influences fatal to life.

WILLIAM:
. . . there arose in my mind the image of an epileptic patient whom I had seen in the asylum, a black-haired youth with greenish skin, entirely idiotic, who used to sit all day on one of the benches, or rather shelves against the wall, with his knees drawn up against his chin, and the coarse gray under-shirt, which was his only garment,

*Henry's first full public disclosure appeared in *Society the Redeemed Form of Man* (1879), and William's in *The Varieties of Religios Experience* (1902).

†A chance remark to a friend who later recorded the acknowledgment in print and a footnote referring the reader to the elder Henry James's book for "another case of fear equally sudden" were the two public links to William himself (Theodore Fluornoy, *William James* [Geneva, 1911], 149n; *VRE*, 161n).

drawn over them enclosing his entire figure. He sat there like a sort
of sculptured Egyptian cat or Peruvian mummy, moving nothing but
his black eyes and looking absolutely non-human.

Each was terrified by this seated figure, but the imagery emphasizes
important differences between them. William's is the imagery of an artist
and a physician—naturalistic, concrete, based on a specific clinical experience that was recaptured through sculptural similes. Henry's image is
vague and more grotesque, so that the reader's imagination fills in the
features of the diabolic shape. Produced by influences raying from the
spirit world, Henry's crisis was frankly supernatural. William couched the
loss of self-control in terms of fate—a turn of the wheel of fortune rather
than an influx from another world. *"That shape am I,* I felt, potentially.
Nothing that I possess can defend me against that fate, if the hour for it
should strike for me as it struck for him." For William the menacing
"other" blended a feared possibility—insanity—and a present actuality—
the state of invalidism from which he watched passively, implacably, while
his peers moved on in life.

Both father and son were overwhelmed by feelings of panic, but this
experience, too, was described in quite different terms. Henry spoke of a
regression, a spiritual fall from adulthood to infancy, while his son called
attention to a material change of the body, familiar ground for a self-
scrutinizing invalid physician.

HENRY:	WILLIAM:
The thing had not lasted ten sec-onds before I felt myself a wreck; that is reduced from a state of firm, vigorous, joyful manhood to one of almost helpless infancy.	. . . it was as if something hitherto solid within my breast gave way en-tirely, and I became a mass of quivering fear. . . . I awoke morn-ing after morning with a horrible dread in the pit of my stomach.

Though William was incapacitated by a surge of feelings of dependency,
he did not label them so precisely. The difference may be accounted for by
William's limited experience. He had no children yet, while Henry had
two infant sons below the age of two when he was overcome. The helplessness of infancy was vivid to Henry but remote from his son. William
formulated his helplessness as a fear of being without a protector from the
terrors of the night. "For months," he admitted, "I was unable to go out

into the dark alone." The child within the grown man was crying out, but it took a father to call him by name.

Mary James figures prominently in both crisis tales. Both father and son polarized their anxious world—the squatting horror at one end and Mary James at the other. For Henry, with his frankly acknowledged childlike feelings, she promised maternal succor. By contrast, William saw his mother as the most prominent person in his world who failed to recognize the awful truth personified by the sinister, implacable inmate. Initially both resisted the impulse to run to her for help, but only William kept to himself to the end.

HENRY:
I felt the greatest desire to run incontinently to the foot of the stairs and shout for help to my wife . . . by an immense effort I controlled these frenzied impulses, and determined not to budge from my chair till I had recovered my lost self-possession. . . . I resolved to abandon the vain struggle, and communicate without more ado what seemed my sudden burden of inmost implacable unrest to my wife.

WILLIAM:
In general I dreaded to be left alone. I remember wondering how other people could live, how I myself had ever lived, so unconscious of that pit of insecurity beneath the surface of life. My mother in particular, a very cheerful person, seemed to me a perfect paradox in her unconsciousness of danger, which you may well believe I was very careful not to disturb by revelation of my own state of mine.

Mary James as wife and mother promised protection and care for a self overwhelmed by diabolic influx. Father initially resisted while struggling unsuccessfully to recover himself. William also held back from telling her of his revelation, but he saw himself as protecting her rather than being tempted by the comfort of her maternal sympathy. This thirty-year-old bachelor, who was still so enmeshed in his family and had not yet made any attempt to support himself, dared not formulate his terror in the dependent terms that were so vivid to his father.

William reported his crisis in a book on religious experience, but at best it was a pale shadow of his father's conversion. He himself saw it in terms of mental pathology. Religion served him as a talisman that afforded a magic cure. Henry's crisis brought him into contact with a religious realm that changed his life. William's crisis increased his understanding.

HENRY:
. . . within two or three months of my catastrophe, I felt sure I had never caught a glimpse of truth. In-

WILLIAM:
After this the universe was changed for me altogether. . . . It was like a revelation: and although the imme-

deed, an ugly suspicion had more than once forced itself upon me that I had never really wished the truth, but only to ventillate my own ability in discovering it. . . . Truth must *reveal itself*. . . . For truth is God, . . . and who shall pretend to comprehend that great and adorable perfection?[15]

diate feelings passed away, the experience had made me sympathic with the morbid feelings of others ever since. I have always thought that this experience of melancholia of mine had a religious bearing.[16]

How remote from Henry's passionate avowal of "God's adorable perfection" was his son's "melancholia" with "a religious bearing"! True, his crisis had shown him the illusory quality of selfhood, and after that revelation he could comprehend the starting point of his father's theology. But that was where he stopped. His was a halfway covenant that admitted him to sacraments that were rituals without belief. "The fear was so invasive and powerful that if I had not clung to scripture-texts like 'The eternal God is my refuge,' etc., 'I am the resurrection and the life,' etc., I think I should have grown insane."[17] Even this detail was imitative. In his introduction to *The Literary Remains of the Late Henry James*, William recalled his father's habit of murmuring the Psalms of David to himself by the hour when he was depressed.[18] What for Henry commenced as an effort to make restitution to William of Albany became, through a lifetime of spiritual contemplation, a basis for contact with the divine. For such a man, repeating the Psalms was an act of devotion. Not so for the son he had forced into science. When overwhelmed by panic, William found those verses "therapeutic" rather than inspired, and his terror a symptom of melancholia rather than a sign of grace. Whereas Henry's crisis brought him closer to God, William's crisis brought him closer to his father.

[4]

Four drawings from his notebooks provide visual evidence of William's crisis. The first, a self-portrait, was obviously drawn while he stared at himself in a mirror (Figure 20). He is dressed in a coat and tie—a nascent professional—and his mouth is set and solemn. The look in his eyes seems to pose the question "Who am I?" while at the same time he appears fearful of hearing the answer. The second, a cartoon of the same frock-coated self, is drawn as a squatting figure with knees drawn up, like the frightful idiot of his crisis (Figure 21). The eyes stare in horror and the hair appears about to stand on end. The questioning, uneasy facade of the

20. WILLIAM JAMES, SELF-PORTRAIT
The problem with the man is less what act he shall now choose to do, than what being he shall now resolve to become. —W. James, 1890

21. TERROR
In civilized life, in particular, it has at last become possible for large numbers of
people to pass from the cradle to the grave without ever having had a pang of
genuine fear. Many of us need an attack of mental disease to teach us the meaning
of the word.   —W. James, 1890

22. EGYPTIAN HEAD
He sat there like a sort of sculptured Egyptian cat or Peruvian mummy. . . . —W. James, 1902

23. WILLIAM JAMES IN DESPAIR

It is in these same castles of despair that we find the strongest examples of . . . people who think they have committed "the unpardonable sin" and are lost forever, who crouch and cringe and slink from notice and are unable to speak aloud or look us in the eye. —W. James, 1890

earlier study has given way to panic. Opposite is an Egyptian head with a timeless gaze and a sinister grin creating an impression of the uncanny (Figure 22). Perhaps this was like the image William recalled in the description quoted earlier. The final drawing shows William seated in an attitude of despair, his head hanging, his shoulders drooped (Figure 23). Above is a caption, "HERE I AND SORROW SIT."* There is a curious slip here. Instead of an *N*, William wrote an *M,* so that it reads, "HERE I AMD SORROW SIT." He never added "M.D." to his signature, but that sign hung depressingly over his head. Having answered the question "Who am I?" with an affirmative "My father's son," he remained stalled in depression into the 1870s. His brother Henry had found his calling. His father had found his God. Yet William still lingered indecisively amid the lost Atlantis of art, the necessity of science, and the allure of philosophy.

*The reference is to Shakespeare's King John, III.i.73, a popular theme for illustrators in this period. I am grateful to Esther Dotson for directing me to this source.

16

Two Brothers at War and a Sister at Home

We were . . . the only two of his children who dared fight through the war for the defense of the family and the only two who attempted while very young to earn their own living.

—Garth Wilkinson James, 1882

[1]

THOUGH JUST three and four years younger than William, Garth and Robertson seemed to belong to a different generation. William and Henry were barely engaged by the Civil War. Like their sister, Alice, they stayed at home. The two younger James boys were borne on a crest of abolitionist enthusiasm into uniform. While the older brothers came of age slowly under the protective cover of ill health and parental bounty, the younger pair was forced into premature manhood by battle, so that this minor theme in the lives of William and Henry became the central chapter, the climax of their work lives. Thereafter uncannily they reenacted the plot laid out in their father's early stories. Like so many of the elder Henry's boyhood friends, in spite of "brilliant promise" and "romantic charm," both younger sons "ended badly."[1]

Garth Wilkinson and Robertson were to bear the mark and the burden of unregenerate prodigality, the shadow of their father's wild youth. Wilky, fiscally expansive and chronically in debt, ultimately went bankrupt. Robertson, an alcoholic, was perpetually in search of a life's work that he would never find. Tragically, Wilky completed the symmetry of his father's battle with William James of Albany. Before he died in 1882, Henry James, Sr., would draw a will that cut Wilky off as his own father had cut him off fifty years earlier. The older prodigal's rationale was financial rather than moral (he believed that loans made to Wilky in his lifetime already accounted for his share of the inheritance), but the impact was just as devastating. Predictably, the disinherited son branded his father "cowardly" for such a "death stab." He, too, vowed to break the will as he knew his father "broke his own father's will for his own benefit" half a century earlier.[2]* Like a family curse, the sins of this father seemed inexorably destined to be visited on his two younger sons.

Their secondary place in the James family structure was established early. In an autobiographical fragment written in his maturity, Robertson James mused: "I never remember being told anything extraordinary about my babyhood." With Jamesian subtlety he characterized his forlorn infant self: "I often like to contemplate myself as a baby and wonder if I was really as little appreciated as I fully remember feeling at that time." It was tempting to look at all children as if they, too, felt that they had been born into an alien world. "I never see an infant now without discerning in their usually solemn countenance a conviction that they are on their guard and in a more or less hostile surrounding."† He remembered himself as a miserable boy who indirectly blamed his parents for his unhappiness. "However that may be in my own case, at a very early age the problems of life began to press upon [me] in such an unnatural way and I developed such an ability for feeling hurt and wounded that I became quite convinced by the time I was twelve years old that I was a foundling." This picture of a melancholy childhood was relieved by the memory of his "never yet forgotten" Irish nurse, whose sparkling green brooch made "something wondrous from heaven" awake within him. He had been so touched by her that even as a man in his sixties, he could still be moved to "weep inwardly" by the play of light on a green crystal. But that comforting recollection was unique. For a time Robertson shared a bedroom with his mother's sister, Aunt Kate, but she did little to relieve his gloom. Rather he was sure she had "hurt" him with her "mandatory ways," contributing to a firm conviction that "a mother does wrong to confide her offspring recklessly to others than herself."[3]

In old age Robertson would study his palms for "portents" and "omens." Finding his "line of Fortune" defined but "badly broken" on the left and "not half so distinct and badly broken" on the right, he would conclude, "Destiny of itself gave me bad fortune and . . . with my own right hand I made that Destiny worse."[4]

---

*This is the only evidence that I have found that explicitly indicates that the James children knew of their father's testamentary battle. And it is not at all clear that Wilky knew why his father had been cut off. Thus the question of his brother Henry's understanding is still in doubt (see pp. 65–66).

†It is remarkable how well this description fits Melanie Klein's object relations theory.

Wilky had been conceived during his father's 1844 crisis, and he was born in New York City the following summer. He remained the youngest James son for barely thirteen months before Robertson was born. We can catch a glimpse of the impact of the new baby from Mary James. By her own report, Wilky was "about to be shoved off" a scant two weeks after his brother's birth. He "took at once into his own hand the redress of his grievances which he seems to think are manifold, and has become emphatically the *ruling* spirit in the nursery." Perhaps Wilky's "*ruling* spirit" contributed to Robertson's sense of being born into a hostile world. What struck the bemused mother was "his strength of arm or of will." Instead of recognizing that the older child needed something more from her, Mary James "too often left [him] to fight his own battles." These were Mary's own words, so she obviously felt uneasy about letting Wilky fend for himself so soon. Her justification is intriguing, foreshadowing as it does her readiness to reward illness in her children when they became older. "Poor little soul!" she sympathized, "my pity I believe would be more strongly excited for him were he less able or ready to take his own part."[5] Fortunately, Wilky grew into an appealing youngster with a gift for attracting friends. A tendency toward overweight seemed inevitably coupled in the family's mind with his sociable nature. Thus in later years Alice would report (not without a hint of envy) that "Wilkie is as fat and good natured as ever and seems to have more friends if possible than ever."[6]

They were also subject to their father's educational enthusiasms. Unlike the older boys, they never became central to their father's quest for self-vindication. Wilky was placed in a Swiss boarding school with William when the family lived in Switzerland in 1855. Barely two months after they arrive in Geneva, this school that Henry, Sr., had extolled in a laudatory letter to the *Tribune* suddenly seemed to him "over-rated" and no longer a reason to stay in Switzerland. So they moved to London, where the boys had a private tutor and a series of governesses. When the crash of 1857 cut their income, the family abandoned a lavish Paris apartment (they had left London in 1856) and moved to Boulogne, where the boys attended a school with the children of local artisans. Robertson remembered this "College Municipale and its stone vaulted ceiling" as one more step in his descent. Both he and Wilky, he recalled, had "failed to take prizes." By contrast, the more "fortunate scholars" got "some symbol of merit which *we* did not get." He observed wryly: "The luck had begun to break early!"[7] After fifteen months in Newport (1858–59), where their older brother's attachment to William Morris Hunt and painting threatened their father's plan, the younger sons were once again dragged along to Europe. Robertson's own painter's eye was beginning to develop, and he remembered with pleasure the "daily growing revelations of heavenly landscape in

Switzerland," with the "purple Jura Mountains" rising in the distance and in the foreground the "Junction of the Soane and the Rhone . . . two streams running side by side—one yellow with mud and the other clear and clean and refusing to be defiled."[8] This time he and Wilky were sent off to a boarding school outside of the city while William, young Henry, and Alice remained with their parents in Geneva. Wilky felt the separation keenly, and wrote: "Father, you cannot imagine how much we miss you. . . . I have a sort of unprotected feeling (not physically so, but mentally)—I feel as if there was something missing—but I have no doubt it does an immense deal of good to both sides to have occasionally these little separations."[9] He had obviously caught his father's moralizing tone and was determined to be a brave boy. He was then fourteen.

Before returning to America, in the summer of 1860, Wilky was bitten by "a serpent." The frightening experience did have one good effect: the bite "on the forefinger of the right hand" caused so much swelling that he couldn't write and was therefore excused from the last two weeks of homework.[10] Unenthusiastic about reading, Wilky was probably relieved. William spoofed his brother's distaste (unique in this literary family) when he drew a picture of him lying asleep on his bed above the caption, "G. W. James hard at work (reading)" (Figure 24).

[2]

When the family returned to Newport in the fall of 1860 for William's painting experiment with Hunt, the younger boys were promptly sent away from the family again. Of all the ventures in Robertson's and Wilky's education, their parents' decision to send them to the Sanborn School in Concord was the most fateful. Their father's graphic letter describing the scene at the Sanborn School gives witness once again to his lavish style, his millennial hopefulness, and his disregard for practical affairs. It also emphasizes the dark place the younger boys held in his imagination. It would be impossible to tell from his beautiful description of their beginning at Concord that the schoolmaster to whose care he consigned them had actively helped to finance and organize John Brown's raid on Harpers Ferry, and had nearly been arrested for his part in it. Innocently, it seemed, Henry and Mary exposed their fifteen- and sixteen-year-old sons to the violent wing of the abolitionist movement, thinking all the while that what lay in store for them was merely a transcendentalist venture in coeducation.

Significantly, Henry began his letter on a morbid note: "I buried two of my children yesterday—at Concord, Mass." He pulled back in midsentence from this undefended death wish to the posture of bereaved

24. GARTH WILKINSON JAMES "READING"
My experience is what I agree to attend to.   —W. James, 1890

parent: "and feel so heartbroken this morning that I shall need to adopt two more instantly to supply their place." This paternal stance matches Robertson's lifelong feeling of being unwanted. Were these younger sons really so expendable that the gap created by their "burial" at Concord could be filled by two others "instantly adopted" to take their place? The "bereaved" father proceeded: "Mary and I trotted forth last Wednesday, bearing Wilky and Bob in our arms to surrender them to the famous Mr. Sanborn." Henry chortled over the imagined temptations put in his sons' path by the coeducational venture.

> We asked to see Miss Waterman, one of the teachers quartered in the house, in order to say to her how much we should thank her if she would occasionally put out any too lively spark she might see fall on the expectant tinder of my poor boys' bosoms; but Miss W. herself proved of so siliceous a quality on inspection—with round tender eyes, young, fair and womanly—that I saw in her only new danger and no promise of safety. My present conviction is that a general conflagration is inevitable, ending in the total combustion of all I hold dear on that spot. Yet I can't but felicitate our native land that such magnificent experiments in education go on among us.

Frank Sanborn had started his transcendentalist-inspired school in 1855 with the encouragement of Ralph Waldo Emerson. Naturally, James visited his friend before leaving his sons to their coeducational fate. He playfully cast the venerable Emerson as a pagan god, a "wondrous Pan so glistening with dewdrops." The schoolmaster would not allow them to leave without seeing the experiment in action, and the irrepressible Mr. James surveyed the scene with his characteristic millennial vision. "Out into the field beside his house Sanborn incontinently took us to show how his girls and boys perform together their worship of Hygeia. It was a glimpse into that new world wherein dwelleth righteousness and which is full surely fast coming upon our children and our children's children; and I could hardly keep myself, as I saw my children's eyes drink in the mingled work and play of the inspiring scene, from shouting out a joyful Nunc Dimittis." "Nunc dimittis," the Gospel's affirmation that the Messiah had come (Luke 2:29–32), would have been a suitable ending for the letter. But James went on to repeat once again a somber death wish for his less favored boys. His son Henry would cite this letter as an example of his father's "irrepressible" optimism, "fed so little by sense of things as they were or are." We can also read it as an injunction directing Wilky and Bob to an unhappy fate. "The short of the story is that we left them . . . hoping that they wouldn't die any of these cold winter days, before the parental breast could get there to warm them back to life or cheer them on to a better."[11]

Sanborn's school was a pleasant place, with ample time for picnics at Esterbrook Farm, bathing and skating at Walden Pond, weekly dances, and camping on Mount Monadnock for a week at a time (unchaperoned). Whether the school prepared aspiring students for college adequately was another matter.*

Though Sanborn's teaching methods were innovative, his political views were far more influential in shaping the lives of the younger James sons. Early in his career at Harvard, Sanborn had been drawn to Theodore Parker, the fiery abolitionist minister whom Emerson had labeled "the Savonarola of the Transcendentalists."† When John Brown came to Boston in 1857 to seek support for a plan to foment a slave rebellion, Sanborn, who was the secretary of the Massachusetts Kansas Aid Society, was the first man he sought out. Brown persuaded the young abolitionist of the need for more violent action. A Cromwellian blend of soldier and deacon, the Bible-quoting farmer attracted many Bostonians with his tales of "Bleeding Kansas." He convinced them that he was "an instrument of God" in the war on slavery. Six Bostonians—the Reverend Theodore Parker, Dr. Samuel Gridley Howe, Gerrit Smith, the Reverend Thomas Wentworth Higginson, George Luther Stearns, and Franklin Sanborn—formed a secret cell to raise funds and help him formulate a plan to encourage slaves to flee into the Alleghenies. Though they had all been moved to violent rhetoric by events in the 1850s, Brown moved them by stealth toward violent action at Harpers Ferry.‡ A romantic revolutionary,

---

*Nathaniel Hawthorne's wife, Sophia, wrote an irate letter to the headmaster questioning the value of the entire transcendental enterprise for her son, Julian. "I actually dread the coming term, because, instead of solemn study and serious, thoughtful mental effort, it is as if Julian, in this last important year, were again about to plunge into the dissipations of society—all sorts of sport, flirtations, trifling, weary sittings up of nights, reluctant risings in the morning; jaded spirits, plans for fun—everything except a brave grappling with knowledge, as a school should be" (Maurice Bassan, *Hawthorne's Son: The Life and Literary Career of Julian Hawthorne* [Columbus: Ohio State University Press, 1970], 28). She consulted James Russell Lowell, who agreed that Sanborn's "aesthetic views of teaching" were not geared to prepare a student for Harvard's entrance examinations.

†Grandson of a Minuteman (the musket from the Battle of Lexington hung over his desk, a constant reminder of the place that force had played in the founding of this country), Parker stirred huge audiences (5,000 on a Sunday) with his preaching that a "higher law" justified the use of violence to overthrow slavery. This was no abstract idea for him. He personally threatened slave catchers with mob violence when they came to Boston looking for runaways (the Fugitive Slave Act of 1850 made such pursuit legal). When the Kansas-Nebraska Act (1854) upset the political balance between slaveholding and free states (a new state's status was to be decided by its new settlers), violence erupted in Kansas. Parker and other abolitionists sent rifles for the free staters' defense against proslavery settlers (George M. Fredrickson, *The Inner Civil War: Northern Intellectuals and the Crisis of the Union* [New York: Harper & Row, 1965], 37–39; Jules Abels, *Man on Fire: John Brown and the Cause of Liberty* [New York: Macmillan, 1971], 118–20).

‡They knew nothing, at the outset, of Brown's part in the Pottawatomie massacre of five proslavery settlers, who were hacked to death and dismembered with broadswords at his

Sanborn was "drawn to the idea of the United States passing through the ordeal of war, of an unrepentant South in flames, in order that the slavery curse might be removed at last."[12] After the fiasco at Harpers Ferry and Brown's capture, the "Secret Six" did not remain secret for long. Brown had "carelessly" left correspondence behind implicating them all. Sanborn fled to Canada and did not return to Concord until he was reassured that it was safe to do so.

Because the James family had left for Europe on October 3, 1859, they were out of the country at the time of Brown's raid (October 17), his hanging (December 2), and a government attempt to abduct Sanborn and force him to appear before a Senate investigating committee (April 3, 1860). Henry James, Sr., obviously knew about these events, however, by the time he handed over his sons to "the famous" Mr. Sanborn. He noted the presence of John Brown's daughter at the school in his letter: "tall, erect, long-haired and freckled, as John Brown's daughter has a right to be."[13] Though Sanborn was drawn to the idea of war, when it actually began in April 1861 with the firing on Fort Sumter he did not answer the call. But Wilky and Bob James, two of his impressionable young students, did.

[3]

In his Fourth of July oration at Newport in 1861, Henry James, Sr., spoke of transforming the American soul through a war against slavery. The war, he felt, was "the hour of our endless rise into all beautiful human proportions, into all celestial vigor and beatitude, or of our endless decline into all infernality and uncleanness."[14]

Clearly he was prepared to support the war against slavery as another opportunity to usher in the millennium. But when it came to sending his own sons off to fight, he held back—at least where his older boys were concerned. "Affectionate old papas like me," he wrote a friend, "are scudding all over the country to apprehend their patriotic offspring and restore them to the harmless embraces of their mamas. . . . I have had a firm grasp upon the coat tails of my Willy and Harry, who both vituperate me beyond measure because I won't let them go. The coats are a very staunch

---

command. Nor did they know of his rumored insanity. It was later alleged that his grandmother, mother, three aunts, two uncles, a brother, a sister, and a niece had all been intermittently psychotic (Stephen B. Oates, *To Purge This Land with Blood: A Biography of John Brown* [New York: Harper & Row, 1970], 133–37; Bruce Catton, ed., *The National Experience: A History of the United States* [New York: Harcourt, Brace & World, 1963], 316).

material, or the tails must have been off two days ago, the scamps pull so hard." His reasons made perfectly good sense from the perspective of a loving parent and radical individualist, but hardly meshed with his Fourth of July rhetoric. Privately he declared that no worldly government was worth dying for, and certainly not before one had experienced the "charm" of marriage. "The way I excuse my paternal interference to them is to tell them, first, that no existing government, nor indeed any now possible government, is worth an honest human life and a clean one like theirs. . . . Secondly, I tell them that no young American should put himself in the way of death, until he has realized something of the good of life: until he has found some charming conjugal Elizabeth or other to whisper his devotion to, and assume the task if need be, of keeping his memory green."[15]

However firmly he held to the coattails of his Willy and his Harry, he let his Wilky and his Bob go without a recorded struggle. Perhaps the carnage of 1862 made him realize that he could not withhold all of his sons from the fight. His friend Oliver Wendell Holmes, Sr., who had urged youth to the colors with his stirring "Listen young heroes! your country is calling! Time strikes the hour for the brave and the true!" was searching the battlefields after Antietam seeking his wounded son.[16] If someone had to go, it might have been easier to let go of the coattails of the sons he had already consigned to "burial" at Concord in 1860. Later, when Bob had second thoughts about his decision to enlist and spoke of coming back in 1864, his father urged him to stay. "Cheer up then my dear boy, and be a man, where you stand." Two days later he repeated the same injunction to remain "manfully at your tracks."[17] The contrast between the treatment of this eighteen-year-old and Henry's protective attitude toward his more favored boys could hardly be clearer.

A year before he died at the age of thirty-eight, in 1883, Wilky recalled his youthful entry into uniform. "When I went to the war I was a boy of 17 years of age. . . . My father accompanied me to the recruiting station, witnessed the enrollment, and gave me, his willing mite, to the cause he had so much at heart." If he had ever heard of his father's reluctance to part with a son so young, the memory had faded. What he did remember by way of contrast with his father's letter about his Willy and his Harry was the family's belief (and Mr. Sanborn's as well) "that slavery was a monstrous wrong, and its destruction worthy of a man's best effort, even unto the laying down of life." The Forty-fourth Massachusetts Regiment, he remembered, was made up of undergraduates of Harvard College, a delegation of devout Methodists "who chanted songs from the 'army of the Lord,'" and an assortment of tradesmen.[18] They drilled twice a day on the Boston Common until they were shipped to North Carolina to fight.

Captain Garth Wilkinson James, c. 1865

Wilky may have been an unenthusiastic student, but he took readily to war. At the end of December 1862 he wrote from New Bern, North Carolina, with the tone of a battle-hardened veteran. He had been so tired after twenty miles of marching that when he reached Whitehall and heard the sound of cannon, he was more relieved than frightened. The expected enemy bullets failed to materialize, however, and the regiment rested till night fell. When they met the enemy on the road to Kingston the following morning, the excitement of battle made him feel possessed by devilish forces that welled up within him, and the sight of defeated Confederates waving flags of surrender moved the elated young soldier to exclaim that he had never felt more gleeful in all his life.[19]

[4]

But a greater challenge lay in store for Wilky. When the regiment returned to New Bern, he and two other officers were sent back to Boston to join the newly forming Massachusetts Fifty-fourth Regiment. His assignment as adjutant to a regiment of black soldiers under the leadership of Colonel Robert Gould Shaw pulled him back into the confusing cross-currents of Northern white sentiment toward free blacks. Many people in the Jameses' Boston circle believed that they and the blacks shared a common humanity, but they hardly represented the majority.* From the beginning of the war there was strong resistance in the Union forces to the arming of blacks, who were grudgingly welcomed as cannon fodder but not as comrades. A popular marching ditty declared: "In battle's wild commotion / I won't at all object / If a nigger should stop a bullet / Coming for me direct."[20] In North and South alike, the arming of Negroes was discouraged. Southerners feared slave rebellion and Northerners believed that black troops would be cowardly under fire.

As an officer of a black regiment, Wilky was exposed to his comrades' prejudice. The soldiers he had fought beside now rebuked and taunted him for taking up his new commission.[21] Many years later his brother

---

*Fearful of alienating border-state slaveholders who were still loyal to the Union, President Lincoln had reluctantly issued the Emancipation Proclamation in January 1863, declaring all slaves free in those states that had seceded from the Union. Reaction in the North was cool. Even Robert Gould Shaw, the man who would command the first regiment of black troops from Massachusetts and a committed abolitionist, thought it would have little practical effect. "Wherever our army has been there remain no slaves, and the Proclamation will not free them where we don't go." And he feared that in retaliation the Confederacy would turn the war to decide the fate of the Union into a racial "war of extermination" (Peter Burchard, *One Gallant Rush: Robert Gould Shaw and His Brave Black Regiment* [New York: St. Martin's Press, 1965], 67, 73).

Captain Robertson James at Jacksonville, Florida, c. 1864

William summarized the challenge succinctly: "In this new negro-soldier venture, loneliness was certain, ridicule inevitable, failure possible."[22] On May 28, 1863, when the new regiment, one thousand strong, marched through the city of Boston, the contrary emotions of the white crowds surrounded the raw troops. "Prejudice of the rankest sort then assailed us," Wilky recalled. He would never forget "the alternating cheers and groans, the alternate huzza and reproach which attempted to deafen each other on our march down State street." Some people in the crowd did not content themselves with catcalls. "Copperheads" (peace Democrats opposed to the war) and "roughs" attacked the rear of the column as it neared the wharves and had to be turned back by police.*

Bob was eager to follow Wilky to war. Rather than join the navy, as he had originally planned, Bob accepted a commission as an officer in a second black regiment, the Massachusetts Fifty-fifth. Like Wilky, he had to face the hostility of Northerners before he went south. On the night of July 14, 1863, antidraft mobs stormed the Cooper Street armory in Boston, only to withdraw before a bayonet charge of defending troops. "Roughs" roamed the streets, breaking into rifle shops in search of arms. "I rode a great big lancers horse," Robertson recalled, "and let my Smith & Wesson off unintentionally in front of the old Boylston Market. It was unintentional 'duty'. At all events it delivered my partner, a German cavalryman and myself from a mob."† Years later in a letter to William, Robertson recalled the draft riots of 1863 when he "shot down two toughs in North Street who were trying to drag me from my horse."[23] Robertson looked back on that memorable week of riots as "the first real week of my life." In New York violent bands roamed the city for four days assaulting blacks. An orphan asylum for black children was plundered and set ablaze. A dozen black men were beaten to death. One was hanged and burned by the jeering mob.[24]‡

*There was no mention of this incident in the *New York Times* of May 29, 1863, in the *Daily National Intelligence* of Washington on May 30, 1863, or in *The Liberator* of Boston on June 5, 1863. On the contrary, *The Liberator* reported, "There was nowhere along the line a word of disapproval—not a sneer was heard, nor an unkind work expressed" as the black soldiers marched through Boston to the tune of "John Brown's Body." By the end of the war 186,000 black men had served in the Union Army and almost as many had worked as laborers for the military. More than 68,000 were listed as dead or missing, 2,751 of them in combat. For whites and blacks the major cause of death was disease (Leon F. Litwack, *Been in the Storm So Long: The Aftermath of Slavery* [New York: Alfred J. Knopf, 1979], 97–98).

†There is no mention of this incident in the regimental history. The *New York Times* reported on July 17 that cavalry from Readville, the camp where Bob was stationed, had helped put down the mob. This is probably the incident referred to (*Record of the Service of the Fifty-fifth Regiment of Massachusetts Volunteer Infantry* [Cambridge, 1868; reprinted 1971]).

‡During the riots in New York, the home of Sergeant R. J. Simmons of the Fifty-fourth was invaded by the mob and his seven-year-old nephew was stoned to death. Simmons was

The Fifty-fifth was originally intended to march to New York for embarkation. In anticipation of riots, the men had been drilled in "street-firing." Their orders were changed, but even a Boston embarkation was dangerous in that volatile atmosphere. Before they set out from camp on the morning of July 21, 1863, muskets were loaded, bayonets fixed, and five rounds of ball cartridges issued to each man.[25] Fortunately the seventeen-year-old officer and his men did not need to use their weapons. When they passed Dr. Holmes's house on Charles Street, Robertson recalled with pleasure, Holmes "came out of his front door supporting my dear old father, who had arrived to say Godspeed to his boy."[26]

When Henry James, Sr., wrote to a friend about the departure of the Fifty-fifth, he declared his "heart-break" at parting "with one so young on a service so hard," and predictably interpreted the moment within his ever-receptive religious frame. "I cannot but adore the great Providence which is thus lifting our young men out of indolence and vanity, into some free sympathy with His own deathless life." The irony is startling. The risking of life in war (for a cause that was deemed unworthy for his leisured Willy and Harry) was now declared admirable work to cure "indolence" by this aging radical who had committed his own days to a perpetual Sabbath. The deeply ambivalent imagery that marked his letter from the Sanborn School also stamped this note with a too-ready death wish for a less favored youngest son dispatched to the front. "I seem never to have loved the dear boy before, now that he is clad with such an aureole of Divine beauty and innocence; and though the flesh was weak I still had the courage, spiritually, to bid him put all his heart in his living or dying."[27] Neither father nor son knew that at that moment Wilky lay wounded from assault on Fort Wagner three days before.

By the time Wilky's regiment entered battle, the Confederacy had been cut in two by Grant's victory at Vicksburg, in the west (July 4, 1863). Lee's Army of Northern Virginia had been decisively turned back at Gettysburg, in the east. Charleston was the major port of entry for rebel blockade runners, and its capture was a logical next step in the effort to cut off supplies and bring the war to an end. But the Sea Islands formed a protective barrier, with Fort Sumter at the center and Fort Wagner on the northern tip of Morris Island effectively blocking the entrance to the vital harbor. Southern engineers had spent two years building Wagner into a

---

wounded and captured in the assault on Fort Wagner. He had an arm amputated and died a prisoner in Charleston (Luis F. Emilio, *History of the Fifty-fourth Regiment of Massachusetts Volunteer Infantry, 1863–1865* [Boston: Boston Book Co., 1891], 93). Robert Gould Shaw's father, Francis Shaw, patrolled the family home on Staten Island, armed to repel rioters, who fortunately did not appear (Burchard, *Gallant Rush*, 131–32).

nearly impregnable structure, protected by compact sand and armed with twenty guns that covered its approach across a moat filled by the high tides and held full by a sluice gate.

At the beginning of July, Robert Gould Shaw, mindful of the symbolic as well as the military significance of his command, wrote: "I want to get my men alongside white troops, into a good fight, if there is to be one."[28] Disgusted by their first action under Colonel James Montgomery, an impulsive, violent man who had forced them to pillage and burn the deserted town of Darien, Georgia, Shaw longed for an encounter worthy of his charge. On July 16 he had his wish. Wilky reported, "At early dawn, while holding the advance position with six companies of my regiment, we were attacked by a rebel cavalry." They repulsed the enemy, while losing some sixty killed, wounded, and missing men in the encounter. The untried black troops had held, and the young adjutant was jubilant, though he was edgy about the reaction of the white soldiers as he reported the action to the commander, General Alfred Terry. "It had become a living, breathing suspicion with us . . . that all white troops abhorred our presence in the army," he recalled. He was relieved and filled with "soldierly satisfaction" when the general did not sneer but instructed him to "tell Col. Shaw that he was proud of the conduct of his men."[29]

Two days later Shaw and his men were ferried across to Morris Island for a suicidal attack on Fort Wagner. Nine ironclads and a fleet of fifty warships had subjected the fort to one of the heaviest bombardments of the war, but Wagner had lived up to its design as a Southern Gibraltar. Not one gun was silenced and there were few casualties, though the Union command assumed otherwise. As the bombardment subsided, Brigadier General Truman Seymour ordered a frontal assault despite the protests of several officers, one of whom was convinced that they were going "into Wagner like a flock of sheep." Adjutant James stood near Shaw when General George C. Strong invited Shaw to lead the column with his black troops. Shaw had had a premonition that he would not survive his next battle, but he did not hesitate. He told Wilky to order the weary regiment forward. The men had eaten little for two days and had had no rest since their first engagement. They were tired and hungry but in good spirits. At twilight the Fifty-fourth moved into position. Six hundred strong they lay stretched out on the beach waiting until dark. Then Shaw ordered the advance. Shaw led the march at quick time before the state and national colors along an increasingly narrow funnel of beach with a swamp on the right and the ocean on the left. They rushed into the brilliant flash of a barrage from the fort. Then they broke into a run and charged up the sandy embankment behind their colonel through merciless point-blank fire only to be repelled in fierce hand-to-hand combat. On the parapet

Shaw's outline was silhouetted briefly by the glare of exploding powder against the dark sky. Suddenly he pitched over dead.

Wilky was wounded first in the side and then in the foot. It had been rumored before the battle that white officers of the Fifty-fourth Massachusetts would be hanged if they were captured, and his determination to avoid this fate probably saved his life. He dragged himself along the beach to a knoll, where he was picked up by two retreating ambulancemen. They placed him on a stretcher, but he was not yet safe: "After being borne for a distance to the rear, and still under the mercy of Wagner's fitful guns," he recalled, "a round shot blew off the head of the stretcher bearer in my rear." James lost consciousness only to find himself aboard ship headed for Port Royal and eventually home.*

On board ship the cannister ball was taken out of the sole of his heel and he was returned to his anxious parents "safe if not sound." Though Henry James, Sr., reported the bodily wound in some detail to his friend Samuel G. Ward, it was the spiritual effect on his son that most impressed him. "He has become manly and exalted in the tone of his mind," he observed, "and weeps with delight at the remembrance of his splendid regiment." Henry expressed surprise at the swiftness of the change in his son, coming as it did not from guilt or divine inspiration but from responsible action in the world. "It is really quite incomprehensible to me to see so much manhood so suddenly achieved."[30] In the carnage of that July night the regiment lost two-fifths of its officers and almost half of its men. Yet many Northerners still questioned the black soldiers' bravery.

After listening to Wilky's ramblings and gingerly putting questions to him, "testing, without in the least awakening his suspicions of my objects," his father concluded "that if any hesitancy was exhibited on the part of the troops in this assault or at any period before the retreat was sounded he was perfectly ignorant and unsuspicious of it." Apparently even abolitionists found it hard to credit reports of black bravery. Yet Bob, too, had favorable things to say about the black soldiers. Henry quoted his report that "the 54th fought like devils, but to no purpose." And Wilky, his father told Ward, "believes with an unaffected belief in the bravery and discipline of the blacks and would be unhappy if he were obliged for any cause to dissolve his connection with them."[31]

When Charleston finally fell to a Northern seige in 1865, Wilky had rejoined his unit and triumphantly marched into the captured city.† He

---

*After the fort had been captured by siege and Wilky had had a chance to inspect it, he was convinced that "the whole tragedy was a totally inconsistent military manoeuvre" (*Milwaukee Sentinel*, December 2, 1888).

†Wilky had been injured again in a fall from his horse in the fighting against General William Hardee before Charleston (*Milwaukee Sentinel*, December 2, 1888).

told his sister that it was "without exception the proudest moment of my life when we stepped into Fort Sumpter and Genl. Gillmore took off his hat & with the whole staff around him called for nine rousing cheers for the good old flag which waved above us."[32]

[5]

Alice James was nearly thirteen when the Civil War began, and she missed being surrounded by her brothers. Bob, who was two years older, had been her nursery mate. They had been sick with the measles together and played house, arranging imaginary "marriage compacts" and calling each other "Henry" and "Mary," in imitation of their parents.[33] Brothers were irritating when they dug their heels into her shins, but for a girl just entering her teens they were also companions and a portal to a larger world. When Emerson's daughter Ellen visited the Jameses at Newport in the summer of 1862, Bob, with Wilky as crew, took the girls sailing in his boat (named the *Alice*) to Lawton Valley, where they picnicked, pulled lint for bandages, and visited with the convalescing soldiers at Portsmouth Grove.[34] Ellen at twenty-two could see how much Alice counted on them for companionship. When she returned to Concord she wrote, "Alice is a dear little creature and of course cannot be happy a minute without her brothers." Alice helped in the war by working with the Newport Women's Aid Society making flannel shirts for soldiers in the field and bandages for the wounded.[35]

Both Wilky and Bob made a special point of writing to Alice separately about their war experiences. Wilky enjoyed playing big brother. "I don't see why this letter should not be addressed to you," he wrote, "as you are my only beloved sister & a very good one at that." He proceeded to excite his little sister's imagination with a description of plans for a cavalry charge through the enemy lines. But the privilege of receiving mail addressed to her alone also carried with it the responsibility of writing letters in reply. And when no letters were forthcoming from her, Wilky drew himself up to the full height of his three years' seniority and was as severe as he had been attentive. "Since you will not condescend to write to me, I will take the 'cow' by the horns & write to it." She had to tolerate a bit of fraternal moralizing. "You must remember my dear child, that remissness in family matters, especially in a young woman, have a more pernicious effect on the character, than remissness in any other common duty."[36] Bob also exaggerated the two-year gulf in age that separated them in his letters to "my dearest little sister." He sometimes flirted with her, too. He closed one letter, for example, with the passionate pledge, "Never while reason holds

Alice James, c. 1856

Alice James, 1862

sway will . . . this heart fail to beat more tumultuously than common when thy name is mentioned!!"[37]

But most of what Alice learned about her brothers at war came from letters addressed to her parents. In February 1864 Bob described the "grumbling" that was taking place among the black troops of the Fifty-fifth because they had not received any pay. Although they had been recruited with the understanding that they were to receive the same pay and enlistment bounty as whites, the agreement was not kept.* "I am not willing to fight for anything less than the white man fights for," wrote a Massachusetts soldier, and he spoke for many of his comrades. As an act of protest, the Fifty-fourth Regiment (Wilky's unit) had refused to accept any pay at all, forcing some of their families to subsist on charity. Bob had heard rumors of mutiny and executions in the Fifty-fourth Massachusetts, and warned that "it would be one of the most frightful things that could possibly occur; and there may be danger of it, if their pay is kept back much longer." But he was as keenly aware as Wilky of the importance of acceptance by white troops. "It was flattering to notice the way in which the men were cheered by the white troops on leaving this morning [for Jacksonville]. It did the men as much good," he thought, "as the pay will."[38]†

Perhaps the most moving of the letters home came from Wilky after Lincoln's assassination in April 1865. Five days after Lee's surrender at Appomattox, Lincoln's plans for a generous peace were extinguished by John Wilkes Booth's bullet. The twenty-one-year-old officer was bewildered by "grief and consternation" over the death of his commander in chief. He was not alone. "Every man feels that his own well-being has been trampled on, that his honor had been violated. I never in all my life felt as inexpressably small & shaky & why I should feel so is more than I can explain." The veteran of Fort Wagner and Charleston felt his grief was

---

*Frederick Douglass was one of many recruiters who had assured fellow blacks of equal treatment. When the Union reneged, Douglass secured an appointment with President Lincoln, but was unable to change the abuse. The government claimed it had to preserve the distinction between white and black soldiers to keep up white morale. White privates were paid $13.00 a month plus a $3.50 clothing allowance, but blacks got $10.00 and no clothing allowance. In effect, they were offered a little more than half of what had been promised.

†When the black troops refused to accept the reduced pay just two months after their daring assault on Fort Wagner, they were subjected to a humiliating harangue by Colonel Montgomery, the same officer who had forced them to pillage over Shaw's objections (Emilio, *Fifty-fourth Regiment*, 130). Two men of the Fifty-fourth were wounded in May 1864 because of the pay issue (ibid., 190–91). When the government finally equalized the pay in June 1864, the ruling applied only to those black soldiers who had been free before the war began. Colonel E. N. Hallowell got around the discrimination against the few former slaves in the Fifty-fourth by having them all swear that they "owed no man unrequited labor" before that date (Litwack, *Been in the Storm*, 79–87).

unmanly, but he could not help himself. "Excuse these expressions of my innermost heart, but if I have ever felt sad it is tonight. We have been talking him over and over ever since we heard of his death, & such a crowd of heart-broken young men you would never see again." Though hardened by battle, he felt himself still a boy who longed to be comforted by his parents: "I ought to go to bed, but I feel for you and Mother tonight the same feeling that I did when you were nursing me in my bed in the summer of 1863." But he was embarrassed by his tears. He marked the letter "Private" and instructed: "Please burn this Father & Mother when you have read it, & don't let any one else see it as it [is] simply my own self talking to you two."[39]

By June the last of the Confederate troops had laid down their guns. The war was over. Now, like so many other young men of their generation, Bob and Wilky had to find work to replace the excitement and sense of purpose that the war had provided. For Alice the shift from wrapping bandages to doing social work for the poor was less dramatic. But she, too, had to find her vocation. In post–Civil War America, that meant courtship with the hope of marriage.

17

Declining Fortunes

> Matrimony seems the only successful occupation that a woman can undertake.
>
> —Alice James, 1876

> We came down and settled in a region where many of the inhabitants had never seen a Yankee, . . . [and] have fully vindicated the principle we started on, that the Freed negro under decent and just treatment can be worked to profit employer and employee.
>
> —Garth Wilkinson James, 1866

> I wish our own father had steered his sons into the soap or Baking Powder lines.
>
> —Robertson James, 1898

[1]

O F THE three youngest James children, it was Alice that was damaged most by the war. When peace returned, Wilky's foot had healed and Bob had recovered from heat prostration that had almost led to his discharge. But 600,000 other young men were dead. They would not come back from the battlefields to court and wed the young women of Alice's generation. Raised for marriage as a vocation, she was condemned to spinsterhood and invalidism, not for the weeks or months it took to heal a wound, but for the remainder of her life. The census figures cast her fate in bold relief. Before the war there was an imbalance in the population of Massachusetts, the result of a predominantly male westward migration which made her chances predictably slim. But between the census of 1850 and the census of 1870 (from the time she was two to the year she turned twenty-two) the disproportion of women over men in her state increased more than 150 percent, from 20,000 to

50,000. And by 1880, when Alice turned thirty-two and had became resigned to single blessedness, the imbalance had increased nearly a third
more, to 66,000.[1] Her photographs and letters show her transformation
from an effervescent, hopeful young woman into an acerbic, wan invalid,
who had, as she confided to her journal, crossed the ocean and "suspended" herself "like an old woman of the sea" around her brother Henry's neck.[2] Her bed became her fortress and legions of physicians were
invited to scale its heights, only to retreat before her ironic disdain. Between these ritualized skirmishes she insistently commanded family and
friends to shore up her invalid's battlements.

The vocational alternatives open to young women such as Alice were
limited. She could occupy herself with good works (not "work" as a
serious career) until a suitor appeared, and turn to the men in her family
for erotically tinged affection while she waited. If no suitor came forward,
she could care for sick or aging parents or become sick herself. Alice's
interest in good works waned as no suitor appeared. When her brothers
were lost to marriage and careers, she turned to a "Boston marriage" with
Katharine P. Loring, a companion who would be her beloved caretaker
until she died.

"The Bee" was Alice's first venture into social work after the family
moved to Cambridge. She wrote to William, who was abroad in 1867,
about it. "I have been invited by the young ladies of Cambridge to join the
'Bee'. . . . It is a sewing society formed at the beginning of the war by the
girls and kept up now for the poor. Miss Susy Dixwell is at the head of it
and all the Cambridge young misses go, so I shall have plenty of gossip to
tell you."[3] With no offers, nine years later she complained, "This reminds
me of the most idiotic conversation I had the other evening with Miss Jane
Norton. . . . She said that she thought all these Boston women instead of
devoting themselves to painting, clubs, societies, etc. ought to stay at
home in a constant state of matrimonial expectation. They were all so
happy together that men said to themselves oh! she's so happy we won't
marry her! wh. was a new view that men were attracted by depressed &
gloomy females, & also that they generally married them from compassion."[4]

Alice's sense of humor in letters to her friends Annie Ashburner and
Sara Sedgwick contrasts sharply with the indulged baby sister or ever-
recovering neurasthenic represented in the family correspondence. Her
lively wit cuts through the Cambridge shadows like sunlight splashed
against a cell wall. Though recognizing that "matrimony seems the only
successful occupation that a woman can undertake," she could be very
funny when she commented on the less alluring aspects of that sought-
after state. "A Mr. J. M. Howe called here a few evenings ago, he seems a

nice man quite amusing; he said that the only remedy he knew of against fleas in Florida was 'to take one's wife down with you.' The horrid man!" She was resigned to not being pretty: "My features," she noted wryly, "I have long since ceased to question as the work of an inscrutable wisdom." And she openly envied beautiful women more sophisticated than she. To Sara, who was visiting New York, she exclaimed, "Aren't the women lovely creatures! I wonder if you were ever torn by pangs of envy and cry aloud as I did, 'why am I not made as one of these!'" She made fun of those more successful than she. Again to Sara she frolicked over a friend's engagement to a Saxon baron: "I think that if I condescended to a title I should draw the line at a duke. Aren't you sick of these flimsy Baron's who are always on hand to be converted into husbands!" And she was not above deriding the competitors who seemed maddeningly to have succeeded where she had failed. "What do you suppose I heard the other day? nothing less than that those dreadful Loverings had had no end of offers! It was insulting, but satisfactory as explaining the mystery of why the article had been so scarce in Quincy Str, for if such ragged growth as the Miss L_____s are what's courted, it no wonder that a rare exotic like— modesty forbids my saying who—is left unplucked upon its stem, to reach a bloom bordering, to put it delicately, on the full-blown."[5]

In the early years after the war she had dared to dream. Annie Ashburner received this breathless confidence about Charles Jackson, a young lawyer Alice knew who was already engaged. "Isn't he lovely & hasn't he got the nicest face & the sweetest smile you ever saw!" She cast an approving eye as well on Dr. James Jackson Putnam, William's friend and famous neurologist-to-be: "He has grown an inch or more physically & Europe has added to his many inevitable Jackson virtues a charm & attraction . . . so that he is a very pleasing object now." Again to Annie she sighed over Charles Jackson. "My passion grows, its fortunate I see him rarely for I am told that it wd. be altogether wild in me to nourish the faintest hope." Unfortunately, all the men seemed already spoken for. Another, Moorfield Story, was already married when he caught her eye. She found him an "adorable creature" and couldn't understand why he had gone all the way to Washington for his "stout washer-womany wife."[6]

Her wit turned more savage with each successive disappointment, and her prose was unmistakably Jamesian. She could toss off an adept cameo with a literary flourish. "Your dear friend Mr. Anderson popped in to call on Lizzy; he sat on the edge of the sofa tight and compact, like a neat little parcel drawn up at Metcalfs and talked for about ten minutes, and almost in the middle of a sentence, popped out again. He treated me with the usual contempt. What is the opposite to elective affinities? whatever it is, he is one and I'm the other."[7]

She could tell a story of the matrimonial chase with verve and a fine sense of timing. "First & foremost I came near having an offer! One old gentleman who came to see us one evening, asked one of the ladies the next day whether she thought Miss James wd. have him. Imagine the flutteration within my bosom! At last I was to have the privilege of declining matrimony & of escaping the mortification of descending to the grave a spinster, not from choice of the sweet lot, but from dire necessity. But, alas! no such fate for me, the man was a wretch, it being his habit to destroy the peace of any maiden who might come along, by this airy little remark. My fate, which if he had only spoken I should look upon as rapturous, is as humdrum and hopeless as ever."[8]

As friends and relatives became engaged and married, the excitement and anticipation of love that marked her early confidences faded. No wonder she greeted the first James grandchild (Robertson's son Ned) with the frank "I am so glad that it is a boy and not a miserable girl brought into existence."[9]

For a brief time she found an intellectual focus for her energies. In December 1875 Alice wrote to Annie of a new plan. She had been invited to teach in a correspondence school for women founded by Miss Anna Eliot Ticknor.* Her friend Fannie Morse had urged her to become one of the "Managers" who wrote essays on various subjects and advised students about further reading. So many women registered during the school's first two years that more teachers were needed. Uncertain of her talent, Alice accepted with some diffidence: "after violently declining I finally meekly succumbed." Although schoolteaching was a profession already open to women, the idea of doing serious work was hard to match with her picture of herself. "You can laugh and think me as much of a humbug as you choose," she told Annie, "you can't do so more than I have myself."[10] By then William was launched on his academic career. Perhaps she could follow in her own way.† William had discovered the utility of work as a balm to invalidism and wrote enthusiastically to Henry of their sister's intellectual venture. "Alice has got her historical professorship which will no doubt be an immense thing for her."[11]

---

*Anna Ticknor, the daughter of George Ticknor (the first professor of modern languages at Harvard), had been an invalid like Alice, and the new society gave her an outlet for her stifled energies. "I am enjoying the feeling that I dare to be busy, for the first time in many years, during which I have been an invalid," Miss Ticknor happily announced to a friend (*AJ*, 171; pp. 170–76 of *AJ* give an extended description of the school and its curriculum).

†The American ideal of individualism was espoused earlier by men than by women. Middle-class women of Alice's generation still held firmly to a belief in submission to men in marriage as the highest ideal. Work as self-expression had yet to become a widely accepted alternative. See Linda K. Kerber, "Can a Woman Be an Individual? The Limits of Puritan Tradition in the Early Republic," *Texas Studies in Literature and Language* 25, no. 1 (Spring 1983):166–78.

Alice James, c. 1870

Much to her surprise, Alice also discovered that she loved the work. During her second year of teaching she was so enthusiastic about it that she urged her friend Annie to find something like it for herself. "I wish that you had some work to do that amused you half as much as my society work does me." She had even begun to develop some self-confidence, though she expressed it somewhat negatively: "I in attempting to teach history am not half the fool that I look." Her contact with women all over the country (she mentioned students in "the wilds" of California, Kansas, Missouri, Michigan, Kentucky, Florida, Iowa, and Illinois) made her appreciate her own good fortune. "We who have had all our lives more books than we know what to do with can't conceive of the feeling that people have for them who have been shut out from them always. They look upon them as something sacred apparently, & some of the letters I get are most touching, girls who write to say that they have longed always for just such help & never hoped to get it, & the difficulties that they will overcome to join the society are incredible." Writing "between thirty & forty letters every month" kept her quite busy.[12] For the first time in her life it seemed that Alice felt genuinely engaged with the great world, like her brothers.

Unfortunately, though her brothers welcomed the change in her, the novice teacher feared that other women would not: "Perhaps you may wonder at my sudden onslaught upon yr. innocent self," she wrote Annie, "but I feared that it must seem very silly to you, & as it is what I care about most just now, I did not want you to judge it without a hearing."[13] The Society to Encourage Studies at Home flourished well into the 1890s, reaching its peak year in 1882, when it enrolled 1,000 students.[14] But Alice gave it up. No reason is mentioned in her letters. Perhaps the work became humdrum and no longer attractive as a labor of love. It is hardly likely that she took Jane Norton's advice that women who were intent on courting should wait at home. There is some indication that the lure of invalidism and a European cure beckoned. She hinted at this development at the end of November 1878 when she wrote of a friend who was abroad, recuperating from an illness: "But how much I envy her!—convalescence in Europe seems such an easy process, where there are so many helps on every hand."[15]

Alice turned to female friends as well as to her brothers for affection. Fannie Morse was her close friend from the 1860s on, and Alice's letters to her overflowed with an unembarrassed expression of love that is rare in the family correspondence. "I love you very much . . . I feel myself to be a more respectable human being when I consider that I have you for a friend, & I have you, haven't I, notwithstanding all my sins?"[16] In her tender declaration, we hear a painfully uncertain woman barely out of the chrysalis of adolescence. When husband hunting began in earnest, Alice talked humorously of men as threats to her ties to her female friends. Thus when Sara Sedgwick was abroad and the separation seemed too long, Alice threatened: "If you don't come soon I shall in desperation elope with the handsome butcher-boy, with whom I have an interview every morning for the purpose of telling him that Mrs. J. does not wish anything. . . . He is very good-looking & is filled with emotion whenever he sees me, so you had better fly to the rescue."[17]

But her friends, too, were lost to marriage. When Sara Sedgwick announced her intention to marry, Alice was furious. Sara went to England in 1877 in search of a husband and drew this withering note from her Cambridge-bound "sister": "So you have betaken yourself, madam, to Yarmouth to find a spouse after the manner of your great grandmother. It seems a strange matrimonial fishing-ground, herring having hither to been my only association with those waters. Good luck to you however! May he only not carry with him too strong a reminder of whence you have hooked him." Though bitter, she still would not declare herself completely out of the race and pleaded, "If they bite in numbers, bear in mind the lone lorn spinsters you have left behind." If humor bore the burden of her loneliness, it also provided relief. With broad strokes she sketched a comic vision of Cambridge suddenly out of marriageable virgins. "But aren't you frightened tho' at the mortality that has overtaken these last since your departure. Cambridge is utterly demoralized & those of us who have been always most resigned & modest are in momentary expectation of presidents, widowers, lawyers, professors, we know not what—dropping at our feet." In this disheartened mood, she felt her own good works turning to ashes. The Society to Encourage Studies at Home seemed a futile "sacrifice" without meaning. "If it goes on much longer all the virtuous little causes of history, art, charitable institutions, etc. from which we have sought and derived so much consolation for our loneliness, will be utterly abandoned & many of us, I am afraid left disconsolate having sacrificed our 'resources'."[18]

Her work at the school did not last, but Alice found there and nurtured a friendship that would fill the void for the rest of her life. She first mentioned Katharine P. Loring in an early letter about the school. "I am with Miss Katharine Loring & have charge of the historical young women. I think I shall enjoy it & I know it will do me lots of good." The two had already met on December 17, 1873, and as their friendship deepened, that day became a private landmark, "an anniversary which we always kept unknown to any" until Alice died. Alice waxed ecstatic over Katharine's virtues to Sara, who was now married. Concluding a long anecdote about an ambitious young woman who wanted to go to normal school, she jealously struck at Sara: "The girl turned out to be a semi-idiot and has since sought refuge in matrimony—like yourself." But she extolled *her* beloved's virtues: "I wish you could know Katharine Loring, she is a most wonderful being. She has all the mere brute superiority which distinguishes man from woman combined with all the distinctively feminine virtues. There is nothing she cannot do from hewing wood & drawing water to driving run-away horses & educating all the women in North America."[19]*

If Sara missed the implication that a match between an androgynous woman and a frail invalid was superior to the more conventional bond between man and woman, she could not have helped laughing uproariously at Alice's attack on William's love of nature and the strenuous life. Alice and Katharine had ventured to the Putnam family's camp in the Adirondacks, which was reputedly "William's panacea for all earthly ills." They hated it. "We made a very thorough trial for between ourselves the shanty lacks nothing in the way of discomfort. . . . I assure you that for purposes of cutaneous refreshment a tub in the hand is worth fifty brooks in the bush." It was not simply that she hated the camp. She hated it in the way that a rejected woman hates masculine things. Her erotic imagery is rich in ironic stabs at the "winged brethren" who dared to lust after these "two virgins of thirty summers." She made fun of a sportive mosquito "who found me quit the loveliest production civilization had as yet sent to him." She pitied "all the dear little crawlers I had come so far to feel and who would no doubt have found me as delectable & succulent a feast as did their winged brethren." The male beasts could not get to her "fair form" because Katharine had protectively placed a rubber blanket as a "cruel barrier" over the log on which Alice was lying. The two women were visited briefly by Dr. Charles Putnam, whom Alice characterized as a bachelor with a figure like that of a "maiden aunt." She disliked the masculine world of the Putnam cabin and relished the literary opportunity to frustrate and emasculate the "brethren," large and small, who had passed her by.[20] The intent of her message was clear. She and Katharine were well rid of all men, including her brothers.

---

*As Carroll Smith-Rosenberg has pointed out, close emotional friendships between women were supported by the dramatic demarcation between the masculine and feminine worlds of eighteenth- and nineteenth-century America. Middle-class women often developed intimate relationships with each other that persisted after marriage and, though passionate in intensity, were not necessarily lesbian. They were well within the socially accepted norms. See Carroll Smith-Rosenberg, "The Female World of Love and Ritual: Relationships between Women in Nineteenth-Century America," *Signs* 1, no. 1 (Autumn 1975):1–31. Whether Alice's relationship with Katharine Loring was actively homosexual is not known. Her sister-in-law Alice Gibbens James thought it was.

[2]

When Alice turned to her brothers for love, as she had done from the nursery days when she and Robertson played at being husband and wife, William seemed the most promising. For years she was the "Chérie de Soeur," the "Süss Balchen," the "Beloved Sisterkin" of William's letters. The affectionate diminutives that streamed from his pen naturally emphasized the gap of six years that separated them as well as the playful affection that drew them together. When she was in her teens, he lectured and advised her in the manner of an older brother. On occasion he cided her, as Wilky and Bob did, for not answering letters. "That you should not have written to me for so long grieves me more than words can tell."[21] But he was appreciative, too, of her "nice letters, which, though rudely and coarsely executed are rather *more* than *less* delightful for it," and encouraged her when the writing was particularly successful. Once when she recounted a *bon mot* of Harry's, William applauded: "Those, those are the incidents with which letters should be filled!"[22] As Alice matured, so did William's letters to her. He wrote his latest observations on the national character of the French or the Germans, or vignettes of the personalities he met in his travels, with the same seriousness of tone as those addressed to his brother Henry. When Alice was teaching history he wrote enthusiastically from Florence: "This is the place for history. . . . It would suit you admirably."[23]

At times their affectionate banter had an erotic flavor. When the family was abroad in December 1859, Wilky was not the least surprised when William pulled him into "the parlor" to hear "a little sonnate on Alice which he has just composed and which he means to perform with much gusto." By his report, the rest of the family enjoyed the performance, which "went off very well, and excited a good deal of laughter" in the group.[24] It was a spoof of romantic love poetry replete with the moon "beaming upon the summer seas" and the poet-lover dreaming, "my Alice sweet, of thee."

> I swore to ask thy hand, my love
> I vowed to ask thy hand.
> I wished to join myself to thee
> By matrimonial band.

But Alice rejected him:

> So very proud, but yet so fair
> The look you on me threw
> You told me I must never dare
> To hope for love from you.

And he threatened to kill himself in despair:

> Adieu to love! Adieu to life!
> Since I may not have thee,
> My Alice sweet to be my wife,
> I'll drown me in the sea![25]

In March he gave a similar performance, and this time Aunt Kate was serenaded as well. Alice obviously preferred someone else to be in the spotlight (she had responded "cooly" to the December caper). "Willie is in a very extraordinary state of mind, composing odes to all the family," she wrote. The one for Aunt Kate, she reported, had "a 'warlike tone' in which her hero is her husband and dies for her."[26] A sister of eleven or a married aunt of forty-six were both "safe" targets for William's playful imaginings about love and marriage at seventeen.*

Typically the fraternal banter was simply warm and affectionate: "If . . you felt yourself strongly hugged by some invisible spiritual agency, you may now know that it was me." But occasionally the letters slipped from decorous flirtation to a frank eroticism. "I am . . . writing *à la seule que j'aime*. . . . Her transparent eyes, soft step and gentle hands, her genial voice and mood, never seemed to me more desirable or more lovable than now."[27] As she grew they squabbled. The tenor of this fighting can be inferred from a note William sent from college, in which he apologized for "the abuse we poured on each other before parting," and confessed contritely that his "expressions of joy at not meeting you again for so many months" were "feigned."[28] He even grew to appreciate Alice's combativeness. "O my beloved child, how much I would like to be with you and have you 'sass' me as of yore," he wrote from Berlin. Surrounded by the effusive German characters, he found Alice more attractive by contrast. "How much more pleasing to *this* heart is a good insolent American girl (like yourself) [who] goads you and spurs you to desperate exertions of manliness."[29]

Flirtation is a game that requires two to play, and it would be a mistake to suggest that Alice was merely a passive partner. Beneath the "coolness" and the "sassiness" she relished William's attentions and was not above coquettishly pitting brother against brother. Mary James was a witness. She commented on William's relationship with Alice to her son Henry in the spring of 1874. "He is very sweet upon her, in his own original way, and I think she enjoys very much his charming badinage." In the summer of 1872 Henry James, Jr., had been a cicerone to Alice during a European

---

*Kate had married a rich widower twenty years her senior in 1853. She lived with him barely two years before returning to her sister's household.

25. Ode to Alice

... the direction of the sexual instinct tends to inhibit its application to other individuals. ... —W. James, 1890

tour, and on her return she made the most of the situation to arouse William's jealousy. Once again Mary James described the scene to Henry: "A is full of the most vivid memories of all your love and care last summer, and is so eloquent on the subject, that she brings wrath upon Will's countenance, while she brings tears to my eyes."[30] By then William was thirty-one and Alice twenty-five; both were still single and without vocation. The stakes were getting steep.

William made five sketches of Alice that indicate the erotic tension between them. The first three (Figure 25) form a triptych, an illustrated accompaniment for an 1859 ode to Alice. We see the same moon, read the same poor verse, and witness the same unrequited love. In these sketches Alice is drawn not as the eleven-year-old girl she was, but as a beautiful young woman, and William is here serenading troubadour. The verse is innocent but the pictures are frankly sexual, unconsciously representing a fantasy of defloration. William the bare-legged troubadour bends over his "instrument" in the basement. His huge head feather does not menace his beloved at the outset, but the long thin neck of his lute protrudes through the open window and foreshadows what will follow. Intrigued and attentive in the first scene, Alice turns away in the second, seeming not to notice as William's body begins to rise and straighten. His "instrument" no longer projects through the window but his head feather moves closer to the barrier (floor) that keeps Alice "upright." Finally he stands completely erect, an ardent youth whose head feather strains against the disconsolate virgin's unyielding obstruction. The same scenario is repeated in two other drawing elements. What was a solid floor (or ceiling) obstructing contact in the first scene gives way line by line so that in the third it has all but disappeared, though the aroused troubadour fails to enter. Indeed, if he had located the receptive opening, Alice might have "fallen." The analogous transformation of a leafy bush between the lovers in scene one to partial defoliation in scene two to the complete disappearance of obstructing foliage in scene three echoes the erotic theme.

The fourth drawing is a head of Alice done in her early teens (Figure 26).* Her eyes are cast down demurely as she poses for her brother. One can only imagine her squeal of delight/indignation when she jumped up to see her picture, only to find a caption, "The loveress of W. J.," beneath it.

---

*Figures 28 and 29 are marked with an *H* in one corner. Originally I thought this meant that they were drawn by Henry. But the sketches were made in a notebook, and whoever removed the pages marked them perhaps to indicate their source. Other pages in the collection of drawings, are marked with letters other than *H* and *W*. Perhaps the same person (it obviously was not the artist) speculated on the subject and the artist with the lightly penciled note "Drawing of Alice James?" and underneath, "H.J." The hand in the caption of Figure 28 is unquestionably William's. The likeness to Alice's photograph taken in Newport in 1862 identifies the subject.

The loveress of W, J

Drawing of Alice James?
HJ.

26. ALICE JAMES, 1860
. . . in the one-sided development of civilized life, it happens that the timely age
goes by in a sort of starvation of objects, and the individual then grows up with
gaps in his psychic constitution which future experiences can never fill.

—W. James, 1890

But that did not prevent her from sitting again. In the fifth sketch she looks much older and is clearly a grown woman with a full bosom (Figure 27). Probably in her late teens, she wears a feathered hat and a tightly fitted bodice. Two details signify the erotic engagement between the artist and his model. Just above the bridge of Alice's nose is a heart pierced by Cupid's arrow. She is in love. To underline their attachment, William signed the drawing in a unique way. He placed his mark on her arm, literally branding Alice as his. The placement also suggests that Alice was smitten by him as well, and carried his initials ("her heart") on her sleeve. Mary James was a keen observer of her children, but one wonders whether she fully appreciated the tragedy of this turn between William, the would-be artist, and Alice, the would-be wife.

[3]

Wilky and Bob went south as soldiers. They returned after the war as ministers of a new gospel of free labor and venture capital. That their plan seemed promising at the beginning is remarkable, as they set out to run a cotton plantation without ever having studied agriculture or managed a business or indeed lived outside of a city (save for vacations) until they helped to rout the armies of the Confederacy. They had never even seen a plantation until 1862, yet four years later the veterans moved to a Florida plantation, backed by their father's capital (which the sons were eager to multiply) and motivated by a sincere desire to prove to a vanquished southern aristocracy that free black labor directed by Yankee discipline would redeem the promise of the Union victory. Their failure, resulting from a combination of bad luck (caterpillars, rain, and a drop in prices) and bad management, was not surprising.

The Florida plantation was a daring six-year-long venture approached with an amalgam of ideologies. Transcendentalism and abolitionism in the mode of Henry James, Sr., were blended with capitalism and a work ethic in the spirit of William James of Albany. The James sons were not alone in their ambition to become southern planters. Tens of thousands of northern men had gone south under arms only to return as civilians to earn a livelihood. One estimate suggests that as many as 50,000 northerners ran cotton plantations in the postbellum South.* The movement began in

---

*Wilky and Bob fitted the modal type of the northern planters in Florida, all of whom came from New England, were young (mean age of 30), not college educated (about one in five had some college), and had no previous agricultural experience (only 15 percent had been farmers). Many had been in the Union army (40 percent), most as officers (88 percent). See Lawrence N. Powell, *New Masters: Northern Planters during the Civil War and Reconstruction* (New Haven: Yale University Press, 1980), 160–78.

27. Alice James, 1870

Sex . . . this strongest passion of all so far from being the most "irresistible," may, on the *contrary*, be the hardest one to give rein to, and . . . individuals in whom the inhibiting influences are potent may pass through life and never find an occasion to have it gratified.   —W. James, 1890

1861, when invading Union generals found themselves with thousands of former slaves within their lines and large confiscated plantations that required new masters. After a brief attempt at government management, the army invited "loyal" men of "pecuniary responsibility" to lease and run the plantations on terms that were financially attractive. In the Sea Islands, northern idealists were asked to aid the transition from slave to free labor. By 1865 this pragmatic program of occupying armies was transformed into a mass movement as hordes of northerners streamed south, eager to prove that Yankees could produce more cotton more efficiently than the slave power had done. The humanitarian aim of aiding the freed slaves was appealing to many people. So was the profit potential. A large, cheap labor force, low-cost land, and high cotton prices attracted so many New Englanders that one Massachusetts cotton agent predicted confidently that northerners would grow most of the South's cotton after the war.[31]

Like so many planters from the North, Wilky and Bob bought land near the site of their regimental battles. Both the Fifty-fourth and the Fifty-fifth had fought in the triangle formed by Jacksonville, Olustee, and Palatka, between the St. Johns and St. Marys Rivers in northeastern Florida, and they purchased land in Waldo, just outside this perimeter.* Wilky approached the enterprise in an impressively businesslike manner, and his earliest letters from Florida exude a tone of orderliness and discipline. While he appealed to Providence for help, he knew that the outcome depended on his own efforts as well. By spring he was enthusiastic about their good fortune. "Everything progresses splendidly. The men are working admirably, and never were happier than they are now. They have already ploughed 40 acres of cotton land, and 8 or 10 acres of vegetable land. It would do your heart good," he told his parents, "to see our barn yard with its horses, mules, cows, chickens, guinea hens, dogs, geese and everything else."[32]

He did not let his eagerness interfere with the practical side of the enterprise. He had tried to drive a hard bargain with the landowner, Colonel Del, offering to pay cash instead of three annual payments for the land if Del would include the mill (valued at $5,000) for no extra charge. After prudently asking advice from more experienced planters, he and Bob decided that the local Florida seed, which was four years old, was too risky to use. They would spend extra money to get fresh seed from Port Royal, where the plantations had been in continuous production and the cotton

---

*General Truman Seymour had led them in a raid in the area in April 1864, specifically disobeying the orders of his commander. He assaulted a superior entrenched force, as he had done at Fort Wagner, with disastrous consequences that were the basis of a congressional inquiry. See Emilio, *Fifty-fourth Regiment*, 149–85.

was of prime quality. "It is astonishing what good luck we are having," he concluded. Even his southern neighbors were "very peaceable and hospitable and treat us with great respect."[33]

The magnitude of the undertaking did not intimidate the youthful veteran. His military experience had taught him how to lead. Nevertheless, one is impressed by the pride and sense of command with which Wilky took charge of a work force of nearly thirty men and their families. The total community came to nearly seventy people. They named the settlement Gordon, after General George Gordon of Massachusetts, and applied for a post office to be established there. Not only were they assuming the responsibility for raising cotton, but they were prepared as well to run an integrated school for both white and black children. Schoolmaster, postmaster, and entrepreneur, Wilky kept his eye on the market. He anticipated a yield of from 150 to 300 lbs of cotton per acre and felt confident that his parents would receive a 35 percent profit the first year, if the market held steady.[34]

No doubt his father was pleased at the prospect of such a handsome return on his investment, but he must have been even more pleased at the moral return. Wilky philosophized about the meaning of his farming venture in a vein that surely warmed his father's transcendentalist heart. He found that working with Nature had opened his eyes to important spiritual truths. Another strand to his thought would have delighted his grandfather as well. How much grief would have been avoided, the shade of William of Albany might have mused, if Henry James, Sr., had been prepared and willing to learn at twenty-one what his grandson had now discovered: he found that his mind worked more clearly than ever and he now believed that systematizing one's duties was essential to making a start in life.[35] Efficiency, hard work, spiritual deepening, and capital appreciation—what more could one ask from a season in the sun?

Perhaps some of the initial kindness of his neighbors was due to the presence of Union troops. When, in April, it was rumored that the troops were to be withdrawn, Wilky became uneasy. He did not think it would be safe for just two of them, but assured his parents that with a group, they could "make out." He confessed that "sometimes I feel blue and feel as if we were going to fail, but after sober reflection a good angel generally comes to the rescue and sets me right again." When the "good angel" was upon him, he was already prepared to declare the experiment a success: "We came down and settled in a region where many of the inhabitants had never seen a Yankee. None of them had faith in Negro labor, and we have fully vindicated the principle we started on, that the Freed negro under decent and just treatment can be worked to profit to employer and employee."[36]

Mary James wrote encouragingly to Wilky of his prospects. But her heart was uneasy over Bob, who had been writing discontentedly all winter about farming and his desire to follow an artistic career, perhaps architecture. Once again one notes that the elder Jameses' attitude toward Bob's desire to experiment differed sharply from their acquiescence in William's various vocational enthusiasms. Henry James, Sr., discouraged the proposal on the grounds that the family was leaving Boston for six months to live in Swampscott. But Mary was more open with Wilky, as the older brother. While she recognized that Bob had artistic sensibility, she doubted that he had the discipline to carry through with the three years of study required for a career in architecture. She was convinced that at a 25 percent return, cotton planting was a better choice.[37]

Bob accepted the family's judgment that he was not intended for an artistic career, though the longing to make the attempt was to recur throughout his life. He did take time out from his work on the plantation to paint, and some of his watercolors survive. One shows several log buildings set down in the raw, bleak Florida flatlands. Bob's delicate rendering of the structural details of the buildings suggests his architectural interest (Figure 28). The second is of a black laborer, upright, powerful, and doing what many southerners still doubted Negroes could do, reading (Figure 29).

Wilky's optimistic reports continued through the summer. His crops looked even better than those produced by more experienced planters, and he predicted a $2,500 profit for his parents.[38] The brothers planned to buy another farm and expand their cotton acreage. Wilky thoughtfully reported to his worried parents that Bob was well and had gotten over his asthma.[39] He was also proud to announce that he had been made postmaster by the citizens of Waldo, but said he would turn the task over to the village storekeeper and only sign papers. Though Wilky carefully tended to business, he kept his eye as well on his mission among the Negroes. Concerned not only about their bodies but about their souls, he asked his parents to send Bibles to give to the hands.[40] Wilky's heartfelt announcement on his twenty-first birthday must have seemed a godsend to his parents, surrounded by the neurasthenic William, Harry, and Alice: He was, he declared, contented with his new vocation.[41] The happy culmination of the saga was a simple note on August 9 enclosing freshly picked cotton, the first yield of their venture.[42]

But the triumph was short-lived. Mary James was the first to hold up the darkened mirror of fate to Wilky. In the fall she reported that Augustus James (Uncle Gus), William James of Albany's favored heir, was bankrupt. Mary James pointed ominously to him as an example of the risks of speculation. Augustus' downfall had begun during the panic of 1857, but

28. The James Plantation at Gordon, Florida, about 1866—"a region where many of the inhabitants had never seen a Yankee."
—Garth Wilkinson James to Henry James, Sr., April 7, 1866

29. BLACK FARM HAND
If we can keep them well interested in the crop and get them happy we shall then
be happy ourselves.
—Garth Wilkinson James to Henry James, Sr., March 24, 1867

according to her, he had been too proud to acknowledge the loss. He tried to cover up and lived beyond his means until tragedy struck and left him pale and thin and weeping like a child, longing for death and threatening suicide.*

Though sympathetic with her fifty-nine-year-old brother-in-law, Mary was severely critical of his moral failings. She acknowledged that Augustus had acted honorably by paying all of his creditors, but she censured him nevertheless for not having the pluck to face the family and the world with the truth. To a man with no interest but money, his life was a wretched failure without it.[43] With Dickensian vision she believed that the victims of the business cycle were not merely at the mercy of market forces of industrial capitalism beyond their control, but were also the victims of their own greed and moral defects. Augustus' failure was a harbinger of Wilky's decline.

The downturn in Florida began slowly. Having expanded their land under cultivation (they now managed three farms), the James brothers needed more labor, but none was available. Wilky wrote disconsolately that Bob had returned after searching for three and a half weeks without a single hand. After two years, Wilky confessed he had begun to lose heart and fear failure.[44] In March he acknowledged sheepishly that the factors he had chosen had sold their cotton for 30 percent less than other planters were getting. All that Wilky could offer by way of explanation was that he had learned a lesson and would not repeat the mistake.[45] They needed cash, so one of their farms had to be sold at a loss. Wilky agreed to hold the mortgage to protect his investment while reducing his expenses.[46]

As the promise of profits disappeared and survival became the primary goal, Henry James, Sr., sent words of encouragement. At bottom, he suggested, disappointments in this visible world occur to aid spiritual growth. It was, to his mind, the universal law that spiritual life must flourish because of worldly failure.[47]

Wilky echoed the same sentiment, but he was beginning to realize that his father's religious insights were a poor guide for the management of a business. He began to speak of their shared optimism as a trait of character to be distrusted. "I know my darling Father that I am of an exceedingly hopeful temperament. I feel it morning, noon and night but I do sincerely feel that in the long run those temperaments come out right. I don't think they do so in the short run however, and I am constantly restraining mine."[48] Nothing seemed to be working out. Bob began to show signs of strain and was alternately elated and depressed. Two South Carolinians

---

*Augustus died three months later, on November 29, 1866.

who had offered to buy some of their land never returned.[49] They had to force a tenant off one of their farms because he was careless and managed the land poorly.

To make matters worse, the political situation aggravated their troubles. Federal reconstruction policies antagonized their southern neighbors. Wilky began to fear for his life. "The fact is, affairs here have assumed such a change, that I no longer feel that safety which I once felt, and to tell the plain truth I feel that any moment, I may be called upon to give up my life for the faith of the principle I professed when I was a soldier in the open field." Even his friends began to turn against him. "To-day one of the best friends I thought I had in the whole country called upon me and informed me that hereafter I was his enemy. He had recently learned that I was an officer of the 54th Mass. and that hereafter all our intercourse must cease."[50] Wilky continued to work hard at raising cotton, but he sank deeper and deeper into the financial mire. The market economy and reconstruction politics formed a rack that insidiously stretched his sanguine nature and religious faith to the breaking point. Though he clung tenaciously to his belief in human goodness, he could not ignore what he saw. He noted bitterly that the men around him were ready to cheat anyone for a few dollars. Increase was God.[51] Finally the project was abandoned in 1871.

If the South would not nurture their fortunes, perhaps the West could. Bob was the first to leave. In 1867 he returned to Boston, but he could not find work. His unpredictable moods had been a trial in Florida, and Wilky was relieved to see him go. Unfortunately, Mary James reported, he was also wretched at home and wanted to move to Wisconsin. Though she was doubtful about the wisdom of a move to so severe a climate, she outfitted him and let him go. Sadly Mary James had come to agree with Wilky's judgment that they, too, would be better off without him.

Bob found a position as a railroad clerk in Milwaukee with the help of John Murray Forbes, a friend of the family.[52] Finding the job dull, he restlessly tried his hand at business, farming, and journalism, but could find no satisfaction in them, either. Ill health (back pain, weakness of the eyes, asthma, arthritis) amplified his discontent. Finally, in the 1880s, he returned east to settle in Concord. He dabbled in painting, read his father's Swedenborgian tracts, and wrote religious poetry in the intervals between alcoholic binges and long stretches (up to two years) as an asylum patient (McLean, the Jackson Asylum at Dansville, the Hartford Asylum).* As his fortunes

*In 1881 Mary James wrote the following vivid description to Bob's wife, Mary, of the tempestuous mood swings that had become so burdensome to the family. Bob was living in Boston, having separated from his wife.

declined, he became suspicious of his father (who continued to contribute generously to his enterprises), accusing him of interfering with his life.[53] After Henry James, Sr., died in 1882, Bob leveled similar accusations at William. As he grew older, Bob berated himself for his vocational failures. He could be ironic, as in a note to William's wife, Alice, who had thanked him for teaching her boys to paint: "I am glad if I was able to help the boys in any way about painting. I wish our own father had steered his sons into the soap or Baking Powder line."[54] Three generations of James family vocational struggle were alluded to in that remark. Now an artistic uncle passed his skill on to another generation, nurturing a painter's talent yet urging a more practical life choice.* In one of his religious poems, Bob's mood turned black over the fundamental question that had stymied him: "With weariness of life we come / And say to Him, 'What shall I be?'" As he mournfully contemplated his hands, "which have not sown," he longed for death: "So be it in Thy perfect plan / A mansion is where I am sent / To dwell among the innocent."[55] His brother Henry summed up the matter sadly: Bob was an "extraordinary instance of a man's *nature* constituting his profession, his whole stock in trade."[56]

Thursday P.M.
1881

My dear Mary,

I have just received your letter, and hasten to relieve your anxieties—Bob came home this morning to say good-bye to Alice who leaves this afternoon. He seems very calm and entirely reasonable about everything, and he has been so ever since he left our house the morning he went to the Asylum. You ask what was the cause of this attack. This is all we know of it. He had been spending a week very pleasantly at Uncle Robertson's, taking a great deal of exercise and feeling every way better. He says he had just written a letter to you, and went to mail it when he suddenly felt a strong feeling to have you come, and a feeling of defiance towards us, because as he said we were keeping you from him, and a determination to get home as soon as possible, and defy father. He rushed upon the car although he was told he would have to wait at Springfield, for five hours. While at Springfield he walked the streets, (it was night) and began to feel so weak that he feared he would fall in the street. This feeling led him to take a glass of ale, indeed he took three while waiting for the car. This he said maddened him and in that state he got home. He expended his violence upon us in angry words, and we told him to leave the house until he was sober and sane, and then he might come back. He went off to William's rooms, and after a couple of hours returned completely subdued, and said he wanted to be taken to the Asylum, where he might rest and be taken care of. William and we all expostulated with him, but he persisted and we took him. He has been very much depressed since, but still calm and content. . . . We have come fully to the opinion, that it is worse than useless for you to stay away any longer alienated from him.

He has a sore burden to bear in the proud, sensitive, irascible temper, which brings him so often in conflict with those he loves best, and makes so large a demand upon their forbearance. But perhaps there is hope of improvement even in his case, and this present-bitter experience, may do more for him than anything that ever happened to him. . . . [Typescript, Vaux]

*The remarkable stability of the prodigal theme can be observed in Robertson's relationship with his son, Edward Holton James (the first James grandchild). As a young man Ned was cut off by his father without honor because he continued to take money from his mother rather than support himself in his twenties. Robertson's bitter reflections on fatherhood echo William of Albany's letters during his son Henry's flight to Boston sixty years earlier. See Robertson James to Alice Gibbens James, February 12 and 23, 1898, MH.

Robertson James in Milwaukee, 1872

Garth Wilkinson James in Milwaukee, c. 1873

Wilky followed Bob to Milwaukee in 1871, and except for occasional visits home, he remained there until he died, in 1883. It was an unhappy move and Wilky felt as if he had been banished to a wasteland. "The west commercially is to be admired, and will continue to grow in that way," he predicted, "but the dreary commonplaceness of its social life is unspeakably demoralizing.[57] Railroad work did not appeal to him any more than to Bob, but he did it as a moral exercise until 1874, when, backed by another infusion of parental capital, he invested in a partnership to manufacture iron chains and bolts. By then Mary James was all too well aware of his tendency to overoptimism. She wrote to her son Henry, who was abroad: "Wilky is so sanguine that one can place no reliance upon his judgment, and little upon his prudence." The only saving grace of the plan that she could see was that "he is to do the routine work which will make things safer."[58] The business failed, as did his other speculations. In 1881, sick with heart and kidney disease (probably chronic glomerulonephritis), he could no longer work and declared bankruptcy, leaving an unpaid debt of $80,000. When he learned the following year that he had been cut off from his father's will because the money advanced on the Florida plantation was considered his share of the estate, Wilky was outraged. From his point of view, he had labored on behalf of the family, and rather than being rewarded for his hard work, he was being punished: "I labored with it for *six* of the best years of my life trying to save it, have never received one dollar of benefit from it since I left there in 1871, but on the contrary, burdened myself for life with indebtedness to other people in order to save it to the family, paid its taxes from my salary for 5 years, and its title remains in my father's name."[59] He had worked (albeit unsuccessfully) as no one in the family had worked since his grandfather, yet try as he might, he could not escape the fate of a prodigal son.

$$18$$

A Sort of Fatality

I originally studied medicine in order to be a physiologist, but drifted into psychology and philosophy from a sort of fatality.
—William James, 1902

[1]

HENRY JAMES, SR., believed that philosophy (by which he meant religious understanding guided by revelation) was the highest form of knowledge. He had casually nurtured his son's speculative talents not by design but by permeating the atmosphere with religious concern. Through conversation and correspondence he made philosophizing seem a vital task even as he continued to prod his favorite son toward a scientific career. But scientific training exposed William to teachers and students who ignored or deprecated his father's truths, being persuaded by the brilliant success of science to make materialism a standard by which all of life was to be comprehended, not just the secrets of the laboratory. Darwin's theory seemed to explain human origins on the basis of physiochemical laws, thus making God superfluous. The theory of the conservation of energy seemed to transform the most cherished human abilities—thinking, willing, believing—into mere illusions, the epiphenomena of bodily changes brought about by preexisting impersonal forces. For the elder Henry James and other theologically minded men, this attitude was merely proof that science could run wild. For such young scientists as William James, the prestige of science gave credibility to a philosophy ("naturalism," "positivism") that threatened to rob them of the belief that they could direct their own lives.

If Henry James, Sr., as William's earliest philosophic mentor, urged him toward theism, two Cambridge friends, Chauncey Wright (1830–75)

298

and Charles S. Peirce* (1839–1914), were his positivist tutors. They formed a skeptical counterweight to his father's religious teaching, and William veered first in one direction and then in the other until he finally discovered his own truth and came to rest respectfully in between. Though impressed by the utility of scientific method, he was aware of its limitations as a standard for all thought. Cognizant of the reality of religious experience (such as his father's) and the life-saving impact of religious belief, he refused to accept atheism and pessimism. Positivism and theism, he decided, were the expressions of different temperaments. Neither the "tough-minded" skeptic nor the "tender-minded" religious idealist could with finality banish the other from the temple for worshiping a false god.

As we have seen, James had promised himself as early as 1865, during the Brazilian expedition, to "study philosophy all of my days." But it was one thing to read philosophy and relish philosophic argument and quite another to become a professional philosopher. Philosophers were supposed to reinforce orthodoxy in nineteenth-century American colleges; James Walker, James McCosh, and Francis Wayland, the presidents of Harvard, Princeton, and Brown, set the tone of philosophic instruction, and all were ministers.[1] If one looked at the lives of Chauncey Wright and Charles S. Peirce (not to mention that of Henry James, Sr.), the prospects for a career in philosophy in America were bleak.

Chauncey Wright, born in Northampton in 1830, was twelve years older than James. His father was a grocer and deputy sheriff; his mother was a somber woman who reportedly had not "a particle of fun in her." He attended the Select High School, an educational experiment for twenty to thirty gifted students in Northampton, where he came under the tutelage of a talented teacher, David S. Sheldon. Sheldon introduced him to astronomy (he constructed some crude instruments for studying the stars) and biology, with particular emphasis on Robert Chambers' *Vestiges of Creation,* a defense of evolution. Wright would later prepare significant papers on cosmology ("Physical Theory of the Universe"), proposing that the solar system was created from original nebulae by expanding heat and the opposing force of gravity, and evolution ("Limits of Natural Selection," 1870; "The Genesis of Species," 1871; "Evolution by Natural Selection," 1872; and "Evolution of Self-Consciousness," 1873), defending Darwin through a philosophic analysis of his method of scientific explanation. In his high school years Wright became the protégé of Ann Lyman, a widow who distracted herself from her grief after her husband's death by nurturing the careers of several promising students in Northampton. It

---

*Peirce changed his name from Charles Sanders Peirce to Charles Santiago Peirce in honor of William James (Santiago = St. James).

was through her influence and support that Wright went to Harvard. He graduated in 1852, having been voted the "homeliest man" in the class.[2]

Wright's subsequent career was one of frustration and unrealized talent, owing in part to character traits that went along with his tough-mindedness. When William wrote his friend's obituary note for *The Nation* in 1875, he reflected on Wright's failure. A great man, he noted, "needs to have *many* qualities great" if he is to be successful. Unfortunately, Wright's remarkable analytic powers were submerged by "his shyness, his want of ambition, and . . . his indolence."[3] William had ample opportunity to see him up close, as Wright had been a frequent visitor to the James household from the 1860s on. Henry, Jr., remembering "his strange conflictingly conscious light blue eyes," considered him "the most wasted and doomed . . . [of] bachelors of philosophy."[4] William appreciated him for his clarity, his unconventional turn of mind, and his powers of expression. Wright wrote for *The Nation* and the *North American Review* and gave two lecture series (with "monotonous fluency" that bored his students) on psychology (1870) and mathematical physics (1874) at Harvard. He never secured a regular teaching position, but supported himself by using his mathematical talents to do calculations for the *Nautical Almanac*. As the job was "piece work," he was able to arrange his own hours and had ample time for speculation.[5] But even this liberal arrangement became onerous, and he soon tried to cram twelve months of calculating into the last three months of the year.

For William, Wright was an archetypal positivist, and he respected him as an expert on the scientific method. Wright looked down condescendingly on James from the Olympian heights of twelve years' seniority. In 1875, when Wright was forty five and James was thirty three, Wright wrote, "I dare say my good opinion of [William] relates rather to possibilities in his development, than to the merits of anything he has done or does." He labeled William "boyish" (in his opinion, "one remains a boy longer in philosophy than in any other direction") but felt confident "that by laboring with him I shall get him into better shape by and by."[6] William wrestled with Wright at monthly meetings of the Metaphysical Club, an informal group that began to meet in Cambridge in the early 1870s. He rarely overcame his antagonist's rigorous logic, but when he did he was jubilant. In 1872 he trumpeted to Alice his glee over "the great Chauncey Wright who now (as to his system of the universe) lies in my arms as harmless as a babe."[7] For Wright, science limited all knowledge to the phenomenal world, which it studied inductively aiming to reduce its elements ("behind the bare phenomenal facts . . . there is nothing").[8] It was his firm conviction that speculation on underlying notions of harmony or divine intent was pointless.[9]

Inevitably, Wright's positivism led to agnosticism, which James rejected.* A world in which rational combinations emerge merely as the result of "aimless drifting to and fro" (what Wright called "cosmical weather") did not satisfy the younger man's philosophic need for "a solid warrant for . . . [his] emotional ends." Until he died, Wright continued to deprecate James's ideas as "crude" and "extravagant," and William judged Wright's austere positivism to be the product of "a defect in the active or impulsive part of his nature."[10]

It is remarkable how often James's criticism of Wright echoed barbs leveled at William by his father. What was he saying, after all, but that science could not intelligently extend its realm into the religious sphere, and that a mind that tended toward science was bad for the soul?

The melancholy quality in Wright's character deepened as he grew older. In 1853 Mrs. Lyman, his benefactor, moved to Cambridge and Wright boarded at her house. She liked to hear his "profound" conversation, and the visits temporarily relieved her gloom. Wright became an essential part of the household. When her granddaughter came to stay for the summer, Wright was her favorite companion. In 1861, out of kindness for what she feared had become a burden to Wright, Mrs. Lyman's daughter placed her in the McLean Hospital. The breakup of this home, coupled with the increasing isolation that Wright felt as his friends married and went their separate ways, plunged him into a severe depression. His habitual heavy drinking intensified.[11] A new friend, Charles Eliot Norton, helped to rescue him temporarily from melancholy,† but Wright continued lonely, unknown beyond his Cambridge Socratic circle, and intermittantly alcoholic until he died from a stroke in 1875.

[2]

Charles Peirce, the son of Benjamin Peirce, professor of mathematics at Harvard, was three years older than William. They met when William was a beginning student at the Lawrence Scientific School and Peirce had nearly completed work for his degree.[12] Like Wright, Peirce was an intimate of the James family. He was particularly fond of the elder Henry and

---

*Bruce Kuklick interprets Wright's agnosticism as "a pose," and says that Wright recognized the importance of faith and developed a "soft" natural theology in which the creation of life stood as proof of divine intervention. See Bruce Kuklick, *The Rise of American Philosophy* (New Haven: Yale University Press, 1977), 64–70, 77–78. In this discussion, William James's interpretation of Wright takes precedence.

†Norton was the son of Andrews Norton, the most prominent spokesman for Unitarianism at the Harvard Divinity School. When Charles Eliot Norton fell away from the church under Wright's influence, there was considerable consternation in Cambridge.

was sympathetic to his Swedenborgian faith. At the gatherings of the Metaphysical Club, Peirce deferred to Wright as the "boxing-master whom we,—I particulary,—used to face to be severely pummelled."[13] As he surveyed the bare Cambridge scene in search of intellectual companions in 1861, James spotted Peirce as "a very 'smart' fellow" and shrewdly observed personality traits that were to hamper him as he struggled to build a career. He was "independent and violent."[14] Later, besides being ill at ease socially, he would become suspicious and arrogant.[15] Henry James, Jr., accepted William's estimate of Peirce's genius but found him "intolerable" when the philosopher was in a bad mood (William called him a "thorny and spinous bedfellow").[16] Peirce's father had directed his education, emphasizing analytical and mathematical habits of mind, and persistently urged him toward a career in science. As an undergraduate Peirce was attracted by Kant and German idealism. (He studied Kant's *Critique of Pure Reason* two hours a day for three years, supplementing his reading by almost daily discussions with Chauncey Wright.) But his perspective was always that of the laboratory scientist, and he moved on to the English empiricists because they proceeded "by surer methods and more accurate logic." Though he was to make substantial contributions to applied science (he invented a pendulum to make geodetic measurements more accurate and developed a theory of conformal map projections that resulted in a quincuncial map that is still used in revised form to depict international air routes) and mathematics (he enlarged Boolean algebra, and edited and extended his father's *Linear Associative Algebra*), Peirce's primary interest was philosophy and the methodology of the sciences.[17] Like William, he was a scientifically trained philosopher, but his grasp of science was more sure and the laboratory was more congenial to his nature.

William was always open to a broad range of idiosyncratic people, generously appreciating the variety of life and human genius. It was a trait that made him beloved as a colleague and teacher. After William's death in 1910, Peirce recalled this quality appreciatively: "His comprehension of men to the very core was most wonderful. Who, for example, could be of a nature so different from his as I. He so concrete, so living; I a mere table of contents, so abstract, a very snarl of twine. Yet in all my life I found scarce any soul that seemed to comprehend,—naturally, my concepts but the mainspring of my life, better than he did."[18] But Peirce did not find many such admirers, and as a model for a philosophic career his experience was grim. In the 1870s Peirce bristled, "I am a man of whom critics have never found anything good to say. When they could see no opportunity to injure me, they have held their peace."[19] He gained a scant livelihood from the Lowell lectures, giving a series on the philosophy of science in 1866 (William "could not understand a word" but "enjoyed the sensation of listening") and a course of lectures at Harvard in 1869 (William found it "incomprehensible"), but he could not find an academic position.[20]

It was as difficult for Peirce to understand why William could not grasp the beautiful precision of mathematics as it was for William to believe that mathematical representation adequately touched the living reality that was so palpable to him. "I . . . knew and loved him for forty-nine or fifty years," Peirce once wrote, "but owing to his almost unexampled incapacity for mathematical thought, combined with intense hatred for logic,—probably for its pedantry, . . . he had, I fear a right to be offended at the contemptuous language that I thought it my duty to use when talking . . . to young men. . . ."[21]

But Peirce, though rigorous, did not banish religious questions as meaningless, as Wright did. He wrote two series of articles, one on doubt (1868) and the other on belief (1878), that influenced William's developing thought.[22] William repeatedly adapted Peirce's ideas as he matured. To emphasize the distinctions between them, Peirce renamed his thought "pragmaticism," a term he considered "ugly enough to be safe from kidnappers." Ralph Barton Perry acutely summarized James's distortion of Peirce as follows: "Perhaps it would be correct, and just to all parties, to say that the modern movement known as pragmatism is largely the result of James's misunderstanding of Peirce."[23] By 1869 Peirce seemed a "poor cuss" to William because he had "no chance of getting a professorship anywhere" and was condemned to work at practical science "for good." James was not sanguine about the prospects of anyone of a scientific cast of mind interested in a philosophic career. "It seems a great pity that as original a man as he is, who is willing and able to devote the powers of his life to logic and metaphysics, should be starved out of a career, when there are lots of professorships of the sort to be given in the country to 'safe,' orthodox men." James thought that Peirce ought to "hang on, as a German would, till he grows gray."[24] Though he published ground-breaking articles on the logic and semantics of science that were to influence philosophy in the twentieth century, Peirce never would find a place as a professional philosopher. He worked for thirty years (1861–91) for the U.S. Coast and Geodetic Survey. His last years were spent in abject poverty, financially supported by William James and other colleagues. He died in 1914.

[3]

The elder Henry James whetted William's appetite for philosophy and Chauncey Wright and Charles S. Peirce made his taste more discriminating, but it was personal experience that provided the primary motive for his philosophizing. Through the 1860s despondency had made him vulnerable to materialism. In March 1869 he complained to Tom Ward, "I'm swamped in an empirical philosophy. I feel that we are Nature through and through, that we are wholly conditioned, that not a wiggle of our will happens save as the result of physical laws. . . ."[25] He was then preparing for final examinations in medical school. Having cooperated apparently with inexorable forces out of devotion and uncertainty, he found himself pushed toward naturalism.

But a reluctant scientific career was only one shackle of felt determinism. The fear of madness was another. The following letter to his cousin Kitty Prince, written in 1863, after he had decided to go to medical school, is the earliest direct expression of this fear in his writing. Kitty had written describing the personal qualities of an ideal practitioner of psychiatry, a field that he said attracted him. "As for 'live lunatics' I am very much afraid that I am little fitted by nature to do them any good and your catalogue of the graces wh. shd. deck any one who undertakes to 'treat' them tends to make my fears a certainty." He nakedly confessed his fear. "I verily believe I shd. catch their contagion & go as mad as any of them in a week for on reading Dr. Winslow on Obscure Diseases of the Mind not long since my reason almost fled, it was so rudely shaken by the familiar symptoms the Doctor gave of insanity."[26] The breakdown of the 1870s lay before him. The preoccupation with insanity stretched back to 1861. True, determinism was in the Cambridge philosophic air, but this young philosopher's vulnerability was uniquely personal.

In 1868 he had embraced his friend Holmes as a kindred spirit to whom he could cling "when all the rest of the world was sunk beneath the wave." He labeled himself crazy. "Believe me, my Wendly boy, what poor possibility of friendship abides in the crazy frame of W. J. meanders about thy neighborhood."[27]

The following November (1869), Bob, his youngest brother, provoked another fearful declaration when he got secretly engaged to their cousin Katharine Temple.* The prospect of marriage between first cousins, both of whom had already experienced nervous symptoms, made William write with painful clarity of his conviction that he and his siblings carried a curse and were morally bound not to inflict it on another generation.† Henry

---

*Katharine Temple was the oldest of four daughters born to Catharine James Temple (1820–54), sister of Henry, Sr. Catharine and her husband, Robert E. Temple, had died of tuberculosis within four months of each other, leaving six orphans. The four girls were raised by the Tweedys of Newport.

†The belief in "tainted inheritance" was important in nineteenth-century psychiatry. In our own time genetic transmission has recaptured the attention of psychiatrists. It must have occurred to some readers to wonder whether the family suffered from some genetically

James, Sr., had already written discouraging the match. William added his voice: "I must tell you that I feel with father, and even more strongly than he does." And there was no doubting why. "After all, what results from every marriage is a part of the next generation and feeling as strongly as I do that the greater part of the whole evil of this wicked world is the result of infirm health, I account it a true crime against humanity for anyone to run the probable risk of generating unhealthy offspring." He was so firmly convinced of this organic determinism that he had already decided never to marry. "I want to feel on my death bed when I look back that whatever evil I was born with I kept to myself, and did so much toward extinguishing it from the world."[28]

The family had very good reason to worry about Bob. He was subject to wide mood swings and had been drinking excessively, qualities that intensified as he grew older. William brought the full weight of scientific expertise to bear on the proposed match. Assuming that Bob would "doubtless rather have that [judgment] in someone else's words" than his, he cited an authority who warned: "If disease exists, if it exists in each parent especially in the same form, it will pronounce itself more & more in the children."[29] As Bob had begun to have back symptoms and Kitty already had a "weak back," William was firmly of the opinion that the proposed marriage would be a civic crime."*

The engagement was broken off, but William continued to worry about his own future. On December 21, 1869, he was convinced that "Nature &

---

determined disorder. Of the eleven children of William James of Albany who reached maturity, three—Henry, the Reverend William, and Jannett—had breakdowns. Jannett is the only one for whom I have found evidence of psychosis, probably a manic episode (see Jannett James to Reverend William James, 1830, Amherst College Library). Henry's illness might be diagnosed as a panic disorder. Howard, the youngest brother, was alcoholic. Of the children of Henry James, Sr., all but one (Wilky) were subject to depressions with psychosomatic features (what William called "dorsal insanity"). Robertson was alcoholic, as his father had been. Their first cousin, Robert Temple, the son of Catharine James, was also alcoholic and had been imprisoned for forgery. Garth Wilkinson James at times may have acted the part of a confidence man. Thus the incidence of affective disorder, alcoholism, and other forms of psychopathology in the first three generations of this family is high. (It may be even higher; my data are far from complete.) Modern large-scale twin studies suggest that these disorders have a genetic element: the incidence rises with the closeness of blood relationship to a diagnosed patient. So William's concern over a consanguineous symptomatic match was scientifically justified, though the correlation between consanguinity and mental disease is by no means so simple as he and his generation believed. Genetic predisposition provides only one factor in the shaping of a life. Complex social and personal influences are also formative, as this study demonstrates.

*It must be kept in mind that William used many terms for nervous illness interchangeably: "weak back," "dorsal collapse," "dorsal insanity." In this chapter I use the term "insanity" as it was commonly employed in the nineteenth century—to indicate any nervous disability, not necessarily psychosis—in order to recapture William's dread of nervous disorder for the reader.

life have unfitted me for any affectionate relations with other individuals." Persistent depression and the fear of transmitting insanity might cut him off from an active life ("I may not study, make or enjoy"), but nevertheless he sounded a brave note of resistance: "I can will. I can find some real life in the mere respect for other forms of life as they pass. . . ."[30]

Even in his darkest periods, when determinism seemed inescapable as he floundered in the Slough of Despond, James maintained a belief in his own powers. Both ideas coexisted and neither was extinguished when the other gained ascendancy. The letter of the previous March in which he confessed that he was "swamped in empiricism" can also be cited to demonstrate his belief in the power of mind (reason) and in his own capacity to resist the deterministic momentum of naturalism.[31]* He confided to his correspondent, "I had a little while ago an experience of life which woke up the spiritual monad within me as has not happened more than once or twice before in my life. 'Malgré la vue des misères ou nous vivons et qui nous tiennent par la gorge'†—there is an inextinguishable spark which will, when we least expect it, flash out, and reveal the existence, at least, of something real—of reason at the bottom of things." Far from being overwhelmed by determinism, he sounded a characteristic note of moral defiance to naturalism: ". . . all is nature and all is reason too. *We shall see, damn it, we shall see.*"[32]

In January 1870 the threat of madness was on his mind again as he wryly proposed a change in the medical partnership first mentioned to Henry Bowditch in 1867. Originally Bowditch was to be the practicioner and James the one who kept abreast of the scientific literature for the firm. Now he suggested that Bowditch become the keeper of an insane asylum where William would be assured a refuge. "The older I grow, the more important does it seem to me for the interest of science and of the sick, and of the firm of B. & J., that you should take charge of a big state lunatic asylum. . . . And if you once took firm root, say at Sommerville, I should feel assured of a refuge in my old and destitute days, for you certainly would not be treacherous enough to spurn me from the door when I presented myself—on the pretext that I was only shamming dementia."[33]‡

---

*Despite this clear conjunction (and many other instances could be cited), Ralph Barton Perry was wedded to the picture of serial development, with James "peculiarly exposed to naturalistic arguments, . . . [during] the whole period of his studies and early illness, down to the crisis of 1870 when the reading of Renouvier gave him the courage to think and believe his way out" (*TCWJ*, 1:471).

†Despite the impoverished view in these parts which has us by the throat.

‡Sommerville later became McLean Hospital. During my research in the Boston area, I was repeatedly told that William James had been hospitalized at McLean in later life. My efforts to gain access to such records or to verify that such records exist were unsuccessful. If the rumor is true, it lends this letter to Bowditch a prophetic quality.

The episode of morbid anxiety described in the previous chapter would only confirm his worst apprehensions. In March the death of his cousin Minny Temple (Katharine's younger sister) of tuberculosis made him feel the "immediacy of death" and "the nothingness of all our egotistic fury."[34] It had been a grim winter.

[4]

A month later William recorded his sober reaction to an essay by the French philosopher Charles Renouvier. "I think that yesterday was a crisis in my life. I finished the first part of Renouvier's second 'Essais' and see no reason why his definition of Free Will—'the sustaining of a thought *because I choose to* when I might have other thoughts'—need be the definition of an illusion."[35] In contrast to the pessimism inculcated by the British empirical school, Renouvier supported William's wish to believe that he might direct his own life.

Charles Renouvier was to become an important influence on William James. He was twenty-seven years older and a leading figure in French intellectual life. James was attracted by Renouvier's pluralist empiricist position, which made experience the basis of reality yet avoided the snare of determinism that held John Stuart Mill and the British empiricists in its grip. Renouvier conceived a world in which representations were both subjective and objective, a world whose parts were separate yet interlaced, thus leaving room of novelty, effective will, and moral choice. He emphasized the shortcomings of logic and experience for the development of a coherent philosophy, and recognized that personal belief (an expression of temperament and practical interests) was a key factor in many issues left unresolved by logical proof and limited evidence. All of these ideas struck a responsive chord in William when he began to read Renouvier in 1868. As they grew older time uncovered many points of difference between them. James would continue to cite Renouvier's pluralism as formative to the end of his life, but the Frenchman's influence was less fateful than some writers have considered it.[36]*

---

* Renouvier's intellectual influence on James was obviously profound, but he has also been credited erroneously with rescuing James from despair. According to Ralph Barton Perry, William read Renouvier while in a depressed mood in 1870, was brought to a "crisis," and subsequently experienced a marked improvement in health and spirits. In Perry's words, "he experienced a personal cirsis that could be relieved only by a *philosophical* insight," and Renouvier's argument for freedom of the will provided that "philosophic cure." In Perry's view, Renouvier offered James a new gospel. "To believe *by* an act of will *in* the efficacy of will—that is a gospel which fits the temper of action, and which may be used to bring the invalid warrior back to fighting trim" (*TCWJ*, 1:324).

Perry's version provides a pleasing literary structure for the biography of an important

The "crisis" that James said he experienced on reading Renouvier is to be distinguished from the breakdown described in the previous chapter, which was unique. Such "crises" as this 1870 episode were not at all unusual in James's life. In 1868, for example, two years before the Renouvier entry, he recorded another "crisis" in his journal. It took place while he was listening to a private concert given by some friends. "While listening to Miss H's magic playing & the Dr. and the Italian lady sing my feelings came to a sort of crisis." He was thrilled by the aesthetic experience but disheartened by his own lack of accomplishment. "The intuition of something here in a measure absolute gave me such an unspeakable disgust for the dead drifting of my own life for some time past." In characteristic fashion, he planned to turn the spontaneous emotion into a stimulus for self-improvement. He concluded hopefully, "It ought to have a practical effect on my own will."[37]

We can see what James meant by the term "crisis" in this entry. It is a moment of intense emotion to be used for moral improvement. The guiding spirit for this primitive attempt at behavior modification was Alexander Bain. James began to study his work in 1868, along with Renouvier's. Bain's conception was simple: mind is dependent on the plasticity of nervous tissue, which is capable of retaining impressions made by sensations. Associative connections are formed between sense impressions by contiguity. Moral action (by which Bain meant such things as getting out of bed in the morning) could be taught by the constant repetition of impressions on the plastic nervous substance; intense emotion accelerated the process of habit formation.

Habit formation was not a cool scientific matter for Bain, but a war to overcome evil. In this archetypal contest it was dangerous to lose a single skirmish. "Every gain on the wrong side," he cautioned, "undoes the effect of many conquests on the right." If the "crisis" emotion was to aid habit formation, it had to be recalled vividly. To make recall easier, William associated the concert with a more general category—men of genius who made him feel anguish over his own inadequacy. Thus think-

---

philosopher. It is a tale of rebirth typical of Christian spiritual biography that depends on three elements for its power to convince: the uniqueness of the "crisis," an ensuing conversion to a new belief, and a marked improvement in health proving its curative value (like the Swedenborgian conversion of Henry James, Sr.). Unfortunately, all three elements depend on a misreading of the sources. A careful reading shows that the Renouvier "crisis" was not unique, nor did it mark a change in William's beliefs, and it had no dramatic impact on his health. Furthermore, Alexander Bain, the associationist psychologist, was more important than Renouvier in James's 1870 struggles. Unfortunately, the editors of the definitive edition of *The Works of William James* have followed Perry, compounding the error (H. S. Thayer, Introduction to William James, *Pragmatism* [Cambridge, Mass., 1975], xiii). See Howard M. Feinstein, "The 'Crisis' of William James: A Revisionist View," *Psychohistory Review* 10, no. 2 (1981):71–80.

ing of men of genius would make him reexperience the "crisis" emotion as "a horror of a wasted life."[38] And if all went well, this exercise would bring an end to the confusion and despondency that had characterized his life since 1861. Unfortunately, the 1868 behavioral program had little effect. William ruefully acknowledged, "The only trouble is that the reverberation dies away so soon in the soul and the bog closes around once again."[39]

The 1870 "crisis" was also harnessed to William's therapeutic plans in accordance with Bain's associationist principles. The diary entry that allegedly marked the Renouvier conversion really illustrates the triumph of Bain's moralizing view of habit formation over philosophy (including Renouvier's) and was tied to James's fear of madness. "For the present then remember: care little for speculation; much for the *form* of my action; recollect that only when habits of order are formed can we advance to really interesting fields of action—and consequently accumulate grain on grain of willful choice like a very miser; never forgetting how one link dropped undoes an indefinite number." Not only did James imitate Bain's language, but he mentioned Bain by name: "Today has furnished the exceptionally passionate initiative which Bain posits as needful for the acquisition of habits."[40]*

If the encounter with Renouvier was a turning point, the new conviction should have resulted in some novel action, some affirmation of authentic striving in the world. In fact, the reverse happened. William invoked Renouvier/Bain to stifle himself. Such works as Renouvier's *Second Essay* gave him pleasure. He enjoyed reading them. But moral exercise (his responsibilities as a dutiful son attempting a scientific career, and the wish to prevent madness) required William to force himself away from the philosophic speculation he loved. "For the remainder of the year," he promised himself, "I will abstain from the mere speculation & contemplative *Grubelei* [meditation] in which my nature takes most delight. . . ."[41] The excitement of Renouvier was to be overwhelmed by the asceticism of Bain.

What of the impact of Renouvier on James's health? There is no evidence that it had any effect at all in 1870 or soon thereafter. A week after the diary entry in which he referred to the Renouvier "crisis" he wrote to his brother, "I feel melancholy as a whip-poor-will," but he sounded his usual note of hope that his latest regimen would change his state. "I have at last, I think, begun to rise out of the sloughs of the past three months."[42]†

*The reference was deleted in Perry's version of the diary entry.

†There is even more persuasive evidence of the limits to Renouvier's healing power. In 1872 William wrote to Renouvier describing the French philosopher's work as "one of the great landmarks in the history of speculation." He also spoke of his own health. "As soon as

Rather than a novel turning point, the Renouvier "crisis" of 1870 was just another episode following the same pattern of moralizing self-constriction that William James had pursued since 1861, when he forced himself away from painting. Desire had to be submerged by duty. Whether the siren call came from art (as in 1860–61) or philosophy (as in 1870) mattered little to the self-deforming structure. Both impulses had to be willfully suppressed.[43]

What William needed desperately was not a new argument to support an idea that he already believed, but a means to stop stifling himself. He had to set himself free from the web of confusion spun around him by his father's vocational struggles with *his* father. Without authentic self-affirmation, his striving only rendered him more helpless. As is so often the case with such rational, willful self-treatment, the cure was part of the disease. Renouvier was undoubtedly important to the development of William's ideas, but from the outset Renouvier was fused with Bain to fashion one more justification for James's effort to restrain himself. Instead of freedom *of* the will, William needed to be freed *from* the will—his own and the testamentary shadow cast by William James of Albany.

William's introspective talent kept him from being taken in completely by his self-manipulations. A diary entry a full three months before the Renouvier "crisis" shows him in skeptical form, his ruminations having been provoked by "a great dorsal collapse" that he took to mean that his program of "stifling all eagerness to study" had failed to bring relief. "I must face the choice with open eyes: shall I frankly throw the moral business overboard, as one unsuited to my innate aptitude, or shall I follow it, and it alone, making everything else merely stuff for it? . . . Hitherto I have tried to fire myself with the moral interest, as an aid in the accomplishing of certain utilitarian ends of attaining certain difficult but salutary habits. . . . But in all this I was . . . more or less humbugging myself."[44]

"The moral business" was the willful forcing of himself in the direction defined by his sense of duty. Here was an insight similar to the one revealed in the note written at Pomfret, which showed, if only briefly, that William was painfully aware of what he was doing. He was still balancing his tolerance of pain against his reluctance to cause pain, as he had been the year before. Unfortunately, he concluded that he had not given self-

---

my health (which has been very bad for several years) allows me to undertake serious intellectual work, I mean to make a more thorough and critical study of it, and write a report of it for one of our reviews" (*TCWJ*, 1:662). If Renouvier's works had produced a dramatic improvement, one would have expected William to acknowledge him as a benefactor. Instead he indicated that he had been ill since the journal entry of 1870.

discipline enough chance. "Who knows," he wrote, consoling himself, "but the moral interest may become developed."[45]*

[5]

When asked by his father the reasons for his dramatic change of heart and mind in 1873, William cited three: reading Renouvier, reading Wordsworth, and "more than anything else, . . . having given up the notion that all mental disorder requires to have a physical basis."[46] Although James himself made this change in his ideas about mental disorder the most weighty of the three, Renouvier has captured the attention of previous biographers. How that change of ideas about mental illness came about is obscure. Perhaps it was the reading of Henry Maudsley's *Responsibility in Mental Disease.*

William was especially enthusiastic about Maudsley's chapter "The Prevention of Insanity" in *Responsibility in Mental Disease,* and thought it so "original" and "valuable" that "it should be reprinted as a tract, and dispersed gratis over the land."[47] True, Maudsley said insanity might be prevented. But his thinking, like Bain's, was based on an associationist psychology that was materialist at the root, moralistic in tone, and determinist in most of its conclusions. "There can be no doubt," Maudsley asserted, "that in the capability of self-formation which each one has in greater or less degree there lies the power over himself to prevent insanity." Here was Maudsley's hope. But what was given with one hand was taken away with the other. Fundamentally, like most other late-nineteenth-century psychiatrists, he believed that insanity was organically determined. Insanity was the stigma of a hereditary "taint," and the scion of such "tainted" stock was at best condemned to a lifelong program of willful resistance to his defective nature. The doctor was none too sanguine about the outcome. "It will be understood then, how it is that when we consider deeply what advice should be given a person who fears that he may become insane, we too often discover that we have none to give which will be of much real use to him. His character, developed as it has been, will not assimilate advice that is counter to its affinities." The only real prevention he felt sure of was to forbid the offspring of afflicted families to marry.

One can only imagine William's fear and trembling as he read the fol-

---

*My interpretation of this passage differs radically from Perry's (*TCWJ,* 1:322). Perry omits James's assessment that he had been humbugging himself and thus gives the passage a different meaning. He sees the passage as illustrative of James's position against evil in general and not against a specific evil, that is, hurting his father.

lowing declaration. "It is a fact that a pathological evolution—or more correctly, a pathological degeneration—of mind does take place through generations . . . in the first generation a predominance of nervous temperament . . . with passionate and violent outbreaks; in the second generation . . . epilepsy, hysteria and hypochondria; in the third generation . . . mental derangement; . . . in the fourth generation idiocy . . . the terminus of the pathological decline being reached."[48] What possible encouragement could a young man take from this authoritative prediction, knowing of his father's nervous temperament and his brother's and his sister's hypochondria? No wonder his most frightening image was of an epileptic idiot, representing as it did one more step in the inevitable decline into insanity. Though "scientific," Maudsley's tract read like a Calvinist sermon. Hereditary taint replaced original sin, and the dim hope of salvation for an elect few appeared bright only by contrast with the black despair of conviction. Like Bain, he offered strength of will, self-control, and habit formation as saving sacraments. This was the climate in which freedom from organic determinism became so urgent for James.

The medical moralists had suggestions to make on the subject of vocation and insanity which make William's attempt to extinguish his philosophic interests more comprehensible. In their view, insanity was best prevented by the study of science and the avoidance of speculation. Maudsley (and he is representative) was convinced that philosophic introspection could contribute to insanity in a person burdened by hereditary taint. We can only hypothesize what impact this statement would have on a young man with introspective talent and a love of speculation who was fearful of going insane. "There can be no doubt that harm is sometimes done to persons of a susceptible mind by encouraging or stimulating them to reflect upon their feelings, instead of inciting them to put the energy of their feelings into a well-ordered mental activity."[49] No wonder that he wanted to use Renouvier and Bain, free will and habit, to force himself away from speculation. Though their reasoning varied, it appeared that the experts James studied for clues to his cure were in league with the elder Henry to force him toward science and against himself.*

[6]

William had been interested in psychopathology and psychiatry from the beginning of his medical career, but he did not confine his psychologi-

---

*There is a slight anachronism here. Maudsley's book appeared in 1874, a few years after the period under discussion. I cite him as representative of a general stance in the psychiatry of the time and because William is known to have looked favorably upon the work.

cal reading to this area. Conversant with German and having traveled abroad during a decade when the field was developing, he read works in experimental psychology as well. Psychological issues had traditionally been the concern of philosophers. With the notable advances in knowledge of the physiology of the nervous system,* a foundation had been laid for the belief that physiological answers might be at hand for the age-old problems of philosophical psychology.[50] James thought the new psychology might solve his vocational dilemma. He wrote to Tom Ward, "I have blocked out some reading in physiology and psychology. . . . It seems to me that perhaps the time has come for psychology to begin to be a science—some measurements have already been made in the region lying between the physical changes in the nerves and the appearance of consciousness . . . (in the shape of sense perceptions), and more may come of it. I am going on to study what is already known, and perhaps may be able to do some work at it." He had proposed to study with Helmholtz and Wundt at Heidelberg, a plan that failed in 1868.[51]

From the outset he was doubtful that experimental psychology exactly suited his nonmathematical mind. "The immortal Helmholtz is such an ingrained mathematician that I suppose I shall not profit much by him," he confided to Henry Bowditch before the ill-fated Heidelberg venture.[52] Yet he felt obliged to push himself in that direction. Science represented self-discipline, a moral and a hygienic good. The Germans he saw around him personified this ideal. He admired "their habits of conscientious and plodding work. . . . It makes one repine at the way he has been brought up, to come here. Unhappily most of us come too late to profit by what we see. Bad habits are formed, and life hurries us on too much to stop and drill."[53] What he needed, he thought, was more discipline of the kind recommended by Bain and Maudsley. But he feared it was already too late. "If six years ago I could have felt the same satisfied belief in the worthiness of a life devoted to simple, patient, monotonous, scientific labor day after day . . . and at the same time have had some inkling of the importance [of] . . . getting orderly habits of thought . . . by intense exercise . . . I might be now on the path to accomplishing something."[54]

Instead of self-expression, the elder Henry's guiding principle, William

---

*Sir Charles Bell's charting of the division of sensory and motor fibers through posterior and anterior roots (1811), Johannes Peter Müller's confirmation that specific nerve energies were attached to various sense modalities (1826), explorations of vision by Goethe (1810) and Johannes Evangelista Purkinje (1825), of hearing by Georg Simon Ohm (1843), of touch by Ernst Heinrich Weber (1834), and of brain localization of speech by Paul Broca (1861), extension of the theory of spinal reflexes and involuntary movement by Marshall Hall (1832), demonstration of the electrical nature of nerve impulses by Emil Du Bois-Reymond (1848–49), and measurement of the speed of such impulses by Hermann von Helmholtz (1850).

scourged himself with the doctrine of habit. The patient, monotonous wearing away of channels in the nervous system held out the hope of success. Rather than the romantic heights of expressed divinity, vocation was turned into work and divine influx into a mechanism, and the self was to be controlled by the straitjacket of science. As a support for an emotional and impatient nature William urged Ward (and himself) toward regimen and routine. "I think the work as a mere occupation ought to be the primary interest with us. . . . I strongly suspect it is the secret of German prowess. . . . Have confidence, even when you seem to yourself to be making no progress, that, if you but go on in your own uninteresting way, [results] must bloom in their good time."[55] Instead of a fallen angel, man was a defective machine that needed a willful shove to keep it moving.

James read the German experimentalists Hermann von Helmholtz, Wilhelm Wundt, and Gustav Fechner. But despite his moral flagellation, he could not force himself into the laboratory. Immediately after receiving his M.D. degree, he announced his plan to "make a creditable use of my freedom, in pretty hard study . . . to make whatever reading I can do bear on psychological subjects."[56] Though his own capacity for laboratory work seemed not to benefit, he continued to urge himself and his friends on with the same exhortations. But even when he was moralizing he could not always contain his sense of humor. It bubbled to the surface and occasionally he ended up making fun of the hortatory lesson. When Bowditch had doubts about continuing in physiology, James urged him on. "I was truly glad to hear of your determination to stick to physiology. However discouraging the work of each day may seem, stick at it long enough, and you'll wake up some morning—a physiologist—just as the man who takes a daily drink finds himself unexpectedly a drunkard."[57] But as we have so often noted, James's jokes pointed to his own despair. He might succeed at the task of self-discipline and do himself more harm than good. There was, he half suspected, something self-destructive in the gospel of habit, though he didn't know what to put in its place.

Yet habit, he felt, helped to prevent him from committing suicide.* A vocation might give life meaning. Perhaps psychology would be his way. "I confess that . . . the only feeling that kept me from giving up was that by waiting and living, by hook or crook, long enough, I might make my *nick,* however small a one, in the raw stuff the race has got to shape, and so assert my reality."[58] In a letter to Holmes he joined the desire to make a contribution to the race with his interest in experimental psychology. "If I were able by assiduous pottering to define a few physiological facts, however humble, I should feel I had not lived entirely in vain." He quite

---

*Suicide was a theme he debated with Charles S. Peirce. See *TCWJ,* 1:531.

rightly saw the need for physiological research, but his heart was elsewhere. "I shall continue to study, or rather *begin* to, in a general psychological direction, hoping that soon I may get into a particular channel. Perhaps a practical application may present itself sometime—the only thing I can now think of," he confided to Holmes, "is a professorship of 'moral philosophy' in some western academy. . . ."[59]

In sum, physiology was what he ought to do out of consideration for his father and his own mental health; philosophy was what he really wanted to do; and psychology was a compromise, scientific enough to support reason yet with important implications for philosophy.

James did eventually set up a laboratory for work in physiological psychology at Harvard. In 1895, where he was fifty-three years old, he freely admitted to G. Stanley Hall that laboratory work was against his nature, but challenged his former student's claim that he and not James had established the first laboratory for experimental psychology. "As an armchair professor, I frankly admit my great inferiority as a laboratory-teacher and investigator. But some little regard should be paid to the good will with which I have tried to force my nature, and to the actual things I have done."[60] By then he had succeeded in getting out of the laboratory. He was a professor of philosophy—at Harvard, not "in some western academy." But twenty years earlier he was still enmeshed in the moralist's task.

19

Professor James

What was the most important thing [Carlyle] said to us? He said: "Hang your sensibilities! Stop your snivelling complaints, and your equally snivalling raptures! Leave off your general emotional tomfoolery and get to WORK like men!"

—William James, 1884

[1]

WILLIAM LANGUISHED for four more years after receiving his medical degree. His contemporaries pursued their chosen careers, putting more and more distance between them: Bowditch in physiology, Ward in business, Holmes in the law. Within his own family, James's self-absorbed attempt to stop time, to remain perpetually poised on the brink, became less tenable. His younger brothers moved on, yet he, despite his favored and early start, apparently stood still. No matter how successful a young person may be in avoiding drudgery, routine, and responsibility, without some tie that connects him in a concrete rather than a transcendental way to the lives of his fellows, he is bound to feel that he has missed an essential experience of his life. James knew this, and he exhorted Tom Ward to strive on. Yet he himself stuck fast. He continued to take on prodigious loads of books, mostly literature and philosophy in French and German. But for want of a destination, they weighed heavily, like ballast rather than profitable cargo.

In 1873, through a happy combination of events—the advent of Charles Eliot to the presidency of Harvard, Henry Bowditch's plan to alter his teaching position for a year, and a little behind-the-scenes meddling on the part of Mary James—he was raised off the shoals and shoved out to sea. If inner conflict prevented him from following his artistic ambition, an outward possibility—the offer of a position at Harvard—was a hopeful and necessary beginning for a man of thirty one who had never worked and whose scientific ability was not matched by love of science. Hesitatingly at first, and then with the pleasure that comes from successful deployment of one's powers, and much to his surprise and relief, he found work his salvation.

When Charles Eliot, his former chemistry professor, had been named president of Harvard, William had tersely announced in a letter to his brother Henry: "Charles W. Eliot President. I ween more bad about him than good but we shall see."[1] Eliot had been appointed over considerable opposition, and James's remark reflected the critical Cambridge gossip. Had he been able to peer into the future, he might have been more enthusiastic. Given James's becalmed state, Eliot's job offer was an act of rescue.

Eliot, like James, was the grandson of a successful merchant. Both of these men who were to figure so significantly in Harvard's history had fathers who rejected Calvinism and the careers that had been marked out for them by their wealthy sires. And both had been intended for unwanted careers by their fathers, William for science and Charles for business. Charles had a more orderly education than William. He graduated from Harvard College when he was nineteen. Health was less of a problem for him, though he had been afflicted with a mysterious visual difficulty in his junior year and had to have his lessons read to him. Eliot also faced the problem of career choice with trepidation. Like James, he was painfully aware of the apparently irrevocable nature of the decision. "The different professions are not different roads converging to the same end," he wrote as a young man; "they are different roads, which starting from the same point *diverge* forever. . . ." And whichever road was taken, business or science, would make him "an entirely different man 50 years hence."[2] Eliot seemed assured of wealth, as his father had nurtured his inherited estate more carefully than Henry James, Sr., had done. But the panic of 1857 was even more devastating to the Eliots' fortune than Henry's prodigality had been to the Jameses'.

Charles chose science without concern for the low salaries, but after the panic he suddenly found himself, at the age of twenty-three, the sole support of his parents and three unmarried sisters. He had to become the financier for the Eliots at the beginning of his career as the first assistant professor of chemistry at Harvard. His academic career did not prosper. A heavy teaching load and extensive administrative responsibilities left him very little time to pursue his own laboratory work. When the Rumford professorship in chemistry was vacated in 1863, he was passed over because he had not done enough research. With Agassiz leading the way, it seemed that Harvard was determined to push Eliot out of science and into the business career his father had intended for him. Undaunted, Eliot set off on a grand tour, hoping that European travel would help him to plan his next step. Like William, he devoted his time abroad to preparing himself for a profession that did not yet exist. William read widely and profoundly in fields that led him to teach the new psychology; Eliot trained himself to manage a modern university.

Being of a more practical temper than William, Eliot had no interest in romantic sightseeing or aesthetic cultivation. "Cathedrals are bad things—," he pronounced, "being costly and not well adapted to other uses when no longer needed for 'idolatry.'" He summed up Italy with a peremptory "Rome *stinks*" and "Ruins don't agree with me." More extensive travel in the countryside did soften him a little. "I have learned much about Art in painting, sculpture and architecture and want to read about them," he admitted, but the Boston chill was not thawed so easily, and he added, "if ever I have time for such self indulgent pursuits."[3] Instead of climbing hills for the view, he mounted ladders to see how buildings were put together. He wanted to know how the continental systems of education prepared students for work at all social levels. Trapped in the same ambivalent stance toward leisure that ensnared William, Eliot was happy abroad yet "almost ashamed" of his enjoyment. William might have lingered indefinitely, but Eliot never. "Deliver me from a life of exile, in however beautiful a land," he implored. His parting judgment of leisured Americans was severe: "I think the most objectless, forlorn, useless people we see are the Americans who live abroad without any profession or occupation but that of time-killer."[4] Though better informed, he left Europe as he came, utilitarian and Unitarian to the core.

Eliot was thirty-five when he was appointed president of Harvard. By then he had taught for over a decade and supported his parents, his sisters, and his wife and three children. By contrast, William had, at thirty-one, assumed neither work nor familial responsibility, and was still nursing ill health in his father's house.

William went to the Maine coast for a vacation in July 1872 and wrote excitedly to his parents: "I was overjoyed yesterday by a letter from Bowditch offering me his college place, if Eliot wd. consent." As Eliot was a neighbor and friend, Mary James decided to take the matter directly to him herself. She described the outcome of her mission to Henry, Jr., who was abroad. "Eliot arrived here yesterday in his yacht. I showed him the letter. He said nothing save that he would write about it to Bowditch; but I have little doubt of his agreeing."[5] Her maternal confidence was warranted. In August Eliot offered her son the job. The beneficial effect was prompt and dramatic. William's spirits rose, his energy revived, and he enthusiastically prepared for classes.

[2]

William was vacationing at Mount Desert when the news of his appointment came. He found the anticipation of teaching exciting, and wrote to his brother Henry about his hopes for improved health through scientific work. "The appointment to teach physiology is a perfect godsend to me just now. An external motive to work, which yet does not strain me, a dealing with men instead of my own mind, and a diversion from those introspective studies which had bred a sort of philosophical hypochondria in me of late and which it will certainly do me good to drop for a year." But William's inner self would not be silenced. The excitement of this new venture paled by comparison with his old artistic enthusiasm, which was troublesomely revived. In the same letter he showed once again the painter's sensitivity to landscape. "I write in the little parlor opposite the office. . . . The steady, heavy roaring of the surf comes through the open window, borne by the delicious salt breeze over the great bank of stooping willows, field and fence. The little horse-chestnut trees are no bigger, the cow with the board face still crops the grass. The broad sky and sea are whanging with the mellow light. All is as it was and will be."⁶

It was not only the beauty of Mount Desert that roused him. The imminent plunge into science threatened to extinguish, once and for all, his hopes for an artistic career and a shared closeness with his brother. "I envy ye the world of art. Away from it, as we live, we sink into a flatter, blanker kind of consciousness, and indulge in an ostrich-like forgetfulness of all our richest potentialities; and they startle us now and then when by accident some rich human product, pictorial, literary, or architectural slaps us with its tail." But the willful stifling of self had done its work. "I feel more and more as if I ought to try to learn to sketch in water-colors, but," he said resignedly, "am too lazy to begin."⁷

His envy and sadness over the artistic life not lived was even more apparent in a letter written six weeks later from Cambridge. "I never so much as this summer felt the soothing and hygienic effects of nature upon the human spirit. Before, when I enjoyed it, it has been as a luxury, but this time 't was as vital food, or medicine. I have regretted extremely letting my drawing die out." James toyed with health as a justification for keeping his artistic self alive. "A man needs to keep open all his channels of activity, for the day may always come when his mind needs to change its attitude for the sake of its health." Rather than the threat to spiritual redemption that his father feared, or the dangerous stimulant of the passions cautioned against by medical experts, painting could be a pastime for the mind in search of health. But art as a hygienic hobby hardly matched the intensity of his longing. "I have been of late so sickened and skeptical of philosophic activity as to regret much that I did not stick to painting, and to envy those like you to whom the aesthetic relations of things were the real world. Surely they reveal a deeper part of the universal life than all the mechanical and logical abstractions do, and if I were you I would never repine that my life had got cast among them rather than elsewhere."[8] By November he was attending Bowditch's laboratory daily.

[3]

James found that the preparation for his classes had the very effect on his health and spirits that he had hoped. "I go in to the Medical School nearly every morning to hear Bowditch lecture, or paddle round in his laboratory. It is a noble thing for one's spirits to have some responsible work to do. I enjoy my revived physiological reading greatly, and have in a corporeal sense been better for the past four or five weeks." He began to meet his own classes in January. It didn't take long for him to become disillusioned by the caliber of the students. His mother recorded his complaints "of the loutish character of the young men," only a few of whom showed "intelligence or interest." Characteristically, Mary James was fearful of the effect that work would have on William's nerves. "I think he finds his lessons all that he can do," she observed. "The intellectual part is easy enough, but the whole thing taxes his weak nerves considerably." She had not yet seen the benefits reported by her son, but she hoped that with "habit and experience" the nervous strain would abate.[9]

However salutary he found the work, William was relieved, like any new teacher, to have a two-week vacation when his students were "condemned to pass examinations" and he was therefore free. He told Henry that he found "the work very interesting and stimulating," and even tentatively considered teaching as an appropriate career for himself. He couched the prospect in negative terms: "I should think it not unpleasant as a permanent thing." This was at best a lukewarm endorsement, but for a man who was raised to be suspicious of any permanent work, it was a major concession. He was pleased with his success in doing something that could win public acclaim, too. "The authority is at first rather flattering to one. So far, I seem to have succeeded in interesting them, for they are admirably attentive, and I hear expressions of satisfaction on their part." As he became more comfortable with teaching, he became more convinced that he had taken a step that was good for his health. "My own spirits are very good, as I have got some things rather straightened out in my mind lately, and this external responsibility and college work agree with human nature better than lonely self-culture." He closed with a new gospel: "Enjoy and produce."[10]

Unfortunately, no sooner was William braced by the exhilaration of work than he was forced to decide whether he would take on even more scientific teaching for the next year. He had been hired initially to teach a course in physiology and hygiene for undergraduates as a shared responsibility with an anatomist, Dr. Thomas Dwight. It was an experiment in Eliot's new elective system, and the class attracted more than fifty upperclassmen. Eliot decided to continue the course the next year and offered James the entire responsibility for teaching both physiology and anatomy. From Eliot's point of view, this was not an unreasonable offer, but it forced James into a period of indecision that resurrected the vocational conflicts that had barely been put to rest. It was one thing to have *some* outward responsibility; it was quite another to find oneself overcommitted to a full-time career in science. The good effects of teaching were now apparent to him. "Bless my soul, what a difference between me as I am now and as I was last spring at this time! Then so hypochondriacal and now with my mind so cleared up and restored to sanity. It's the difference between death and life."[11] Yet he was troubled by Eliot's proposal.

Instead of a beacon that promised to guide William toward wished-for health and career stability, Eliot's proposal flashed a warning of a returning storm. The elements were the same that had drawn him for twelve years, but now the pace was accelerated. Was he headed for Europe or America? Art or science? Introspection or action? Philosophic speculation or laboratory research? Work or leisure? Health or disease?

From the time Eliot made his offer, in February, until the following March, when William returned from a five-month sojourn in Europe, he tacked frenetically, first to one point, then to the opposite. The flush of enthusiasm for teaching physiology pointed to science in February: "I decide today to stick to biology for a profession," but that declaration was immediately corrected by the next clause: "in case I am not called to a chair of philosophy. . . ."[12] A month later he swung away from physiology and toward psychology. Despite his success at teaching and his conviction that it would be easier the next time around, he "had resolved to fight it out in the line of mental science," and could not afford to make "an expedition into anatomy." He was fully aware that if he accepted Eliot's offer, it could develop into an appointment that had the virtue of being permanent "though less native to my taste."[13] Four days later he jerked on the tiller once again, heading toward science; but the move was no more decisively executed than the previous maneuver. "Yesterday I told Eliot I would accept the anatomical instruction for next year, if well enough to perform it, and would probably stick to that department."[14] He was preparing for the familiar tug of ill health to save him from science once again.

But illness, as we have seen, is a sword with a double edge. It might save him from physiology in 1873, as it had saved him from medicine in 1867.

But this time his redemption meant giving up what he wanted as well as avoiding what he didn't want. "I came to this decision mainly from the feeling that philosophical activity as a *business* is not normal for most men, and not for me."[15] A month later he informed his brother that he was still on the same reluctant scientific course, having veered away from psychology. "By the way, I believe I told you in my last that I had determined to stick to psychology or die. I have changed my mind, and for the present give myself to biology. . . ." He was obviously humiliated by the thought that the decision was the "tamer" rather than the "nobler" of the two. And sadly, his imagery was couched in the awareness of self-murder, just as in 1861, when "death, death, death" was the predicted end of scientific study. Acceptance of Eliot's offer, he mused, "is virtually tantamount to my clinging to those subjects for the next ten or twelve years, if I linger so long."[16]

By the end of May, illness had become an irresistible force pushing him away from science, work, and America and toward art, leisure, and Europe. Suddenly the work that had proved salutary to all observers was labeled dangerous. "I have succeeded in doing my college work this half-year without losing ground, so far as I know, in health, but also without gaining an inch." He told his brother Henry that he might spend a winter in Europe for his health. There was the usual concession to science: "It would also in a scientific point of view not be so very bad, since I could carry on with advantage a certain line of study there," and the equally familiar prescription for art: ". . . the appeal to the senses, and so forth, would prevent my postponement of 'business' from affecting my spirits as unpleasantly as would be the case were the winter so spent in Cambridge."[17]

By summer vacation, William had so arranged matters that he could back out of teaching at the very last minute, if his health so dictated. With his future course to be organically determined, he set off for the shore. In the ease of summer, nature seemed a healing balm and leisure to enjoy it the only normal life. Goethe was the guiding muse of that respite, and William pronounced himself "free and happy again." He wondered "how people can pass years without a week of that *normal* life . . . —life in which your cares, responsibilities and thoughts for the morrow become a far-off dream. . . ." But the dream could not last. He had to prepare for classes. "I have to deliver about thirty new lectures next year and have hardly yet made a stroke of preparation."[18]

His parents and brother Henry watched William's erratic course with concern, but like a well-drilled crew they leaped to their appointed stations. Henry was responsive to William's every direction. Henry was sure that when William began "to lecture or teach or preach, or whatever it is," his pupils would be charmed "by his accents like the forest-brutes by

Orpheus."[19] When all seemed well and William thought of continuing, he hoped "the thing [would] develop and bring you larger opportunities."[20] When William was for a career in physiology, so was Henry. "I am glad to hear you have decided on the physiology and anatomy place for next year." Yet he was gently aware of the lure of psychology and philosophy. "But I shall be interested to hear how you have compromised with the desire to give time and strength to other things."[21] And he perceptively underscored William's sadness over the move toward science. "There seems something half-tragic in the tone with which you speak of having averted yourself from psychology." Yet he was content to accede to his brother's stoicism. "You know best, and one must do not what one plans, but what one can."[22]

Though fraternally supportive, Henry's letters were filled with his enthusiasm for the sunny glory of Rome. His talk of society and artistic success could hardly help make William painfully aware of the bare Cambridge scene. Henry only occasionally mocked William's quest for health. In the spring, for example, having heard that William and Alice were using an exercise machine for the lifting cure, he quipped, "I am glad to hear Alice and William are at the lifting business again; they ought by this time between them to have lifted the world into a higher plane."[23] But for the most part he was generous, and self-assured. Writing brought him an income of $3,000 a year. His brother faltered under the burden of earning one-fifth as much. When William seemed headed toward Europe and sought advice about the "safety" of Rome for a man in his "state," Henry's reply was prompt and inviting. "I'm strongly inclined to think that you might subsist very comfortably *in Rome* on the footings you set forth." There was, he noted, enough society to "make your idle hours tolerable . . . without counting the galleries."[24] If William decided to come, Henry promised to spend the winter with him.

As soon as the health issue was raised, both parents took their characteristic position—against work. Mary James viewed the invalid with maternal solicitude. "Poor fellow! I wish it was possible for him to learn to live by the day, and not have to bear today the burden of coming months and years. He says the question of being able to do his work that lies before him next winter, and indeed his whole future career weighs so heavily upon him that it keeps him from rallying." Mr. James urged his son to quit. Though William was embarked on the scientific career he demanded, his threatened illness aroused his father's suspicions of all work. "After a serious talk with him yesterday, Father's advice to him was to give up the idea of working next winter." By midsummer, both parents were convinced that "the wiser decision would be to go abroad and rest for a year."[25]

But a barely perceptible shift was at work in their invalid son. True, he was using the tactics that had served him for twelve years. But this time he sounded genuinely interested in resisting the repetition of that familiar pattern. The semester of teaching had been a new and potentially saving experience. He had not had time to weigh it sufficiently in the balance before being forced to make his decision. That work, even work in science, might be satisfying was hardly a new idea to him. It had been his major theme in correspondence for years. But the experience of work and responsibility *was* new. It had been a "godsend" and not the disaster avoided by the elder Henry. Mrs. James seemed puzzled that William held back instead of fleeing immediately as he had done in 1867: ". . . he seems unwilling under the circumstances to do it, unless absolutely forced by a feeling of entire incompetency for his work."[26] Experience had wrought a change. But first, as if nostalgically visiting his youthful haunts, William had to complete the rest of the cycle. At the very last minute he left for Europe, promising to visit Heidelberg. He did not; instead he made one more ambivalent pass at the art treasures of Europe. This time he did not have to write to Henry because he was accompanied by "my in many respects twin brother."[27]

[4]

William was probably interested in reaffirming the shared aesthetic sensibility of their youth, yet the visit with Henry served rather to confirm their differences. To be sure, Henry still admired William's flashes of critical artistic insight. But Henry was working part of every day at his writing, his established career, and William was a not too welcome distraction. Furthermore, there was a notable shift in William's reaction to art. Compared with his enthusiastic reveling in 1867–68, his responses were cramped and lacked vitality. The years of forceful stifling of self for moral and healthful gain had slowly transformed him, and he seemed intent on underscoring that transformation in the presence of his artistic brother—as if dismissing what Henry loved would make more secure the foundations he had willfully constructed to support a career in science. He noted the change in a letter to Wilky: "For ten days after my arrival [in Florence] I was so disgusted with the swarming and reeking blackness of the streets and the age of everything, that enjoyment all took place under protest, as it were. But," he assured him, "I've left all that behind me, and can take the picturesque now without any moral afterthought." Unfortunately for his relations with Henry, that was not true. "My old love of art returns, but not in its full force. The years have weakened it, I am afraid."[28]

That was how he summarized the matter for Wilky, but it was a vast understatement. Gone from his correspondence are the enthusiastic descriptions, lovingly executed in every detail, of his earlier visit. The acme of his epistolary enthusiasm was reached in Venice, where he briefly exclaimed, "Such glory of painting," and immediately paired the glory with "and such actual decay. . . ."[29] Decay rather than creation was very much on his mind. Even when he resorted to criticism in the privacy of his notebook, he was troubled by decline as a theme. "Why does a school of art retrograde into mannerism, etc., as soon as it ceases to advance?" was the puzzle he posed for himself. A painter can treat his first discoveries without losing the "sting of interest," but followers, he thought, have to exaggerate for effect.[30] Decline was the theme, especially decline in vitality as imitators followed leaders. He was thinking of Correggio and Michelangelo and Rembrandt, but the observation was equally true of himself. By impulse he was an artist, but he was even more determined to be his father's son. Rather than luxuriating in art, he was now prepared to moralize about it, and produce a mannered imitation of a sermon against art by the elder Henry.

The remarkable effectiveness of the transformation is evident in a November letter to his father. It begins with mordant imagery reminiscent of his early sketches. "We left Florence day before yesterday . . . passing on the way by a set of little towns perched on hill spurs which would have brought from your moral consciousness certain hearty and picturesque expletives that I would have been glad to hear; so wicked and venomous did they look, huddled together and showing their teeth as it were to the world. . . ." Rome was worse. His report of a nighttime visit to the Colosseum made it sound like the setting for a Gothic horror tale. "Finally when we entered under the mighty Coliseum wall and stood in its mysterious midst, with that cold sinister half-moon and hardly a star in the deep blue sky—it was all so strange, and, I must say, inhuman and horrible, that it felt like a nightmare." Once again he imagined himself as his father. "Again would I have liked to hear the great curses which you would have spoken. . . . I think if Harry had not been with me I should have fled howling from the place." As if recounting this moonlight visit to "that damned blood soaked soil" were not enough to suit father, William enlarged, in the same mood, on his visit to St. Peter's. "Yesterday . . . another 'unsympathetic' experience, *viz.* St. Peter's, to complete the enjoyment of which I again needed your denunciatory presence. . . . it so reeks as it stands now with the negation of that Gospel which it pretends to serve, is so perfectly explosive a monument of human pride, insolence, presumption or whatever . . . that for the moment I felt fully like . . . any modern evangelical fanatic who sees in Rome the incarnation of Satan."[31]

This was a common reaction of Protestant New Englanders to Catholic

Rome. But unlike most Americans (Charles Eliot, for example) who found Rome repugnant, William had previously shown an artist's sensibility and a romantic appreciation of ruins and the picturesque. These aesthetic perceptions reflect rather the tragic solidifying of a heroic stance in defense of his own and his father's stability. If he were obliged to be scientist rather than artist, a square peg forced into a round hole, then some wholeness must be sacrificed.

No matter how noble the intent, this type of willful throttling of self is likely to provoke a storm of inner protest. The rage that was evident in William's oral-destructive drawings of 1859 was revived once again, though muted in intensity. The image of a village "showing its teeth" to the world and a drawing from his notebook survive to mark it. His father was not present to bring moral pressure to bear, but his presence was no longer necessary. William had firmly implanted his father's views within himself. Now *he* could moralize just as caustically against what he once had loved. The architectural detail that stirred him to take up his sketchbook, a doorway in the Via Gregoriana in Rome, was emblematic of his inner conflict and the devouring imagery it evoked (Figure 30). The doorway forms the mouth for a fierce visage with bushy brows and bulging eyes. The arch of the doorway suggests a man about to scream, as in James's earlier drawings. It also invites comparison with the devouring ogre whose victim's remains hang from his cruel mouth. What is different this time is the perspective and the scale. Earlier drawings leave the viewer outside, an onlooker to a world much smaller than himself. This drawing places one in the picture with the artist, who, instead of having to be captured in a struggle, is about to deliver himself into the grotesque maw. With this drawing the trickle of James's artistic productions ceased.*

In "Habit," one of the most reprinted chapters from his textbook *The Principles of Psychology* (1890), James's wistful references to the interaction between person and work must have built upon his own experience.

> Habit is thus the enormous fly-wheel of society, its most precious conservative agent. . . . It dooms us all to fight out the battle of life upon the lines of our nurture or our early choice, and to make the best of a pursuit that disagrees, because there is no other for which we are fitted, and it is too late to begin again. . . . Already at the age of twenty-five you see the professional mannerism settling down on the young commercial traveller, on the young doctor, on the young minister, on the young counsellor-at-law. You see the

---

*This is an inference. Because the drawings were removed from their original notebooks by an early executor, the dating of many is uncertain. Judging by the subject matter, however, as well as the notebook identifications that are available, this picture from the Roman visit of 1873 is the last.

Door in the Via Gregoriana
Rome

30. Doorway in the Via Gregoriana, Rome
. . . in the very act of murdering the vanquished possibility the chooser realizes how much in that instant he is making himself lose. It is deliberately driving a thorn into one's flesh. —W. James, 1890

little lines of cleavage running through the character, the tricks of thought, the prejudices, the ways of the "shop" in a word, from which the man can by-and-by no more escape than his coat-sleeve can suddenly fall into a new set of folds. On the whole, it is best he should not escape. It is well for the world that in most of us, by the age of thirty, the character has set like plaster, and will never soften again.[32]

[5]

The contrast between William's departure from Europe in 1868 and his homecoming in 1874 was dramatic. Then he returned at his parents' insistence, having stayed longer than ill health and family resources could justify. This time he returned early, of his own accord, because he wanted to work. Henry chronicled the change in health and directedness to his parents. "He left here so intensely impatient to get home and return to work that I shall not be surprised at his decision [to sail earlier than planned]. . . . I think you'll find he's a much better man."[33] The work experience of the previous year had come to belated fruition. On the surface, it had looked like a complete capitulation to science; in fact, it proved a satisfactory compromise between duty and desire. Work and science were theoretical constructs for Henry James, Sr. He knew little at firsthand about either. William's semester of teaching provided a test of father's romantic apotheosis of divine labor, and of the reality of his fears. The experience was neither as good nor as bad as he had been trained to believe. It was not all uplifting expression of the divine, but neither was it dangerous and depleting. William discovered that he could teach science and derive satisfaction from the deployment of his energies, the admiration of his students, and the social confirmation symbolized by a salary. Actual work in a specific position moved him beyond his father's reach.

Upon his return, he commented on the transition to work and America in a letter to Bob. "I don't think I shall care to go again to Europe soon, as it upsets one's content with the small scale of passive delights which he has learned to use and enjoy here. . . . I think one can learn the secrets anywhere, and end by getting as deep satisfaction out of a new wooden paling in the place where one belongs, as out of a picture-gallery abroad."[34] He had to make even more clear to Henry, who was convinced of the superiority of art and Europe, that a mundane American life might suit him. "I'm in a permanent path, and it shows me how for our type of character the thought of the *whole* dominates the particular moments. All my moments here are inferior to those in Italy, but they are parts of a long plan which is good, so they content me more than the Italian ones which only existed for themselves. I have been feeling uncommonly strong for almost three weeks . . . and done a good deal of work in Bowditch's laboratory."[35] The remarks have the familiar ring of his exhortations to Ward. But this time was different. This was a statement of *his own intentions*. William had finally decided to work, not like his father, in quixotic isolation, or like his brother, as an artist abroad, but as a scientist in America—the task for which nurture and early choice had fitted him. Fortunately the world was receptive to his genius.

Epilogue

A man with a broadly extended empirical Ego, with powers that have uniformly brought him success, with place and wealth and friends and fame, is not likely to be visited by morbid diffidences and doubts about himself which he had when he was a boy. . . . Whereas he who has made one blunder after another, and still lies in middle life among the failures at the foot of the hill, is liable to grow all sicklied o'er with self-distrust, and to shrink from trials with which his powers can really cope.

—William James, 1890

IN 1902, when he was sixty and near the end of his career, William James wrote: "I originally studied medicine in order to be a physiologist, but drifted into psychology and philosophy from a sort of fatality."[1]

Perhaps when he described the "fatality" of his career, William had forgotten how hard he had to work to extricate himself from physiology or the administrative hurdles that had been overcome to permit him to teach psychology when a senior faculty member, Francis Bowen, considered the matter adequately covered by *his* course. He may have thought it indiscreet to disclose how vigorously he had campaigned to gain recognition from the faculty, first as a psychologist and then as a philosopher, so that he could free himself once and for all from the burden of the laboratory. To tell this story we need to descend from the high ground of William's intellectual development to the swamp of university politics. It is not a tale of "a sort of fatality" at all, but a characteristic Jamesian play of will and self-determination.

It is a testament to James's genius that he shaped his opportunities so that the psychologist in him might emerge along with the philosopher, one at center stage while the other waited (often impatiently) in the wings. He continued to talk and write as if his painting experience irrevocably set his vocational pattern, as if only one self could survive at the expense of the others, but he fashioned a different way for his middle years. True, he still experienced yearnings toward painting, but that ghost no longer blocked his path as it had done in the 1860s. In his beginnings at Harvard, he pursued physiology as he had pursued medicine—as a natural science that provided needed discipline. Philosophy, like painting in his youth, was labeled a self-indulgence that threatened mental stability. Psychology was a compromise between the two. Though ill health continued to be a reliable support to the structure of his life, providing justification for leisure to write and sanction for abandoning unappealing tasks, it ceased to be a mainstay. Between 1873 and 1890, his fourth and fifth decades, William James succeeded in balancing his talents and his possibilities; as in a mobile sculpture, disparate and even deformed elements contributed to the moving, vital tension of the whole. In that process a new dynamism emerged, barely visible at first, like thin wire linking the more obvious masses. Having decided to work, he dared to become ambitious.

One of the more vivid and personally revealing chapters in James's *Principles of Psychology*, "The Consciousness of Self," contains unmistakable evidence of this internal shift. He intended to write about people in general, but the references to his own experience are unmistakable. He noted that "self-feeling" (self-esteem) normally depends on one's "actual success or failure" and the "position one holds in the world." Then he contrasted the successful man (himself) with the failure (his father) in terms that remind us of the plight that has chronicled thus far. By 1890, when the book was published, James had reached the top of the academic ladder at Harvard. He could look back on his past and dissociate himself both from the uncertain boy he had been and from the negative vocational possibility modeled by his father and his younger brothers. Like the hypothetical idealized man he sketched for his readers, *his* powers had "uniformly brought him success" so that it was no longer likely that *he* would "be visited by the morbid diffidences and doubts about himself which he had when he was a boy." Nor was *he* any longer in danger of being one who "still lies in middle life among the failures at the foot of the hill." He had dared to be ambitious and triumphed.

Two literary allusions in his discussion of self-esteem underline that fact, one boyish and the other imperial. Like the images of a dream, they allude to successive layers of personal history. "He put in his thumb and pulled out a plum, and said what a good boy am I" exudes a boyish sense of phallic triumph. And "Is not this great Babylon, which I have planted?" resounds with the imperious satisfaction of a conqueror. Both emphasize his sense of professional accomplishment. He had arrived.

He declared to his readers in an uncharacteristic gesture of public breast beating that he had decided to risk all, to stake his salvation on psychology: "I, who for the time have staked my all on being a psychologist, am mortified if others know much more psychology than I." It is perfectly plain from his subsequent illustrations—"the paradox of a man shamed to death because he is only the second pugilist, or the second oarsman in the world"—that he meant not only to be a good psychologist but to be the best psychologist in the world. He had turned his back on his youthful self. Gone is "yonder puny fellow" who lives by the timid maxim "With no attempt there can be no failure; with no failure there can be no humiliation."[2] In his place we have the public man, a secure professional prepared to match himself against all challengers in an academic battle for the survival of the fittest.

The contrast between the confident professional of *The Principles of Psychology* and the diffident instructor of 1873 is striking. The change was gradual, and signs of his rising ambition can be detected very early in his Harvard career. Eliot offered him a position but it remained for William to create a place for himself. Even in the small institution that Harvard was in the 1870s, a new teacher who aspired to teach a new discipline had to move a previously well-established professor out of the way. Thus the introduction of novelty was inevitably linked with university politics. The young instructor of psychology showed himself equal to the task. He took advantage of support from the Board of Overseers, President Eliot, publicity in *The Nation,* and a carefully cultivated job offer from Johns Hopkins to overcome departmental barriers. The new professor learned quickly that political maneuvering had to prepare the way for his intellectual talents before he could metamorphose into the eminent psychologist of 1890.

Such psychology as there was before James joined the Harvard faculty was taught in the philosophy department. The overseers had been openly critical of the teaching of psychology at Harvard in its 1871 report (the year before James was hired). They declared: "Psychological studies cannot be said to rank very high among us. They are neither taught by as many teachers, nor studied by as many students as they might be; . . . we confess that we are moved to ask for a revival of Psychology."[3] Whether the overseers intended to focus their discontent on Francis Bowen, the Alford Professor of Philosophy, is not clear. But Bowen responded by introducing a "new" course called "psychology" into the philosophy department the following year.

Francis Bowen survived from an earlier era at Harvard. The same age as William's father, he had been teaching for forty years by the time James became an instructor. He was a spokesman for a Unitarian version of theism and had successfully represented orthodoxy at Harvard against the transcendentalist assault of the 1830s. Though expert in the history of philosophy, he was a boring teacher devoted to the inculcation of Christian truths. He opposed President Eliot's innovations at Harvard, and tried to block the introduction of the elective system, lectures, and the move toward specialization. He was to oppose William James's move into the philosophy department, and would attempt to block his promotions after the young scientist-psychologist turned philosopher.[4]

Unfortunately Bowen merely changed the title of his course to accommodate the overseers. Bowen's "new" course used the same texts he had always used (Noah Porter, John Locke, Victor Cousin, and James Mill) to demonstrate that the scientific study of the mind had nothing to teach philosophers. No one was fooled.

In 1873 James Eliot Cabot spoke for the overseers, noting simply that "in psychology there has been no change, so far as we are aware."[5] Bowen's defense of orthodoxy was based on Cartesian dualism. If mind and body were forever distinct, then physiological psychology, like other scientific attempts to reduce man to mechanism, were irrelevant to philosophy. Predictably, Bowen was a foe of evolutionary theory, too. But in the 1870s students wanted to know more about the new scientific methods of studying the mind (the "new psychology"), and Bowen's data blend of Scottish realism and Unitarian natural theology did not satisfy the appetite.

The new instructor of physiology was a multiple threat to his senior colleague: he was a dynamic teacher; he was the son of an outspoken critic of natural theology; he was a scientist familiar with the new psychology and an avowed supporter of Darwin's theory; and perhaps most important, he was Eliot's man.

In 1874, his second year as a full-time teacher of physiology, William introduced a graduate course called "The Relations between Physiology and Psychology." This was his first wedge into the established curriculum and a preliminary incursion into Bowen's territory. James Eliot Cabot must have been pleased that his criticism had finally been taken seriously. He tried to pour oil on troubled waters, however, noting in the Overseers' Report for 1875–76 that scientific training was not necessarily a threat to religion. Indeed, scientific knowledge could lead to a more informed defense of Christianity. "We are glad to learn that a course upon the relations of Physiology to Psychology has been established, and we hope that it is to be incorporated into the department of Philosophy. The ignoring by philosophers of the physical side of mental phenomena has had the natural effect of exaggerating the importance of materialistic views." Cabot waxed enthusiastic about James's new course. The Alford Professor of Philosophy must have been made distinctly uncomfortable by the barely veiled reprimand that concluded Cabot's report: "It is not the immediate business of Philosophy to edify, but to help us understand the facts of life; and to do this, we must take care not to turn our backs upon any, because they do not suit our preconceived opinions."[6] It is no wonder that George Herbert Palmer, Bowen's young colleague in the philosophy department, was afraid of James, too. He had been trained in classics and divinity. He had no scientific experience of the sort the overseers were demanding. But, unlike Bowen, he *was* willing to use psychological texts, such as Bain's *Mental Science,* in his teaching. Under no circumstances could he pretend to James's competence. To his credit, Palmer would fight for James's course on Spencer's psychology when it was proposed for the department of philosophy in 1877.[7]

In December 1875 James learned that he was to be considered for promotion as assistant professor of physiology. He wrote a politically deft letter to Eliot in support of his case, defining his field ("mental science") so as to include yet circumscribe Bowen. His definition made the presence of a teacher who combined scientific training with the talents of a metaphysician essential for Harvard's future. The letter is worth quoting at length, as it shows how effectively William served as his own advocate in the academic scramble. It is significant that as he moved to solidify his scientific teaching position, James used a metaphor drawn from the painting episode that had caused him so much grief. He likened the Harvard faculty to a painter's canvas that could be stretched (within limits) to include him.

> Dear Sir,
>
> Since you are about to confer with the Corporation about my general position in the College program, it may not be improper for me to give you on paper my notion of the way in which my proposed teaching would fit in without stretching unduly the canvas.

He divided the field of mental science into four parts—logic, history of philosophy, metaphysics, and psychology—and indicated that the present curriculum (under Bowen) dealt mainly with the history of philosophy (by implication the three other areas were neglected); suggested that orderly progressions would be just as well served by three courses (there were four in the catalogue) if size were no consideration (thus making room for *his* course); and then proposed that physiological psychology be added to the undergraduate offerings. He emphasized his colleagues' inability to teach the new psychology with a sharp rhetorical question.

> The question is shall the student be left to the magazines on the one hand and to what languid attention professors educated in an exclusively literary way can pay to the subject? Or shall the college employ a man whose scientific training fits him fully to realize the force of all the natural history arguments, whilst concomitant familiarity with writers of a more introspective kind preserved him from certain crudities of reasoning which are extremely common in men of the laboratory pure and simple?

The answer, of course, was obvious. The reluctant physician and armchair scientist unabashedly made a virtue of his dual training.

> Apart from all reference to myself, it is my firm belief that the College cannot possibly have Psychology taught as a living science by any one who has not a first hand acquaintance with the facts of nervous physiology. On the other hand, no mere physiologist can adequately realize the subtlety and difficulty of the psychologic portions of his own subject until he has tried to teach, or at least to study, psychology in its entirety. A union of the two "disciplines" in one man, seems then the most natural thing in the world, if not the most traditional."[8]

During the next year James participated in a series of events orchestrated to force Bowen to retire. It's not likely that he organized all of the elements (people who were more powerful than he were most certainly involved), but he played an active part in the cabal along with Cabot, Eliot, and G. Stanley Hall. President Eliot responded to James's December 1875 letter promptly with promises of future opportunities at Harvard. Eliot clearly had the power to bring William along, though he proved unable to dislodge Bowen. William reported his prospects to his brother Henry on December 12: "I had an interview with C. W. Eliot the other day, who smiles on me and lets me expect $1200 this year and possibly hope for $2000 the next, which will be a sweet boon if it occurs." He added a comment on his health, confirming the good effects that working (and political infighting) had on him. "As the term advances I become sensible that I am really better than I was last year in almost every way; which gives me still better prospects for the future."[9]

His undergraduate course, Natural History 2, was approved for the academic year 1876–77, and he was promoted to assistant professor of physiology. Eliot could do that much. Though he and the Board of Overseers smiled upon James and funds were allocated to support a small laboratory for research and demonstrations of physiological psychology, William was restive, feeling misplaced as a professor of science.[10] He had been corresponding with Charles Renouvier, the French philosopher, since 1872. In July 1876 he confided his problem to Renouvier. The teaching of physiology or the new psychology inevitably required work in the laboratory, for which he felt himself unsuited. He needed time to study, write, and think, and laboratory scientific duties interfered. He made his usual bow to ill health as justification, but his intent was clear. He wanted to move out of science into philosophy. He was after Bowen's job. "I long for leisure to study up these questions [pluralism versus monism]. I have been teaching anatomy and physiology in Harvard College here. Next year I add a course of physiological psychology, using, for certain practical reasons, Spencer's *Psychology* as a textbook. My health is not strong; I find that laboratory work and study, too, are more than I can attend to. It is therefore not impossible that I may in 1877–1878 be transferred to the philosophical department, in which there is likely to be a vacancy."[11] Renouvier replied with words of encouragement, acknowledging his correspondent's philosophic talent. "We have not enough real philosophers, and it is very desirable for all concerned that those who have a real calling for it should employ their power in the field of general ideas. That calling you unquestionably have."[12]

The next move in the attempt to dislodge Bowen was a public one involving James's first graduate student, G. Stanley Hall. Two years younger and a graduate of Union Theological Seminary in New York City, Hall had shown a keen interest in philosophy in his undergraduate days at Williams College. He was on his way to Germany to study psychology with Wundt when an offer to teach English brought him to Harvard. Hall stayed on to complete a Ph.D. in psychology (Harvard's first) under James. A minister of the Gospel who turned to the new psychology with an almost religious fervor, Hall, like James, looked longingly at the Harvard philosophy department and Bowen's professorship. Speaking of his original plan to study in Europe, he recalled, "I only reached Cambridge, however, for I was met by the offer of an instructorship in the English department at Harvard under Professor Childs . . . and reluctantly accepted in the hope that I might acquire a foothold to teach philosophy, as it was rumored that Professor Bowen was about to retire, which the sequel showed he had no thought of doing for some time."[13]

While James clearly had priority, what was good for his teacher might be good for Hall's possibilities, too. As we shall see, this would not be the last time that professor and student would angle for the same catch. In the fall of 1876 Hall published an open letter in *The Nation,* criticizing the teaching of philosophy in American colleges. The letter was accompanied by an unsigned statement of agreement written by Professor William James. Perhaps the two hopefuls conjectured that public opinion would help budge Bowen.

In his open letter, Hall complained that in America's best institutions "there are few if any branches which are so inadequately taught as those generally roughly classed as philosophy." He was careful to note that Harvard's offerings were broader than most, but the ploy can hardly have deceived Bowen. "The whole field of study is generally given into the hands of one of the older and 'safer' members of the faculty, under the erroneous belief that it should be the aim of the professors of this department to indoctrinate rather than to instruct . . . to tell *what* to think, than to teach *how* to think."* The motive for the letter became even more apparent when Hall later expanded it into an article. "It is, in any case plain that there is very small chance that a well-equipped student of philosophy in any of its departments will secure a position as a teacher of the subject."[14]

James opened his letter with an affirmation of Hall's criticism: "Needless to say we fully agree." He contrasted the political enslavement and metaphysical freedom in Germany with the limitations set by organized religion in the political freedom of the United States. Henry James, Sr., would no doubt have applauded his son's vigorous attack on the clergy, but Bowen and *his* friends must have had their uneasy suspicions confirmed. Young Dr. James was as dangerous as his radical father. In the United States, James asserted, metaphysical thought "has always been haunted by the consciousness of the religious orthodoxy of the country. . . . The form of philosophical problems and discussions, in short, is too apt to be *set* for us by the existence of the Church." James made an impassioned plea for "openness of mind" in philosophical teaching, so that the colleges would "make men and not machines." Like Hall, he indicated that matters were changing for the better at Harvard, but it is doubtful whether that palliative distracted informed readers in Cambridge from his bald assertion: "The sleepiest doctor-of-divinity-like repose must soon be awakened at its teaching-desk, and, getting disquieted at the novel agitation around its throne, end by abdicating in favor of teachers of more alert temperament."[15]

Bowen did not budge. James taught his undergraduate course with great success, and for the first time Harvard students had an opportunity to gain experience with the laboratory procedures of experimental psy-

---

*Notice how Hall's criticism echoes the Board of Overseers' report concerning indoctrination.

chology. If Bowen wouldn't retire, then the canvas would have to be stretched to include James along with him. Over Bowen's strenuous objections, James's course on Spencer moved to the philosophy department. Cabot and the Board of Overseers continued to praise James's teaching and to remind the philosophy department that in spite of increased enrollment and improvements in its courses, "the purely philosophical work of the college is still very inadequately represented." We must note how closely Cabot observed James's progress, how consistent an ally he proved to be in the internecine struggle for place, and how closely his arguments echoed those James put forward on his own behalf. "The course in Psychology offers a great deal of interest and stimulus to thought, which cannot fail to be of great advantage to those of the students who are sufficiently grounded in the matter to be able to test for themselves the methods of investigation and the fundamental assumptions which prevail in the 'scientific' school of philosophy at the present day." He cautioned that without adequate preparation (by implication there needed to be more instruction of the type offered by the assistant professor of physiology) students might merely substitute "the facts of one order for the facts of another order, to the confusion of all right thinking." But with William James teaching at Harvard, the risk of indoctrination was small (compared with the risk represented by unnamed members of the faculty). "We do not think, however, that with the eminently liberal and inspiring method pursued in this course, the danger in our case is a serious one."

Cabot concluded his report on philosophy (1877–78) with a comment on the need for a new textbook to teach psychology. This is yet one more clear indication of his alliance with James, who had just signed a contract to write such a text. "It is, no doubt, a misfortune that the only available text-books, and most of the material for collateral reading, should be so generally pervaded by inadmissible postulates as to give to the instruction, to a great extent, a polemical character; but this is, perhaps, unavoidable."[16] It appears that the overseers, the president, and William James were in complete agreement about what was best for Harvard's future. It was not Professor Bowen.

James was determined to get into the promised land of philosophy and abandon the fleshpots of science. His next move on his own behalf was to cultivate an outside offer from Johns Hopkins University (opened in 1876) to bring futher pressure to bear on Harvard. G. Stanley Hall was the first to hear about this job possibility. He passed the word on to James. On April 23, 1877, William wrote to President Daniel Coit Gilman of Hopkins: "The double field of psychology and physiology which I now cover is too broad for my working powers. . . . I should prefer to drop the physiology rather than the psychology. I accordingly told President Eliot some weeks ago that I wished to be regarded as a candidate for the first philosophical vacancy that should occur here. But since nothing is to be counted on blindly in whis world, I think it behoves me also to let my position be known in wider circles, and accordingly I take the liberty of acquainting you with it." He offered to meet Gilman in Newport (where Gilman had a house) and cited J. Eliot Cabot as the referee in the best position to make a "philosophic" estimate. His friend Charles Peirce also wrote a glowing letter of recommendation, emphasizing the importance of the new psychology and indicating that James was "the only man in the country" adequately prepared to teach the subject.

James was characteristically modest when Gilman immediately jumped at the opportunity to raid Harvard for badly needed faculty. On April 29 William acknowledged Gilman's "extremely friendly letter." Finding that the bait had been taken, he pulled up gently on the line. "I made my application to you merely in obedience to the general principle that if one wishes anything in this world he had better let his wish be as widely known as possible; not because I thought I was in any *particular* way suited for the place you want to fill. In fact I am wholly ignorant of what the special requisitions may be which the JH University will make of its Professors of Philosophy." The hook was set. Gilman held on and arrangements were made for William to teach a two-week series in Baltimore "in a general way expository and critical of recent speculations concerning the connection of mind and body." Hopkins would thereby gain a badly needed course and students and faculty would have the opportunity to look over the prospective candidate. In his formal acceptance William politely but firmly raised the delicate issue of money. "You made no mention of compensation, but I suppose that was accidental."[17] Though a late starter, he was learning how to play the academic game.

Henry James, Jr., was much less circumspect. The drama being enacted in the academic halls of Cambridge evoked a favorite imaginative theme, the rich American imperiously trying to buy whatever captured his naive fancy. He wrote from Europe urging his mother to tell him how William's political maneuver was faring. "I desire greatly to hear the upshot of Gilman's visit with his money-bag, and William's liability to be tempted by him. The College would be very shabby to permit itself to be outbid, and I should be very sorry to hear of his having to give up the superior civilization of Cambridge."[18] From Henry's already established European base, "the superior civilization of Cambridge" could only have been meant ironically. William was to prove himself as intractable as Henry's Madame de Cintré in *The American*. But not before Gilman, Eliot, and James played out the drama to its favorable (for William) denouement.

The lecture series of February 1878 was well received and the negotiations advanced yet one more step. In the fall William told Gilman, "As to a permanent appointment—were one offered me of which the conditions as to salary and duties were agreeable, I think I can now say I should not decline it. It is barely possible that promotion into some (now not to be expected) vacancy here might prove an effective counter-temptation—but the lighter drudgery in Baltimore would outweigh even that."[19] Eliot began to worry. Harvard blocked a plan for James to abandon his course in physiology to allow him more time to lecture at Hopkins. Sensing that his time was short, Gilman came forward with a clear intention to offer James a permanent appointment. The next move was up to Eliot. Once again the lure of Bowen's Alford professorship was dangled before William. Eliot assured James that he had "better chances than any other candidate of succeeding to the principal philosophic professorship." Though William didn't mention it in his letter to Gilman, Eliot must have been even more forthcoming than that since Bowen was still firmly in place and would remain so for another decade. James must have bargained hard. He didn't get Bowen's job but he got everything else he wanted. In 1879 he was allowed to offer his first exclusively philosophical course, Philosophy 5 (on Renouvier), he was completely freed from teaching physiology, and his appointment was formally changed to assistant professor of philosophy in 1880.[20] He had escaped at last the physiology laboratory and the scientific direction his father had imposed on him. President Gilman took defeat in gentlemanly fashion (though when James attempted to open the issue again he complained of having "his advances spurned by Harvard men").[21] He wrote, "To be frank with you, as you have been with me, I have felt confident all along that Cambridge had too strong a hold upon you for us to break."[22]

The "hold" that President Gilman referred to was less academic than familial. William confessed as much in his letter of refusal: "You know the immense strength of family ties. My father is infirm, my sister is an invalid and I think they would suffer from my absence."[23] As was his habit, he put the matter in terms of illness, but President Gilman (a familiar of the family in Newport) must have been able to fill in the rest for himself. William had lived under his father's roof until July 1878, when he married at the age of thirty-six.* Becoming separate was not easy in the James family.

The process of individuation, establishing one's unique psychological integrity, was inextricably bound to the search for vocation and the attempts of the children of Henry and Mary James to found their own families. Of the five James children, Alice and Henry never married, and of

---

The average age at marriage of Harvard graduates at the end of the century was 29 to 31.

the three who did, one, Robertson, spent his years separated from his Milwaukee-bound wife while he lived near his family in Boston. As we have seen, the two younger brothers were yoked, moving in tandem through school, the Union Army, and the postwar plantation experiment in Florida. Bob was married first and Wilky a year later to women who were close friends. Both couples had two children, first a boy and then a girl, less than two years apart. These were the first breaks out of the James family circle, and the family reaction provides some insight into the tenacity of the family grip. Whatever social amenities may have been observed, Mary James was decidedly cool to her daughters-in-law and the advent of grandparenthood.

Bob married Mary Holton in November 1872. The young couple visited Boston after the honeymoon and Mary James wrote tartly to her son Henry, "You have heard a great deal about Mary from everyone. There is not much to learn about her, I mean that does not appear on the surface. . . . Alice took to her beautifully, and although she could not make a companion [she] could make a pet.[24] When Wilky became interested in Caroline Eames Carey, his mother showed the same condescension toward yet another western addition to the family. She wrote to Alice, "These girls are neither of them I should judge at all intellectual." But that was not the only defect she noticed. In Mary Holton she detected a practical, managerial ability akin to her own, and rewarded it with haughty disdain. She cattily predicted that "little Mary" would end up taking them all over. "Perhaps one of these days they might join their resources and live together, and let little Mary manage for them all, for I imagine she would be equal to any emergency, so great a little power she is."[25]* To Henry she gloated over a family friend's impending visit to Milwaukee, where she expected to make the acquaintance of the prospective brides: "Miss Cary may be up to it; but I am sure that little Mary won't."[26]

Mary James was less disapproving of Wilky's bride-to-be, though she was far from enthusiastic. "Miss Cary" might, she thought, provide a stimulus for Wilky to work hard. "With his tendencies and temperament he needs some strong motive to stimulate him to work, and if she is only a woman of sentiment, and strength of character, and strongly enough attached to him to help him in the struggle, we might rejoice in it."[27] But

---

*Caroline Carey's background was similar to those of Mary Walsh James and William's wife, Alice Gibbens James. They were all women whose mothers had died or abdicated parental responsibility, so that as children they had assumed a parental role in their families. Wilky described his fiancée to his mother: "She has had no mother since she was 8 year old & ever since she has been able she has been the head of her father's house, directing it & managing it for him" (*AJ*, 151n). Mr. and Mrs. Henry James, Sr., eventually developed a good relationship with Mary Holton James, but Wilky's wife was never accepted, and bitterness over this rejection lingered even after his death.

several months later she was less sanguine: "Poor Wilky! . . . I am afraid she is not a strong helpful woman."[28] Apparently to Mrs. James a proper family was composed of strong women and weak men. But another powerful matriarch in the family was an unwelcome intruder.

She continually referred to the newly married sons in diminutive terms, as if they were playing house and hers was the only real grown-up family. Her son Henry received the following sardonic note when the first grand-child was born: "Our news from Bob's little household, and the pictures he draws of Mary and the boy have something more of heaven than earth in them. I wish you could read some of the daily bulletins he has sent us. You would feel that he is the most enviable of men."[29] When summer came, she referred coolly once again to her grandson Edward: "Alice sent you a photograph of our little off-shoot, which certainly looks vigorous. We hear from Wilky that he too is looking forward to blessing us in the same way. . . . Carrie will not have much sentiment about it but she may make a good mother for all; and Wilky's business prospects are so good, it is not to be regretted."[30] "Not to be regretted" was the most enthusiastic endorsement she could muster for the blooming of this branch in her family.

A rather skeptical sixty-three-year-old grandmother, she hardly ap-peared to be recommending marriage and family to her bachelor son Henry. Indeed, most of her references to the marriages of his friends repeat the same negative refrain. She skewered Sarge Perry's bride-to-be: "No doubt her cleverness has attracted him, but I should have thought that the high estimate she places upon it herself would have weakened the spell."[31] John La Farge's marriage also drew her barbs, in this case though it was the husband's self-centeredness that she deplored. "I know no man who strikes one so disagreeably . . . he is *so* selfish and filled with preten-sions and conceit. He lives in New York and leaves that long suffering wife of his with the whole burden of the family."[32]

Having nourished Henry and Alice on such negative views of marriage, Mrs. James urged Henry toward matrimony in the spring of 1874 with surprisingly passionate intensity. He planned to make his life in Europe, away from the family, and that prospect unleashed a flood of emotion that is unique in her correspondence. It blended maternal tenderness toward a favorite son with the passion of a lover.

My darling Harry,
Although I have not written to you so much of late, I believe I have never thought so much about you as since Willy came home. I feel so often that I want to throw around you the mantle of the family affection, and fold you in my own tenderest embrace. It seems to me darling Harry that your life must

need this succulent fattening element more than you know yourself. That not withstanding the charm and beauty that surround you, and that so inspired and vivified your intellectual and asthetic life, your social life, the life of your affections must need the moisture and sunshine, which only home or the intercourse of a circle of familiar friends can give. I know only one thing that would solve that difficulty, and harmonize the discordant elements in your life—You would make dear Harry according to my estimate, the most loving and loveable and happiest of husbands.[33]

But Henry showed absolutely no inclination toward the "succulence," the "moisture," or the "embrace." He steered clear, and kept an ocean between them.

Alice James in London, 1891

343

William James, 1893

William had little experience with women. Aside from a flickering interest in Fanny Dixwell (who later married Oliver Wendell Holmes, Jr.), his affections were securely tied to the family. As we have seen, he was playful and teasing with his sister. Through the 1860s and 1870s his correspondence with her glowed with fraternal affection.

When William James chose another Alice to marry in the summer of 1878, his sister fell ill, losing all the gains of health and good looks that had been carefully recorded in the family correspondence. She closed like a blossom chilled by a premature frost. Near death in 1892, she wrote in the privacy of her journal, "The fact is, I have been dead so long and it has been simply such a grim shoving of the hours behind me . . . since the hideous summer of '78, when I went down to the deep sea, its dark waters closed over me and I knew neither hope nor peace."[34] As William admitted to President Gilman, her invalidism was a tie that could still bind a married brother's affections.

William was the only one of the James children to make a marriage that had the wholehearted approval of his parents. Having chosen a scientific vocation for his son, Henry James, Sr., also selected William's wife. The first fiat of creator to creature had, as we have seen, become law only after a painful struggle. The second went down more easily, perhaps because William felt sure enough after his success in reshaping his profession to see the merit of the twenty-seven-year-old schoolteacher his father selected. What drew Mr. James to the short, stocky, brown-haired Alice Gibbens is not recorded. They met at the Radical Club, a Unitarian group devoted to attacking supernaturalism in religion, so she shared his interest in unorthodox ideas. Perhaps he sensed the nurturing strength (so like his wife's) that a difficult life had fixed in her character. The eldest of three daughters born of a fragile, unhappy marriage, she became virtually the head of her family at the age of sixteen, when her long-separated physician father returned from the Civil War and a long battle with alcoholism, and committed suicide. Her mother had collapsed and Alice had taken over. Alice Gibbens knew how to be a helpmate. If not a rib from the same flesh, she was comfortably Bostonian and firmly tethered to the vicinity of the paternal garden.*

William's sister was not the only family member to be upset by his decision to take a bride. It was an act that cut a deep fraternal link as well. Henry, Jr., was abroad during the courtship and wedding, pursuing his successful literary career. On receiving notice of the engagement, he offered congratulations with attempted humor that shaded into bitterness.

---

*The only source of information on Alice Gibbens James is *WJ*, 214–23. Among the James Papers, 1,300 letters from William James to his wife remain unavailable until 2022.

The James family home, 95 Irving Street, Cambridge

"You have my blessings indeed, and Miss Gibbens also; or rather Miss Gibbens particularly, as she will need it most. . . . I was not surprised at all, for I had been expecting to get some such news as this from you. . . . I believe almost as much in matrimony for most other people as I believe in it little for myself—which is saying a good deal."[35] He offered "a tender bridal benediction," declaring, "I was divorced from you by an untimely fate on this occasion." Henry's next novel, *Confidence,* tells of two very intimate young men who fight to win the affections of the same woman (who was named Angela, a feminized version of Angel, Harry's pet name in the family).[36] Though he had succeeded in individuating from William through his literary career and his chosen London residence, Henry continued to ruminate on the puzzling connection of twinlike male figures in his fictive world. Imaginatively he cast himself as one of the closely linked men trying to work out a separate fate and also as a woman, both witness to and cause of a rift between them.

William moved out of the family home to honeymoon in the Adirondack Mountains, where he often went to retreat from his academic, city-bound life. His new bride immediately became part of his work world. Mary James had been writing William's dictated letters to "spare his eyes." Now a second Mrs. James stepped into the role of amanuensis. The new marriage had to take its place beside the new psychology in his life. As he had contracted to write his textbook two months before the wedding, a playful letter from Francis J. Child, professor of English literature at Harvard, poked fun at the newlyweds for the odd conjunction of textbook making and lovemaking ("Psychology and Psyche"). His joke drew an equally playful reply from William: ". . . what is this mythological and poetical talk about Psychology and Psyche and keeping back a manuscript composed during a honeymoon? The only Psyche now recognized by science is a decapitated frog whose writings express deeper truths than your weakminded poets ever dreamed." Apparently his bride was enthralled by the doctrines of the new psychology: "*She* (not Psyche but the bride) loves all these doctrines which are quite novel to her mind. . . . She swears entirely by reflex action now. . . . Hope not with your ballad-mongering ever to gain an influence."[37] Beneath the lusty humor, the essence of his conflict with his father, Bowen, and his future critics was evident. Science conflicted with art, and materialism threatened to overwhelm religion and philosophy. For the rest of his life, his task would be to explain psychological science with literary grace, while defending the meaning of religious experience (such as his father's) against the tyranny of scientific materialism.

Notes

Preface

1. Cushing Strout, "Ego Psychology and the Historian," *History and Theory* 7(1968):281–97; "William James and the Twice-Born Sick Soul," *Daedalus* 97 (Summer 1968): 1062–82; "The Pluralistic Identity of William James: A Psychohistorical Reading of *The Varieties of Religious Experience*," *American Quarterly* 23 (May 1971): 134–52.

Prologue

1. *TCWJ*, 1:469.
2. Leon Edel, ed., *The Complete Tales of Henry James* (Philadelphia: J. B. Lippincott, 1962), 3: 353.

BOOK ONE. GRANDFATHER

Epigraph: *PP*, 1:289.

1. *Tenants Become Landlords*

Epigraph: R. J. Dickson, *Ulster Emigration to Colonial America, 1718–1775* (London, 1966), 75.
1. Dickson, *Ulster Emigration*, 8.
2. W. E. H. Lecky, *A History of Ireland in the Eighteenth Century* (London, 1892), 2: 163.
3. Dickson, *Ulster Emigration*, 86, 157–58, 209, 217, 272.
4. *L. W. J.*, 1:2, calls the story of William's resistance to his parents' efforts to make a minister of him a legend. Harold Larrabee speaks with more certainty in "The Jameses: Financier, Heretic, and Philosopher," *American Scholar* 1 (1932):

4 02. The earliest source is an unsigned obituary in the *Boston Evening Transcript,* December 20, 1882.

5. Dickson, *Ulster Emigration,* 75.

6. Katherine Hastings, "William James of Albany, N.Y. (1771–1832) and His Descendants," *New York Geneological and Biographical Record* 55 (1924):1.

7. The James McBride Day Book, 1820–1854, NN, contains numerous references to this trade.

8. Hastings, "William James," 2, 39–40.

9. Darius A. Orcutt, interview, *Syracuse Courier,* July 22, 1879. Orcutt got this information from a conversation with Burnet in 1835.

10. William James to John R. Williams, July 22, 1825, cited in Harold Larrabee, "From Salt Merchant to Artist: The James Family in Syracuse," lecture, 1962, Onondaga Historical Association, Syracuse.

11. Elias K. Kanes to William James, April 8, 1819, New York State Library, Albany. The Goldsbrow Banyar Papers include records of the management of James properties.

12. Arthur James Weise, *The History of the City of Albany, New York from the Discovery of the Great River in 1524, by Verrazzano to the Present Time* (Albany, 1884), 460–62, contains a description of the festivities based on eyewitness accounts.

13. Joel Munsell, *Collections on the History of Albany from Its Discovery to the Present Time* (Albany, 1867), II:444–46, contains speeches by William James delivered at two canal celebrations, in 1823 and 1825.

14. Ibid., 466–67.

15. Franklyn H. Chase, *Syracuse and Its Environs: A History* (New York, 1924), 1:63, 68.

16. Joshua Forman to William James, November 3, 1824, NN.

17. Hastings, "William James," 4–5.

18. Ibid., 6.

19. William B. Sprague, *Address Delivered on the Occasion of the Funeral of Rev. William James* (Albany, 1868), 12–13.

BOOK TWO. FATHER

Epigraphs: *LRLHJ,* 117–18; William James, *Pragmatism* (New York: Longmans, Green, 1907), 292.

2. *A Crime against Childhood*

Epigraph: *LRLHJ,* 182.

1. Henry James, "Immortal Life, Illustrated by a Brief Autobiographic Sketch of the Late Stephen Dewhurst," in *LRLHJ,* 182–83.

2. *LRLHJ,* 173.

3. *LWJ,* 1:7–8.

4. Jannett James to Marcia Ames James, November 16, 1827, MH.

5. Augustus James to Rev. William James, May 6, 1828, Amherst College Library.
6. *LRLHJ*, 147.
7. Howard Feinstein, "The Double in the Autobiography of the Elder Henry James," *American Imago* 31 (Fall 1974):293–315.
8. *LRLHJ*, 185–86.
9. *MC*, 13.
10. M. De Wolfe Howe, *Memories of a Hostess* (Boston, 1922), 76.
11. Julia Ward Howe, *Reminiscences, 1819–1899* (Boston, 1899), 325.
12. *LRLHJ*, 139.
13. *LRLHJ*, 190–91.

3. *Flight from Union*

Epigraph: A. Bronson Alcott, "Orphic Sayings," *The Dial*, July 1840, cited in Perry Miller, *The Trancendentalists* (Cambridge, Mass., 1950), 304.
1. Codman Hislop, *Eliphalet Nott* (Middletown, Conn., 1971), 15. This book contains a detailed account of the lottery manipualtions.
2. Cornelius Van Santvoord, *Memoirs of Eliphalet Nott, D.D., L.L.D.* (New York, 1876), 150.
3. Ibid., 152.
4. Ibid., 386.
5. A. Franklin Ross, "History of Lotteries in New York," *Magazine of History*, February–June 1907, 265.
6. *Documents Relative to the Dispute between the Trustees of Union College and Yates and McIntyre* (Schenectady, 1934), paras. 60, 119.
7. Ross, "History of Lotteries," 322.
8. *Documents Relative to Dispute*, paras. 386, 389.
9. Hislop, *Eliphalet Nott*, 287.
10. Ibid., 291.
11. *Documents Relative to Dispute*, para. 191.
12. Ibid., para. 21.
13. Van Santvoord, *Memoirs of Eliphalet Nott*, 386–89; Jabez D. Hammond, *History of Political Parties in the State of New York* (Syracuse, 1852), 2:93; Hislop, *Eliphalet Nott*, 483–91.
14. *EHJ*, 17.
15. Ibid.
16. *EHJ*, 16.
17. Archibald McIntyre to Henry James, November 12, 1829, typescript, MH. This letter is published in part in *EHJ*, 17.
18. William James to Archibald McIntyre, December 2, 1829, MH. This letter is published in part in *EHJ*, 17–18.
19. Harold Larrabee, "The Flight of Henry James the First," *New England Quarterly*, December 1937, 774–75.
20. Ibid., 774, 775.

21. *EHJ*, 19.

22. Van Santvoord, *Memoirs of Eliphalet Nott*, 155–56.

23. *EHJ*, 20. See also Henry James to Isaac Jackson, January 13, 1830, MH. *EHJ* gives the date incorrectly as January 30, 1830.

24. *Christian Examiner and Theological Review* 3 (January 1826).

25. Sampson Reed, *Observations on the Growth of the Mind* (Boston, 1859), 30, 39, 95.

26. William James to Archibald McIntyre, n.d., typescript, MH.

27. Henry James, Sr., to Robertson James, n.d., Vaux.

4. *A Conflict of Wills*

Epigraph: The will of William James of Albany (July 24, 1832). See Alonzo C. Paige, *Reports of Cases Argued and Determined in the Court of Chancery of the State of New York* (Saratoga Springs, 1865), 5:318.

1. *Albany Argus*, July 6 and 23, 1832.

2. Ibid., June 22, 1832.

3. Ibid.

4. Paige, *Reports of Cases*, 5:318.

5. "The Syracuse Partition Suit," MH. The original will is on file in the Surrogate's Court, Albany, New York. It was also reprinted with the legal opinions resulting from litigation connected with it. See "Hawley v. James" in Paige, *Reports*, vol. 5.

6. Paige, *Reports*, 5:473.

7. "Syracuse Partition Suit," 2.

8. *EHJ*, 31.

9. Ibid.

10. *NSB*, 267–68.

11. *NSB*, 268.

12. Henry James, *Roderick Hudson* (Leipzig, 1879), 1:20–23.

13. Grattan, *Three Jameses*, 39.

14. "Syracuse Partition Suit," 2, 25.

15. *LRLHJ*, 58–59.

16: John Bunyan, *The Pilgrim's Progress* (New York and London, 1848), 15.

17. Ibid, 2.

18. *TCWJ*, 1:43.

19. Ibid.

20. *TCWJ*, 1:50.

21. *TCWJ*, 1:42.

22. *TCWJ*, 1:16; Clement J. Wilkinson, *James John Garth Wilkinson* (London, 1911), 41.

23. Wilkinson, *Wilkinson*, 15–16, 23.

24. *LRLHJ*, 62.

25. Genesis 19:17.

26. *SRFM*, 56.

27. *S&S*, 126.
28. *S&S*, 25–27.
29. *SS*, 161.

5. *Ideology for a Prodigal*

Epigraph: Ralph Waldo Emerson, "Nature," in *Selections from Ralph Waldo Emerson: An Organic Anthology,* ed. Stephen E. Whicher (Boston: Houghton Mifflin, 1960), 55.

1. *MC*, 40. This discussion focuses on the personal utility of transcendentalist ideas for Henry James, Sr.; many others participated in the movement for their own reasons. See O. B. Frothingham, *Transcendentalism in New England* (1876; reprint ed., New York: Harper & Row, 1959); Perry Miller, *The Transcendentalists: An Anthology* (Cambridge: Harvard University Press, 1950); William Hutchison, *The Transcendentalist Ministers: Church Reform in the New England Renaissance* (New Haven: Yale University Press, 1959); Taylor Stoehr, *Nay-Saying in Concord: Emerson, Alcott, and Thoreau* (Hamden, Conn: Archon Books, 1979); Anne C. Rose, *Transcendentalism as a Social Movement, 1830–1850* (New Haven: Yale University Press, 1981).

2. *MC*, 87, 90.
3. *LM*, 11.
4. *LM*, 62.
5. *LM*, 46.
6. *LM*, 346–49.
7. *CLC*, 105.
8. James Freeman Clarke, review of James's *Substance and Shadow,* in *Christian Examiner* 75 (1863):212–24.
9. *LM*, 213.
10. *LM*, 70.
11. *LM*, 120.
12. *NE*, 20–21.
13. *NE*, 24.
14. *LM*, 187.
15. *NE*, 61.
16. *NE*, 183.
17. *LM*, 205.
18. Henry James, "The Church of Christ," *New York Tribune,* August 24, 1855, cited in *PHJ*, 302.
19. *LM*, 281.
20. *MC*, 62–63.
21. *NE*, 98–101.
22. *NE*, 218–20.
23. *NE*, 256–58.
24. *NE*, 130–31.

6. *Words and Work*

Epigraph: *PP* 288.

1. Henry James, "Theological Differences in Association," *Harbinger* 6 (1848): 26. For an excellent discussion of the social dimension of the conflict between work and leisure, see Daniel T. Rodgers, *The Work Ethic in Industrial America, 1850–1920* (Chicago: University of Chicago Press, 1978), especially chaps. 4, 7, 8.

2. William Perkins, *A Treatise of the Vocations, or Callings of Men, with the Sorts and Kinds of Them, and the Right Use Thereof* (Cambridge, 1608).

3. *MC*, 136.

4. Henry James, "The New Jerusalem Magazine," *Harbinger* 6 (1847):8.

5. *TCWJ*, 1:36.

6. *S&S*, 74.

7. Ibid.

8. *SS*, 172–73.

9. *CCE*, 71–72.

10. *LM*, 102.

11. Henry James, "The Divine Life in Man," *Harbinger* 7 (1848):9.

12. *PHJ*, 190.

13. James, "Divine Life in Man," 9.

14. *MC*, 59.

15. *SBO*, 207.

16. James, "Theological Differences," 26.

17. *LM*, 242–43.

18. *MC*, 126, cited in *PHJ*, 83.

19. *LM*, 134.

20. *TCWJ*, 1:191.

21. *SRFM*, 296–97.

22. Henry James, "On the Philosophical Tendencies of the Age—J. D. Morell," *Harbinger* 7 (1848):3.

23. *S&S*, 305.

24. *SS*, 196.

BOOK THREE. SON

Epigraph: *PP*, 1:379.

7. *A Painter's Vocation*

Epigraph: William James to Thomas Sergeant Perry, August 15, 1860, in Virginia Harlow, *Thomas Sergeant Perry: A Biography* (Durham, N.C., 1950), 261.

1. Ibid.

2. *LWJ*, 1:23.

3. *SBO*, 269–72.

4. Neil Harris, *The Artist in American Society: The Formative Years, 1790–1860* (New York, 1966), 262.

5. *SBO*, 266–68.

6. *SBO*, 204–5.

7. *SBO*, 337–38.

8. *SBO*, 314.

9. Benjamin Robert Haydon, *The Autobiography and Journals of Benjamin Robert Haydon (1786–1846)*, ed. Malcolm Elwin (New York, 1950), 164.

10. Ibid., 21.

11. *SBO*, 47–49.

12. Haydon, *Autobiography*, 14.

13. Ibid.

14. *SBO*, 315.

15. Jeffrey Maas, *Victorian Painters* (New York, 1969), 126.

16. John Ruskin, *Pre-Raphaelitism* (New York, 1851), 12.

17. Ruskin, *Pre-Raphaelitism*, 10–11.

18. *The Portable Dante*, ed. Paolo Milano (New York, 1947), 40.

19. William James, "The Dilemma of Determinism," in *The Writings of William James: A Comprehensive Edition*, ed. John J. McDermott (New York, 1967), 602.

20. *HJ*, 1:138.

21. *NSB*, 62.

22. *NSB*, 68.

23. Henry James, Sr., to Howard James, April 12, 1861, MH.

24. *MC*, 72.

8. *The Murdered Self*

Epigraph: William James, "Great Men and Their Environment," in *"The Will to Believe" and Other Essays in Popular Philosophy* (New York, 1897), 227.

1. Henry C. Angell, *Records of William M. Hunt* (Boston, 1881), 50.

2. Helen Knowlton, *Art-Life of William Morris Hunt* (Boston, 1899), 12.

3. Robert L. Herbert, *Barbizon Revisited* (New York, 1962), 10–13.

4. Percy MacKaye, *Epoch: The Life of Steele MacKaye, Genius of the Theatre, in Relation to His Times and Contemporaries* (New York, 1927), 1:44–52, 59–61, 63, 170–73, 215.

5. Virginia Harlow, *Thomas Sergeant Perry: A Biography* (Durham, N.C., 1950), 26.

6. MacKaye, *Epoch*, 1:76.

7. Royal Cortissoz, *John La Farge: A Memoir and a Study* (New York, 1911), 26, 45, 50, 57, 67, 68, 73, 79, 90–91, 109, 117, 121.

8. *TCWJ*, 1:186.

9. Ibid.

10. *WJ*, 55.

11. Ibid.
12. *TCWJ*, 1:192.
13. *TCWJ*, 1:188–89.
14. *TCWJ*, 1:191.
15. *TCWJ*, 1:196.
16. *TCWJ*, 1:199–200.
17. *NSB*, 62.
18. Neil Harris, *The Artist in American Society: The Formative Years, 1790–1860* (New York, 1966), 106, 108, 122, 218, 255, 287–88.
19. *TCWJ*, 1:197.
20. *NSB*, 81.
21. *NSB*, 45, 109, 17.
22. Henry James, Sr., to Rev. William James, December 21, 1860, MH. Henry's mention of Una Hawthorne's successful galvanic treatment permits the letter to be dated precisely.
23. William James, "Great Men and Their Environment," 227.

9. Evolution at Harvard

Epigraph: Louis Agassiz, "Methods of Study in Natural History," *Atlantic Monthly,* February 1862, 214.
1. Richard J. Storr, *The Beginning of Graduate Education in America* (Chicago, 1953), 1–55.
2. Stephen P. Sharpless, "Some Reminiscences of the Lawrence Scientific School," *Harvard Graduate Magazine* 26 (1918):532–40.
3. Charles Eliot, "The New Education," *Atlantic Monthly,* February 1869, 203–20.
4. Edward Lurie, *Louis Agassiz: A Life in Science* (Chicago, 1960), 31.
5. Ibid, 48.
6. Ibid., 63.
7. Edward W. Emerson, *The Early Years of the Saturday Club, 1855–1870* (Boston, 1918), 420–41.
8. A. Hunter Duprée, *Asa Gray, 1810–1888* (Cambridge, Mass., 1959), 351.
9. Ibid., 15–16.
10. Ibid, 23–24.
11. Ibid., 32.
12. Ibid., 25–26.
13. *NSB*, 123.
14. Lurie, *Louis Agassiz,* 309.
15. Agassiz, "Methods of Study in Natural History," 214, 222.
16. *TCWJ*, 1:211.
17. Lurie, *Louis Agassiz,* 254.
18. Duprée, *Asa Gray,* 229.
19. Ibid., 270, 323.

10. *Basic Science vs. the Humbug of Medicine*

Epigraph: *LWJ*, 1:44.
1. LSS
2. *LWJ*, 1:34, 40.
3. *TCWJ*, 1:212.
4. *LWJ*, 31–32.
5. *LWJ*, 1:43.
6. *TCWJ*, 1:211.
7. *NSB*, 129.
8. *LWJ*, 1:37–39.
9. *LWJ*, 1:43–44.
10. *NSB*, 129.
11. *LWJ*, 1:42.
12. William James to Henry and Mary Walsh James, December 1861, MH.
13. William James to Henry and Mary Walsh James, December 15, 1861, MH.
14. William James, Account Book, 1861, MH.
15. *LWJ*, 1:50.
16. William James to Henry and Mary Walsh James, Spring 1862, MH.
17. William James to Henry and Mary Walsh James, 1863, MH.
18. *LWJ*, 1:43–44.
19. *LWJ*, 1:45–46.
20. *LWJ*, 1:50.
21. *TCWJ*, 1:216.
22. Samuel Eliot Morison, *The Development of Harvard University since the Inauguration of President Eliot, 1869–1929* (Cambridge, Mass, 1930), 558, 560.
23. *The Harvard Medical School, 1782–1906* (Boston, 1906), 23.
24. *Harvard Medical School*, 6, 8.

11. *Vacation in Brazil*

Epigraph: William James, "Vacations," *Nation* 16 (1873):90–91.
1. Edward Lurie, *Louis Agassiz: A Life in Science* (Chicago, 1960), 344–45.
2. Louis and Elizabeth Agassiz, *A Journey in Brazil* (New York, 1869), v.
3. *TCWJ*, 1:217–18.
4. *LWJ*, 1:57.
5. *TCWJ*, 1:219.
6. *LWJ*, 1:65–66.
7. *LWJ*, 1:58.
8. *TCWJ*, 1:220.
9. *TCWJ*, 1:219.
10. *LWJ*, 1:61.
11. *LWJ*, 1:69.
12. *TCWJ*, 1:225.

13. William James to Henry and Mary Walsh James, June 3, 1865, MH.
14. Ibid.
15. *LWJ*, 1:66.
16. Ibid.
17. *TCWJ*, 1:222.
18. *LWJ*, 1:56.
19. *TCWJ*, 1:225.
20. Lurie, *Louis Agassiz,* 253–80.

12. *The Use and Abuse of Illness*

Epigraphs: Henry James, Sr., "Physical and Moral Maladies," *Liberator,* July 22, 1859; William James, "Stanford's Ideal Destiny," in *Memories and Studies* (New York: Longmans, Green, 1917), 365–66.
1. *LWJ*, 1:79.
2. *TCWJ*, 1:231.
3. *TCWJ*, 1:300–301.
4. F. O. Matthiessen, *The James Family* (New York: Alfred A. Knopf), 271n.
5. Mary Walsh James to William James, May 27, 1867, MH.
6. Mary Walsh James to Alice James, April 1867, MH.
7. Mary Walsh James to Henry James, Jr., April 5, 1870, MH.
8. Mary Walsh James to Henry James, Jr., September 6, 1869, MH.
9. William James to Henry James, Jr., May 11, 1873, MH.
10. George Miller Beard, *A Practical Treatise on Nervous Exhaustion: Neuraesthenia, Its Symptoms, Nature, Sequences, Treatment* (New York, 1880), 20, 184, 180.
11. *Boston Evening Transcript,* November 10, 1882.
12. *TCWJ*, 1:23.
13. Mary Walsh James to William James, May 27, 1867, MH.
14. Mary Walsh James to Alice James, January 14, 1870, MH.
15. Mary Walsh James to Henry James, Jr., December 8, 1873, MH.
16. *TCWJ*, 1:519.
17. Mary Walsh James to Henry James, Jr., August 8, 1869, MH.
18. Mary Walsh James to Henry James, Jr., April 1, 1873, MH.
19. *TCWJ*, 1:373.
20. *HJL*, 1:131.
21. *TCWJ*, 1:239–40.
22. William James to Mary Walsh James, June 12, 1867, MH.
23. *HJ*, 1:44.
24. Mary Walsh James to Henry James, Jr., September 22, 1873, MH.
25. *LWJ*, 1:80.
26. *HJ*, 1:47, 49.
27. Mary Walsh James to Alice James, July 18, 1872, MH.
28. *HJL*, 1:115.

29. *HJL*, 1:124.

30. *HJL*, 1:124–25.

31. Mary Walsh James to Henry James, Jr., July 24, 1869, MH.

32. Alice James to Sara Sedgwick, March 23, 1874, MH.

33. *DAJ*, 48.

34. Henry James, Sr., to Anna Hazard (Barber) Ward, March 12, 1856, MH.

35. Henry James, Sr., to Anna Hazard (Barber) Ward, November 2, 1857, MH.

36. *NSB*, 292.

37. *NSB*, 299–301.

38. *DAJ*, 36.

39. *HJL*, 1:119, 121.

40. *SS*, 172.

41. *HJL*, 1:187.

42. Mary Walsh James to Henry James, Jr., March 17, 1874, MH.

43. *DAJ*, 149.

44. Anna Robeson Burr, ed., *Alice James, Her Brothers, Her Journal* (New York: Dodd, Mead, 1934), 43.

45. Mary Walsh James to Henry James, Jr., August 8, 1869, MH.

46. *DAJ*, 149.

47. George Beard, *Salem Witchcraft* (New York, 1882), 94–95.

48. *HJL*, 1:98–99.

49. *HJ*, 2:95.

50. *HJL*, 1:136, 142, 155–56.

51. Mary Walsh James to Henry James, Jr., July 24, 1869, MH. A vivid description of rest turned into a trial of sensory deprivation is to be found in Charlotte Perkins Gilman, *The Yellow Wall Paper* (Old Westbury, N.Y.: Feminist Press, 1973 [1899]). It is an indictment of the Weir Mitchell rest cure.

52. *HJL*, 1:163.

53. Rev. William James to Kitty Prince, January 25, 1861, Colby College Library.

54. *HJL*, 1:256.

55. Alice James to Sara Sedgwick, May 5, 1883, MH.

56. Beard, *Nervous Exhaustion*, 140.

13. *An Invalid Physician*

Epigraph: William James to Hugo Munsterberg, July 8, 1891, *LWJ*, 1:313.

1. Mary Walsh James to Alice James, April 1867, MH.

2. Mary Walsh James to William James, November 21, 1867, MH.

3. Ibid.

4. *LWJ*, 1:99.

5. William James to Tom Ward, September 12, 1867, MH. This passage was excised from the letter published in *TCWJ*, 1:244.

6. *LWJ*, 1:129.

7. *TCWJ*, 1:518.

8. *LWJ*, 1:95.

9. William James to Tom Ward, November 7, 1867, MH. This passage was excised in *LWJ*, 1:118.

10. Henry James, Sr., to Samuel G. Ward, April 1, 1867, MH.

11. *LWJ*, 1:86.

12. *TCWJ*, 1:235.

13. *LWJ*, 1:87, 91.

14. *LWJ*, 1:92–93.

15. *TCWJ*, 1:238, 239.

16. *TCWJ*, 1:242.

17. William James to Henry James, Sr., September 5, 1867, MH.

18. *LWJ*, 1:95–96.

19. Ibid., 98.

20. *TCWJ*, 1:513, 514.

21. *TCWJ*, 1:509, 510.

22. *TCWJ*, 1:275.

23. *TCWJ*, 1:286.

24. *LWJ*, 1:128.

25. *LWJ*, 1:129, 130.

26. *TCWJ*, 1:287.

27. *LWJ*, 1:121, 123.

28. *LWJ*, 1:124.

29. *TCWJ*, 1:254.

30. *LWJ*, 1:133–34.

31. Henry James, Sr., to Samuel G. Ward, January 14, 1868, and October 9, 1868, MH.

32. *TCWJ*, 1:258–59.

33. *TCWJ*, 1:262.

34. Ibid.

35. *TCWJ*, 1:268.

36. *TCWJ*, 1:275.

37. *TCWJ*, 1:282.

38. Ibid.

39. *TCWJ*, 1:288.

40. *TCWJ*, 1:289.

41. *TCWJ*, 1:295.

42. *TCWJ*, 1:298.

43. William James, Notebook, 1868, MH.

44. *LWJ*, 1:154.

45. *LWJ*, 1:155.

46. Mary Walsh James, to Henry James, Jr., July 24, 1869, MH.

47. Mary Walsh James to Henry James, Jr., August 8, 1869, MH.

48. Mary Walsh James to Henry James, Jr., September 21, 1869, MH.

49. *TCWJ*, 1:301–2.

14. *A Singular Life*

Epigraph: *PP,* 2:408.
1. *TCWJ,* 1:244.
2. *NSB,* 444.
3. *SBO,* 9.
4. *SBO,* 221.
5. *SBO,* 264.
6. *SBO,* 314, 315, 345.
7. Leon Edel has emphasized the rivalrous aspects of the twin theme (see *HJ,* 1:240–52); I am interested in a different psychological problem, individuation. For a modern instance of psychological fusion in identical twins, see Linda Wolfe, "The Strange Death of the Twin Gynecologists," *New York,* September 8, 1975, 43–47.
8. *TCWJ,* 1:236, 241, 268, 267.
9. *TCWJ,* 1:251.
10. *HJL,* 1:80.
11. William James to Henry James, Jr., June 12, 1869, MH.
12. William James to Henry James, Jr., May 25, 1873, MH.
13. *TCWJ,* 1:245.
14. *HJL,* 1:96, 105.
15. *HJL,* 1:146.
16. *HJL,* 1:186, 216.
17. Henry James, *Roderick Hudson,* ed. Leon Edel (London, 1961), 47.
18. William James to Henry James, Jr., October 25, 1869, MH.
19. William James to Henry James, Jr., November 1 and December 5, 1869, MH.
20. William James to Henry James, Jr., June 1, 1869, MH.
21. Henry James, "De Grey: A Romance," in *The Tales of Henry James (1864–1869),* ed. M. Aziz (Oxford: Clarendon Press, 1973), 277–79, 293.
22. Ibid., 306.
23. Henry James, "The Romance of Certain Old Clothes," in ibid., 210–26.
24. *TCWJ,* 1:263.
25. James, "Romance of Certain Old Clothes," 210, 211.
26. *TCWJ,* 1:264.
27. James, "Romance of Certain Old Clothes," 213, 216.
28. Ibid., 217, 226.
29. *HJ,* 1:249–50.
30. James, "A Light Man," in *Tales of Henry James,* ed. Aziz, 359, 367.
31. Ibid., 346, 347, 353.
32. Ibid., 348.
33. Ibid., 348–49.
34. Ibid., 359.
35. Ibid., 357, 358, 361–63.
36. Ibid., 356, 371, 372.

15. *An Ontological Window*

Epigraphs: William James to Henry James, Jr., September 5, 1867, in *TCWJ*, 2:705; Henry James, "Eugene Pickering," in *The Complete Tales of Henry James,* ed. Leon Edel (Philadelphia: J. B. Lippincott, 1962), 3:308.

1. *TCWJ*, 2:711.
2. Henry James, "The Ontology of Swedenborg," *North American Review* 105 (1867):89–123.
3. The significance of this correspondence was obscured by Perry, who lifted the letters out of context and published them as a separate appendix to vol. 2 of *TCWJ*, 705–16.
4. *TCWJ*, 2:713.
5. *TCWJ*, 2:714.
6. *S&S*, 102–3, cited in *PHJ*, III.
7. *TCWJ*, 2:706.
8. *TCWJ*, 2:711.
9. *TCWJ*, 2:712.
10. *TCWJ*, 1:518.
11. *TCWJ*, 2:710.
12. *TCWJ*, 2:713.
13. *TCWJ*, 2:706, 712, 714, 716.
14. *TCWJ*, 2:714.
15. *LRLHJ*, 58, 59, 60, 62, 63.
16. *VRE*, 160, 161.
17. *VRE*, 161.
18. *LRLHJ*, 73.

16. *Two Brothers at War and a Sister at Home*

Epigraph: Garth Wilkinson James to Robertson James, December 26, 1882, Vaux.

1. *SBO*, 47–49.
2. Garth Wilkinson James to Robertson James, December 26, 1882, Vaux.
3. Vaux.
4. Robertson James to Alice Gibbens James, February 24, 1898, MH.
5. *HJ*, 1:43.
6. Alice James to William James, August 6, 1867, MH.
7. *HJ*, 1:123, 132, 133, 136.
8. Robertson James to Alice Gibbens James, February 24, 1898, MH.
9. *TCWJ*, 1:187–88.
10. James Joseph Lawson Sisson Diary, March 10, June 9, June 16, 1860; by permission of Houghton Library, Harvard University.
11. *NSB*, 221–24.
12. Stephen B. Oates, To Purge This Land: A Biography of John Brown (New York: Harper & Row, 1970), 62–63, 230.

13. *NSB*, 222.

14. Henry James, Sr., *The Social Significance of Our Institutions, an Oration Delivered at Newport, R.I., July 4, 1861* (Boston, 1861), 33–34.

15. *HJ*, 1:171–72.

16. *HJ*, 1:171; George M. Frederickson, *The Inner Civil War: Northern Intellectuals and the Crisis of the Union* (New York: Harper & Row, 1965), 79.

17. Henry James, Sr., to Robertson James, August 29, 31, 1864, Vaux.

18. *Milwaukee Sentinel*, December 2, 1888.

19. Garth Wilkinson James to Henry and Mary Walsh James, December 29, 1862, in a private collection.

20. Saunders Redding, *The Lonesome Road* (Garden City, N.Y., 1958), 15.

21. *Milwaukee Sentinel*, December 2, 1888.

22. William James, "Robert Gould Shaw," in *Memories and Studies* (New York: Longmans, Green, 1917), 45.

23. Robertson James to William James, Tuesday (n.d.), MH.

24. *New York Times*, July 14 and 17, 1863.

25. Luis F. Emilio, *History of the Fifty-fourth Regiment of Massachusetts Volunteer Infantry, 1863–1865* (Boston: Boston Book Co., 1891), 7–8.

26. Robertson James to Edward Henry Clement, November 22, 1900, typescript, MH.

27. *AJ*, 75–76.

28. Peter Burchard, *One Gallant Rush: Robert Gould Shaw and His Brave Black Regiment* (New York: St. Martin's Press, 1965), 116.

29. *Milwaukee Sentinel*, December 2, 1888.

30. Henry James, Sr., to Samuel G. Ward, August 1, 1863, MH.

32. Ibid.

32. Garth Wilkinson James to Alice James, February 22, 1865, MH.

33. Robertson James to Fannie Morse, March 14, 1892, typescript, MH.

34. *DAJ*, 128; *AJ*, 74.

35. *AJ*, 75, 79.

36. Garth Wilkinson James to Alice James, January 5, 1865, and August 6, 1866, MH.

37. Robertson James to Alice James, January 21, 1867, MH.

38. Robertson James to Henry and Mary Walsh James, February 14, 1864, MH.

39. Garth Wilkinson James to Henry and Mary Walsh James, April 27, 1865, MH.

17. *Declining Fortunes*

Epigraphs: *AJL*, 72; Garth Wilkinson James to Henry James, Sr., April 7, 1866, in *Alice James, Her Brothers, Her Journal*, ed. Anna Robeson Burr (New York: Dodd, Mead, 1934), 44–45; Robertson James to Alice Gibbens James, February 23, 1898, MH.

1. *AJ*, 87–88.

2. *DAJ*, 104.

3. *AJL,* 51.

4. *AJL,* 72–73.

5. *AJL,* 72, 53, 61, 63–65.

6. *AJL,* 60, 69–70.

7. *AJL,* 64.

8. *AJL,* 66.

9. *AJL,* 67.

10. *AJL,* 70.

11. *AJ,* 175.

12. *AJL,* 76.

13. *AJL,* 77.

14. *AJ,* 174.

15. AJL, 78.

16. *AJ,* 92.

17. *AJL,* 63.

18. Alice James to Sara Sedgwick, Septemper 20, 1877, MH.

19. *AJL,* 70, 82.

20. *AJL,* 81.

21. *LWJ,* 1:49.

22. *TCWJ,* 1:213, 238.

23. *LWJ,* 1:176.

24. *TCWJ,* 1:188.

25. *AJ,* 53.

26. *TCWJ,* 1:188.

27. *LWJ,* 1:108.

28. *LWJ,* 1:49.

29. *TCWJ,* 1:257, 282.

30. Mary Walsh James to Henry James, Jr., April 3 and April 27, 1874, MH.

31. Lawrence N. Powell, *New Masters: Northern Planters during the Civil War and Reconstruction* (New Haven: Yale University Press, 1980), xi–7. See also Willie Lee Rose, *Rehearsal for Reconstruction: The Port Royal Experiment* (New York, 1964).

32. Garth Wilkinson James to Henry James, Sr., March 2, 1866, in *Alice James, Her Brothers, Her Journal,* ed. Anna Robeson Burr (New York: Dodd, Mead, 1934), 43.

33. Ibid., 44.

34. Garth Wilkinson James to Henry James, Sr., March 27, 1866, in a private collection.

35. Ibid.

36. Garth Wilkinson James to Henry James, Sr., April 7, 1866, in *Alice James,* ed. Burr, 45.

37. Mary Walsh James to Garth Wilkinson James, May 14, 1866, in a private collection.

38. Garth Wilkinson James to Henry James, Sr., April 27, 1866, in a private collection.

39. Garth Wilkinson James to Henry James, Sr., June 26, 1866, in a private collection.

40. Garth Wilkinson James to Henry James, Sr., April 14, 1866, in a private collection.

41. Garth Wilkinson James to Henry James, Sr., July 21, 1866, in a private collection.

42. Garth Wilkinson James to Henry James, Sr., August 9, 1866, in a private collection.

43. Mary Walsh James to Garth Wilkinson James, September 3, 1866, in a private collection.

44. Garth Wilkinson James to Henry and Mary Walsh James, February 1, 1867, in a private collection.

45. Garth Wilkinson James to Henry James, Sr., March 24, 1867, in a private collection.

46. Garth Wilkinson James to Mary Walsh James, January 27, 1868, in a private collection.

47. Henry James, Sr., to Garth Wilkinson James, February 8, 1867, in a private collection.

48. Garth Wilkinson James to Henry James, Sr., March 24, in *Alice James,* 1867, ed. Burr, 47.

49. Garth Wilkinson James to Henry James, Sr., October 17, 1868, in *Alice James,* ed. Burr, 47.

50. Garth Wilkinson James to Henry James, Sr., November 15, 1868, in *Alice James,* ed. Burr, 47–48.

51. Garth Wilkinson James to Henry and Mary Walsh James, December 31, 1868, in a private collection.

52. F. O. Matthiessen, *The James Family* (New York: Alfred A. Knopf, 1961), 267.

53. William James to Robertson James, January 27, 1877, in a private collection.

54. Robertson James to Alice Gibbens James, February 23, 1898; MH.

55. *NSB,* 377–78.

56. *DAJ,* 48.

57. Garth Wilkinson James to John C. Gray, January 20, 1882, MH.

58. Mary Walsh James to John C. Gray, January 20, 1882, MH.

59. Garth Wilkinson James to Robertson James, December 26, 1882. MS. (Vaux).

18. *A Sort of Fatality*

Epigraph: A. Menard, *Analyse et critique des principes de la psychologie de W. James* (Paris, 1911), 5.

1. Edward H. Madden, *Chauncey Wright and the Foundations of Pragmatism* (Seattle: University of Washington Press, 1963), 24. See also Joseph L. Blau, *Men and Movements in American Philosophy* (New York: Prentice-Hall, 1952); William R.

Hutchison, *The Transcendentalist Ministers* (New Haven: Yale University Press, 1959); Bruce Kuklick, *The Rise of American Philosophy* (New Haven: Yale University Press, 1977).

2. Madden, *Chauncey Wright* chap. 1.
3. *CER,* 20.
4. *TCWJ,* 1:521.
5. *TCWJ,* 1:267.
6. *TCWJ,* 1:530.
7. *TCWJ,* 1:520.
8. *CER,* 23.
9. Chauncey Wright, *Philosophical Discussion,* ed. Charles Eliot Norton (New York: Henry Holt, 1877), 244–50.
10. *CER,* 23, 24.
11. Madden, *Chauncey Wright,* 13.
12. *TCWJ,* 1:533.
13. *TCWJ,* 1:535.
14. *LWJ,* 1:35.
15. *TCWJ,* 1:538.
16. *TCWJ,* 1:536.
17. Carolyn Eisele, *Studies in the Scientific and Mathematical Philosophy of Charles S. Peirce* (The Hague: Mouton, 1979), 1–9.
18. *TCWJ,* 1:541.
19. Charles Frankel, *The Golden Age of American Philosophy* (New York: George Braziller, 1960), 52.
20. *TCWJ,* 1:534.
21. Charles S. Peirce, *Collected Papers of Charles Sanders Peirce,* ed. Charles Hartshorne and Paul Weiss (Cambridge, Mass., 1935), 6:184.
22. *TCWJ,* 1:542.
23. *TCWJ,* 1:409.
24. *LWJ,* 1:149.
25. *LWJ,* 1:152.
26. William James to Kitty Prince, December 13, 1863, Amherst College Library.
27. *LWJ,* 1:127.
28. William James to Robertson James, November 14, 1869, Vaux.
29. Ibid.
30. William James, Journal, December 21, 1869, MH.
31. The letter dated March 1869 (*LWJ,* 1:152) refers to yet a third "crisis" not fully described.
32. *TCWJ,* 1:473.
33. *LWJ,* 1:150.
34. *TCWJ,* 2:356.
35. *LWJ,* 1:147.
36. *TCWJ,* 1:654–69.
37. Diary of William James, May 22, 1868, MH.
38. Ibid.
39. *TCWJ,* 1:277.

40. *LWJ*, 1:148, cited in part in *WJ*, 169. Gay Wilson Allen recognizes that Bain was an important influence here but he does not show how this influence changes the usual view of the episode.

41. *LWJ*, 1:147.

42. *LWJ*, 1:157–58.

43. Howard Feinstein, "Fathers and Sons: Work and the Inner World of William James, an Intergenerational Inquiry," Ph.D. dissertation, Cornell University, 1977.

44. Diary of William James, February 1, 1870, MH.

45. Ibid.

46. *TCWJ*, 1:339–40.

47. William James, review of Henry Maudsley, *Responsibility in Mental Disease*, in *Atlantic Monthly* 34 (1874):365.

48. Henry Maudsley, *Responsibility in Mental Disease* (New York, 1874), 270, 274, 279.

49. Ibid., 298.

50. Edwin G. Boring, *A History of Experimental Psychology* (New York, 1950), 27–30.

51. *LWJ*, 1:118–19.

52. *TCWJ*, 1:274.

53. *LWJ*, 1:121–22.

54. *LWJ*, 1:119.

55. *LWJ*, 1:133.

56. *LWJ*, 1:154.

57. *LWJ*, 1:156.

58. *LWJ*, 1:132.

59. *TCWJ*, 1:275–76.

60. *TCWJ*, 2:9.

19. *Professor James*

Epigraph: William James, "The Dilemma of Determinism," in *The Will to Believe and Other Essays in Popular Philosophy* (New York: Longmans, Green, 1897), 174.

1. *TCWJ*, 1:294.

2. *CWE*, 1:57.

3. *CWE*, 1:134, 142, 151.

4. *CWE*, 1:128, 149.

5. Mary Walsh James to Henry James, Jr., July 26, 1872, MH.

6. *TCWJ*, 1:327–28.

7. *TCWJ*, 1:327.

8. *TCWJ*, 1:329.

9. *TCWJ*, 1:332, 334–35.

10. *TCWJ*, 1:336–37.

11. *LWJ*, 1:169.

12. *TCWJ*, 1:335.

13. *TCWJ*, 1:341.

14. *TCWJ*, 1:343.

15. *TCWJ*, 1:343.

16. *TCWJ*, 1:344.

17. *TCWJ*, 1:346–47.

18. *TCWJ*, 1:350.

19. *LHJ*, 1:325, 332.

20. *LHJ*, 1:367.

21. *LHJ*, 1:386.

22. *LHJ*, 1:390.

23. *LHJ*, 1:388.

24. *LHJ*, 1:393.

25. Mary Walsh James to Henry James, Jr., July 1, 1873, MH.

26. Mary Walsh James to Henry James, Jr., August 4, 1873, MH.

27. *TCWJ*, 1:340.

28. *TCWJ*, 1:351.

29. *TCWJ*, 1:354.

30. *TCWJ*, 1:352.

31. *TCWJ*, 1:162–64. Perry took this letter out of context and loses its psychological significance.

32. *PP*, 1:121.

33. *LHJ*, 1:431.

34. *TCWJ*, 1:355.

35. *TCWJ*, 1:355.

Epilogue

Epigraph: *PP*, 1:306–7.

1. A. Menard, *Analyse et critique des principes de la psychologie de W. James* (Paris, 1911), 5n.

2. *PP*, 1:306–7.

3. Board of Overseers, *Report of the Committee on Resolutions*, December 19, 1871, 17, Harvard University Archives.

4. *TCWJ*, 2:12; Bruce Kuklick, *The Rise of American Philosophy: Cambridge, Massachusetts, 1860–1930* (New Haven, 1977), 30; Sheldon M. Stern, "William James and the New Psychology," in *Social Sciences at Harvard, 1860–1920: From Inculcation to the Open Mind*, ed. Paul Buck (Cambridge, Mass., 1965), 177–78.

5. Stern, "James and the New Psychology," 179.

6. Board of Overseers, *Report of the Committee on Resolutions, 1875–76*, Harvard University Archives.

7. *TCWJ*, 1:453; Samuel Eliot Morison, *Three Centuries of Harvard University* (Cambridge, Mass., 1946), 353; Samuel Eliot Morison, *The Development of Harvard University* (Cambridge, Mass., 1930), 216–18.

8. William James to Charles Eliot, December 2, 1875, MH; published in part in *TCWJ*, 2:10–11.

9. *TCWJ*, 1:364.

10. Stern, "James and the New Psychology," 185.

11. *TCWJ*, 1:666.

12. *TCWJ*, 1:667.

13. G. Stanley Hall, *Life and Confessions of a Psychologist* (New York, 1923), 203.

14. G. Stanley Hall, "The Teaching of Philosophy in Our Colleges," *Nation* 23 (September 21, 1876); "Philosophy in the United States," *Mind,* January 1879, 91.

15. William James, "The Teaching of Philosophy in Our Colleges," *Nation,* 23 (September 21, 1876):178–79.

16. Board of Overseers, *Report of the Committee on Resolutions, 1877–78,* 5–6. This entire discussion is based on the correspondence in Jackson I. Cope, "William James's Correspondence with Daniel Coit Gilman, 1877–78," *Journal of the History of Ideas* 12 (October, 1951):609–27.

17. Cope, "William James's Correspondence," 614–17.

18. *TCWJ*, 1:380; Cope, "William James's Correspondence," 620.

19. Ibid., 619n.

20. Ibid., 620.

21. Ibid., 627.

22. Ibid., 622. Parts of this story have already been told in Kuklick, *Rise of American Philosophy,* 27; Dorothy Ross, G. Stanley Hall: The Psychologist as Prophet (Chicago, 1971), 63, 79, 105.

23. Cope, "William James's Correspondence," 621.

24. Mary Walsh James to Henry James, Jr., December 15, 1872, MH.

25. Mary Walsh James to Alice James, July 18, 1872, MH.

26. Mary Walsh James to Henry James, Jr., July 23, 1872, MH.

27. Mary Walsh James to Henry James, Jr., March 21, 1873, MH.

28. Mary Walsh James to Henry James, Jr., March 25, 1873, MH.

29. Mary Walsh James to Henry James, Jr., July 6, 1874, MH.

30. Mary Walsh James to Henry James, Jr., July 6, 1874, MH.

31. Mary Walsh James to Henry James, Jr., May 25, 1873, MH.

32. Mary Walsh James to Henry James, Jr., March 21, 1873, MH.

33. Mary Walsh James to Henry James, Jr., May 18, 1874, MH.

34. *DAJ*, 230.

35. *HJL*, 2:174.

36. *HJ*, 2:385.

37. *LWJ*, 1:196.

Index

Page numbers in italics indicate illustrations.